Turkmenistan

THE BRADT STORY

The first Bradt travel guide was written in 1974 by George and Hilary Bradt on a river barge floating down a tributary of the Amazon. In the 1980s and '90s the focus shifted away from hiking to broader-based guides covering new destinations – usually the first to be published about these places. In the 21st century Bradt continues to publish such ground-breaking guides, as well as others to established holiday destinations, incorporating in-depth information on culture and natural history with the nuts and bolts of where to stay and what to see.

Bradt authors support responsible travel, and provide advice not only on minimum impact but also on how to give something back through local charities. In this way a true synergy is achieved between the traveller and local communities.

* * *

We receive quite a few proposals for new guidebooks but this one stood out. The fact that the potential writer was the current British ambassador for Turkmenistan drew our attention, but it was how he presented this least-known of the 'Stans that persuaded us to publish. I liked the fact that it was part of the Silk Road, so full of archaeological sites, and I remembered that the Queen once received a beautiful golden Ahal Tekke horse as a gift from a former president. The book fitted our niche so we commissioned it. A year later, on reading the manuscript, I was convinced by the end of the introduction that I was dying to visit Turkmenistan. Paul's ability to convey the essence of the country is the hallmark of a good Bradt guide, and I am proud to publish his book.

Hilary Bradt

23 High Street, Chalfont St Peter, Bucks SL9 9QE, England
t 01753 893444 f 01753 892333
e info@bradtguides.com www.bradtguides.com

Turkmenistan

THE BRADT TRAVEL GUIDE

Paul Brummell

Bradt Travel Guides Ltd, UK
The Globe Pequot Press Inc, USA

First published December 2005

Bradt Travel Guides Ltd
23 High Street, Chalfont St Peter, Bucks SL9 9QE, England
www.bradtguides.com
Published in the USA by The Globe Pequot Press Inc, 246 Goose Lane,
PO Box 480, Guilford, Connecticut 06437-0480

British Library Cataloguing in Publication Data
A catalogue record for this book is available from the British Library

ISBN-10: 1 84162 144 7
ISBN-13: 978 1 84162 144 9

Photographs
Front cover: Monument to the desert explorers, Balkanabat (Paul Brummell)
Text: Paul Brummell

Illustrations Carole Vincer
Maps Alan Whitaker

Typeset from the authors' disc by Wakewing, High Wycombe
Printed and bound in Italy by Legoprint SpA, Trento

Author/Acknowledgements

AUTHOR

Paul Brummell is a career diplomat, who joined the Foreign and Commonwealth Office in 1987. He has served in Islamabad and Rome, and as British Ambassador to Turkmenistan from 2002 to 2005. He was shortlisted for the 1999 Shiva Naipaul Memorial Prize for an article on the San Remo Song Festival. He is a Fellow of the Royal Geographical Society.

ACKNOWLEDGEMENTS

My thanks go to everyone at the British Embassy in Ashgabat for their wonderful support during my time in Turkmenistan. Thanks to Tim Williams and the archaeologists of the International Merv Project for helping to unravel the mysteries of Ancient Merv, and to Viktor Sarianidi and his team for doing the same at Gonur. Thanks to all at Ayan Travel for responding so enthusiastically to my requests to travel to out-of-the-way corners of Turkmenistan. Thanks to Dominic Schroeder, Andrew Page, Mike Welch and Andrew Plummer at the Foreign and Commonwealth Office, and to Hilary Bradt, Tricia Hayne, Adrian Phillips and all at Bradt Travel Guides for their faith in the project. Above all, my thanks go to the people of Turkmenistan, without whose delight in presenting the treasures and traditions of their country this book could not have been written. The comments presented herein do not necessarily reflect the views of the Foreign and Commonwealth Office.

A CAUTION

Central Asia is a potentially volatile region, and the comments contained in any published travel guide can never be fully up to date. You are therefore strongly urged to consult the travel advice issued by your government before you plan your trip for the latest information as regards the security situation in Turkmenistan and the wider region. Website addresses for the British Foreign and Commonwealth Office and US State Department travel advice are given on page 232. You should seek advice from your travel agent, or nearest Turkmen Embassy (see page 30), as regards the current rules and regulations surrounding visits to Turkmenistan, as these have been subjected to frequent change. Finally, while the prices, timetables and other information given in this book were those encountered at the time of research, do be aware of the possibility that they may have changed by the time you visit.

Contents

LIST OF MAPS

For a key to map symbols, see page VIII.

FEEDBACK REQUEST

While all efforts have been made to ensure that the details within this guide are as accurate and up to date as possible, Turkmenistan is changing fast. Surviving Soviet-era monuments continue to be demolished, while grand new white marble-faced structures gradually transform the urban landscape of Ashgabat. Rules and regulations are also subject to frequent change. Any information regarding changes, recommendations about new sights of interest, good restaurants and comfortable hotels, or warnings about unpleasant ones, would be gratefully received and will help in the updating of the guide.

Bradt Travel Guides Ltd, 23 High Street, Chalfont St Peter, Bucks SL9 9QE
t +44 01753 893444; f +44 01753 892333;
e info@bradtguides.com; www.bradtguides.com

KEY TO STANDARD SYMBOLS

- International boundary
- Province/region
- Capital city
- Main town or city
- Small town or village
- Airport (international)
- Airport (other)
- Railway
- Railway station
- Bus station etc
- Main road (dual)
- Main road
- Other road
- Track (4x4)
- Featured hike/trek
- Other footpath
- Canal
- Land depression
- 1 km Distances between interrupted road cases
- Nature reserve
- Urban park (town plans)
- Market area (town plans)
- Embassy
- Bridge
- Car park
- Post office
- Hospital, clinic
- Telecommunication centre
- Bank
- Hotel, inn etc
- Restaurant
- Mosque
- Cathedral or church
- Buddhist stupa
- Museum/art gallery
- Theatre
- Zoo
- Botanical garden/site
- Stadium
- Statue
- City wall etc
- Earth wall/rampart
- Ancient/Archaeological site
- Scenic viewpoint
- TV/Radio antenna
- Other place of interest
- Summit (height in metres)
- Crater
- Relief hachures

The size of some symbols may vary to suit an individual context.
Other map symbols may be shown. These may be explained in key boxes on individual maps.

Introduction

Why come to Turkmenistan? The prospect of negotiating a letter of invitation, obtaining a visa and grappling with a body named the State Service for the Registration of Foreign Citizens, all in order to visit a little-known country in Central Asia consisting mostly of desert, is not, perhaps, instantly alluring. Yet this is a remarkable place.

Turkmenistan emerged as a newly independent state only in 1991, but the land has been shaped by the legacies of many occupants. The Kugitang Mountains in the east bear traces of the footprints of dinosaurs. At Margush in the heart of the country, archaeologist Viktor Sarianidi has toiled for decades in the hot desert to unearth a civilisation of Bronze Age fire-worshippers. Major sites representing different ages and rulers can be visited without fear of encountering jostling crowds of visitors. The Silk Road city of Ancient Merv was long one of the most important capitals of the Islamic world, where the recently restored mausoleum of Sultan Sanjar stands as a proud tribute to the Seljuk Empire. Yet the camels here outnumber the tourists. The visitor can feel a pioneer too at Konye-Urgench, capital of the once mighty Khorezm Empire, or the Parthian royal residence of Old Nisa, where fabulous carved drinking horns were unearthed.

The legacy of Turkmenistan's membership of the Soviet Union during much of the 20th century is recalled in many unusual monuments quietly decaying across the country. The MiG plane standing outside a fire station in the town of Mary. A spring deep in the western desert, where surely no Bulgarian has ventured for years, which announces itself as a monument to friendship between Bulgaria and the Soviet Union. The apartment blocks in the oil town of Balkanabat decorated with symbols of the 1980 Moscow Olympics.

These fragments of Turkmenistan's recent Soviet past are, however, disappearing fast, to make way for the structures and symbols of its present. Turkmenistan has been ruled since independence by President Saparmurat Niyazov, the local Communist Party boss when the Soviet Union collapsed, who has consolidated his hold over the state. The capital, Ashgabat, once an unremarkable provincial Soviet city, is being transformed into a fantasy of white-marble palaces, modern apartment blocks and large fountain complexes. In the centre of the city is the three-legged Arch of Neutrality, a monument to the United Nations General Assembly Resolution which gave Turkmenistan its neutrality status. It is topped by a golden statue of President Niyazov, which revolves to face the sun. The president is known as Turkmenbashy, the father of the Turkmen. His image is everywhere, from billboards to vodka bottles. The country's main port has been renamed Turkmenbashy, as has the month of January.

But the major impression the visitor will take away from Turkmenistan is of the Turkmen people. Of ladies wearing elegant velvet dresses, with intricate embroidered trims. Of white-bearded elders sporting apparently oversized woollen hats, *telpeks*, throughout the height of summer. Of small children, whose initial shyness when confronted by foreigners soon gives way to a barrage of questions about the mysteries of life in far-off countries. This is a people proud of its traditions: the magnificent Ahal Tekke horses; the burgundy-toned Turkmen carpets; the brides bedecked in heavy silver jewellery who are the bashful centres of attention in lavish and noisy wedding celebrations. Turkmenistan may not be an easy destination for the tourist, but for those who come here the rewards are great.

Part One

General Information

TURKMENISTAN AT A GLANCE

Location Central Asia, bordering Iran, Afghanistan, Uzbekistan, Kazakhstan and the Caspian
Area 488,100km^2
Status Republic
Head of state President Saparmurat Niyazov
Population Official figures just over 6 million; most unofficial estimates 4–5 million
Capital Ashgabat
Other main towns Turkmenabat, Mary, Dashoguz, Balkanabat, Turkmenbashy
Major exports Natural gas, oil, textiles, cotton
Language Turkmen; Russian also fairly widely spoken, especially in urban areas
Religion Predominantly Sunni Muslim
Currency Manat
Exchange rate US$1 = 5,200 manat at official exchange rate
International telephone code +993
Emergency phone numbers Fire brigade 01; police 02; ambulance 03
Time GMT +5 hours
Electricity 220 volts, 50 Hertz
Weights and measures Metric
National flag Green, with a vertical maroon stripe near the hoist decorated with a pattern of carpet designs, representing the five regions of Turkmenistan, and two olive branches, symbolising Turkmenistan's permanent neutrality. In the upper left corner of the largest green field is a white crescent and five white five-pointed stars.
Public holidays 19 February (Flag Day), 27 October (National Day or Independence Day), 12 December (Neutrality Day). See also page 48.

1 Background Information

GEOGRAPHY AND CLIMATE

Turkmenistan is the fourth largest of the states emerging into independence in 1991 from the collapse of the Soviet Union. Russia, Kazakhstan and Ukraine are the three larger states; Uzbekistan is slightly smaller. But its population is low. Official Turkmen government estimates put this at little more than 6 million, and this is probably decidedly generous. Much of the country is covered by the sparsely inhabited desert known as the Kara Kum ('Black Sands'), and the main population centres are dotted around the edge of Turkmenistan, particularly the piedmont oases at the foot of the Kopet Dag Mountains in the south, the Amu Darya River valley in the east and the Khorezm Oasis in the north. The west of the country abuts the Caspian.

The climate is a severe continental one. Between December and February, temperatures frequently fall below freezing while, at the height of summer, temperatures above 40°C are common, and 50°C not unknown. There is very little rainfall during the summer months, and overall annual rainfall is low: a tiny 80mm in parts of the north of the country, rising to 300mm or so in the mountains in the south.

NATURAL HISTORY AND CONSERVATION

Flora and fauna

With 80% of Turkmenistan's territory desert, the flora and fauna of Turkmenistan is focused strongly around species able to withstand arid conditions. The desert ecosystems of the Kara Kum are varied, including expanses of barchan sand dunes, the flat clay desert known as *takyr*, and large stretches dominated by the gnarled saxaul trees. The mountain ecosystems of the Kopet Dag and Kugitang ranges include the pistachio savannahs of Badkyz (see page 223) and, above around 1,000m, landscapes dominated by juniper. River valley environments include the remarkable salt-resistant *tugay* forests of the Amu Darya (see page 190). In spring, the deserts and hillsides of Turkmenistan, moistened by the winter rains and snows and warmed by the sun, briefly erupt into colour, as ephemeral and other flowering plants put on a wonderful display. The brilliant reds of the poppies and tulips turn uneventful landscapes into scenes to inspire any artist.

Among the wildlife of Turkmenistan, two species of hoofed mammals, protected in the country's nature reserves, have become almost symbols of the country. The goitred gazelle or *jieran*, the name deriving from its enlarged larynx, and the Central Asian wild ass, known as *kulan*, are both found in large herds. Badkyz Nature Reserve is a particularly good place to see both, as well as herds of the Transcaspian urial, a wild sheep. Other rare mammals include the Bukhara deer of the *tugay* forests and small populations of leopard in the Kopet Dag Mountains. You are highly unlikely to see either. The Turan tiger and Asiatic cheetah are both now extinct in Turkmenistan. One large hoofed mammal you will have little problem in encountering in Turkmenistan is the camel: domesticated single-humped dromedaries, which are kept for their wool, milk and meat. Ambling in front of oil derricks in the Balkan Region, or the Mausoleum of Sultan Sanjar at Merv, these creatures add a certain exoticism to many a tourist photo taken in Turkmenistan.

The Turkmen deserts are home to large rodent populations, which survive the harsh conditions by spending much of their time underground, where temperatures are milder and more equable. Amongst the most common species are ground squirrels, known as *susliks*; great gerbils, much larger than the creatures common as pets in Western households; and the nocturnal jerboas, with huge eyes and long hind legs. The holes made by burrowing rodents cover many desert slopes. The desert nights also accommodate porcupines, foxes and striped hyenas. The rodents form a major food source for the many birds of prey, which include eagles, buzzards, falcons and vultures, and which are often to be seen gliding above the desert terrain. Hunting with falcons is also popular, and is carried out both by local Turkmen clubs and hunting parties from the Gulf states.

Turkmenistan has a fearsome collection of reptiles, including several species of highly poisonous snakes, among them Central Asian cobras and saw-scaled vipers. Among the lizards, the desert monitor, known as *zemzen*, is the giant, reaching a length of up to 1.8m, and a weight of 2.5kg. This almost prehistoric-looking creature delivers both a fierce bite and a painful blow with its tail, but is traditionally regarded as a welcome neighbour by nomadic Turkmen families because it keeps down the snake population.

Among the domesticated animals, two distinctive Turkmen species of dogs deserve mention. You may well come across the large Central Asian sheepdog known as *alabai*, whose ears and tail are traditionally docked to make the animals less vulnerable in fights. Turkmens also believe that cutting the ears down improves the animals' hearing. *Alabais* are resilient to large temperature variations and modest in their food needs. While they can be highly affectionate, be wary of approaching any *alabai* guarding a flock. Much less common is the *tazy*, a lean and alert hunting dog of the borzoi family. *Tazys* are often used in conjunction with falcons for hunting.

Conservation and water management

Many of the rarest species and most precious ecosystems are protected in eight nature reserves (*zapovedniks*), which cover desert, mountain, coastal and riparian environments. But the nature of Turkmenistan faces considerable challenges. Hunters threaten rare species such as the leopard. In the Caspian, the arrival of the comb jelly, *mnemiopsis*, probably carried in on the hulls of ships, threatens the stocks of indigenous fish by devouring the plankton on which the fish feed. The major environmental challenge facing arid Turkmenistan, however, remains, as it always has been, the sustainable use of water.

Agriculture in Turkmenistan is almost entirely dependent on irrigation. The control and management of water resources has long been crucial to human settlement in the area. The focus in the Soviet period on cotton ('white gold') involved a large expansion in areas under irrigation. In the post-independence period, to cotton has been added a major drive to achieve self-sufficiency in wheat production, and these two state-order crops dominate Turkmenistan's irrigated lands. The government increases its production targets for both cotton and wheat every year, adding to the pressures to bring more land under irrigation and to increase yields through more intensive farming. More than 90% of irrigation waters in Turkmenistan are taken from the Amu Darya River, under an agreement with Uzbekistan, especially through the Kara Kum Canal (see box opposite). This

THE KARA KUM CANAL

The longest irrigation canal in the world, the construction of the Kara Kum Canal was a remarkable Soviet-era engineering feat, taking waters from the Amu Darya some 1,100km westwards to Gazanjyk (now Bereket) in Balkan Region. From here, water is piped even further westwards, to Turkmenbashy on the Caspian, making a total length of 1,370km. A planned extension of the canal, from Bereket to Etrek in the far southwest of Turkmenistan, has however yet to materialise. Construction of the canal began in 1954. It had reached Ashgabat by 1962, and Bereket in 1981. It takes almost 13km^3 of water annually from the Amu Darya, the largest single recipient of waters from that river. It supports close to a million hectares of irrigated cropland, and a much larger area of rangeland. The area served by the canal produces around half of the cotton and most of the grain output of Turkmenistan.

I was once shown a Soviet-era *Book for Honoured Guests visiting the Kara Kum Canal named after V I Lenin*. Most of the comments had been penned by visiting Communist Party delegations from around the globe. Those from the USA were particularly effusive, in an ideological kind of way. 'Dear Turkmenia Comrades. The Canal is a glowing example of proletarian internationalism and of the Leninist approach to the solution of the national question. We wish you many more victories on your road to building a Communist society.' That kind of thing. The canal is now named in honour of Saparmurat Turkmenbashy rather than Lenin. It also tends to be described not as a canal at all but as the Kara Kum River, as if it was a natural work, rather than an artificial one.

A series of large hydraulic structures, mostly around the Merv and Tejen oases, control the level and flow of the water and facilitate diversions for irrigation. There are three main reservoirs along the canal system: Zeid, in Lebap Region; Hanhowuz, at the eastern edge of the Tejen Oasis; and the Kopet Dag Reservoir near Geok Depe. The Zeid Reservoir acts as a large settlement tank, to attempt to cope with the heavy sediment load in the Amu Darya. But silting of the main canal remains a considerable problem. Inadequate central control and information systems hinder informed decision making. The state of maintenance of the Kara Kum Canal is a cause for concern, and water efficiency is poor.

heavy off-take from the Amu Darya has been one of the contributory factors in the gradual drying up of the Aral Sea, an environmental problem with significant regional consequences.

The main method of irrigation used is traditional surface irrigation. Over-watering is endemic. Coupled with often inadequate drainage, this has led to rising water tables and soil salinisation as salts are drawn to the surface. Abandoned fields, covered by a white dusting of salt, are a common sight across Turkmenistan, especially in Dashoguz Region. Water is taken off the fields by a network of drainage channels, feeding large 'collectors' whose waters form the input for artificial bodies of water such as Lake Sarygamysh. These waters are often highly polluted. Large quantities of inorganic fertilisers have been used since Soviet times to try to generate high yields on Turkmenistan's poor desert soils. And herbicides are widely applied to defoliate cotton plants to make the cotton easier to harvest, especially mechanically.

HISTORY

Earliest times to the Parthians

The earliest sites of human occupation in Turkmenistan include the caves of Dam Dam Chashma and Jebel along the flanks of the Big Balkan massif in the west, which were inhabited in Mesolithic times. In a series of Neolithic settlements along the piedmont of the Kopet Dag range, pastoralism and the cultivation of wheat and barley were practised as early as the middle of the 6th millennium BC. Known by archaeologists as the Jeitun Culture, these sites include the village of Jeitun itself, the oldest known agricultural settlement in Central Asia.

From the middle of the 3rd millennium BC, larger proto-urban settlements emerged in this piedmont belt. By the middle Bronze Age, sites such as Namazga Depe and Altyn Depe occupied a significant size, contained multi-roomed houses with open courtyards and had clearly defined artisans' quarters. Excavations at Altyn Depe revealed a large ziggurat-like monumental structure. Another area of Bronze Age occupation, the northern part of the Merv Oasis, where the ongoing excavations of archaeologist Viktor Sarianidi continue to yield fascinating treasures, may have been settled by emigrants from the foothills of the Kopet Dag.

Archaeologists have described a period of cultural decay in the piedmont area around the mid-2nd millennium BC, when Altyn Depe and Namazga Depe were abandoned. By the early Iron Age, settlements centred around fortified citadels were dotted around the Kopet Dag piedmont and the Merv Oasis. Another early Iron Age culture had developed in Dekhistan in the southwest of the country, where extensive irrigation systems brought water from the River Etrek.

The first of the major Central Asian empires was that of the Achaemenians, Persians of Zoroastrian faith. The empire, founded by Cyrus the Great, stretched at its height from Egypt to northern India and held sway from around 550–330BC. The settlement of Erk Kala at Merv was founded at this time. The Achaemenian Empire fell to the great conqueror from Macedonia, Alexander the Great. Following Alexander's early death in 323BC, those parts of his territory in present-day Turkmenistan went to Seleucus Nicator, ushering in the Seleucid Dynasty. Merv, then known as Antiochia Margiana, was rebuilt by Seleucus' son, Antiochus I.

While a successor Hellenistic state continued to hold Bactria in present-day Afghanistan, Greek rule in Turkmenistan ended with the arrival of the Parthians around 250BC. The Parthians were highly skilled warriors: the famous Parthian shot was a sting in the tail provided by archers on horseback, who turned round in the saddle to fire back on their opponents whilst riding away from them. In 53BC, at Carrhae in Mesopotamia, the Parthians defeated the Roman General Crassus, whose head and hand were delivered after the battle to the Parthian ruler. Many Roman soldiers taken prisoner at Carrhae were resettled at Merv. The most important Parthian site in Turkmenistan is Nisa.

From the Sasanians to the Khorezmshahs

The long-lived but weakly cohesive Parthian Empire was brought to an end around AD220 by the defeat of the Parthians by the Sasanians, Zoroastrians from present-day southern Iran. Their first major ruler, Ardashir, was by tradition a descendent of a Zoroastrian high priest named Sasan. The Sasanians, who ruled for four centuries, are often associated with religious persecution, though in Merv there is evidence that Judaism, Christianity and Buddhism flourished at this time, alongside Zoroastrianism. In the west, the Sasanians continued to fight with Rome, and later Byzantium. In the east, problems were caused by incursions of Hephthalite Huns, and later Turks from the Altai Mountains.

The conflict-wracked Sasanian Empire faced a new challenge: Islam. Following the death of Prophet Mohammed in 632, the Arab expansion, spreading the Islamic religion, proceeded rapidly. The last Sasanian ruler, Yazdigird III, was killed near Merv in 651. The city of Merv became a centre of Arab colonial expansion, receiving settlers from crowded Mesopotamian cities such as Basra. It was in Merv, in the 740s, that the Abbasid commander Abu Muslim proclaimed the start of the Abbasid rebellion against the Umayyads. Baghdad became the capital of the Islamic world, and Merv the capital of the great province of Khorasan, which gradually moved towards independence from Baghdad's control.

The area was ruled as a fully independent administration from 875 by the Samanids, who held sway for around a century. The Samanids were succeeded by two Turkic dynasties: the Karakhanids in the Syr Darya basin to the north; and in Khorasan the Ghaznavids, whose capital was Ghazna in present-day Afghanistan. Mahmud of Ghazni, who established much of the Ghaznavid Empire, transferred from Gurganj to Ghazna the renowned Academy of Ma'mun after his conquest of Khorezm.

In the 11th century the Turkic Seljuks, from the lower Syr Darya, advanced into the area, securing a decisive victory over the Ghaznavids in 1040 at Dandanakan, between Merv and Serakhs. The Seljuks were to establish a mighty empire stretching right to the Mediterranean, with Merv as its capital. The Seljuk Empire faltered following the death of Sultan Sanjar in 1157 and the region fell under the control of another Turkic dynasty, the Khorezmshahs. Based in the Khorezm Oasis, the Khorezmshahs were former vassals of the Seljuks who were able to expand their territories rapidly to exploit the vacuum created by the Seljuk decline.

Genghiz Khan and Timur

The Khorezmshahs were, however, to find themselves pitted against a terrible foe, the Mongols of Genghiz Khan. The latter initially toyed with the establishment of commercial contacts with the Khorezmshahs. But in 1218 a caravan of merchants with a Mongol envoy was put to death at the Khorezm border town of Otrar. Genghiz Khan prepared for war. The Khorezmshah Mohammed II adopted a defensive strategy based around his fortified towns. They were sacked one after the other. Gurganj was taken in April 1221, and most of the inhabitants massacred. A similarly brutal fate met the citizens of Merv. The oldest son of Mohammed II, Jelaladdin, secured a reputation for valiant resistance against the Mongols in theatres from Afghanistan to Azerbaijan, until his death in 1231. But this was but a minor nuisance to the all-conquering Mongols.

Mongol dominance of the region brought a long period of relative peace, and the revival of trade. This was the period of Marco Polo's travels to China. Some cities, however, including Merv, were never fully to recover from the severity of their sacking.

A future leader whose notoriety is almost as great as that of Genghiz Khan was born in 1336 into the Barlas clan of Shakhrisabz, near Samarkand. Timur, known in the west as Tamerlane ('Timur the lame'), became the ruler of Samarkand in 1370. Claiming ancestry from Genghiz Khan, he was to conduct 30 years of almost continuous campaigning. His actions could be hugely brutal, for example in his razing of Urgench, in part motivated by the consideration that the Khorezm Oasis represented a rival caravan route to that centred on his heartland of Samarkand and Bukhara. Timur's death ushered in a struggle for power between his sons and relatives. His fourth son, Shah Rukh, based in Herat, emerged the strongest. Shah Rukh established a new city at Merv, Abdullah Khan Kala. But within a few years of his death in 1447, the Timurid Empire had collapsed.

From the Shaybanids to the Russians

From the late 15th century, the maritime trade route to India started to eclipse the traditional land routes of the Silk Road. The decline of the great Central Asian oasis settlements was further accelerated by the loss of strong centralised power. For several centuries, the territory of present-day Turkmenistan was a battle for influence between Uzbek and Persian rulers, in which these dynasties frequently managed no more than notional control over the local Turkmen tribes and caravans were vulnerable to raids.

Mohammed Shaybani, a descendent of Shayban, grandson of Genghiz Khan, ruling from the territory of modern Uzbekistan, attempted to control the wider region, but was defeated in 1510 by the Persian Safavids, who incorporated Merv into their domains. A later Safavid general named Nadir Shah briefly created a significant empire of his own, establishing the Afsharid Dynasty in 1736, with its seat at Mashhad. The Afsharid Dynasty did not long survive Nadir Shah's assassination in 1747. The three Uzbek Khanates of Khiva, Bukhara and Kokand also made various attempts to extend their domains. The Emir of Bukhara, for example, took Merv in 1785, having destroyed its main dam.

In 1860 an appeal for assistance by Turkmens of the Sarik tribe, having been displaced from the Merv Oasis by Tekke Turkmen, unleashed the so-called Qajar War. The forces of the Persian Qajars advanced towards Merv, but were comprehensively defeated by the Tekkes. Among the prisoners taken by the Tekkes was a French cartographer named Henri de Blocqueville, who had been in the service of the Persians. De Blocqueville was later to publish an account of his fourteen months in Turkmen captivity. The defeat of the Qajars left Merv under Tekke Turkmen control.

Nineteenth-century travellers such as the Hungarian Arminius Vambery, who crossed the territory in 1863, found the Turkmen deserts a frightening place, controlled by nomadic Turkmen tribes of fearsome reputation, frequently at war with each other, menacing of caravans crossing the desert, and zealous in their slaving expeditions against the Persians.

It was into this environment that the Russians arrived in the late 19th century, carried there by the momentum of imperial expansion. Russian interest in Central Asia had first been ignited during the reign of Peter the Great, when Prince Alexander Bekovich landed on the eastern shores of the Caspian to pursue Peter's interest in the trade routes of Central Asia. But the Bekovich expedition was snuffed out by the Khan of Khiva, and a determined Russian attempt to secure the territory of modern Turkmenistan did not take place until the late 1860s, by which time Tashkent was already under Russian control, and the Russians needed Transcaspia to provide improved supply lines to its new territories further east. A permanent fort was established at Krasnovodsk in 1869. The Russians secured a devastating defeat of the Tekke Turkmens at Geok Depe in 1881, and took Merv without a fight three years later.

The rapid Russian advance across Transcaspia caused considerable disquiet in Britain, where there was great concern about possible Russian designs on India. The Transcaspian theatre was one of the arenas of the so-called Great Game, played out by agents of these two powers. Britain and Russia indeed appeared to come perilously close to war in 1885, when the Russians seized the oasis of Panjdeh from its Afghan defenders, who were backed by the British. The Joint Afghan Boundary Commission eventually settled the frontiers, and the Russians strengthened their control over their new territories with the construction of the Transcaspian Railway. The Transcaspian Region was established, with Ashgabat as its capital.

The Turkmen Soviet Socialist Republic

Following the Russian Revolution, the Transcaspian region experienced several reversals of power. Control in Ashgabat was initially taken by the Social Revolutionary Party, formed from a nucleus of railway workers. The Social Revolutionaries were unseated by the Bolsheviks, only to rise up again against the new and thuggish Bolshevik administration, in the process hanging nine of the Bolshevik Ashgabat Commissars and thereby inadvertently creating a set of future Soviet martyrs.

The new Social Revolutionary government enlisted the support of the British, who saw the Ashgabat administration as an ally against the threat posed to India by their Turkish enemies, who were then preparing to attack Baku, across the Caspian. In a now barely remembered military engagement of October 1918, Anglo-Indian forces and their Transcaspian allies were pitted against Bolshevik troops in a battle based around the small railway town of Dushak, in present-day Ahal Region. But the end of World War I, and the consequent removal of the perceived Turkish threat to India, resulted in the recall of the British Transcaspian mission. Without British support, the Social Revolutionary Transcaspian government was unable to stand up to the Bolsheviks, who had taken the whole region by February 1920.

The Turkmen Soviet Socialist Republic (TSSR) was established on 27 October 1924, one of a series of republics in Central Asia founded on the basis of a distinct 'nation', as part of a Soviet policy which aimed to discourage tendencies towards pan-Islamism and pan-Turkism within the region. In May 1925 the TSSR became one of the republics of the Union of Soviet Socialist Republics. The activity of anti-Bolshevik guerillas known as *basmachi* was a thorn in the regime's side in its early years, and briefly intensified following the commencement of the hugely traumatic policy of collectivisation in the late 1920s, when traditionally nomadic Turkmens were forcibly settled onto collective farms.

Soviet policy encouraged the TSSR, and the other Central Asian component republics of the Union, to focus their economies on a small range of products, to ensure dependence on the USSR as a whole. The industrial sector was not developed. As in Uzbekistan, the agricultural sector was strongly oriented towards the production of cotton, a task which was given a boost by the construction of the Kara Kum Canal in the 1960s, but with little regard for the environmental consequences. The exploitation of Turkmenistan's hydrocarbon reserves was also prioritised. During the 1970s and 1980s, the production of natural gas soared, but it was sold for a pittance to other Soviet Republics. Turkmenistan was dependent on an annual subsidy from Moscow which it would not have needed had it received a proper price for its gas.

The status of the ethnic Turkmen majority within the TSSR was always a sensitive issue. In 1958, Sukhan Babaev, the then First Secretary of the Central Committee of the Communist Party of Turkmenistan, made clear his concern that ethnic Russians were occupying too high a proportion of the leading jobs. He was sacked. Membership of the Soviet Union certainly brought some benefits for Turkmens: an education system open to all, producing high rates of literacy; a reasonably progressive approach to the role of women, who had relatively good opportunities to study and work; and health care that was available to everyone. But the downsides outweighed the up. In the late 1980s, a movement of Turkmen intellectuals, Agzybirlik, formed a manifesto based around concerns surrounding the Turkmen language and culture, as well as wider economic and environmental issues.

But the last years of the USSR were not marked in Turkmenistan by the emerging success of a popular nationality-based movement. Rather, the transition to independence was managed by the local regime. The post of First Secretary of the Communist Party of Turkmenistan had fallen in 1985 to Saparmurat Niyazov. The new First Secretary strengthened his hold on the republic in 1990, when he was first elected Chairman of the Supreme Soviet and then, on 27 October, elected to the newly created post of executive President of Turkmenistan. He was not opposed in the latter election, in which he secured a reported 98.3% of the vote. He combined a strong line against movements such as Agzybirlik with concern about the prospect of the break-up of the USSR, fearing the consequences of the loss of the subsidy received from Moscow. In the all-Union referendum on the status of the USSR held in March 1991, a higher proportion of the voters of the TSSR (more than 95%) opted for the preservation of the USSR than of any other republic. But as the flow of events through 1991 increasingly clearly spelt the end of the USSR, a national referendum on 26 October produced, according to the official figures, an overwhelming vote for independence. On the following day, independence was declared by the Turkmen Supreme Soviet.

GOVERNMENT AND POLITICS

Presidential rule

The politics of post-independence Turkmenistan has been dominated by one man, Saparmurat Niyazov. Born on 19 February 1940, he was orphaned as a child. His father, Atamurat, was killed in World War II, and his mother and brothers died in the Ashgabat earthquake of 1948. He was raised first in an orphanage, and later with distant relatives. Niyazov graduated from the Leningrad Polytechnic Institute with a degree in power engineering, and started his working career at the Buzmeyin (now Abadan) power station, west of Ashgabat. He had joined the Communist Party in 1962, and rose through its ranks, becoming the head of the Ashgabat administration in 1980 and First Secretary of the Communist Party of Turkmenistan in 1985.

On Turkmenistan's independence in 1991, Niyazov had already established a stronghold on the organs of power, and was able to consolidate his control thereafter. The Communist Party of Turkmenistan was simply renamed the Democratic Party of Turkmenistan, with Niyazov as its chairman. The new constitution of May 1992 further focused powers on the president, stipulating that the head of state was also the head of government, as chairman of the cabinet of ministers. President Niyazov also serves as the commander-in-chief of Turkmenistan's armed forces.

In June 1992, Niyazov was re-elected president, again unopposed, this time securing a reported 99.5% of the vote. At the end of 1993, Turkmenistan's parliament voted to extend President Niyazov's term of office until 2002, to allow the completion of the president's ten-year development programme. This extension was ratified in a referendum on 15 January 1994 when, according to the official results, a mesmerising 99.99% of the electorate voted in favour. The December 1999 session of Turkmenistan's People's Council (*Halk Maslahaty*) voted to make Niyazov president for life. Niyazov has since repeatedly suggested, usually to staged cries of disapproval from his supporters, that he will aim to retire on or around 2010, when he will be 70. In April 2005, he announced that new presidential elections, with a range of candidates, would be held in 2009, and that he would himself stand down at that time.

The *Halk Maslahaty*, with more than 2,500 members, is in theory the supreme legislative body of Turkmenistan, empowered to amend the constitution and approve the overall direction of government policy. Only a small minority of the delegates are elected; the majority are state officials and functionaries of organisations supporting the regime. The *Halk Maslahaty* has met since 1996 in conjunction with the Council of Elderly and the Galkynysh National Revival Movement. It meets roughly once a year: President Niyazov has traditionally announced the date and venue, set the agenda, and chaired the meeting. His proposals, except where these concern the possibility of new presidential elections, are invariably approved with unanimity. The speeches from delegates are centred on praise for the president's work and ideas and on proposals to grant new awards to the president

Turkmenistan's parliament (*Mejlis*) comprises 50 deputies, elected every five years from single-member constituencies. Although the 2004 *Mejlis* elections were contested, all candidates were supporters of the regime, whose pre-election manifestos proudly emphasised their commitment to implementing the policies of President Niyazov. In practice, the *Mejlis* is a legislative rubber-stamp.

Niyazov frequently fires his ministers and senior officials, accusing them of corruption or incompetence, as part of an apparent policy to ensure that no potential rivals can develop a power base. Domestic opposition is not allowed, and rare small-scale demonstrations, for example against the demolition of houses in Ashgabat, are quickly broken up by the authorities. While Niyazov has talked in general terms about the eventual emergence of a multi-party system in Turkmenistan, the one (artificial) experiment in this direction, the announcement in 1993 of a Peasants' Justice Party to serve as a champion for agrarian interests, was not developed. There is some exiled opposition to Niyazov's government, whose leaders include former ministers and officials dismissed by the Turkmen president.

On November 25 2002, a group of exiled oppositionists led by former Foreign Minister Boris Shikhmuradov organised, according to the Turkmen government version of events, an assassination attempt against Niyazov, in which they had enlisted the help of foreign mercenaries. The alleged plotters of the coup attempt, including Shikhmuradov, were rounded up, tried and convicted in a summary way as 'betrayers of the motherland', the nature of the detentions and trials raising considerable international concern over the apparent abuses of human rights involved.

The concentration of power by President Niyazov has been made on the basis of what he perceives as a social contract with the people of Turkmenistan, as part of which certain basic goods are provided at free or heavily subsidised rates, including free gas, and petrol at 300 manat a litre. In a book of poetry, *Spring of My Inspiration*, completed in 2004, Niyazov sets out his conception of a democratic state in the poem '*My Democracy*'. Free water, gas and electricity are a core part of the vision, as are televised Cabinet meetings, national unity and the hard and honest work of the president.

Nation-building

Since 1991, Niyazov has paid great attention to nation-building, with at its core the identification of the state of Turkmenistan with the Turkmen people, and a strong focus on the history and achievements of the Turkmens. The iconography of the newly independent state of Turkmenistan is developed in Niyazov's books of poetry and, especially, in the two volumes of his book *Ruhnama* (see box, page 13).

The regime's nation-building programme has placed the figure of President Niyazov himself firmly at its heart, as the leader to have brought Turkmenistan to independence, and the Turkmen people to a new Golden Age (*Altyn Asyr*). One of the most strongly emphasised cults of personality found anywhere in the world has developed in Turkmenistan. Niyazov has adopted the title Turkmenbashy, 'The

Father of the Turkmen', later amended to 'Beyik Turkmenbashy', thereby adding 'Great' to the title. The slogan '*Halk, Watan, Beyik Turkmenbashy*' ('People, Homeland, Great Father of the Turkmen') is printed on billboards around town, written in whitewashed pebbles on hillsides overlooking roadways, and chanted by soldiers during military parades. Photographs of the smiling president beam down from office walls and billboards, adorn the cabins of every Turkmenistan Airlines aircraft and grace officially produced greetings cards. In one particularly favoured pose, Niyazov's chin cupped in his left hand, the president bears a notable resemblance to a mid-career Dean Martin. Golden statues of the president are everywhere.

The cult of personality in Turkmenistan has expanded its range to encompass Niyazov's parents. His father Atamurat is presented as a war hero, whose statue forms the centrepiece of the war memorials built since independence. His mother, Gurbansoltan Eje, is also depicted on numerous statues, her virtues those of motherly love and sacrifice for her children. The front covers of Niyazov's books are themselves pictured on many posters, and *Ruhnama* is the subject of book-shaped monuments. Cities, towns and even geographical features across Turkmenistan have been renamed in honour of President Niyazov and his family. The name Turkmenbashy has, for example, been allotted to the country's largest port, its highest peak, a brand of vodka and the month of January.

The developing cult of personality is such that some early post-independence renamings have now been deemed insufficiently grand. Thus in May 2003 the *Mejlis* decreed that Saparmurat Niyazov District in Lebap Region would henceforth be renamed Saparmurat Turkmenbashy the Great District. The real and legendary historical figures identified in Niyazov's writings as representing past Golden Ages of the Turkmen people, from Oguz Han to Magtymguly, have also been commemorated in many renamings. Thus almost every Turkmen town seems to have one main street named after Niyazov/Turkmenbashy, usually intersecting with another named after Magtymguly.

President Niyazov's personal style of leadership, in which Cabinet meetings are frequently dominated by his homilies, has over the years given the Western media a rich source of copy. One story to tickle the tabloids came in April 2004 when, at a meeting at the Agricultural University, Niyazov noted the gold teeth in the mouth of one of the students. He informed young Selbijan that her teeth would look much better if they were white. His Minister of Health was a dentist, and Niyazov suggested that he could do the necessary work. Turkmens should look after their teeth by gnawing on bones, as a dog looked after by the young Niyazov had done. That dog had excellent teeth.

Niyazov has complained about beards sported by students, sacked his chief meteorologist for getting the weather forecasts wrong, and urged television cameramen to change the angle from which they were filming Turkmenistan's female singers, as they were making them look too fat. But international media excitement at Niyazov's announcement about the construction of an ice palace in this desert republic turned out to have been prompted by an error in translation. He had been talking about a skating rink.

ECONOMY

Turkmenistan's economic policy is guided by ten- and 20-year strategies, which set production targets in every sector of the economy, underpinned by state investment programmes. The unreliable official Turkmen statistics announce considerable success in the attainment of these ambitious targets, with reported

RUHNAMA

In September 2001 appeared a book with a distinctive pink and pastel green cover, *Ruhnama: Reflections on the Spiritual Values of the Turkmen*. Its author was President Niyazov, and the purpose of the book was to help develop the nation-building process in Turkmenistan by emphasising the geographic identity between the present-day territory of Turkmenistan and the Turkmen people, stressing the historical and future greatness of the Turkmens, and identifying and praising the values of Turkmens as a group.

The book presents the many empires founded by Turkic peoples, from Seljuks to Ottomans, as evidence of the past glories of the Turkmens. One of Niyazov's books of poetry, published in 2003, develops more explicitly the theme, explored in *Ruhnama*, of past Golden Ages of the Turkmen people. Five such Golden Ages are identified. The first is associated with Oguz Han, legendary ancestor of the Turkmens. The second with Gorkut Ata, legendary spiritual leader around whom the epic *Book of Gorkut* was based. The third with Georogly, legendary warrior hero. The fourth with Magtymguly, a real 18th-century poet. The fifth Golden Age, continuing today, is associated with Saparmurat Niyazov.

In *Ruhnama*, Niyazov stresses that the key to securing such Golden Ages is unity among the Turkmen people, avoiding the tribal divisions which historically allowed the Turkmens to be dominated by external powers. *Ruhnama* praises family values, honest labour and patriotism. It sets out the inventions and achievements of the Turkmens, which include, apparently, giving the world the first robots as well as a yellowish-coloured sheep.

Through the sponsorship of foreign businesses working in Ashgabat, *Ruhnama* has been translated into numerous foreign languages. The Turkmen press even reported at one stage that a Zulu version was planned. Some of these translations have involved rather hasty work, but I like the juxtaposition in the English text of a reference to the Ahal Tekke horse with one to a stable state. Turkmen schoolchildren and university students take compulsory lessons and exams in *Ruhnama*, slogans from Niyazov's book appear on billboards, and readings from *Ruhnama* are given in Turkmen mosques during Saturday (*Ruh*-day) prayers. The Turkmen media refer to *Ruhnama* as a 'sacred' book, and newspapers run crosswords to test the knowledge of their readership on its finer points. You can read the text online at www.rukhnama.com. In September 2004, volume two appeared.

annual GDP growth rates regularly above 20%. Foreign investment is hampered by the dual exchange-rate system, by Turkmenistan's heavy bureaucracy and by the strong state control. The role of the private sector is weakly developed, with key strategic sectors remaining firmly in state hands. Turkmenistan remains, then, in large measure a command economy.

Hydrocarbons

Turkmenistan is blessed with major reserves of oil and, especially, natural gas, and its hydrocarbons wealth forms the bulk of its export earnings. Its oilfields in the west of the country, and offshore in the Caspian, are operated either by the state concern Turkmenneft, or by foreign hydrocarbons companies under production-sharing agreements with Turkmenistan. The government is particularly keen to attract more foreign companies to the Caspian, where the costs and risks associated with the exploration and development of new fields are high. The absence of an agreed demarcation of the Caspian between the five littoral states remains, however, an impediment to new foreign investment in the many disputed areas. Crude oil is either exported or sent to the oil refineries at Turkmenbashy and Seydi, where the government is carrying out a considerable investment programme, aiming to bolster revenues through the production of a wider range of oil products.

Natural gas production is in the hands of Turkmen state concerns. Throughout the post-independence period, the question of export routes for Turkmenistan's gas has remained a major concern of the Turkmen government. With the exception of a small gas pipeline from fields in southwest Turkmenistan to Iran, opened in 1997, the gas pipelines infrastructure remains that of the Soviet period, running north to the countries of the former Soviet Union. Turkmenistan's main customers have been Russia and Ukraine, under deals which have given Turkmenistan a relatively low price for its gas, and often in a formula which has involved part payment in goods, rather than a straight cash arrangement. The state of repair of the pipelines infrastructure, and the claims on the pipelines made by the other gas-producing states of Central Asia, also limit the export capacity of these routes in respect of Turkmen gas.

Possible new pipelines across the Caspian to the South Caucasus and thence to Turkey, and across Afghanistan to Pakistan, have been the subject of feasibility studies and lengthy negotiations, but without as yet any concrete outcomes. The government has responded to its difficulties over gas pipelines by trying to bolster the export of natural gas in other forms, through the development of liquefied gas plants, electricity exports, and industries relying on natural gas as an input, such as fertiliser production.

Agriculture and textiles

In agriculture, Niyazov implemented a programme of land reform involving the conversion of the Soviet collective farms into 'peasants' associations' (*dayhan birleshik*), with a stated policy of the progressive transfer of land to private ownership, through the interim step of a leasehold arrangement. But leaseholders are still required to grow cotton or wheat to fulfil production quotas set by the state. They use machinery, seeds and fertilisers provided at cheap rates by state concerns, and in return must sell their harvest at low prices to monopolistic state purchasers. Real private-sector development in the peasants' associations has so far been largely limited to the small household plots on which farmers are allowed to grow, and market, whatever they choose.

The Soviet emphasis on cultivation of cotton has been retained, though Niyazov has attempted to boost Turkmenistan's revenue through the construction, usually in partnership with Turkish companies, of modern textiles factories, producing for export cotton yarns or ready-made fabrics rather than just raw cotton. Niyazov also embarked soon after independence on an ambitious programme to expand Turkmenistan's production of wheat, based around the stated goal of securing self-sufficiency in grain. The announcement of the successful fulfilment of the annual grain production target is marked by bread-focused government celebrations, with the quota figures inscribed on huge loaves. The new emphasis on wheat production, combined with environmental problems such as soil salinisation, the absence of productivity-motivating prices paid to the farmers and the overall inefficiencies of the state-controlled system, however, have all joined the vagaries of the weather in contributing to a series of disastrous cotton harvests.

Government spending

The receipts from Turkmenistan's export earnings have been used to finance an ambitious state-directed construction programme, whose most striking result has been the remodelling of the city of Ashgabat with a white marble face. Export receipts, often channelled into the opaque Foreign Exchange Reserve Fund rather than into the state budget, have also financed such purchases as Turkmenistan Airlines' Boeing aircraft, the black Mercedes cars allotted to Turkmen ministers and local governors, and a formidable fleet of large tractors and cotton harvesters. Funding for sectors such as health and education has remained modest.

PEOPLE AND CULTURE

The ethnic groups of Turkmenistan

Ethnic Turkmens are a large majority of the people of Turkmenistan. The 1995 census figures recorded that Turkmens comprised around 77% of the population. Uzbeks made up 9.2%, and Russians 6.7% (down from 9.5% in the 1989 census). Other significant communities included Kazakhs, Ukrainians, Armenians, Azeris and Tatars. Since 1995, the proportion of ethnic Turkmens has certainly increased further, through a combination of a high birth rate among the ethnic Turkmen group, and out-migration of other communities in response to the government's Turkmenisation policies. President Niyazov, while stressing the importance of friendship and harmony between ethnic groups, closely identifies the state of Turkmenistan with the Turkmen people. The Turkmen language is the medium of education and government, non-Turkmen cultural outlets are now rarities, and few senior government posts are held by non-Turkmens. Significant non-Turkmen minorities remain, however, in the main towns, and Dashoguz and Lebap regions have large ethnic Uzbek populations.

Turkmen people

According to *Ruhnama*, the Turkmens originated from Oguz Han, who had six sons, each of whom had four sons of their own. From these 24 boys originated 24 clans, from which all of the Oguz people of the world are descended. While Turkic tribes had started to arrive in this part of Central Asia from around the 5th century, historians believe that there was a major westwards migration of Oguz tribes from the area of present-day Mongolia in the 10th century. One of the new homes of the Oguz was the region of the Aral Sea and Syr Darya Basin. The use of the word 'Turkmen' began to appear around this time, possibly to distinguish those Oguz tribes which had accepted Islam. From this area emerged the Seljuks, who expanded their territories southwestwards in the 11th century, forming a great empire. The Oguz peoples moving into the area at this time were the ancestors of the modern Turkmen.

The Turkmens are a tribal people. The main tribes include the Tekke, based around the Ahal, Tejen and Merv oases; the Ersari, along the Amu Darya; the Yomud, in the western Balkan Region and Khorezm Oasis; the Goklen, in the far southwest; and the Sarik and Salor, in the southern part of the Merv Oasis and along the Murgab River. Historically, divisions between the tribes have been strong. Visiting in the 1860s, the Hungarian traveller Arminius Vambery found for example that the Yomud lived 'in an inveterate and irreconcilable enmity with the Goklen' while the Sarik were at that time in hostile relations with almost everybody else. The 18th-century Turkmen poet Magtymguly stressed the need for unity among the Turkmen tribes, better to withstand external aggression, and this theme has been taken up strongly by Niyazov's government. Tribal background remains important in many spheres of life, from patronage networks to determining marriage partners, though is not necessarily a decisive factor. Differences between the tribes are reflected in styles of dress, carpet designs, dialect and, many Turkmens will claim, even in personal character.

Turkmen culture

Since independence, the nation-building programme of the Turkmen government has placed great emphasis on the promotion of the traditional culture of the Turkmen people, although this is often presented in a stylised version. Turkmen-style dress, for example, is required to be worn by most school and university students and teachers, and increasingly in government offices more widely. Television channels show frequent concerts of Turkmen music, based around the two-stringed *dutar* and a guttural singing style. The Turkmen carpet, Ahal Tekke horse and the poetry of Magtymguly are all commemorated in national holidays. Traditional dances such as the energetic *gush depdi* from the western Balkan Region have been adapted to suit large state concerts.

Some Turkmen traditions have not been strongly emphasised by the post-independence government. One example, perhaps because of its associations with nomadism, rather than an urban, state-building tradition, is the *yurt*. This circular, wooden-framed, felt-covered dwelling could be packed up and carried by camel between nomadic encampments. Vambery notes that the *yurts* of the Turkmens were categorised into one of two types. The *gara oy* ('black house') was a standard *yurt*, blackened with the smoke of countless fires, and the *ak oy* ('white house') was a pristine dwelling, reserved for newly-weds and honoured guests. *Yurts* are still found today in Turkmen desert communities, in the courtyards of some Turkmen families nostalgic for the old ways, and in a few urban restaurants wishing to offer a traditional Turkmen dining environment.

The dresses worn by Turkmen women add colour and style to the streets of Turkmen towns. They are long dresses of silk or velvet, descending to the ankle, most frequently a burgundy colour, though deep blue and green are also favoured. The necks are enlivened with intricately embroidered trims, which descend in a bar down the front of the dress. Married women wear a colourful headscarf. An embroidered Turkmen skull-cap, *takhya*, is a standard part of the uniform at school and university for both girls and boys. Younger schoolgirls have their hair tied with two fluffy white pom-poms.

Male office-wear combines a dark three-buttoned suit with a white shirt. Government employees and students are encouraged to wear a lapel pin bearing President Niyazov's head in silhouette. Older men, the respected *aksakals* ('white beards'), still frequently sport the shaggy sheepskin hats known as *telpeks*, worn on top of the *takhya*. Baggy black trousers, tucked into black boots, white shirts with a modest embroidered trim, and a long coat complete the traditional male dress, though it is rarely worn by young men, except during concert performances.

LANGUAGE

The official language of Turkmenistan is Turkmen, part of the Ural-Altaic language group which includes the family of Turkic languages. Within this group, Turkmen is one of the Oguz or Southern Turkish languages, along with Turkish and Azeri. There are many Turkmen dialects, broadly corresponding to the different Turkmen tribes. The standard Turkmen language is based most strongly around the Yomud and Tekke dialects. During the Soviet period, the Turkmen language adopted many Russian words, especially to describe new items of technology. The Turkmen government is encouraging their replacement by equivalent terms derived from authentic Turkmen roots.

Turkmen has been written in a range of alphabets, reflecting changing political priorities. It was written in an Arabic script until the late 1920s, when the Latin-based Unified Turkish Latin Alphabet was introduced, similar to the alphabet currently in use for the Turkish language. A Cyrillic script was introduced in 1940. Following independence, President Niyazov introduced a switch to another Latin alphabet, known as the New Alphabet (*Taze Elipbiy*). The president even patented the script. For an introduction to the basics of the Turkmen language, see *Appendix 1*, page 225.

Russian-language teaching was given a high priority in the Soviet period. Better-off families in urban areas, members of the Russian and other non-Turkmen minority groups and many older Turkmens speak Russian, and so a knowledge of this language is invaluable for getting around and making conversation in Turkmenistan. The Russian-language ability of the young generation is, however, markedly weaker than that of their parents. While Russian is still taught in many schools, it is as a foreign language rather than a medium of wider instruction. In rural communities you may struggle to communicate in Russian.

English is also taught as a foreign language in some schools, but the standard of tuition is patchy at best. You will certainly find many Turkmens eager to practise their English, but this often extends to little more than a few standard phrases.

RELIGION

The large majority of the population is Sunni Muslim, but the religious practices of Turkmens have always incorporated strong pre-Islamic elements, some drawn from Zoroastrianism and Shamanism. The attachment of Turkmens to amulets and talismans, the important place of ancestor worship, including visiting the graves of ancestors, and traditions such as the 'swinging away of sins' during the *Kurban Bayram* festival, are all examples. The influence of the mystical Sufism movement in Turkmenistan is particularly strong, probably because it appeared to enable the fusion of Islamic worship with traditional practices. Local Sufi leaders often incorporated music, even dance, into their rituals, and their tombs have become some of the most highly venerated places of shrine pilgrimage in Turkmenistan.

The constitution declares Turkmenistan to be a secular state, but President Niyazov has tended to identify Islam as part of the national heritage of Turkmenistan, and the Islamic religion as an integral part of Turkmen identity. Niyazov's speeches frequently emphasise the freedom to practise Islam recovered following independence, comparing the four mosques which remained open during the Soviet period with the more than 300 built since 1991. Niyazov himself made the *hajj* in 1992, the first leader of one of the newly independent states of Central Asia to do so. Islamic marriage and funeral traditions are practised openly.

The government, however, concerned about the possible emergence of radical or political Islam, has taken steps to ensure that the state exerts control over religious structures, for example through the establishment of a Council for Religious Affairs, reporting to the president. The state controls the selection of clergy, often favouring local elders with limited formal theological training. *Madrasas* and other religious schools have not been permitted to operate. The annual *hajj* delegation from Turkmenistan is typically of around 188 people: this figure represents the capacity of one of Turkmenistan Airlines' Boeing aircraft. The state decides on the delegation and pays for the flight. Turkmens traditionally have no strong tradition of attendance of mosques, usually praying at home and at shrine pilgrimage sites. The largest of the mosques built since independence, including those at Geok Depe, Gypjak and the Ertogrul Gazy Mosque in Ashgabat,

SHRINE PILGRIMAGE

Shrine pilgrimage (*ziarat*) is one of the strongest features of religious belief among the Turkmens, and is closely associated with the tradition of veneration of ancestors. Almost all Turkmen cemeteries are based around the tomb of a revered figure who, as the *gonambashy* ('head of the cemetery'), extends his or her positive influence over the cemetery as a whole. Within Turkmen society, there are some 'non-Turkmen' lineage groups, known as *owlat*, or holy, groups. These groups, of perceived Arab origin, trace their ancestry not to Oguz Han but to the Prophet Mohammed. The *owlat* lineages usually include a respected Sufi figure. Those cemeteries in which the *gonambashy* is a well-known Sufi of *owlat* line tend to be important places of pilgrimage.

But there are a wide variety of shrine pilgrimage sites, and by no means all are located at the place of burial of a well-known Sufi or other respected figure. Some are based around natural objects such as caves or particularly ancient trees, around which legends are woven. In some cases, there is no tomb at these sites. Others are the purported burial sites of major figures of the Islamic world, although these are in many cases known to have been buried elsewhere, or of legendary figures.

Alongside the tomb or mausoleum of the venerated figure, the largest shrine pilgrimage sites include a complex of buildings, including a mosque, a guesthouse for pilgrims, and a covered area for the holding of sacrificial meals. The last, known as *hudaiyoly*, form an important part of the pilgrimage. They are given as part of the process of making a request to the venerated figure during a pilgrimage, or to give thanks when a previous request was answered positively. They can also be given at home, for example on specific days following a death of a close relative, or to give thanks for a piece of luck or achievement. The offering of part of the sacrificial meal to other visitors to the pilgrimage site is considered particularly praiseworthy, so you may well find that visits to places of shrine pilgrimage include the receipt of a bowl of *plov*.

Visits to shrine pilgrimage sites involve a complex series of rituals. These differ from site to site, but a common feature is the circling three times of the tomb or mausoleum, while repeatedly touching the tomb with both hands and then holding the hands to the face. At the end of this process, pilgrims often squat down in the company of the caretaker of the site, himself respected as a 'holy man', while the caretaker recites a blessing. The caretaker is usually given a small payment for performing this service. Many sites incorporate a feature known as a *chile agach*, comprising one or more trees or constructed from

owe their grand designs more to the requirements of the regime than to those of the local religious communities.

Freedom of religious expression is enshrined in Turkmenistan's constitution but, under restrictive legislation passed in the mid-1990s, only Sunni Muslim and Russian Orthodox communities were able successfully to secure the necessary registration. In 2004 and 2005, following a relaxation of the rules surrounding registration, several further religious communities have secured it, including Baha'is, Seventh-Day Adventists, Hare Krishnas and Baptists, though reports of various forms of harassment of minority religious communities continue.

pieces of wood, sometimes taking the form of a basic wooden gateway. Passing through this is believed to cure the sick and bring children to the infertile.

Votive offerings are very common. The most widespread are small strips of cloth, usually tied to the branches of a gnarled and ancient tree or *chile agach*, each signifying a prayer. Two bricks placed on the ground in a small hut shape are another prayer signifier. The nature of the votive offerings gives a good indication that desire for a child is a particularly common prayer: plastic rattles, dummies, and little cribs modelled from cloth are seen at almost every site. An open pair of scissors also represents the wish for a child – the allusion is to the severing of the umbilical cord. The colour of the strip of cloth placed at pilgrimage sites may reflect the desired sex of the child: a white strip reflecting the wish for a boy, a colourful strip for a girl. There are always more white strips than coloured ones. The majority of pilgrims to many of the sites are women. Parau Bibi in particular is strongly dominated by female pilgrims.

At many sites you will see collections of unusually shaped stones, often including fossils such as ammonites, stones which appear to bear the print of a hand or foot, stones which resemble fruits or household items, or simply attractive rounded pebbles. Larger stones are balanced on the thumbs of two pilgrims. Smaller ones are balanced on the thumb and first two fingers of one pilgrim. If the stones gently rotate, it is believed that no sin has been committed. Other unusual traditions include girls rolling down the hill at the Kyrk Molla site, in a bid to promote fertility, and pilgrims staring down into a well at Ak Ishan, in search of the moon.

There are many hundreds of shrine pilgrimage sites across Turkmenistan. My personal recommendation of the ten most interesting sites for the casual visitor is as follows:

Ak Ishan, Ahal Region (see page 119)
Malik Baba, Ahal Region (page 128)
Parau Bibi, Balkan Region (page 155)
Shibly Baba, Balkan Region (page 158)
Ismamut Ata, Dashoguz Region (page 169)
Mausoleum of Nedjmeddin Kubra, Dashoguz Region (page 174)
Kyrk Molla, Dashoguz Region (page 178)
Ibrahim Sultan, Dashoguz Region (page 180)
Kyrk Gyz, Lebap Region (page 198)
Mausoleum of Mohammed Ibn Zayd, Mary Region (page 217)

2 Practical Information

WHEN TO VISIT

Lying in the heart of the Central Asian land-mass, Turkmenistan's climate has been described as extreme continental. Summers are hot, winters cold, there is little rainfall and low humidity.

The summer months, from June to early September, are probably the worst time to visit Turkmenistan. Temperatures frequently climb above 40°C in the shade, and make a stroll around an archaeological site a tough proposition. Applications for visits to nature reserves during this period are often refused, because of the risks of fire. The deep blue skies of the Turkmen summer offer some compensation for the burdens of the heat, though, and a summer holiday can be pleasant here with the right preparations. Ensure that all accommodation booked has air conditioning (the summer is not a time to cut costs by staying in the cheapest hotels, where you will swelter in airless rooms), avoid trying to do too much, and stay close to your water bottle.

Winter, which lasts roughly from the end of November until February, is nothing like as severe as the snowbound months faced in more northerly parts of the former Soviet Union. Temperatures rarely fall far below freezing, except in the Kopet Dag Mountains, and any snowfall lingers for days or weeks, not months. Winter is a perfectly possible time to visit, and you may be lucky and experience only clear, crisp days. But this period can show Turkmenistan at its dreariest, with pallid skies and frequent cloud cover. Turkmen women cover their bright velvet dresses with dark leather jackets, almost as a metaphor for the wintry gloom. This time of year also sees the highest risks of flight delays (the Turkmenistan Airlines flights to the UK seem particularly prone to delays resulting from fog at the point of departure in India).

Most Turkmens will advise foreign visitors to come in springtime. The country is at its most beautiful in April and May, with the Kopet Dag Mountains covered in red poppies and tulips, and even the desert in bloom. Temperatures are pleasantly warm, though the Turkmen spring can be unpredictable, with rainy spells sometimes lingering.

Autumn too is a good time to visit. The landscape, scorched by the heat of summer, is much browner than in springtime, but warm temperatures and frequent blue skies make the period from mid-September until early-November ideal for tourism. Autumn is, however, also the time of the cotton harvest, when many Turkmens are bussed to the cotton fields to pick Turkmenistan's 'white gold'. Most museums outside Ashgabat are closed during this period, and bazaars in cotton-growing areas are kept shut by the local authorities during the daytime, to encourage people to stay in the cotton fields. They open for a few hours in the evenings.

Approval to visit Turkmenistan is particularly difficult to get in the run-up to the Independence Day holiday on October 27, when the government focuses its attention on the official delegations visiting Turkmenistan. Difficulties in securing the necessary visit approval from the Turkmen government are also frequently reported in the run-up to two other holidays: Flag Day on February 19 and Neutrality Day on December 12. All three dates are therefore best avoided, unless you are part of an official delegation.

HIGHLIGHTS

Depending on whether you are a lover of archaeology or scenery, monuments or carpets, the following are the core highlights around which a good Turkmenistan programme may be built.

Ashgabat With Turkmenistan's only international airport, most hotels, and the hub of the domestic transport network, Ashgabat is difficult to avoid. Not that you would wish to do so. Its white marble buildings, golden statues and fountains are an evolving monument to the nation-building programme of President Niyazov. The National, Fine Arts and Carpet museums are interesting and help set the context for a visit to Turkmenistan. And there are worthwhile side trips to the Parthian fortress of Old Nisa and ruins of the mosque at Aneu.

Historical sites The two top attractions are Merv and Konye-Urgench, both of which make obvious building-blocks around which to construct a Turkmenistan programme. Other, less widely known, sites which also fascinate include the ongoing Bronze Age excavations at Gonur, the remote city site of Misrian in western Turkmenistan, and the cave settlement of Ekedeshik near Tagtabazar.

The mountains The Kopet Dag may be modest as mountain ranges go, its peaks never troubling the 3,000m mark, but it offers good riding and trekking, and some splendid scenery, for example around Nohur and in the Sumbar Valley. The Kugitang Nature Reserve in the far east of the country, which does have a 3,000m peak, is another excellent upland destination, offering potentially superb but largely untapped prospects for speleological tourism and, for non-troglodytes, a remarkable plateau pock-marked with the footprints of dinosaurs.

The desert The Kara Kum Desert, the vast empty heart of Turkmenistan, demands respect. Trips here require careful planning, but considerable rewards can be earnt from the effort. Targets include the stunning polychrome canyon at Yangykala and the burning gas crater near Darvaza, but the attractions of the desert are captured too around a camp-fire on a still, silent evening, beneath a rich canopy of stars.

The people The Turkmen people, welcoming and curious, will offer the real highlight of your trip wherever you go. Some travel agencies in Turkmenistan offer specially designed 'ethnographic' excursions, to see traditional village life in places like Erbent or the desert oasis of Damla. In many parts of the world, such trips would be artificial touristic kitsch, but here they are much more authentic. Turkmenistan's bazaars, especially the sprawling Tolkuchka market outside Ashgabat, are ideal places to watch and interact with local people. And I recommend the inclusion of at least one of Turkmenistan's main shrine pilgrimage sites on your itinerary. These sites, which provide an insight into the religious beliefs of the Turkmen people, are often at their most animated on Thursdays and Fridays. The hillside mausoleum of Parau Bibi, near the town of Serdar, is one of the most interesting.

TOUR OPERATORS

Overseas operators

UK

Adventure Overland 9 Ridge Rd, Mitcham, Surrey CR4 2ET; t/f 020 8640 8105; e info@adventureoverland.com; www.adventureoverland.com. Tailor-made itineraries. Sample programmes include nine days horseriding in the Kopet Dag Mountains and ten days off-road through the Kara Kum Desert.
Coromandel Andrew Brock Travel Ltd, 29A Main St, Lyddington, Oakham LE15 9LR; t 01572 821330; f 01572 821072; e abrock3650@aol.com; www.coromandel.com. Individually tailored itineraries. Sample programmes include the 11-day 'Essence of Turkestan', covering Ashgabat and Merv as well as destinations in Uzbekistan.
Dragoman Camp Green, Debenham, Stowmarket, Suffolk IP14 6LA; t 0870 499 4475; f 01728 861127; e info@dragoman.co.uk; www.dragoman.com. Offers a wide range of tour permutations including Turkmenistan. For example, a 14-night Ashgabat to Tashkent trip includes Ashgabat, Tolkuchka Bazaar, the Kara Kum Desert and Konye-Urgench. A 23-night tour from Istanbul to Ashgabat features Turkmenbashy, the Kow Ata underground lake, Geok Depe and Old Nisa.
Regent Holidays 15 John St, Bristol BS1 2HR; t 0117 921 1711; f 0117 925 4866; e regent@regent-holidays.co.uk; www.regent-holidays.co.uk. Individually tailored itineraries.
Steppes East 51 Castle St, Cirencester GL7 1QD; t 01285 651010; f 01285 885888; e sales@steppeseast.co.uk; www.steppeseast.co.uk. Specially tailored itineraries.

Australia

Sundowners Travel Ste 15, Lonsdale Court, 600 Lonsdale St, Melbourne, Victoria 3000; t +61 (0) 3 9672 5300; www.sundownerstravel.com. A good range of tours including Turkmenistan. The 16-day 'Turkoman traveller' between Ashgabat and Tashkent includes Old Nisa, Tolkuchka Bazaar, Merv and Konye-Urgench. A 35-day trip from China to Turkey includes a journey on the Transcaspian Railway from Ashgabat to Turkmenbashy.

Canada

Bestway Tours Suite 206, 8678 Greenall Av, Burnaby, British Columbia V5J 3M6; t +1 604 264 7378; f +1 604 264 7774; e bestway@bestway.com; www.bestway.com. Programmes featuring Turkmenistan include a 17-day Central Asia tour, visiting Ashgabat, Old Nisa, Merv, Dashoguz and Konye-Urgench, and a train-based tour from Beijing to Moscow.
Silk Road Tours 300-1497 Marine Dr, West Vancouver BC V7T 1B8; t +1 604 925 3831; f +1 604 925 6269; e canada@silkroadtours.com; www.silkroadtours.com. Specially-tailored itineraries.

Germany

Studiosus Reisen 25 Riessestrasse, D 80992 Muenchen; t +49 89 500 60505; f +49 89 500 60100; e tours@studiosus.com: www.studiosus.de. Programmes featuring Turkmenistan include a 16-day tour covering Konye-Urgench, Merv, Ashgabat, Old Nisa and Anau, as well as destinations in Uzbekistan.
Ventus Reisen 8 Krefelder Strasse, 10555 Berlin; t +49 30 391 00332; f +49 30 399 5587; e office@ventus.com; www.ventus.com. Offers a nine-day off-road tour in Turkmenistan, including Ashgabat, Erbent, the Kara Kum Desert, Mary, Merv, Gonur and Meana Baba.

Kazakhstan

Stantours 163/76 Kunyaeva, Almaty; tel +7 3272 631344; f +49 89 14882 41382; e info@stantours.com; www.stantours.com. Stantours' David Berghof, a German national with a penchant for extreme sports, formerly worked in the travel business in Ashgabat, and this Almaty-based agency retains a good level of experience in organising tailored packages to Turkmenistan.

United States

Mir Corporation Suite 210, 85 S Washington St, Seattle WA 98104; ☎ +1 206 624 7289; f +1 206 624 7360; e info@mircorp.com; www.mircorp.com. Offers a range of tours, including a 21-day programme around the five former Soviet Central Asian Republics, seeing Merv, Ashgabat and Old Nisa in Turkmenistan.

Travel agencies in Turkmenistan

The large number of regulations surrounding the tourism sector in Turkmenistan mean, in effect, that all visitors coming to Turkmenistan on a tourist visa must use the services of a registered Turkmen travel agency in order to secure their invitations (see *Red tape*, below). Overseas tour operators likewise must work through one of the local Turkmen firms. Turkmen travel agencies are either state or private concerns. Most travellers report that the private agencies offer a generally more efficient service, and foreign tour operators mainly work with one of the private firms. All the agencies below are based in Ashgabat.

State travel agencies

State Committee for Tourism and Sport 17 1984 Kochesi; ☎ 12 396663; f 12 397703; e turkmentour@online.tm; www.tourism-sport.gov.tm. Turkmenistan's 'Ministry of Tourism', usually referred to by the shortened Turkmen title Turkmensyyahat, is responsible for the overall regulation of the tourism sector in Turkmenistan, including the registration of individual travel agencies and the management of a number of hotels. But they do not really act as a travel agency in their own right, and you are unlikely to need to contact them direct. The address on 1984 Street somehow seems appropriate.

Ashgabatsyyahat 7 Georogly Kochesi (in the Sheraton Grand Turkmen Hotel); ☎ 12 396666, 351110; f 12 352015, 396660; e ashgabadsiyakhat@online.tm. Organises letters of invitation, hotel accommodation, short tours in and around Ashgabat, and a small range of longer tours, including to Merv, Nohur and Kugitang. Also arranges horseriding. English-speaking guides available.

Ahalsyyahat 94 Magtymguly Shayoly; ☎ 12 395642, 354260; f 12 350675; e ahal-travel@online.tm. Arranges letters of invitation, accommodation, and a range of tours focusing on destinations in Ahal Region.

In addition to the above agencies, there are state travel agencies based in Balkan, Dashoguz, Lebap and Mary regions, each providing visa support services and offering tour programmes focused on their regions. Their contact details are listed under *Getting there and away* for the relevant regional capitals.

Private travel agencies

Of the registered private agencies in Turkmenistan, the following are the most experienced in working with foreign tourists. All can arrange letters of invitation, accommodation, local transportation and tailored in-country programmes with English-speaking guides. Most offer horseriding tours. Most are able to work with tour companies in neighbouring countries to set up wider Silk Road tours.

Ayan Travel 108-2/4 Magtymguly Shayoly; ☎ 12 352914, 350797; f 12 393355; e ayan@online.tm; www.ayan-travel.com

Dag-Syyahat 69 2011 Kochesi; ☎ 12 392559, 356097; f 12 352643; e dag_syyahat@online.tm. Formerly known as the Amado Tourist Company.

DN Tours 48/1 Magtymguly Shayoly; ☎ 12 479217, 470121; f 12 420503;
e dntour@online.tm; www.dntours.com
Elhan Syyahat 19 Turkmenbashy Shayoly; ☎ 12 398406; f 12 357128;
e elkhantour@online.tm
Latif 19 Bitarap Turkmenistan Shayoly; ☎ 12 392808, 392809: f 12 392930, 392931;
e latif@online.tm; www.turkmenistan-latif.com
Owadan Tourism 65 2011 Kochesi; ☎ 12 391825; f 12 354860; e trowadan@online.tm

RED TAPE

A great deal of bureaucracy is involved in getting into Turkmenistan. There are many grey areas, and the rules are subject to frequent change and reinterpretation. You should seek up-to-date advice from your travel agent, or from the nearest Turkmen embassy.

All foreign nationals require a visa. With the single exception of transit visas, all visas are issued on the basis of a Letter of Invitation (LOI) from your hosts in Turkmenistan. As from February 2005, the LOI must be approved by the State Service for the Registration of Foreign Citizens (the task previously fell to the Ministry of Foreign Affairs). State Service approval takes at least ten working days, though you should allow three weeks. Approval is not always forthcoming, and explanations for refusal are rarely offered. If your application is refused, you are not permitted to apply again within the next six months. The LOI is valid only for three months from the date of certification by the State Service.

There is a wide variation in the cost of a Turkmen visa, depending on where you obtain it, duration of stay and whether you used a 'fast-track' service to get it. At the time of research, the cheapest single-entry visa obtainable from the Turkmen Embassy in Washington, for visits of up to ten days, was US$31; but a 12-month multiple-entry visa purchased under an expedited service would have set you back more than US$1,000. Visas obtained at the border generally cost more than those purchased through the non-expedited service at Turkmen embassies overseas, with charges at Ashgabat Airport higher than those at the land borders.

LOIs for business visitors to Turkmenistan will normally be issued by the firm's local business partner or inviting ministry. Where the foreign firm has not as yet established a local partner, LOIs can be sought from the Chamber of Commerce and Industry. It is located at 17 2037 Kochesi, Ashgabat (☎ 12 354717; f 12 351352). The Chamber has, however, become more reticent of late about taking responsibility for foreign business visitors, and may be willing to issue invitations only to firms attending exhibitions organised by the Chamber. For tourist visitors to Turkmenistan, the basic options are to seek either a transit or tourist visa.

Transit visas

As the name suggests, transit visas are primarily designed for travellers aiming simply to cross Turkmen territory en route to somewhere else. They offer two great advantages over other Turkmen visas: you do not need an LOI from an organisation in Turkmenistan, and you will not be chaperoned by the representative of a local travel company during your time in the country. You are free to book whatever accommodation you choose, and are not restricted to state-run hotels. The downside is that they are valid for only a relatively short period, typically five days. They do nonetheless offer a good means of getting a brief exposure to the country as part of a wider regional tour. Note that the period of validity of the visa is not calculated by the hour. Thus, the day on which you enter Turkmenistan counts as day one of your transit visa, even if you arrive in the late afternoon. The day of your departure also counts as a full day, irrespective of the time at which you actually cross the border.

The length of time you will be granted for your transit visa may be different depending on where you apply. There is no consistent pattern, but as a very general rule Turkmen embassies and consulates closer to Turkmenistan, including those in Iran and Uzbekistan, seem less willing to grant longer transit visas: you may find that you are given only three days. Travellers occasionally manage to secure transit visas for seven or even ten days, mainly from some of the Turkmen embassies in Europe.

Although an LOI is not required for transit visas, applications still have to be approved by the State Service for the Registration of Foreign Citizens in Ashgabat, which again involves a processing time of at least ten working days. Additionally, if you require a visa for your country of destination on leaving Turkmenistan, you will be required to produce this before the transit visa will be issued.

The transit visa will stipulate your point of arrival into and departure from Turkmenistan, and you are expected to stick to the obvious route between these two points. With a transit visa you cannot apply to visit restricted areas, except where the transit route crosses them. Transit visas are not normally extendable, and they cannot be obtained direct at Turkmenistan's border crossings.

Tourist visas

If your plans involve more than the short exposure to Turkmenistan allowable with a transit visa, you will need a tourist visa, and with it necessarily comes an intimate relationship with an authorised local travel agency, such as those listed in the previous section. If you have booked through an overseas tour operator, they will handle much of the bureaucracy for you, through their partner Turkmen agency. If not, you will need to contact one of the local travel agencies direct yourself.

You will need to tell the agency your chosen dates and places of entry and departure into/from Turkmenistan, and agree your route within the country. The agency will then draw up an LOI, and submit this to the State Service for the Registration of Foreign Citizens, together with a scanned or faxed copy of the photo page of your passport. If your plans involve visits to any designated restricted areas, the agency will need to specify these in the LOI, as these require special permission. The LOI requires the usual 10–15 working days for processing by the State Service.

Once the LOI is through, the travel agency will send it to you by fax or email, and you can apply for your Turkmen visa at the nearest embassy or consulate. Since approval has already been given by the Turkmen authorities in Ashgabat, this should be straightforward (though make sure that your passport is valid for at least six months from the proposed date of departure from Turkmenistan). Nonetheless, Turkmenistan's embassies usually claim to require a further processing time of a week or so, while offering a 'fast-track' service, for an additional fee, for those who need their passports back more quickly. Most Turkmen embassies, including the one in London, will take visa fees only in US dollars.

With an approved LOI, you can also apply for your visa direct at the Turkmen border rather than having to do so through a Turkmen embassy or consulate overseas. But you should seek the advice of your Turkmen travel agent about this well in advance, as they may have to alert the relevant authorities of your arrival. This is particularly important if you are planning to arrive by land or sea, where an official authorised to issue visas may need to be despatched to the relevant border post to meet you. One further drawback in obtaining your visa on arrival is that this will be issued for no more than ten days. If your approved LOI gives permission for a longer stay, however, a visa extension can be purchased from the State Service in Ashgabat.

The main problem with your tourist visa is that the rules require a representative of your travel agency to accompany you almost everywhere during your stay in Turkmenistan. There are some good guides working in the travel business in Turkmenistan, and will add to the insights you receive about the country. Many guides are bright, engaging and illuminating, though they face some pressure to stick to authorised language about the achievements of post-independence Turkmenistan. But however good the guide, to the independent-minded traveller the requirement can come to feel like the imposition of a minder. And a minder for whose services the tourist is paying (albeit not exorbitantly. usually around US$30 or so per day).

The Turkmen government has in recent years introduced progressively tighter rules on travel agencies, removing much of their earlier discretion to leave tourists in their charge to their own devices. As from 2004, for example, travel agencies have been required to accompany tourists on journeys between regional capitals. Tourists are also usually required to book a minimum of three excursions with the travel agency organising their LOI. And they must be accommodated in state-run hotels throughout their stay. In practice, the agencies are still generally willing to leave tourists to wander freely around Ashgabat and the main provincial capitals, but will accompany their charges on all journeys between the main towns and into rural areas.

Arrival and registration requirements

Successful negotiation of the hurdles involved in obtaining a Turkmen visa, however, by no means marks the end of the red tape. Anyone entering Turkmenistan on a tourist visa is required to have an **Entry Travel Pass**, which must be brought to the border post of arrival by a representative of their travel agency. Being met at the point of arrival by your tour guide is thus not so much a polite service on the part of the travel agency as a formal requirement of the Turkmen authorities. The travel agency will have completed this document in advance, in quadruplicate. One copy goes to the tourist. Most travel agencies wrap the fee for the preparation of this pass into their overall bill. Your segment of the pass will be stamped at passport control on arrival. You will need to keep it carefully, as the Entry Travel Pass is considered by the Turkmen authorities as an essential part of the tourist visa, and must be presented on departure.

A further **immigration card** was introduced in March 2003, as one of a series of measures designed to keep a closer watch on foreign visitors to Turkmenistan following the reported coup attempt of November 2002. This card is required by all foreigners entering Turkmenistan, regardless of the type of visa possessed. A US$10 fee is involved, which should be paid in cash on arrival at the border. The authorities have fortunately dropped the 2,000 manat fee, initially levied as an administration charge for the preparation of this card, which caused visitors great bafflement as to where they were expected to obtain a small sum in manat at Ashgabat Airport in the early hours. Again, a portion of the card is stamped and given to the visitor for retention until final departure from Turkmenistan. Again, it should be kept safe.

If you will be in Turkmenistan for longer than three days, you will need to **register**. As part of the new rules introduced in March 2003, registration procedures were placed in the hands of the State Service for the Registration of Foreign Citizens. You are required to register within three days of your arrival in Turkmenistan, excluding Saturdays, Sundays and public holidays. If you have entered Turkmenistan on a tourist visa, registration will be sorted out through your travel agent, and you should not have to go to the State Service in person. If you do need to contact the State Service direct, their address is 57 2011 Kochesi, Ashgabat (☎ 12 391337). They are open for enquiries Mon–Fri 09.00–12.00. Under the rules, state travel agencies are entitled to register tourists themselves, but private agencies are not. If you have used a private agency, the latter will typically take your documents to a state agency, such as Ashgabatsyyahat, who will register your passport on payment of a small fee.

One of the most irksome conditions of registration as a tourist is that you must stay in a state-run hotel. The hotel is required to provide a certification that you are their guest as part of the registration procedures. This requirement excludes some of the more progressive hotels in Turkmenistan, such as the Margiana in Ashgabat, as well of course as private homestays. Some tourists have reported that their travel agent agreed they could check out of their state-run hotel, and into a private one, as soon as the registration procedures were completed, but not all agencies seem to allow this. Camping, however, is fine, provided that your camping trip has been organised through your local travel agent, who will have had to obtain the approval of the State Committee for Tourism and Sport to arrange such a package. And, yes, a representative of the travel agency is required to accompany you, though not necessarily to sleep in the same tent.

Restricted zones

Large swathes of Turkmenistan are designated restricted or border zones, and require special permission to enter. You will need to discuss with your travel agent, or whoever is inviting you, whether your itinerary includes any designated border areas, as they will need to specify these in your letter of invitation. When you collect your visa, make sure that the issuing embassy or consulate has included reference to these border areas, as it will involve effort and expense in Ashgabat to have these added on if they have omitted to do so.

The geography of Turkmenistan, with a large desert in the centre, and much of the population having always lived along the rivers and in the oases which lie around the edges of the country, means that many of the most interesting places to visit sit in restricted border zones. The latter are subject to change: for example, the Nohur Valley was added to the list in 2004, an event marked by the sudden appearance of a new checkpoint at the base of the valley. For the most recent consolidated list of restricted zones which seems to be available, see box.

Major tourist attractions falling within border zones include Konye-Urgench, Dekhistan, Yangykala, Ekedeshik, Badkyz and Kugitang. Ashgabat, Merv, Turkmenabat and Balkanabat are not in restricted areas. An additional restricted zone permit does not seem to be required for travellers passing straight through a restricted zone on the direct main route to a border crossing, provided that this is the place specified on their visa.

Nature reserves

Special permission is also required to visit any one of Turkmenistan's eight nature reserves. Proposed visits to these areas should again be discussed with your local travel agent, who will need to apply for permission from the Ministry of Nature Protection at 102 2035 Kochesi, Ashgabat (☎ 12 396002). Processing time can take two to three weeks. Permission is rarely given between May 1 and October 1, except to the Repetek Reserve, because of the high risk of fire during the summer months. It can occasionally be turned down for more eccentric reasons. One application to visit the Hazar Reserve on the Caspian coast was refused with the argument that 'the birds have flown away', and therefore, the authorities reasoned, there was presumably nothing of interest to the visitor.

RESTRICTED BORDER ZONES OF TURKMENISTAN

The Ministry of Foreign Affairs circulated in 2004 the following list of restricted zones.

Ahal Region

- Ak Bugday, Kaka and Serakhs districts
- Archabil, and the villages in the hills near Ashgabat of Bagabad, Kasamly/Julge, Ipaykala and Germab
- The village of Uchbirleshik in Geok Depe District
- The villages of Nohur, Garawul and Konyegummez in Baharly District

Balkan Region

- The sub-districts of Garabogaz, Jangra, Guwly, Hazar and Gyzyl Gaya
- Turkmenbashy, Hazar, Esenguly, Etrek and Magtumguly districts. (The reference to Turkmenbashy District here is to the rural district lying outside the town; the latter is not considered to be part of a restricted zone.)

Dashoguz Region

- Dashoguz town
- Georogly, Niyazov, Gubadag, Boldumsaz, Konye-Urgench and Saparmurat Turkmenbashy districts
(This list suggests that only two districts of Dashoguz Region, Akdepe and Gurbansoltan Eje, are *not* restricted zones. Since it is not possible to reach either without passing through a designated restricted zone, this means that access to the whole of Dashoguz Region is effecively restricted.)

Lebap Region

- Atamurat, Beyik Saparmurat Turkmenbashy, Koytendag, Magdanly, Hodjambaz, Farap and Birata districts

Mary Region

- Tagtabazar and Serhetabat districts

Various fees are payable to the local reserve director during the visit, including a basic entry charge (typically around US$15). In most of the reserves, the authorities can arrange basic accommodation, usually in a hut used by rangers. A small amount in dollars is charged for this. The reserve director may also enforce a photography fee, sometimes calculated on a per-shot basis.

EMBASSIES

In Ashgabat

Afghanistan 94 Georogly Kochesi; ☎ 12 348046, 348089; **f** 12 348681, 348068; **e** embaf@online.tm

Armenia 14 Georogly Kochesi; ☎ 12 354418, 395549; **f** 12 395538; **e** eat@online.tm

Azerbaijan 62A 2023 Kochesi; ☎/**f** 12 391102; **e** azsefir_ashg@online.tm

Belarus 17 2011 Kochesi; ☎ 12 350737; **f** 12 396488; **e** embblr@online.tm

China Hotel Kuwwat, Archabil Shayoly, Berzengi; ☎ 12 488105, 488131; **f** 12 481813; **e** chemb@online.tm

France 3rd floor, Office Building, Hotel Four Points Ak Altyn, 141 Magtymguly Shayoly; ☎ 12 363550; f 12 363546
Georgia 139A 2011 Kochesi; ☎ 12 344838; f 12 343248; e georgia@online.tm
Germany 1st floor, Office Building, Hotel Four Points Ak Altyn, 141 Magtymguly Shayoly; ☎ 12 363515; f 12 363522; e grembtkm@online.tm
India International Business Centre, 1951 Kochesi; ☎ 12 456152; f 12 456156
Iran 3 2070 Kochesi; ☎ 12 341452; f 12 350565
Japan 2nd floor, Office Building, Hotel Four Points Ak Altyn, 141 Magtymguly Shayoly; ☎ 12 364450; f 12 364453
Kazakhstan Garassyzlyk Shayoly; ☎ 12 480469, 480472; f 12 480474, 480475; e turemb@online.tm
Kyrgyzstan 14 Georogly Kochesi; ☎/f 12 355506; e kg@online.tm
Libya 17A 2011 Kochesi; ☎ 12 354917; f 12 390569
Netherlands (Consulate) 17 2070 Kochesi; ☎ 12 346700; f 12 344252; e mirbuza@online.tm
Pakistan 92 2035 Kochesi; ☎ 12 350097; f 12 397640; e parepashgabat@online.tm
Romania 107 2023 Kochesi; ☎ 12 347633; f 12 347620; e ambromas@online.tm
Russia 11 Turkmenbashy Shayoly; ☎ 12 353957, 357041; f 12 398466; e konsul-rf@online.tm
Saudi Arabia International Business Centre, 1951 Kochesi; ☎ 12 454964; f 12 454968; e ksaembss@online.tm
Tajikistan 14 Georogly Kochesi; ☎ 12 355696; f 12 393174; e embtd@online.tm
Turkey 9 Shevchenko Kochesi; ☎ 12 351461; f 12 391914; e tcembassy@online.tm
Ukraine 49 2011 Kochesi; ☎ 12 391373, 395294; f 12 391028; e ukremb@online.tm
United Arab Emirates Khalifa Centre, 124 Turkmenbashy Shayoly; ☎ 12 456923; f 12 456920
United Kingdom 3rd floor, Office Building, Hotel Four Points Ak Altyn, 141 Magtymguly Shayoly; ☎ 12 363462; f 12 363465; e beasb@online.tm; www.britishembassy.gov.uk/turkmenistan
United States 9 1984 Kochesi; ☎ 12 350045, 398764; f 12 350049; www.usemb-ashgabat.usia.co.at
Uzbekistan 50A Georogly Kochesi; ☎ 12 342419; f 12 342337; e muzbek@online.tm

Turkmenistan embassies overseas

Armenia 19 Kievyana, Yerevan; ☎ +3741 221029; f +3741 222172
Austria 22 Argentinierstrasse, Vienna; ☎ +43 1 5036470; f +43 1 5036473
Belarus 17 Ulitsa Kirova, Minsk; ☎ +375 172 293427; f +375 172 223367
Belgium 106 Av Franklin Roosevelt, Brussels; ☎ +32 2 6481874; f +32 2 6481906
China Diplomatic Office Building, 1-15-2, San Li Tun, Beijing; ☎/f +86 10 65326976
France 13 Rue Picot, Paris; ☎ +33 1 47550536; f +33 1 47550568
Germany 14 Langobardenalle, Berlin; ☎ +49 30 30102451; f +49 30 30102453
India C-17 Malcha Marg, Chanakyapuri, New Delhi; ☎ +91 11 6118054; f +91 11 6118332
Iran 39 5 Golestan St, Pasdaran Av, Tehran; ☎ +98 21 2542178; f +98 21 2580432
Kazakhstan 64 Otyrar, Astana; ☎ +7 3172 280823; f +7 3172 280882
Pakistan 22A Nizam-ud-din Rd, F-7/1, Islamabad; ☎ +92 51 2278699; f + 92 51 2278799
Russia 22 Filipovskiy Pereulok, Moscow; ☎ +7 095 291 6636; f +7 095 291 0935
Tajikistan 22 Chekov, Dushanbe; ☎ +992 372 216884; f +992 372 215749
Turkey 28 Koza Sokak, Chankaya, Ankara; ☎ +90 312 441 7122; f +90 312 441 7125
Ukraine 6 Pushkinskaya, Kiev; ☎ +380 44 229 3363; f +380 44 229 3034
United Kingdom George House, 14-17 Wells St, London W1 3FP; ☎ 020 7255 1071; f 020 7323 9184
United States 2207 Massachusetts Av, NW, Washington, DC; ☎ +1 202 588 1500; f +1 202 588 0697

Uzbekistan 10 1 Bol. Mirabadskaya, Tashkent; ☎ +998 71 120 5278; f +998 71 120 5281

GETTING THERE AND AWAY

By air

Turkmenistan has one international airport, Saparmurat Turkmenbashy Airport in Ashgabat. The terminal, built in the 1990s, is clean and rarely crowded, though offers little in the way of facilities for departing or transit passengers. Anyone arriving at Ashgabat with an onward flight connection but no transit visa will not be allowed out of the airport's transit area. A little more comfort on arrival and departure can be gained by use of the 'commercially important persons' (CIP) lounge. This costs US$20 in each direction. The travel agency or other organisation which has invited you must apply in advance for permission for you to use the CIP lounge (☎ 12 378701). CIP does nothing to insulate you from the bureaucracy of getting into and out of the country, and it is probably not worth the extra hassle and expense.

Turkmenistan Airlines

The country's national carrier offers a pleasant surprise to travellers used to the ageing Soviet planes of some other alirlines in the region: it has an all-Boeing passenger fleet. President Niyazov has ordered an ambitious expansion programme, to take Turkmenistan's fleet to 40 Boeings by the year 2020. Turkmenistan Airlines has good flight connections to London (two direct flights weekly) and Birmingham (four). Relatively few passengers on these flights start or finish their journeys in Ashgabat, however. The flights head on to Delhi/Amritsar, and most of the passengers are members of the Sikh community in the UK.

Turkmenistan Airlines has the only direct flights from Ashgabat to the UK, and is much cheaper than other options between Ashgabat and western Europe. The major downside is that the flights can be difficult to book. Turkmenistan Airlines has not signed up to the agreements which allow most UK travel agents to make direct bookings, and their UK agent, the delightfully monickered Cozy Aviation, can be elusive. The contact details for the latter (seasoned veterans recommend sending a fax with your request and telephone number if you cannot get through by phone) are as follows:

London office 494 Great West Rd, Hounslow, Middx TW5 OTF; ☎ 020 8577 2211; f 020 8577 9900, 020 8577 8400
Birmingham office 16–18 South Rd, Smethwick, Warley, West Midlands B67 7BN; ☎ 0121 558 6363; f 0121 558 3456

Turkmenistan Airlines also currently offers direct flight connections to Frankfurt (one flight per week), Abu Dhabi (two), Bangkok (two), Dubai (two), Peking (one), Istanbul (four), Almaty (two), Kiev (one) and Moscow (daily). Its other overseas offices are as follows:

Germany Terminal 1, Frankfurt Airport; ☎ +49 69 690 70169; f +49 69 690 59739
India N1 BMC House, Middle Circle, Connaught Place, New Delhi; ☎ +91 11 3721085; f +91 11 3713869
Kazakhstan 182 Auezova, Almaty; ☎ +7 3272 623531; f +7 3272 506154
Russia 22 Filipovskiy Pereulok, Moscow; ☎ +7 095 290 5483; f +7 095 291 1223
Thailand Nailert Plaza, 644/3 M4 Petchburi Rd, Rajthevee, Bangkok; ☎ +66 2 6565805; f +66 2 6565804
Turkey 171/1 Cumhuriyet Cadesi, Elmadag, Istanbul; ☎ +90 212 233 9306; f +90 212 246 2208

Ukraine 18 Ulitsa Popudrenko, Kiev; ☎/f +380 44 559 2429
United Arab Emirates 202 Sheikh Zayed St, Abu Dhabi; ☎ +971 2 6327100; f +971 2 6344486

The main Ashgabat office is at 82 Magtymguly Shayoly; ☎ 12 354857, 12 393900. It is open every day, 08.00–20.00, with a lunch-break 14.00–15.00.

A survey carried out in 2004 by Skytrax Research awarded Turkmenistan Airlines a decidedly modest two-star rating (on a one to five scale) as regards its quality of service. Certainly the in-flight entertainment is thin, consisting on most flights of a route map display, which also incorporates calls from President Niyazov for everyone to glorify the motherland. When a movie is shown, usually a Bollywood musical, you may wish that it hadn't been, as the airline does not bother with personal headphones, so the sound echoes full volume around the cabin. The food is unlikely to win many awards, and check-in staff at both London and Birmingham take a tough approach to hand baggage (some passengers report being told that all hand baggage is 'forbidden' on Turkmenistan Airlines, though the official line from the airline seems to be that up to 5kg is allowed). But the service is basically fine.

Other carriers

The listings below give the Ashgabat offices of the overseas airlines currently serving Turkmenistan.

Aerosvit Turkmenistan Trade Centre, 73 Magtymguly Shayoly; ☎/f 12 350164; www.aerosvit.com. Office open Mon–Fri 09.00–18.00, Sat 09.00–12.00. A Ukrainian airline, which offers one flight a week to Kiev.
Armavia 15 Turkmenbashy Shayoly; ☎ 12 390548; f 12 350392; e anna13@online.tm. Office open Mon–Fri 10.00–18.00. An Armenian airline, with one flight weekly to Yerevan.
Lufthansa Ashgabat Airport; ☎ 12 232 056, 510 694; f 12 510 728; e asbgutea@dlh.de; www.lufthansa.com. Open Mon–Fri 09.30–18.00, Sat 09.30–13.30. Three flights weekly to Frankfurt, via Baku.
Turkish Airlines Turkmenistan Trade Centre, 73 Magtymguly Shayoly; ☎ 12 392919, 392924; f 12 392843; www.turkishairlines.com. Open Mon–Fri 09.00–17.00, Sat 09.00–13.00. Three flights weekly to Istanbul.
Uzbekistan Airways Ashgabat Airport; ☎ 12 378203; f 12 232026. Curious hours of business: Mon, Tue, Fri 09.00–18.00; Wed, Sat 09.00–14.00; Thu 14.00–18.00. One flight a week to Tashkent.
British Airways Hotel Sheraton Grand Turkmen, 7 Georogly Kochesi; ☎ 12 510799, 510801; f 12 510798; e exair@online.tm. Office hours Mon–Fri 09.00–18.00, Sat 09.00–13.00. No flights to Ashgabat; the office specialises in providing onward flights to destinations not served by Turkmenistan Airlines.

For passengers on airlines other than Turkmenistan Airlines (for whom it is included in the price of the ticket), a departure tax of US$25 is payable at Ashgabat Airport.

By sea

The only regular passenger option is the ferry route between Baku and Turkmenbashy. The main business of the ferry is goods transport: the human cargo is something of an afterthought, and the ferries leave not to a regular timetable, but when they are loaded. The number of passengers who can be taken is also influenced by the nature of the goods being transported (potentially dangerous cargoes such as oil products mean fewer passengers). So there is a certain unpredictability about using the route, and potentially a good deal of waiting around, but at least one ferry seems to make the trip on most days, and most tourists report that they secured a place on the first available ferry. The journey takes around 14 hours. Ticket prices for foreign nationals range from US$45 for a seat on deck to US$100 for the nicest available cabin. Motor vehicle charges range from US$87 to US$214, depending on the length of the vehicle. Motorcycles are charged between US$22 and US$35. Bicycles are US$5.

The ferry terminal at Turkmenbashy is at the eastern end of the port (see page 137). The port facilities in Baku were being reconstructed when I visited, and the location of the ticket office for the Turkmenbashy ferry was remarkably obscure. If it has not moved to a more central location by the time of your visit, look for the modern ten-storey building at the east end of the Gagarin Bridge, across the railway tracks from the centre of Baku. From here, take the minor road running along the city-centre side of this building, marked with a sign for the 'Parom Restaurant'. Some 300m along this road, you will see a stretch of crumbling wall decorated with a mosaic of Lenin's head. The unmarked white metal door on the opposite side of the road is the Caspian Shipping Company booking office. The unhelpful ladies inside will sell you a ticket for the ferry, and may even be willing to offer a vague opinion as to when it is likely to depart.

By land

There are no cross-border buses or passenger trains. The train from Dashoguz to Turkmenabat crosses Uzbek territory, but passengers are not allowed to join or leave the train in Uzbekistan. Other train routes across the Turkmen border, such as the crossing into Iran at Serakhs, are currently freight only. So the use of land borders requires you either to use your own transport, or to take a taxi or any available public transport to the border, walk across, and pick up another taxi at the other side. Most travel agencies in Turkmenistan can sort out taxis to collect their departing clients from the Uzbek or Iranian borders, and take them on to their first night's accommodation in the neighbouring country.

If you are planning to bring your own vehicle into Turkmenistan, and are applying for anything other than a transit visa, this fact will have to be made clear in your LOI. A valid international driving permit is required. In addition, you will be charged a not inconsiderable entry and transit fee (irrespective of your type of visa) at your point of arrival, payable in US dollars cash. The fee varies according to what you are driving and the route to be taken across Turkmenistan. One element of this fee is what is termed 'petrol difference', charged at the time of research at six cents per kilometre for petrol-driven cars; four cents per kilometre for diesels. Buses and lorries are charged at 13 cents per kilometre. The authorities will work out the distance in kilometres between your designated arrival and departure points, and charge you a lump sum. The logic here is that petrol prices in Turkmenistan are heavily subsidised: the fee serves to counterbalance the subsidy received by the foreign visitor at the pumps, so that the government is not out of pocket.

The fee also includes an element for third-party insurance: this is mandatory, even if you already have (as you are strongly advised to take out) your own fully comprehensive insurance cover. At the time of research, the insurance element was US$50 for cars, US$20 for motorbikes and US$70 for lorries. There is also an additional transit fee, of US$30 for cars, US$15 for motorbikes and US$100 for lorries, as well as a sum for 'disinfection procedures' – US$10 for cars, US$5 for motorbikes, and US$20 for lorries (you pay whether or not any 'disinfection procedures' are actually carried out). The entry and transit fee bundle is completed by a US$5 handling fee, and US$2 described as 'bank charges'.

The main land crossing points are:

With Uzbekistan

- Between Farap and Karakul. The main route between Turkmenabat and Bukhara.
- Between Dashoguz and Urgench. Useful for Khiva. May, however, be closed to foreign visitors on the Uzbek side.
- Between Konye-Urgench and Hodjeyli. Serves Karakalpakstan.

With Kazakhstan

- North of Garabogaz on the Caspian coast. An isolated border post. Travel arrangements need careful pre-planning, and 4x4.

With Iran

- At Gudurolum, convenient for the Mausoleum of Gonbad-I Qabus. 4x4 probably necessary.
- Between Gaudan and Badzgiran. The main route between Ashgabat and Mashhad.
- At Serakhs. Alternative route to Mashhad via Iranian Sarakhs.

With Afghanistan

- Between Serhetabat and Torgundi. The main route between Mary and Herat.
- At Imamnazar. Links Atamurat with Andkhoy. A 4x4, dry conditions and careful pre-planning required. Given the security situation in Afghanistan at the time of writing, you should be particularly careful to check the latest travel advice from your government before attempting to visit. (See *Appendix 3, Further Information*, for details of websites.)

Turkmenistan's border crossings are generally open from around 09.00 – 18.00, but there is some variation both between crossings and seasonally, and you should plan to get to the Turkmen side of the border in good time. Crossing procedures can be lengthy.

HEALTH

Before you go

You should seek up-to-date advice in good time (at least two months) before your trip from your general practitioner, or a specialised travel clinic such as those in the following list, but recommended **immunisations** are likely to include diphtheria, tetanus, typhoid, hepatitis A and hepatitis B. Rabies is also a risk in Turkmenistan, so you may additionally wish to consider a course of rabies inoculations, usually given as three separate injections across a one-month period, especially if you are planning to hike or spend long periods in rural areas. Keeping away from unknown animals is also obvious but nonetheless sensible advice.

Malaria is currently believed to pose a risk only in a relatively small area of Turkmenistan close to the Afghan border. If you are planning to visit the Serhetabat or Tagtabazar districts in the southern part of Mary Region between May and November, you should seek advice about suitable anti-malaria prophylaxis. This area includes the cave settlement of Ekedeshik and the Badkyz Nature Reserve, as well as the towns of Serhetabat and Tagtabazar themselves. You should also bring supplies of mosquito repellent (good advice for Turkmenistan more widely since there are mosquitos aplenty, even if not everywhere is malarial).

A mosquito net is also worth considering, especially if you are contemplating using cheaper-range accommodation without air conditioning.

Pharmacies in Turkmenistan offer a poor range of **medicines**. You should bring with you a full supply of any prescription medication, and it is well worth packing a few basic medicines, including oral rehydration salts. Suncream with a high protection factor is vital.

Travel clinics and health information

A full list of current travel-clinic websites worldwide is available from the International Society of Travel Medicine on www.istm.org. For other journey preparation information, consult www.tripprep.com. Information about various medications may be found on www.emedicine.com.

UK

Berkeley Travel Clinic 32 Berkeley St, London W1J 8EL (near Green Park tube station); ☎ 020 7629 6233

British Airways Travel Clinic and Immunisation Service There are two BA clinics in London, both on ☎ 0845 600 2236; www.ba.com/travelclinics. Appointments only Mon–Fri 9.00–16.30 at 101 Cheapside, London EC2V 6DT; or walk-in service Mon–Fri 09.30–17.30, Sat 10.00–16.00 at 213 Piccadilly, London W1J 9HQ. Apart from providing inoculations and malaria prevention, they sell a variety of health-related goods.

Cambridge Travel Clinic 48a Mill Rd, Cambridge CB1 2AS; ☎ 01223 367362; e enquiries@cambridgetravelclinic.co.uk; www.cambridgetravelclinic.co.uk. Open Tue–Fri 12.00–19.00, Sat 10.00–16.00.

Edinburgh Travel Clinic Regional Infectious Diseases Unit, Ward 41 OPD, Western General Hospital, Crewe Rd South, Edinburgh EH4 2UX; ☎ 0131 537 2822; www.link.med.ed.ac.uk/ridu. Travel helpline (☎ 0906 589 0380) open weekdays 09.00–12.00. Provides inoculations and anti-malarial prophylaxis and advises on travel-related health risks.

Fleet Street Travel Clinic 29 Fleet St, London EC4Y 1AA; ☎ 020 7353 5678; www.fleetstreetclinic.com. Vaccinations, travel products and the latest advice.

Hospital for Tropical Diseases Travel Clinic Mortimer Market Building, Capper St (off Tottenham Ct Rd), London WC1E 6AU; ☎ 020 7388 9600; www.thehtd.org. Offers consultations and advice, and is able to provide all necessary drugs and vaccines for travellers. Runs a healthline (☎ 0906 133 7733) for country-specific information and health hazards. Also stocks nets, water purification equipment and personal protection measures.

Interhealth Worldwide Partnership House, 157 Waterloo Rd, London SE1 8US; ☎ 020 7902 9000; www.interhealth.org.uk.Competitively priced, one-stop travel health service. All profits go to their affiliated company, InterHealth, which provides health care for overseas workers on Christian projects.

MASTA (Medical Advisory Service for Travellers Abroad) London School of Hygiene and Tropical Medicine, Keppel St, London WC1 7HT; ☎ 09065 501402; www.masta.org. Individually tailored health briefs available for a fee, with up-to-date information on how to stay healthy, inoculations and what to bring. There are currently 30 MASTA pre-travel clinics in Britain. Call 0870 241 6843 or check online for the nearest. Clinics also sell malaria prophylaxis memory cards, treatment kits, bednets and net treatment kits.

NHS travel website www.fitfortravel.scot.nhs.uk. Provides country-by-country advice on immunisation and malaria, plus details of recent developments and a list of relevant health organisations.

Nomad Travel Store/Clinic 3–4 Wellington Terrace, Turnpike Lane, London N8 0PX; ☎ 020 8889 7014; travel-health line (office hours only) 0906 863 3414;

LONG-HAUL FLIGHTS, CLOTS AND DVT

Dr Jane Wilson-Howarth

Long-haul air travel increases the risk of deep vein thrombosis. Although recent research has suggested that many of us develop clots when immobilised, most resolve without us ever having been aware of them. In certain susceptible individuals, though, large clots form and these can break away and lodge in the lungs. This is dangerous but happens in a tiny minority of passengers.

Studies have shown that flights of over five-and-a-half-hours are significant, and that people who take lots of shorter flights over a short space of time form clots. People at highest risk are:

- Those who have had a clot before – unless they are now taking warfarin
- People over 80 years of age
- Those who have recently had a major operation or surgery for varicose veins
- Someone who has had a hip or knee replacement in the last three months
- Cancer sufferers
- Those who have ever had a stroke
- People with heart disease
- Those with a close blood relative who has had a clot

Those with a slightly increased risk:

- People over 40
- Women who are pregnant or have had a baby in the last couple of weeks
- People taking female hormones or other oestrogen therapy
- Heavy smokers
- Those who have very severe varicose veins
- The very obese or the very tall (over 6ft/1.8m) or short (under 5ft/1.5m)

e sales@nomadtravel.co.uk; www.nomadtravel.co.uk. Also at 40 Bernard St, London WC1N 1LJ; ☎ 020 7833 4114; 52 Grosvenor Gardens, London SW1W 0AG; ☎ 020 7823 5823; and 43 Queens Rd, Bristol BS8 1QH; ☎ 0117 922 6567. For health advice, equipment such as mosquito nets and other anti-bug devices, and an excellent range of adventure travel gear.

Trailfinders Travel Clinic 194 Kensington High St, London W8 7RG; ☎ 020 7938 3999; www.trailfinders.com/clinic.htm

Travelpharm The Travelpharm website, www.travelpharm.com, offers up-to-date guidance on travel-related health and has a range of medications available through their online mini-pharmacy.

Irish Republic

Tropical Medical Bureau Grafton Street Medical Centre, Grafton Buildings, 34 Grafton St, Dublin 2; ☎ 1 671 9200; www.tmb.ie. A useful website specific to tropical destinations. Also check website for other bureaux locations throughout Ireland.

USA

Centers for Disease Control 1600 Clifton Rd, Atlanta, GA 30333; ☎ 800 311 3435; travellers' health hotline 888 232 3299; www.cdc.gov/travel. The central source of travel information in the USA. The invaluable *Health Information for International Travel*, published annually, is available from the Division of Quarantine at this address.

A deep vein thrombosis (DVT) is a blood clot that forms in the deep leg veins. This is very different from irritating but harmless superficial phlebitis. DVT causes swelling and redness of one leg, usually with heat and pain in one calf and sometimes the thigh. A DVT is only dangerous if a clot breaks away and travels to the lungs (pulmonary embolus). Symptoms of a pulmonary embolus (PE) include chest pain that is worse on breathing in deeply, shortness of breath, and sometimes coughing up small amounts of blood. The symptoms commonly start three to ten days after a long flight. Anyone who thinks that they might have a DVT needs to see a doctor immediately who will arrange a scan. Warfarin tablets (to thin the blood) are then taken for at least six months.

Prevention of DVT

Several conditions make the problem more likely. Immobility is the key, and factors like reduced oxygen in cabin air and dehydration may also contribute. To reduce the risk of thrombosis on a long journey:

- Exercise before and after the flight
- Keep mobile before and during the flight; move around every couple of hours
- During the flight drink plenty of water or juices
- Avoid taking sleeping pills and excessive tea, coffee and alcohol
- Perform exercises that mimic walking and tense the calf muscles
- Consider wearing flight socks or support stockings (see www.legshealth.com)
- Taking a meal of oily fish (mackerel, trout, salmon, sardines, etc) in the 24 hours before departure reduces blood clotability and thus DVT risk
- The jury is still out on whether it is worth taking an aspirin before flying, but this can be discussed with your GP.

If you think you are at increased risk of a clot, ask your doctor if it is safe to travel.

Connaught Laboratories PO Box 187, Swiftwater, PA 18370; ☎ 800 822 2463. They will send a free list of specialist tropical-medicine physicians in your state.
IAMAT (International Association for Medical Assistance to Travelers) 1623 Military Rd, 279, Niagara Falls, NY14304-1745; ☎ 716 754 4883; e info@iamat.org; www.iamat.org. A non-profit organisation that provides lists of English-speaking doctors abroad.
International Medicine Center 920 Frostwood Drive, Suite 670, Houston, TX 77024; ☎ 713 550 2000; www.traveldoc.com

Canada

IAMAT Suite 1, 1287 St Clair Av W, Toronto, Ontario M6E 1B8; ☎ 416 652 0137; www.iamat.org
TMVC (Travel Doctors Group) Sulphur Springs Rd, Ancaster, Ontario; ☎ 905 648 1112; www.tmvc-group.com

Australia, New Zealand, Singapore

TMVC ☎ 1300 65 88 44; www.tmvc.com.au. Twenty-three clinics in Australia, New Zealand and Singapore including:
Auckland Canterbury Arcade, 170 Queen St, Auckland; ☎ 9 373 3531
Brisbane 6th floor, 247 Adelaide St, Brisbane, QLD 4000; ☎ 7 3221 9066
Melbourne 393 Little Bourke St, 2nd floor, Melbourne, VIC 3000; ☎ 3 9602 5788

Sydney Dymocks Building, 7th Floor, 428 George St, Sydney, NSW 2000; ☎ 2 9221 7133
IAMAT PO Box 5049, Christchurch 5, New Zealand; www.iamat.org

South Africa

SAA-Netcare Travel Clinics Private Bag X34, Benmore 2010; www.travelclinic.co.za. Clinics throughout South Africa.
TMVC 113 DF Malan Drive, Roosevelt Park, Johannesburg; ☎ 011 888 7488; www.tmvc.com.au. Consult the website for details of eight other clinics in South Africa.

Switzerland

IAMAT 57 Chemin des Voirets, 1212 Grand Lancy, Geneva; www.iamat.org

In Turkmenistan

The hot Turkmen sun needs to be treated with respect. The generally low humidity means that it is easy to underestimate how much water is being lost through evaporation from the skin. You should drink copious amounts of water throughout the day, apply a good-quality suncream before venturing out into the sun, and try not to overdo any sunbathing.

Diarrhoeal diseases are fairly common in Turkmenistan, and drinking untreated tap water is not recommended. Use bottled water, ideally including to clean your teeth, and avoid ice in drinks. Dairy products also need to be treated with care. Local milk is mostly unpasteurised: imported cartons of long-life milk, available in the main urban bazaars, are safer. As in many parts of the world, it is wise to treat with caution seafood, fruits which cannot be easily peeled, salads and mayonnaise.

Turkmenistan's fauna includes a number of poisonous species, including snakes, spiders and scorpions. Snakes will slither away from humans if approached, but you should try to avoid inadvertently cornering one. Particular care needs to be taken at archaeological sites, especially when walking into mud-brick buildings. It is unwise to turn over stones or to explore crevices in walls in a search for treasures. Good footwear such as desert boots, as well as not walking bare-legged, can help protect against bites from snakes and ticks. You should also be wary of snakes in thick vegetation at the base of river valleys. Turkmen children are bitten every year while berry-picking in such locations. If you are hiking, horse trekking or planning a long trip into the desert, you might ask your travel agency about supplies of anti-venom, as hospitals in Turkmenistan do not usually stock any. If you are bitten by a snake, clean the wound, apply a firm dressing, immobilise the limb if possible (for example, with a splint) and seek urgent medical care.

SAFETY

Levels of violent crime in Turkmenistan are low, but there is a stronger risk of petty theft. You should be wary of the risk of pickpockets in busy markets, especially Ashgabat's Tolkuchka Bazaar. Avoid keeping money or other valuables in backpacks, as these are vulnerable to thieves. Aggressive begging is starting to become a problem, especially in the provincial capitals where rates of poverty and joblessness are much higher than in the capital, but numbers involved are still small.

A more frequent complaint by foreign travellers is that of experiences at the hands of aggressive, intrusive or otherwise annoying security officials. Uniformed officials are everywhere. You may well be stopped and asked to show your passport, visa or other documentation. You should carry your passport with you everywhere you go in Turkmenistan, protected securely, for example in a money-belt concealed beneath clothing. In most cases officials are reasonably polite, and

Previous page Mausoleum of Turabeg Khanum, Konye-Urgench

Above Tolkuchka Bazaar, Ashgabat

Right Old Lady, Tolkuchka Bazaar, Ashgabat

Below right Turkmen skull-caps (*takhyas*). Tolkuchka Bazaar, Ashgabat

Below left Street-sign featuring carpet motifs representing each region, Ashgabat

the best advice is to remain friendly, helpful and above all calm. Questioning can, however, occasionally become aggressive, especially where the tourist is deemed to have committed some misdemeanour. Photography is one potential cause of problems. You should avoid photographing anyone in a uniform, or any military or civil aviation subjects, and should not take photographs while waiting at one of the many road checkpoints or border crossings. In Ashgabat, taking photographs around the Turkmenbashy Palace or other government buildings is likely to earn you a rebuke, and possibly even the destruction of your film.

The local security authorities may also place foreign visitors under surveillance, and you should be aware of the possibility that email messages sent from Turkmenistan may be read, telephone conversations monitored, and hotel rooms searched or bugged.

The likelihood of being stopped on the street by security officials increases after 23.00, when bars and restaurants shut, and some members of the law enforcement agencies seem to take the view that anyone still out and about is likely to be up to no good. Another more practical problem in getting around on foot after dark is the potentially dangerous combination of poorly illuminated streets and pot-holed roads and pavements. A pocket torch can be a godsend.

Turkmenistan is certainly not among the highest-risk countries for women travellers, but the usual personal safety precautions should be followed. All visitors, but especially women, should where possible avoid walking alone after dark. In Ashgabat, it is safer to use the telephone taxi service rather than hailing a car on the street. If you do hail a car, and have any concerns about the occupants of the one which stops for you, it is perfectly acceptable simply to decline to get in and wave it on. The locals do this all the time.

Road safety

The quality of the best roads in Turkmenistan is high. There are some wide and modern stretches of road around Ashgabat, such as a 14km stretch of multi-lane highway from the suburb of Berzengi towards the hill resort of Archabil, which features everything from flyovers to overhead electronic boards. Not coincidentally, this route links Ashgabat with the president's main residence. But most roads are not the best. There are many uneven and pot-holed streets, including in the capital, road markings are sparse and illumination poor, and many rural settlements are accessible only by rutted track.

Standards of driving are relatively low. Lane discipline is poor, and you should expect the unexpected, such as drivers heading the wrong way down one-way streets. The range of vehicles on the roads is wide, stretching from clapped-out Soviet makes to new Mercedes and Toyota imports, usually driven too fast. And in rural areas, some of the traffic has four legs, not four wheels. This all makes driving in Turkmenistan more hazardous than the relatively low overall number of vehicles would suggest. You should avoid if at all possible driving at night, especially outside of town. Among the more unorthodox hazards are camels, which have a nocturnal habit of lying down on roads, since the asphalt preserves the heat of the day better than the surrounding desert. The hour or so immediately before nightfall is also potentially dangerous, as declining visibility coincides with the movement of flocks of sheep and goats from their pastures back to pens in the villages.

There are numerous road checkpoints of varying degrees of severity. Some involve no more than ad hoc checks of certain vehicles. At others the boots of cars are checked for firearms and smuggled goods. Others involve the full registration of passport and automobile documentation, by officials who write everything down with agonising deliberation in large ledgers. Considerable queues can build up at the latter checkpoints. You should remain calm, co-operative and patient throughout. Attempts to urge officials to speed things up are almost invariably counterproductive. At some of the more remote checkpoints, delays may have nothing to do with the weight of traffic. When entering one restricted zone, the rather bored official on duty insisted that I challenge him to a game of *nardi,* akin to backgammon, and would not open the barrier until he had beaten me. Fortunately this did not take him long.

The speed limit is 110km/h on new dual carriageways, but these are few in number, and on other main roads it is 90km/h. It drops to 60km/h when the road passes through a settlement, and may drop further to 50km/h or 40km/h (indicated by signs). You should obey the speed limit, both because of the risks of driving too fast and because Turkmen traffic police are well-equipped with speed guns. If you do receive a traffic fine, be aware that failure to pay results in a doubling of the fine every 12 hours, with possible seizure of the vehicle after 72 hours.

WHAT TO TAKE

You should consider the following items.

- **Plug adaptors**. Sockets in Turkmenistan are the twin round-pin, continental European type. The voltage is 220 Volt.
- A **torch**. Invaluable for getting around at night, and for exploring archaeological sites.
- Good **suncream**, **sunglasses** and a spare set of any **prescription glasses**; a basic supply of **medicines**, including any **prescription medication**; a **lip salve.**
- A **wide-brimmed hat** against the sun.
- Sturdy **footwear** which protects the ankles (such as hiking or desert boots).
- If you are planning to stay in cheaper-range accommodation, a **sheet sleeping-bag**, of the kind used by youth hostellers, as the bedding provided in Turkmenistan's cheaper hotels is often unspeakable; and a **sink plug**, as there often isn't one.
- A **corkscrew**, if you are planning any wine-fuelled picnics. Wine is widely available in Turkmenistan, but corkscrews are not.
- Spare **batteries**, if you have any equipment which takes anything other than standard AA or AAA batteries (for example, lithium camera batteries).
- Small **gift items**, such as postcards and maps of your home country (see *Giving something back*, page 60).

MONEY

The newly independent Turkmenistan introduced its new national currency, the manat, on 1 November 1993, an anniversary which is still celebrated each year, with exhortations from President Niyazov to the Turkmen people to love their money. Officially, there is a sub-unit of the manat, the tenne, with one manat made up of 100 tennes. But the latter is worth an infinitesimally small sum, and tenne coins have in practice long been removed from circulation. Some of the smaller-value manat notes have now joined them, including the 1, 5, 10 and 20 manat notes. The 50 and 100 manat notes are still around; you are likely to have use for them only to pay for the absurdly cheap fares on public buses in Ashgabat. The four denominations you will use regularly are 500 and 1,000 manat coins (the old notes for these sums have been phased out, though remain legal tender), and 5,000 and 10,000 manat notes.

The manat is a soft currency, and although there do not seem to be any rules against the importation or exportation of manat, you cannot buy it at foreign banks or exchange offices, and you cannot exchange any manat that you do take out.

The official exchange rate in Turkmenistan has been set at around 5,200 manat to US$1 for years. This is the only legal rate of exchange, and is the rate you will receive at every Turkmen bank. However, conversion of money in the other direction (back into US$) is only granted in a tightly defined set of circumstances (usually for a firm operating under a contract for which such official-rate conversion is specified), and even then must be authorised on every occasion by the Central Bank. Official rate conversion back to hard currency is thus not available for foreign tourists. The fact that you are able to produce exchange receipts demonstrating that you have obtained your manat legally, at the official rate, will not help. You should therefore ensure that you acquire only as much manat as you know you will definitely need.

There is, however, a black-market rate of exchange; the gap between the two rates is wide and growing. At the time of writing, the black-market rate was close to 25,000 manat to US$1. The black market is easy to find: a cry of 'dollar change?' from individuals clutching plastic bags filled with piles of manat greets you around every major bazaar in Turkmenistan. Receptionists or porters at most of the main hotels in Ashgabat organise the exchange of money, at a rate slightly below the black-market one, for foreign tourists reluctant to deal with the money-changers direct. The black market is closely monitored by the Turkmen authorities, which reportedly regulate the activities of the money-changers. President Niyazov has even on occasion appeared to countenance the use of the black market: for example, when telling officials in the city of Mary that he was giving them funds for a new mosque, he announced that he would convert his dollar donation at the black-market rather than the official rate, as they would get more money that way. And the black-market rate is the only one at which manat can be converted back to dollars.

None of this, however, removes the fact that the use of the black market in Turkmenistan is illegal, though the penalties in force in respect of a breach of the rules are unclear. I clearly cannot do anything other than recommend that you obey the law, and you may in any case need to produce certificates proving that you have obtained manat at the official rate for certain purposes (the two main examples are the purchase of domestic flight tickets and paying for accommodation at a small number of the cheaper state-run hotels, where prices are denominated in manat). But the black-market rate is the one against which Turkmen citizens calculate their prices, and the use of the official exchange rate therefore makes Turkmenistan a more expensive place to visit than it should be. It can also have some decidedly perverse consequences: for example, a night at a flea-pit hotel (denominated in manat) can end up costing you more than one at a top-of-the-range international hotel (denominated in dollars).

There are certain items for which you will be required to pay in US dollars. These include the services of your travel agency, most hotel accommodation, admission to the main museums and charges for various permits and taxes. It is not, however, legal to use hard currency at ordinary shops, or at bars and restaurants other than those in the main hotels.

You should bring US dollars in cash with you to Turkmenistan. Although euros are starting to become somewhat more widely accepted, the dollar remains king. Credit cards are accepted in very few establishments (though the main international hotels in Ashgabat now do take them). Few banks will cash travellers' cheques, and those that do charge commission of anything up to 10%.

You should make sure that your dollar bills were issued after 1996, and that they are all in good condition. Dollar bills with only relatively minor tears, or no more than moderate levels of all-round distress, may be refused. You should bring a range of denominations, as change may not be available. There do not seem to be any limits on the amount of foreign currency you may import, though you have to declare it on your customs form on arrival. You should retain the stamped version of this form, since you are not allowed to take out from Turkmenistan more hard currency than you declared on arrival.

BUDGETING

Turkmenistan should be a cheap country for the traveller, but the operation of the dual exchange rate, constraints on independent travel, and a dual-pricing system for hotel accommodation and museum entry as between foreign and Turkmen nationals all conspire to raise the cost of your holiday. As a rough guide, you might expect to pay around US$60 a night for discounted top-range accommodation. US$10–20 will get you a basic hotel room with a grotty bathroom. You can eat reasonably well outside Ashgabat for 100,000 manat a day, but will need to budget at least double this in Ashgabat, unless you are restricting yourself to cheap cafés.

For most visitors to Turkmenistan on tourist visas, costs of accommodation, transport, guide services and the various costs associated with visa support (though not the visa fee itself) are paid in a single dollar sum to the travel agency. Charges vary greatly (you will, for example, probably pay more if you book through a foreign operator rather than direct with a Turkmen agency, and more too for an individually tailored trip than as part of a larger group). The charge levied by travel agencies for the basic visa support package, including preparation of the LOI, meeting at the border with Entry Travel Pass, and registration, tends to be around US$60–80. Guides are charged at around US$30 per day.

GETTING AROUND

Urban transport

Ashgabat has a well-developed, very cheap and reasonably modern **bus** system. The picture in other towns is less good, with stronger reliance on informal taxis. Urban buses, where they can be found, are usually old and battered. Women usually gravitate towards the front of the bus, men to the rear, though this is a matter of custom rather than regulation.

Taxis are a more flexible yet still cheap means of getting around town. While a bookable taxi service exists in Ashgabat, most people simply flag down cars on the street. Anything that stops is a taxi. With unemployment high, and petrol prices low, many people in urban Turkmenistan make ends meet by driving around town in the hope of picking up an occasional fare. Having determined that the driver is willing to go to the chosen destination, the usual practice is just to get in and pay the local standard fare at the end of the trip. But there is no harm in agreeing the fare with the driver before you set off. If there are already other people in the taxi, you may find that the driver takes a circuitous route to your destination, dropping other passengers off first.

By road

All manner of vehicles ply the routes between the main towns. There are **government buses** (with green number-plates), which run to a timetable, but are few in number. A small number of 'luxury' buses have started to appear, which offer all modern comforts for an increased price. There are **private buses** (with white number-plates), which depart when full, or when the driver decides he is ready to go, but which tend to be more frequent. A wide range of smaller private vehicles, operating on a similar 'depart when ready' principle, include Toyota minivans, whose drivers seem happy to take risks with their human cargoes in an effort to shave a few minutes off the journey time, and smaller six-seater Toyotas. As a general rule, the fare increases and journey time decreases with a reduction in the size of the vehicle. **Intercity taxis** can be taken either on a shared basis, in which case you wait around until the taxi is full (they are considered to have four seats), or as a single-occupancy taxi, in which case you pay for the empty seats. Drivers often assume that foreigners will want to take the latter option. Be aware that services to some destinations dry up in the early evening, even where there has been a frequent service during the day. The prices charged by intercity taxis vary considerably according to the make of car: a place in a Russian car without air conditioning comes considerably cheaper than one in a modern German or Japanese make. Minibuses and taxis also charge more for overnight journeys (which are, in any case, to be avoided on road-safety grounds).

To get to some tourist attractions of no great day-to-day interest to the locals, such as many archaeological sites, your only option other than booking a tour with a travel agency is to hire a taxi to take you there and back and wait while you are at the site. This is usually negotiable for a reasonably modest sum. Self-drive car hire is not currently available in Turkmenistan.

By rail

The origins of the railway system in Turkmenistan lay in the late 19th-century variant of the Great Game between Britain and Russia. From the Russian settlement of Krasnovodsk on the Caspian, the Transcaspian Railway headed eastwards, to consolidate Russian control over its newly acquired territories in Central Asia, and provoking a good deal of nervousness in British India. The present-day railway network of Turkmenistan is substantially based around the tsarist lines: the route of the Transcaspian Railway from Turkmenbashy to Turkmenabat, via Ashgabat and Mary, with a branch to Serhetabat on the Afghan border. The service is cheap: the longest route, in the best available standard of carriage, costs less than 60,000 manat. The trip will also give you a good opportunity for (lengthy) conversations with your Turkmen fellow passengers. But the arrival and departure times are often inconvenient, and the service is agonisingly slow. It seems to have been ever thus; Lord Curzon, travelling on the new railway in 1888 as far as Samarkand, found that he had averaged 12 miles per hour.

A new railway currently under construction across the Kara Kum Desert from Ashgabat to Dashoguz will at least make the train a more realistic option to Turkmenistan's northern region: until now the trip has involved heading first to Turkmenabat, far to the east, and then reaching Dashoguz via a route along the Amu Darya.

By air

Internal flights are an outstanding bargain in Turkmenistan. Ticket prices range from around 23,000–60,000 manat. Under new rules introduced in 2004, foreign nationals are likely to be asked to produce, at the time of booking their ticket, a bank certificate demonstrating that they have obtained their manat at the official rate of exchange. All internal flights use Boeing 717 aircraft, although one downside to the decision to have a Boeing-only passenger fleet was the axing of passenger flights in 2004 to four small airports, unable to take Boeings, and previously served by Yak or Antonov turboprops. So Gazochak, Atamurat, Magdanly and Hazar airports are now silent.

With cheap flights on modern aircraft, the inevitable catch is that flight tickets can be fiendishly difficult to obtain. Tickets on the flights between Ashgabat and Dashoguz are particularly hard to get, since the alternatives by road or rail involve arduous trips. Flights to the coastal town of Turkmenbashy are especially difficult to get hold of during the summer months, but all internal flights book up quickly. If you have no joy at the Turkmenistan Airlines office, local travel agents may be able to secure a seat where you could not, though a 'commission charge' of several times the ticket price will probably be involved.

ACCOMMODATION

Hotels

Hotel accommodation in Turkmenistan involves two contrasting pictures: Ashgabat and the provinces. The construction of hotels as prestige projects, rather than in response to market demands, has resulted in a heavy over-provision of hotel rooms in the Turkmen capital. As a result, there is a wide choice of rooms available at all price levels, from around US$10 (for something rather grim) upwards. Good bargains are available at the upper end of the market, with hotels desperate for custom offering large discounts on their listed prices. Maintenance budgets in even the grandest hotels are low, and the smartest places can start to look rundown after just a few years.

Outside Ashgabat, options narrow considerably. The regional capitals are all able to offer at least a limited choice, and serve as useful bases from which to explore their regions. State-run hotels in the smaller district capitals are scarce, and usually dire. The coastal town of Turkmenbashy, and the adjacent village of Awaza, are being developed for domestic summer tourism, and offer the best selection of accommodation outside Ashgabat. Prices here in summer are the highest in Turkmenistan, though large discounts are available in winter.

Other accommodation

The organisation of **private home-stays** with Turkmen families has become more difficult in recent years. The Turkmen government claims that some of the foreign 'mercenaries' allegedly involved in the reported coup attempt of November 2002 were able to stay undetected in a private house in Ashgabat for several months. New rules were introduced, heavily restricting the possibilities for foreigners to stay in private accommodation in Ashgabat. Outside the capital the position is less clear, and the prospects of securing a home-stay are greater in more rural areas. Some travel agencies will include a night or two with a Turkmen family in one of the hill villages of the Kopet Dag, as part of a trekking package.

Several **private hotels** offer better alternatives to the state-run places in the mid-price bracket. Travellers on tourist visas are not, however, allowed to stay in these, or in home-stays. For trips into the Turkmen desert, or the remoter parts of the Kopet Dag Mountains, your only option is to **camp.** Several local travel agencies are experienced in setting up packages under canvas, which can offer memorable insights into wild Turkmenistan.

EATING AND DRINKING

Food

The centre-piece of the Turkmen diet is bread (*chorek*), traditionally eaten as a flat, round loaf, stamped for decoration with patterns of dots supplied by a small wooden hand-stamp. Bread is treated by Turkmens not as a simple food, but as something sacred, a building-block of life. Many superstitions surround it. It is considered unlucky, for example, to leave your *chorek* upside down. Official visitors to a Turkmen institution such as a school are greeted by a girl in long velvet dress holding out a *chorek*, from which they are expected to break off a piece as a sign of the acceptance of the hospitality of the institution. If you are invited to a meal with a Turkmen family, the first food offered is likely to be a *chorek*, carefully unwrapped from the cloth in which it has been kept warm. You should break off a piece, and hand the *chorek* on to your neighbour. When you leave your hosts, you may be again offered a piece of bread, as a talisman for the journey. *Chorek* is delicious when fresh and warm, but hardens quickly, rather losing its appeal.

The *chorek* is made in a conical clay-oven, or *tamdyr*. You will see these in the courtyards of houses throughout Turkmenistan, in towns as well as rural areas. The *tamdyr*, like the bread itself, is treated with reverence. It is considered unlucky ever to destroy a *tamdyr*, which is why you will sometimes see a bright new *tamdyr* standing next to an old, abandoned one.

Bread also features heavily in one of the most traditional Turkmen dishes, *dograma,* a heavy soup containing torn pieces of *chorek*, onions and roasted meat. Families tend to reserve *dograma* for religious festivals, especially *Kurban Bayram,* and a more omnipresent soup is *chorba*, usually made with large lumps of fatty mutton, halved potatoes, and whatever vegetables are available. Soups are usually eaten with brightly coloured papier-mâché spoons.

Turkmen cuisine features several other dishes well known across Central Asia, including *manty*, like large ravioli, usually filled with minced meat and onion. These are served with sour cream and eaten by hand, the juices from the ravioli parcels dripping down your arm. Another Central Asian staple is *plov,* a rice dish incorporating meat (usually chunks of mutton), onion, garlic and carrots, cooked up in a heavy round pot called a *kazan* with the aid of huge quantities of cottonseed oil, which gives the finished dish a distinctly oily taste. Along the Caspian coast, you can sometimes find a fish *plov*, made with sturgeon and raisins, which makes a great alternative to the fattier meat version.

As everywhere in the region, kebabs (here usually known by the Russian word, *shashlik*) are very popular. You will see the special barbecue stands, *mangal*, outside restaurants and cafés across the country. Purists argue that *shashlik* tastes at its best only when the gnarled, twisted wood of the desert saxaul is used for the barbecue. The *shashliks* are skewered lumps of lamb, mutton, chicken, pork or sturgeon, or a version called *lyulya*, a long sausage of minced lamb, all served with pieces of raw onion and some sprinkled greenery. Turkmen kebabs tend to be fatty.

The more traditional Turkmen dishes are not always easy to find in Turkmenistan's restaurants. Most Turkmens rarely eat at a restaurant, except at weddings and other celebratory events, when special menus featuring Turkmen fare will be prepared, and many restaurant menus retain a somewhat Russian feel. They typically include a long list of mainly mayonnaise-heavy salads. *Olivye* is what is known in Britain as Russian salad. *Selyodka pod shuboy*, literally 'herring in a fur coat', involves pickled herring buried by layers of beetroot and mayonnaise. Russian staples such as the beetroot soup *borscht, golubtsy*, which are meat-filled cabbage parcels, and various types of breaded cutlets, fill up the menu and will do the same to the diner.

Turkmen dishes are easier to find in cheaper cafés around markets, and roadside truck-stops. Markets are also good places to try the popular hot pastries, most of which have a minced-meat and onion filling. *Somsas* are small triangle-shaped pastries, and make a good snack. Those made by the ethnic Uzbek communities in Dashoguz and Lebap regions are said to be the best. *Fitchi* are larger, and circular. *Ishlekli* are the largest of all; coronary-inducing large round pies.

MADE IN THE TAMDYR

'Come and watch a goat being slaughtered in your honour!' With this irresistible offer from my Turkmen hosts at a small house in the Kugitang Nature Reserve, I was introduced to the Turkmen dish known as *tamdyrlama*, literally something 'made in the *tamdyr*'.

The bleating goat was expertly despatched, a bowl of its blood brought to the family's tethered dog, who happily lapped it up. The goat was hung up on a tree branch; its intestines disgorged into a bowl with a single cut of the knife. It was then dissected into large slabs of meat, each liberally sprinkled with salt. Smaller pieces of the goat's meat were mixed in a metal bowl with tomatoes, onions, potatoes and cabbages. Salt and chilli peppers were added, together with pieces of dried plants from a mysterious-looking plastic bottle. I was told that these were herbs collected from the mountains. The contents of the metal bowl were poured into the goat's stomach. This was then tied shut with a loop of metal wire. More meat was cut up into chunks, and placed into a metal pot. To this was added vegetables and hot water, making a soup. Further loops of wire were tied around the handles of the pot.

The family's conical clay-oven, *tamdyr*, had meanwhile been fired up with kindling, and was burning fiercely. The soup pot was carefully placed in the bottom of the *tamdyr*. The loop of wire around the goat's stomach was tied to a metal pole, which was balanced across the top of the oven, leaving the stomach to dangle into the furnace. Two large cuts of meat were hung onto another metal pole, and likewise suspended into the fire. Sprigs of mint and juniper were draped around these, to add flavour. Our host then sealed up both the top and side openings of the *tamdyr* with wet mud. He placed an inverted cooking pot on the top of the sealed oven, and a small gobbet of mud on the upturned base of the pot. When that mud had dried, he said, our meal would be ready.

Some traditional dishes are served as a particularly high honour to a guest, though if you find yourself the recipient of a sheep's head, you may wish that you had been accorded a lesser honour. One particularly impressive dish, whose name refers more to a way of cooking than the dish itself, is a *tamdyrlama* (see box). Other unusual food items you might come across include *nabat,* a yellow crystallised sugar, and *gurt,* salty balls of dried curd, eaten as a savoury snack with beer. Another popular bar snack is dried fish.

Dessert is generally fruit, ice-cream, or a cake decorated with alarmingly garish icing. Fruit is definitely the best option. Turkmen grapes are sweet and juicy and, in the autumn, pomegranates are popular. Turkmenistan is, however, most famous for its melons. Huge piles of different types of melons and watermelons dominate Turkmenistan's bazaars during the summer months. The Turkmen government released in 1999 a *Turkmen Melons Atlas*, which listed a total of 378 types of Turkmen melon, plus 54 watermelons and 55 pumpkins. Among the most prized of Turkmen melons is the rugby ball-shaped yellow- and green-skinned *waharman*.

Drink

Tea and soft drinks

The most important drink in Turkmenistan is tea. Turkmens drink both green and black teas, often the former when they wish to relax, the latter to boost levels of alertness. It is served from the pot, into little bowls without handles, called *piyalushka*. It is never drunk with milk, except by the ethnic Kazakh community.

Almost as many superstitions and rituals surround the taking of tea as those involving bread. A fresh pot of tea should, for example, first be poured three times into a cup before it is drunk. If you see bubbles on the surface of your tea cup, this means that you will come into money. But you must 'catch' the bubbles, by dabbing them with your finger and then tapping this on the top of your head, before they reach the side of the bowl, or your new-found wealth will drain away. If bits of stalk from the tea float on the top of your cup, then be prepared to welcome guests to your home.

Coffee usually means either Nescafé, served black, or a rather synthetic drink called 'three-in-one', involving sachets of ready-mixed coffee, sugar and creamer. The most popular brand, Stars and Stripes adorning the packet, is called 'Golden Eagle: True American Flavour', and is produced in Malaysia. There is a reasonably wide selection of carbonated soft drinks, both locally produced and imported. The product of Ashgabat's Coca-Cola bottling plant apart, domestic fizzy drinks tend towards lurid colours and mildly unpleasant flavours. There is also a good quality locally produced fruit juice named Serdar (Leader) in honour of the president, though some of the flavours use imported concentrate rather than local fruit.

Alcohol

Almost three-quarters of a century as part of the Soviet Union has left Turkmenistan with a legacy of beer and vodka drinking. The picture as regards the consumption of alcohol is changing, with a gradual increase in the number of Turkmen Muslims avoiding it on religious grounds. But alcohol remains widely available throughout the country, and for foreign visitors problems tend to be less to do with any difficulty in obtaining alcohol than with fending off the demands of enthusiastic and increasingly inebriated Turkmen hosts to take large vodka toasts (see *Interacting with local people*). Among the better locally produced vodkas are two dedicated to President Niyazov. Special presentation bottles of Beyik Turkmenbashy, in a green cylindrical carton, were produced to commemorate the tenth anniversary of Turkmenistan's independence. And the frosted-glass bottles of Serdar, the flagship Turkmen vodka, feature a clear-glass window through which you can gaze at a smiling portrait of the president. Turkmenistan also produces palatable, if rather sweet, brandy, and a herbal liqueur called *balsam* which is a rather more acquired taste.

Once on a Turkmenistan Airlines flight I asked for a glass of wine.

'I'm sorry, we have no wine. We only have Turkmen wine,' replied the stewardess.

Turkmenistan's wine industry has gone through a turbulent time, hit by Gorbachev's anti-alcohol drive, and then by the loss of its markets following the break-up of the Soviet Union. But a small number of wineries remain across the country, producing a bewildering variety of wines, in small production runs, for the domestic market. Local varieties of grapes are used, especially the black *gara uzum* and white *terbash*, as well as European varieties such as cabernet and muscat. The product is a wine which is very strong (most Turkmen wines have an alcohol content of 16–19%), and very sweet; more like sherry than the table wines familiar in Europe or North America. So in a way that Turkmenistan Airlines stewardess was right: wine as a European passenger would understand it and Turkmen wine are two quite different drinks.

Imported bottled beers are widely available. Local market leaders include the Russian Baltika and the Turkish Efes. But two privately produced Turkmen beers are more palatable than their names might suggest: Berk and Zip. The latter is available either in football-shaped plastic bottles, or on tap at several 'Zip bars' across the country. Check the alcohol content of your beer carefully: high-alcohol varieties, such as the treacly Baltika 9, are popular in Turkmenistan, especially in rural areas where incomes are lower, because they provide a cheaper route to drunkenness.

PUBLIC HOLIDAYS AND FESTIVALS

Turkmenistan has a large number of public holidays, many though celebrated on Sundays in order not to disrupt the working week. Most are creations of President Niyazov and form part of his nation-building project for the young state of Turkmenistan. Holidays celebrate the independence of the country, significant dates (such as the UN General Assembly resolution granting Turkmenistan its status of permanent neutrality), the most famous symbols and products of Turkmenistan (its horses, carpets and even melons) and the achievements of key groups of workers, from singers to employees of the oil and gas sector. Some Islamic festivals, such as the end of *Ramadan*, and pre-Islamic ones, such as the spring festival, are also commemorated.

All these Turkmen holidays are celebrated through special programmes on state-run Turkmen television and news broadcasts incorporating the texts of holiday messages from the president. But in many cases, there is not a great deal in which the foreign tourist can get involved. The most prestigious of the state concerts held to mark the events, often in the Ruhyyet Palace or Olympic Stadium in Ashgabat, involve an invited audience, whose role is to applaud and wave Turkmen flags. With most of the audience having been instructed to attend, provision is not usually made for visitors actually *wanting* to come. But these concerts, which feature songs and dramatic sketches, often either in praise of President Niyazov or using the texts of his poetry as lyrics, are of interest as a graphic visual demonstration of the personality-driven focus of the Turkmen regime. Securing attendance at smaller concerts outside Ashgabat is usually easier, as is getting to see the parades usually held in the capital around the Flag Day, Independence Day and Neutrality Day holidays. These major holidays also frequently include public firework displays, as well as other cultural events, including concerts of Turkmen pop music. But many of the smaller newly created holidays have not really generated any resonance in the lives of most Turkmens, and pass unnoticed by most people.

The holiday calendar

1 January: **New Year's Day** Restaurants hold sumptuous ticket-only events on New Year's Eve, with dancing and party games, fuelled by sweet sparkling wine. The trees in town centres are decorated with tinsel, and kids let off firecrackers in the streets. Shops decorate their windows with fake snow.

12 January: **Memorial Day** Commemorates the Turkmens killed at the battle of Geok Depe in 1881. Each year President Niyazov leads a memorial service at the Geok Depe Mosque.

19 February: **Flag Day** Commemorates the adoption of Turkmenistan's new state flag in 1992. The flag is rather attractive: a crescent moon and five stars on a green background, with a vertical red strip decorated with five carpet motifs, each representing one of the five regions of Turkmenistan. In 1997, two crossed olive branches were added to the base of this vertical strip, to symbolise Turkmenistan's foreign policy of permanent neutrality. The date 19 February has another significance; it is also President Niyazov's birthday.

20–22 March: **National Spring Holiday** Based around the vernal equinox, the spring holiday, known as *Novruz Bayram*, is celebrated across Central Asia as the time of the arrival of spring, and in Iran as the start of the new year. One Turkmen tradition associated with *Novruz Bayram* is the preparation of a caramel-coloured paste known as *semeni*, made from sprouted wheat and flour. Turkmen families believe that if you leave a dish of newly prepared *semeni* overnight, the handprint of Fatima, daughter of the Prophet Mohammed, may be visible on the surface of the food in the morning. But not every Turkmen family is able to make *semeni*. One Turkmen friend told me that the first time his paternal grandmother tried to make the dish, her oven blew up. On the second occasion, her mother-in-law fell ill. On the third, she herself fell ill. Thereafter, she paid heed to the bad omens and stopped trying to make the stuff. The family now receive their supplies from his mother's side. In 2003 Niyazov announced that he was moving Women's Day, previously celebrated in Turkmenistan as elsewhere on 8 March, to link it up with the spring holiday, which henceforward would be celebrated over three days.

First Sunday in April: **Drop of Water – Grain of Gold Day** This holiday, named from a traditional Turkmen proverb, is the occasion for an annual message from the president about the importance of the effective management of Turkmenistan's water reserves.

Last Sunday in April: **Holiday of the Turkmen Horse** Celebrates the famous Ahal Tekke horses of Turkmenistan. The main focus of the day is, predictably enough, horse races, held at tracks in all the regional capitals.

8–9 May: **Remembrance and Victory Days** One of the few Turkmen holidays which maintains a Soviet-era tradition. Many Turkmens were killed in what is still referred to as the Great Patriotic War, and 8 May is marked by the laying of wreaths at war memorials as well as by family visits to the graves of those who died. This public holiday is also the focus of a developing personality cult around President Niyazov's father, Atamurat, killed in World War II.

18 May: **The Day of Revival, Unity and the Poetry of Magtymguly** The date 18 May was celebrated as the Day of Revival and Unity until 1999, marking the anniversary of the adoption, in 1992, of the constitution of the new state of Turkmenistan. In 2000, in an attempt at rationalising the spiralling number of holiday events, Niyazov combined this holiday with the annual celebration of the 18th-century Turkmen poet Magtymguly, which had up to then been held on the following day. The science-fiction author Brian Aldiss includes a fictional account of Magtymguly Day celebrations in his novel *Somewhere East of Life*. But the reality of the day is more low key than that of Aldiss's fiction, centring on the laying of flowers at the various monuments to Magtymguly around the country.

Last Sunday in May: **Carpet Day** An exhibition of carpets and carpet-making, coupled with an open-air concert, is usually organised at the back of the Carpet Museum in Ashgabat.

Third Sunday in July: **Grain Day** A celebration of the wheat harvest, greeted with great fanfare if the annual production target is deemed to have been met.

Second Sunday in August: **Melon Day** In 2003 this event was marked by a melon-themed exhibition at Independence Park in Ashgabat, to which visitors were greeted by small girls dressed in inflatable melon and watermelon outfits. The following year, less eccentrically, the centrepiece of the celebrations was a music concert.

Second Saturday in September: Day of the Employees of the Oil and Gas, Energy and Geological Industries First commemorated in 2003, a holiday devoted to Turkmenistan's largest exports earner. State-organised events are focused on the main centres of the industry, such as Balkanabat.

Second Sunday in September: Day of the Turkmen *Bagshy* On the heels of the oil workers come the folk singers. Musical performances are the order of the day.

October 6: Remembrance Day for those killed in the Ashgabat earthquake of 1948 Wreaths are laid at the earthquake monuments in Ashgabat and Gypjak. The Turkmen government holds a sacrificial meal at the Gypjak Mosque.

October 27–28: Independence Day The anniversary of the independence of the young state of Turkmenistan is the most important date on the government's calendar: such an important day, in fact, that it lasts 48 hours. There is usually a parade in Ashgabat, watched over by the president, in which a display of Turkmenistan's (mostly Soviet-era) military hardware is followed by a procession involving Ahal Tekke horses, employees of various state organisations and brightly coloured dancers. There are concerts, plays, an annual song competition and fireworks.

First Saturday in November: Health Day Usually marked by government officials walking the Health Paths in Ashgabat and other Turkmen cities.

Last Sunday in November: Good Neighbourliness and Harvest Days Good Neighbourliness Day is an event intended to reinforce the Turkmen tradition of support for neighbours. The focus of this day, which until 2002 was celebrated on the first Sunday in December, is the sharing of food with one's neighbours. In 2003, Niyazov amalgamated this holiday with Harvest Day at the end of November.

December 12: Neutrality Day A holiday commemorating the anniversary of the 1995 United Nations General Assembly resolution granting Turkmenistan its status of permanent neutrality. As from 2003, Neutrality Day has been combined with the Day of Student Youth, moved from its earlier slot of 17 November.

Islamic holidays

Turkmenistan also commemorates some key Muslim holy days, whose dates are set by the lunar calendar. These are as follows.

***Kurban Bayram* (*Eid ul-Adha*)** This Muslim festival marks the willingness of Ibrahim to obey the word of Allah by agreeing to sacrifice his son. Allah spared the boy, and allowed Ibrahim to sacrifice a lamb instead. In Turkmenistan, families sacrifice a sheep, arranging for most of the mutton to be distributed to the poor. The boiled mutton is often used to make the dish *dograma*. The family themselves will eat the *dograma* as a soup. But they will also arrange for little parcels of the dried mixture of mutton, bread and onion used to make the dish to be sent to the needy, as well as to their neighbours and relatives. The *Kurban Bayram* celebration is the most colourful in Turkmenistan, and is held over three days, starting 70 days after the end of *Ramadan*. Aspects of the celebration in Turkmenistan draw from a pre-Islamic tradition. These include jumping over fire, which seems to hint at Zoroastrianism. The most visible feature of the *Kurban Bayram* holiday for the visitor to Turkmenistan is, however, the tradition of 'swinging away sins'. Across Turkmenistan, you will see large metal frames, often in open spaces on the edges of settlements. During *Kurban Bayram* a swing, usually little more complex than a plank of wood, is suspended from these frames, and youngsters ride on the swings, by tradition losing one sin with every swing. Courting couples face each other on the swings, an action which can be taken as a betrothal. Foreign visitors will be enthusiastically welcomed on to the swings, usually by small children who will be only too keen to propel you ever higher. This can turn into an extreme sport to rival anything dreamt up by adventure travel companies, so is not to be attempted lightly.

***Oraza Bayram* (Eid ul-Fitr)** The holiday marking the end of the month of *Ramadan*. Bars and restaurants remain open throughout the day during *Ramadan*, and business visitors will often still be offered tea and coffee at meetings by their hosts. Rates of observance of the daylight *Ramadan* fast are however on the increase in Turkmenistan. The night between the 26th and 27th days of *Ramadan* is known as *Gadyr Gijesy* (Omnipotence Night), when by recent tradition President Niyazov orders the release of many petty criminals from Turkmenistan's jails. In 2002, Niyazov wrote a poem to commemorate the action. It was called *Taking Oneself Home*.

SHOPPING

The bazaars at the heart of every town in Turkmenistan are the basic port of call for both food and general shopping. Opening hours are usually roughly from 08.00–20.00. Bazaars are generally open every day, including Sundays, though close for occasional 'cleaning days', which are taken unpredictably (though the first Monday in the month seems to be a common choice). Larger out-of-town markets, like the Tolkuchka Bazaar outside Ashgabat, usually open only on two or three mornings a week. Note that during the cotton harvest in the autumn, most bazaars outside Ashgabat are closed during daylight hours. Government-run shops are generally closed on Sundays, and may also close for lunch. Privately run shops usually open every day.

The top item on the shopping list of many visitors to Turkmenistan is one of the country's prized carpets, though the complex and potentially expensive export regulations can prove a real headache (see box, pages 52–3). Another good souvenir is a felt rug, or *keche* (known as a *koshma* in Russian). The making of felt rugs is a deep-seated Turkmen tradition. *Keches* were once used to line the *yurt*, and a modern Turkmen family will picnic on a *keche*, whose thick woollen mat is said to offer good protection against scorpions and other unwelcome visitors. One distinctive kind of *keche* is used as a *namazlyk*, or prayer rug. These are generally white in colour, and often contain 'wavy' designs resembling snakes.

Another traditional craft of Turkmenistan is jewellery-making. Turkmen women often wear large quantities of heavy silver jewellery; especially on their marriage, when they may be weighed down by several kilogrammes of jewels. There is jewellery for the head, ears, neck, plaits, arms and fingers, as well as breast plates, dorsal jewellery and a wide range of amulets. The jewellery typically features mounted cornelians, a stone believed to offer protection against disease and to lift the spirits of the wearer. Jewellery made by craftsmen of the Yomud tribe of western Turkmenistan often contains small pieces of turquoise, which cluster around a single large cornelian. There are stringent restrictions on the export of silver jewellery, but most of the pieces you will find in the bazaars of Turkmenistan are not silver. You are not allowed to export any antique items, a rule which seems to be interpreted by Turkmen customs officials as meaning anything vaguely old-looking, and which may cause you problems in respect of other items purchased at bazaars, such as *samovars*.

Brightly coloured Turkmen paintings also provide evocative memories of your trip. Representational painting was introduced to the area by the Russians;

TURKMEN CARPETS

Carpets, usually predominantly deep red in colour, and featuring a repeated motif known as a *gul* ('flower'), are a great source of pride to the Turkmen. They were among the most prized possessions of Turkmen nomads, the walls and floors of whose *yurts* were decorated with carpets. Turkmenistan celebrates an annual Carpet Day, and the national flag incorporates the *guls* typical of carpets from each of the country's five regions.

The *gul* is, in effect, an emblem of the tribe. There is much debate as to the meaning of each of the patterns. The guides at the Carpet Museum in Ashgabat will weave for visitors elaborate explanations, though much of this is guesswork. They will tell you, for example, that the *gul* characteristic of the Tekke tribe is divided into four parts to represent the seasons, its alternating white and dark colours symbolising day and night. Within each of the four parts, the three designs resembling birds' feet may each signify a month, which I suppose makes the whole design a kind of calendar *gul*. The four colours used in the making of the carpet – orange, white, red and black – are said to represent the elements, respectively, of earth, air, fire and water. The guides identify in the *gul* of the Yomud tribe, which occupies the Caspian shores of western Turkmenistan, many marine-related items. Thus the elongated shape of the *gul* is said to represent a boat, or possibly a fish, and the design features repeated anchor shapes. Around the edges of Yomud carpets may be identified a pattern resembling seashells intertwined with seaweed.

Carpets have traditionally been used to make many other items. Folded in two, with the edges sewn together, they form storage bags. The largest type of bag, traditionally hung on the walls of a *yurt* and used to store clothes, is known as a *chuwal*. A *torba* is a smaller bag, used for utensils. There are many specialised designs of storage bag. The *uk ujy*, for example, was designed for the carriage of *yurt* poles between encampments. Carpetwork saddle-bags, *horjun*, also make an attractive souvenir.

Carpets have traditionally been woven by women, and the Turkmen carpet industry is still based firmly around hand weaving. At the carpet factories across Turkmenistan run by the state concern Turkmenhaly, most of the employees are teenaged girls and young women, who sit, several weavers to a loom, building the remembered pattern at a furious pace. Most of the wool is,

Turkmen art had traditionally been based around the abstract designs of its textiles and jewellery. The workshops around the Artists' Union buildings in Ashgabat and Mary, as well as two private art galleries in Ashgabat (see page 85) are the best places to buy paintings in Turkmenistan. An export licence is, however, required: this is issued by the Artists' Union in Ashgabat for a fee of 10% of the value of the painting.

The intricate embroidered trims which decorate Turkmen dresses can look good framed and hung on the wall. Souvenirs of post-independence Turkmenistan include lapel pins, watches and vodka bottles decorated with portraits of President Niyazov, and English-language copies of *Ruhnama*, at 50,000 manat. Bottles of Turkmenbashy aftershave are, however, now a rarity.

ARTS AND ENTERTAINMENT

Since independence, President Niyazov has strongly encouraged those arts outlets which express the traditions of Turkmenistan, or at least the official version of

however, coloured with synthetic rather than natural dyes, a legacy of Soviet 'modernisation'.

With the cost of a carpet from one of the bazaars of Turkmenistan considerably less than the price of a 'Bukhara' (as Turkmen carpets are often misleadingly described) in the West, a Turkmen carpet would seem the obvious souvenir to bring back from your visit. This happy picture is, however, clouded by the complex export regulations surrounding carpets. If you have purchased your carpet from a bazaar or private shop, before you can take it out of the country you will need to get it certified by the 'Expert Commission', based at the Carpet Museum in Ashgabat. The 'Expert Commission' (✆ 12 398879; f 12 398887) is open 14.30–17.30 Mon–Fri, and 10.00–12.00 Sat. The entrance is around the back of the Carpet Museum building. Commission staff are in principle willing to provide certifications out of hours, but charge double in this case. For a fee of 115,000 manat per square metre, the Commission will certify that the carpet is not more than 50 years old, and may be exported. Carpet-related products such as *chuwals* must also be certified.

Carpets above a certain size are additionally subject to an export duty, payable at customs on departure. For carpets in what is categorised as the 'Tekke group' (including Tekke, Sarik and Salor designs), duty is payable on all carpets above 1.36m^2. For carpets in the 'Yomud group' (including Yomud, Beshir and Choudur designs), duty is payable above 2m^2. Duty is charged at 2,005,000 manat for each additional square metre, payable in dollars at the official rate of exchange. This quickly racks up to a prohibitive cost.

The alternative is to buy your carpet at one of the state carpet shops (see page 85). Although the basic price of carpets purchased in these stores is more expensive, the shop will provide the necessary certification (make sure you request the certificate) at no extra charge, and you should not have to pay export duty on larger carpets purchased in state shops. The customs authorities instead charge a small 'commission fee', of 0.2% of the cost of the carpet.

Travellers visiting Turkmenistan as part of a regional tour should also be aware that Turkmen customs authorities may charge a small 'transit fee' in respect of carpets purchased in neighbouring countries but brought through Turkmenistan.

them, while other cultural forms have been closed down, or simply allowed to wither without government support or acknowledgement.

Theatre

The Turkmen government has embarked on an ambitious programme to construct new theatres in every regional capital. Plays are usually epic dramas, based around heroic Turkmen figures of the past such as Oguz Han or Georogly, often drawing from proverbs mentioned in Niyazov's book *Ruhnama*. A night at the theatre can offer an interesting insight into the way in which the arts establishment presents Turkmen history, provided your tour guide or a Turkmen friend is willing to act as interpreter. Ticket prices are low.

Music

Types of music using traditional Turkmen instruments have been encouraged since independence, and outlets for Western classical music closed, including both

TURKMEN MUSICAL INSTRUMENTS

The ***dutar***, a two-stringed guitar with a rounded body, is the most important musical instrument of Turkmenistan, providing the musical accompaniment to the epic sung poetry known as *destans* which are the stock-in-trade of Turkmenistan's traditional singers, or *bagshies*. The *dutar* typically has a body made of mulberry wood, or occasionally walnut, its neck of apricot wood. The teaching of the *dutar* has become a major focus of post-independence musical education, and it is now common in Turkmenistan to see schoolchildren clutching the instrument, protected in a velvet carrying-case.

The ***gyjak*** is a three- or four-stringed instrument, played with a bow whose string is made of hair from a horse's tail. The instrument is stood upright, resting on a little peg at its base, and produces a sound which might evoke for you the ever-changing landscapes of the desert of the Kara Kum. Or it might just remind you of a long screech. The *gyjak*, which is also usually made from a mixture of mulberry and apricot woods, is typically used to accompany the *dutar*.

The ***gargy-tuyduk*** is a long reed flute which produces a wonderful, melancholic sound. This really *will* evoke the sound of the wind blowing across the desert. The ***dilli-tuyduk*** is a much shorter flute, producing a shriller sound.

The ***gopuz*** is a small metal instrument, which in other parts of the world is known as a Jew's harp. It is placed in the mouth, from which a protruding stainless steel reed is strummed by a quickly moving hand. The mouth serves as a sound chamber, and the breath varies the pitch. The *gopuz* is mostly played by women, and produces a distinctive twanging sound.

the opera and ballet. However, a small number of groups using Western instruments have continued to receive government support, such as the Saparmurat Niyazov Violin Ensemble led by Harold Neimark. Some Soviet-era Turkmen composers, of whom the most famous was Nury Halmammedov, incorporated traditional Turkmen styles into their classical compositions, and such artists provide the focus of the repertoires of these groups.

The songs of the Turkmen *bagshies* can sound harsh and unfamiliar to the Western ear, with guttural sounds and loud wailing. Very much in this vein is Djamal Saparova, a singer close to the regime, who has made a speciality of adapting President Niyazov's poetry into song. She also acts as artistic director of the largest government concerts. Turkmen pop music is softer in style, very similar to Turkish pop. Leading exponents include Lachyn Mammedova. A few bands have experimented with Turkmen techno. Archabil is one name to check out. Concerts of popular music are advertised around town, and tend to be most frequent on and around major public holidays. Admission prices are low. Turkmen weddings are another good place to hear both traditional and modern forms of Turkmen song: families pay out considerable sums to hire big-name stars. Bands offering cover versions of Western pop music perform at weekends in some of the Ashgabat bars most popular with expatriates.

Dance

State-sponsored dance is focused on the provision of large, well-choreographed extravaganzas for government events in celebration of national holidays. The dancers, often university students, are dressed in shiny outfits modelled on traditional Turkmen dress: the boys with shaggy *telpek* hats, shirts and breeches; the girls in long flowing dresses and plenty of silver jewellery. The dancing of the boys is energetic, with gymnastic moves designed to demonstrate athleticism, while the girls are required to show grace and poise. Away from government events, other forms of dance can be found. Particularly within the ethnic Russian community, break-dance remains surprisingly popular, practised by groups with names like Dance Boyz and Dance Power.

Sport

There are some prestigious sports facilities in Ashgabat, crowned by the Saparmurat Turkmenbashy Olympic Stadium. But this is used more for state-sponsored concerts than sporting events. Outside the capital, most sporting facilities are pretty run down. Turkmenistan has a small football league, with teams representing the main towns, plus organisations such as the Turkmen Army. Tickets are cheap (around 3,000 manat), the spectators almost entirely male. Huge quantities of sunflower seeds are chewed on the terraces of a typical match. The league is fought with a passion: I watched one match in Mary at which the coach of the visiting Turkmen-Turkish University team had to be led off by police after attempting to thump the referee. Horse racing is another popular spectator sport, and an excellent opportunity to see Ahal Tekke horses in action (see page 82 for details of racing in Ashgabat).

Physical fitness training is popular in Turkmenistan, as is tae kwan do and Central Asian wrestling. Staple pastimes of the Soviet period such as chess and, especially, Russian billiards remain popular.

MEDIA AND COMMUNICATIONS

The Turkmen domestic media are state controlled to a very high degree. Newspapers are mostly four-page broadsheets, their contents focusing heavily on the engagements of President Niyazov. A photograph of the president adorns almost every front page. One national newspaper, *Neutralniy Turkmenistan*, is in Russian; all other dailies are in the Turkmen language. There is also a range of specialist newspapers and magazines, such as *Eshger*, the newspaper of the armed forces.

There are four state television channels. Three are aimed at domestic audiences, one at foreign viewers. The three Turkmen-language channels are *Altyn Asyr* (Golden Age), *Miras* (Culture) and *Yashlyk* (Youth). Although the programming differs to a mild degree – with, for example, a little more youth-related output on *Yashlyk* – in practice the three channels offer a similar mix of documentary programming about the attractions and successes of Turkmenistan, concerts of Turkmen music and dancing, and some anodyne dubbed foreign feature films. Bollywood output is a particular favourite. A golden silhouette of President Niyazov's head in profile is displayed in the top-right corner of the screen on every channel. All three show the evening news programme, *Watan*, at 21.00.

The fourth television channel, logically enough titled *TV-4*, was born in 2004, the product of President Niyazov's determination to advertise the achievements of post-independence Turkmenistan to a wider international audience. The channel broadcasts in six languages, including English, for 24 hours a day. The programming mostly involves documentary segments offering a glimpse into a modern hospital ward, well-stocked supermarket or successful school.

There are constraints on the access of Turkmen citizens to some foreign media. In 2002, subscriptions to foreign-language newspapers, previously obtainable

HINTS ON PHOTOGRAPHY

Nick Garbutt and John Jones

All sorts of photographic opportunities present themselves in Turkmenistan, from simple snaps to that one-off festival, although do be aware of restrictions on photography (see page 39). For the best results, give some thought to the following tips.

As a general rule, if it doesn't look good through the viewfinder, it will never look good as a picture. Don't take photographs for the sake of taking them; be patient and wait until the image looks right.

Photographing **people** is never easy and more often than not it requires a fair share of luck. If you want to take a portrait shot of a stranger, it is always best to ask first. Focus on the eyes of your subject since they are the most powerful ingredient of any portrait, and be prepared for the unexpected.

There is no mystery about good **wildlife** photography. The secret is getting into the right place at the right time and then knowing what to do when you are there. Look for striking poses, aspects of behaviour and distinctive features. Try not only to take pictures of the species itself, but also to illustrate it within the context of its environment. Alternatively, focus in close on a characteristic which can be emphasised.

Photographically, the eyes are the most important part of an animal – focus on these, make sure they are sharp and try to ensure they contain a highlight.

Look at the surroundings – there is nothing worse than a distracting twig or highlighted leaf lurking in the background. Getting this right is often the difference between a mediocre and a memorable image.

A powerful flashgun adds the option of punching in extra light to transform

through the Central Post Office, were curtailed. Foreign newspapers are now extremely difficult to obtain in Turkmenistan. The same year, the government banned the practice of onward cabling from satellite televisions, which had previously allowed all households in an apartment block to be served from the single satellite dish of an enterprising resident. But the possession of a satellite dish itself remains legal in Turkmenistan, and satellite ownership is high, especially in urban areas, as a glance at any Ashgabat apartment block will confirm. Russian or Turkish channels, depending on the linguistic background of the household, are the main programmes of choice.

Internet access is in the hands of a single (state monopoly) service provider, Turkmen Telecom. Internet use is monitored, and some websites containing material critical of the regime are blocked. Levels of internet access amongst the Turkmen population are low. There are scarcely any internet cafés in Turkmenistan in the Western sense: the best option for tourists to check emails lies in the business centres at the top-range hotels.

BUSINESS

Turkmen government officials usually require permission from their own authorities before they can agree to any formal meeting with foreign nationals, and business appointments should therefore always be made in advance. Business meetings tend to be rather formal in character. You should dress smartly. Male Turkmen officials usually wear a white shirt and dark suit, often with a small gold or silver pin of President Niyazov in the lapel. Female officials wear traditional long

an otherwise dreary picture. Artificial light is no substitute for natural light, though, so use it judiciously.

Getting close to the subject correspondingly reduces the depth of field. At camera-to-subject distances of less than a metre, apertures between f16 and f32 are necessary to ensure adequate depth of field. This means using flash to provide enough light. If possible, use one or two small flashguns to illuminate the subject from the side.

Landscapes are forever changing, even on a daily basis. Good landscape photography is all about good light and capturing mood. Generally, the first and last two hours of daylight are best, or when peculiar climatic conditions add drama or emphasise distinctive features. Never place the horizon in the centre – in your mind's eye divide the frame into thirds and either exaggerate the land or the sky.

Film

If you're using conventional film (as against a digital camera), select the right film for your needs. Film speed (ISO number) indicates the sensitivity of the film to light. The lower the number, the less sensitive the film, but the better quality the final image. For general print film, ISO 100 or 200 fit the bill perfectly. If you are using transparencies for home use or for lectures, then again ISO 100 or 200 film is fine. However, if you want to get your work published, the superior quality of ISO 25 to 100 film is best.

- Try to keep your film cool. Never leave it in direct sunlight.
- Don't allow fast film (ISO 800 and above) to pass through X-ray machines.
- Under weak light conditions use a faster film (ISO 200 or 400).

Turkmen dresses, with elegantly embroidered collars. Business meetings usually start on time, and the giving of business cards is common practice. Meetings with ministers and senior officials are subject to last minute cancellation, for example if the minister concerned is called by the president's office to attend a Cabinet meeting. Most senior officials are able to conduct business in both Turkmen and Russian, though knowledge of the latter is declining, and younger Turkmen officials in particular may be fluent in Turkmen only. Few officials speak good English.

Business hours tend to run roughly from 09.00 to 18.00 Monday to Friday. Many offices are also open on Saturdays, though tend to close rather earlier in the day. Turkmens tend to take their holidays in either July or August.

CULTURAL DOS AND DON'TS

Turkmens are relatively conservative as regards **dress**, though you would not necessarily realise this from some of the fashions sported by young women around town in Ashgabat. The wearing of shorts, especially by men, is considered rather odd. Other items of dress which will make you stand out instantly as a culturally insensitive foreigner include T-shirts with prominent logos and brightly coloured backpacks (unless you are a seven-year-old schoolgirl, in which case a Barbie backpack seems *de rigueur*). Walking boots and loud training shoes are considered appropriate footwear for the mountains and sports field, respectively, not for wearing around town. Turkmens wear clean, neatly ironed clothes. Even in a dusty provincial town, with blown sand swirling around the main street, Turkmens always seem to manage to keep their shoes shiny. This is an art you may not be able

THE EVIL EYE

Turkmens use a wide range of talismans in an attempt to ward off the evil eye, and the misfortunes that this will bestow upon a family. Above the front door of Turkmen houses it is common to see one or more of a range of these: small phials of salt; dried chilli peppers; ram's horns; and, especially, a few twigs of the shrub *yuzaerlik*, fashioned into the shape of a small broom. Turkmens suffering from a cold or the flu will sometimes 'disinfect' their homes with the smoke from a burning *yuzaerlik* shrub, carried from room to room in a suitable container, such as an old tin can. Another plant which is considered particularly good at keeping the evil eye at bay is the *dagdan* tree, which grows at high altitudes where the air is clean. Many Turkmens carry in their pockets a small piece of *dagdan* wood, a few centimetres long, which they will touch in times of stress.

In the responses of Turkmens to the evil eye, the mixing of pre-Islamic superstitions with the Islamic faith is clearly shown. Some Turkmen families display verses from the Koran in the porches of their homes as further protection against the eye. Koranic texts are also placed inside some items of female silver jewellery, such as the triangular *tumar*, worn over the breast. Three is considered a particularly sacred number, and the triangular shape is thus prominent in the fight against the forces of evil. Embroidered triangles are often worn around the neck or placed over doorways. One practice adopted by some Turkmens, though highly criticised by others, is the use of a pig's tooth as a talisman against evil; the principle being that an item taken from an unclean animal is itself effective at warding away all else that is bad.

The camel is considered to be a powerful ally in the fight against the evil eye. Bracelets of camel hair intertwined with black, white, red and orange wool are worn by many Turkmens. Longer pieces are often wrapped around car steering wheels, to protect the driver.

to emulate, but the basic message, that scruffy, dirty-looking clothing goes down badly in Turkmenistan, is well worth heeding.

A small **gift** should be taken if you are invited to a Turkmen family home for a meal. You will need to take a larger gift to a wedding. Flowers are always an acceptable gift, but you should ensure that you bring an odd number; even numbers are considered unlucky. The ready-made bouquets available at Turkmen markets always provide an odd number of flowers. Flower sellers, however, have a tendency to embellish their wares by spray-painting the flowers in garish colours to make them look livelier, and adding such non-natural features as glitter, polythene and even little plastic birds. None of this poses a problem in terms of the Turkmen recipients of your gift, but it may deflate the spirits of the giver. Alcohol is a suitable gift only if you are sure that the host family partakes. Gift items linked to your home country are usually particularly welcome.

You should **remove your shoes**, but not socks, upon entering any Turkmen house, or any mosque or mausoleum. Point the shoes towards the interior of the house, not the door. Non-Muslims should not attempt to enter any mosque during prayer times, though outside of these hours, visiting tourists are welcome, providing they behave in a respectful manner.

Turkmens are highly **superstitious**, and it is all too easy to commit some form of behaviour perceived as likely to draw the unwanted attentions of the evil eye.

Spicy food should, for example, be handled with care. You should not pass anything spicy direct to anyone else at the dinner table, but should place it on the table in front of them, where it may easily be reached.

INTERACTING WITH LOCAL PEOPLE

Turkmenistan has long been a relatively isolated land, and Turkmens are endlessly curious about life in foreign countries. Expect to be asked detailed questions about salary levels, the price of gas, and agricultural husbandry techniques back home. The curiosity, friendliness and natural hospitality of Turkmens towards foreigners may be tempered, though, by concern that public interaction with foreign visitors might result in unwanted attention from the local law-enforcement agencies. So the Turkmen studiously avoiding your smile may not simply be rude. But in most cases, particularly outside Ashgabat, natural friendliness wins out.

An invitation to a Turkmen house is an opportunity not to be missed. Traditional Turkmen homes are sparsely furnished, as families eat, and sleep, on the floor, which is usually covered by rich, red Turkmen carpets. These may also be used as wall-hangings. Garish murals of alpine scenes or Caribbean beaches are also common wall decorations. Food is usually laid out on a large plastic mat in the centre of the guest room, to which you will be ushered. In some parts of the country, especially Lebap and Dashoguz regions, a low table, or *desterkhan*, will be used. In either case, you will need to squat or sit around the food. Lounging on one of the cushions usually provided is considered perfectly acceptable, and unless you are particularly good at yoga will probably be necessary at some stage during the meal to ward off leg cramp.

Turkmen traditions of hospitality dictate that you will be served far more food than it would be physically possible to consume. You are not expected to try, although your host will continually be urging you to eat more. But simply picking at your food is not really considered polite. The array of salads, fruit, bread, sausage, cold chicken, sweets and biscuits which will probably already be spread out on the mat when you arrive represents only the tip of the food iceberg. Expect a large bowl of *chorba* to follow, plus at least two main dishes, frequently including *manty*, *shashlik* and *plov*.

A word about toasts. Some Turkmen men do not drink alcohol, but many do. One of the legacies of spending much of the 20th century as part of the Soviet Union is the persistence of a tradition of toasts taken with small glasses of vodka or, less frequently, brandy. There is a considerable risk of coming under pressure to drink far more than you wish, with hosts frequently urging that the subject of the current toast is so important that drinking 'down in one' is required. It is usually possible, after a fair amount of negotiation, to refuse to drink. But if you do decide to agree to take vodka toasts, the best advice is probably to down your first toast, at which your drinking habits will be most closely watched, but thereafter to take only small sips. Follow each toast with a large gulp of mineral water or fruit juice and, unless you particularly like hangovers, avoid the beers which will often also be offered. Beer is not considered an acceptable drink with which to take a toast, so if you take a beer you will end up drinking this *plus* the vodka toasts. You can try to moderate the amount of vodka poured into your glass by whoever around the table has been deputised to dispense the drink. The Russian phrase '*chyt chyt*' ('just a little') is useful in this context.

Toasting etiquette is less formal in Turkmenistan than in some parts of the former Soviet Union, but a designated toastmaster will sometimes be appointed, to let everyone know when their turn has arrived. Toasts need not be elaborate: simply thanking the host and family for their hospitality is all that is really required, though if you can weave in an appropriate simile, metaphor or proverb, so much the better, and a toast made in, or using words of, Russian or Turkmen will be particularly appreciated. A toast made 'to the ladies' usually involves all the men at the meal standing up, and a toast taken down in one. To attempt to leave, you can call for a *pasashok*, a Russian word literally meaning a small staff, and the rough equivalent of 'one for the road'. Turkmen women rarely drink, and female visitors will generally come under far less pressure to get involved in rounds of toasting than will males.

In some Turkmen households, particularly in rural areas, the women of the household will keep to the kitchen and out of sight of visiting foreign guests, especially where these include males. In other households everyone, male and female, will eat together. The best advice is to respect the wishes of the household, which will usually be pretty clear, as regards who you get to meet.

GIVING SOMETHING BACK

Non-governmental organisations (NGOs) in Turkmenistan face major constraints on their freedom of operation. Under the 2003 Law on Public Associations, all such organisations were required to seek re-registration, which at the time of writing has not been forthcoming for many. Most civil society organisations are fledgling groups, operating on small budgets, and highly deserving of help. There are groups active in a range of areas, from teaching schoolchildren about ecological issues to helping to disseminate the techniques of profitable bee-keeping to Turkmen farmers. However, any donations received from foreign organisations and individuals are subject to official scrutiny. As a result, it is not straightforward to make donations to NGOs and other civil society groups in Turkmenistan. Because of the constraints on foreign support for the sector, if you are interested in finding out more about civil society in Turkmenistan you might first contact your embassy in Ashgabat for up-to-date advice about who to contact and whether to do so.

Turkmenistan's relative isolation, and the paucity of information about distant lands, mean that one good way of giving something back is to bring with you a small quantity of picture-books, maps, postcards and other information about your home country to hand out as gifts to those you meet on your travels. Books such as English dictionaries and simplified readers of classic tales also make excellent gifts for young Turkmen learners of English. Attempting to bring in more than a very small number of such books (say, three or four), however, or any items of an apparently religious nature, may well generate difficulties with the customs authorities on arrival, and should be avoided.

Part Two

The Guide

3

Ashgabat: the White City

Destroyed by an earthquake in 1948, Ashgabat (telephone code 12) was rebuilt as the unremarkable capital of the Turkmen Soviet Socialist Republic. A selection of postcards printed in 1990 clearly struggled to identify striking urban sights, offering such subjects as plane tree, a theatre, and 'a new residential area'. The city was characterised by three- and four-storey apartment blocks, of at best indifferent quality, in its central districts. Single-storey dwellings around central courtyards, favoured by Turkmen families, dominated the outer suburbs. The main streets were lined with trees, and fringed with little canals known as *arryks*.

Turkmenistan's independence in 1991 was, however, to set in motion a programme of urban change of great ambition. The creation of a beautiful capital city, worthy of the 'Golden Age' of Turkmenistan, is at the centre of President Niyazov's nation-building project. New palaces, ministries, hotels and residential buildings, faced with white marble tiles, have reshaped the urban environment of large areas of the city. Elaborate fountains and golden statues adorn the central squares and thoroughfares. A large share of Turkmenistan's export earnings from its hydrocarbons resources has been invested in the redesign of its capital, and the many building sites across the city testify to the continued rapid pace of change.

Niyazov served as the head of the Ashgabat city administration in the early 1980s, and takes an intensely personal interest in the new urban design. At one meeting with municipal officials in August 2000 he even turned his attention to the state of the toilets at the city's bazaars, complaining that the facilities at the Tekke Bazaar could be smelled from 3km away. The remodelling of Ashgabat is one of the most personalised urban redesign projects taking shape anywhere in the world. It involves not private investment but a series of government contracts, awarded to a small group of overseas construction companies. The French firm Bouygues has built many of the most prestigious projects, including the Presidential Palace, Ruhyyet Palace, Central Bank, and the Ministries of Defence, Justice and Oil and Gas. The Turkish company Polimeks has designed some of the more striking monuments, including the Neutrality Arch and Independence Monument. Another Turkish firm, Gap Construction, is involved in projects ranging from apartment blocks to the construction of a theme park based around Turkmen fairy tales. In every case, the specifications are drawn up tightly by the Turkmen government, on the instructions of the president, such that, for example, all new major buildings are faced by white marble tiles, which must be 80cm long, 40cm wide and 3cm thick. For the residents of Ashgabat, the downside to this programme of urban redesign includes the frequent demolition of large areas of older housing, with provision for relocation usually available only to those able to demonstrate legal title to their property.

The post-independence reconstruction of the city has at the time of writing impacted most heavily in central districts of the city, and in the area running southwards from the centre to the suburb of Berzengi, at the foot of the Kopet Dag Mountains. In other parts of town, a cityscape largely inherited from the Soviet era still predominates. But the rapid pace of redevelopment means that the look, plan and sights of Ashgabat are particularly vulnerable to change.

Ashgabat street names have also been the subject of recent change. In 2003, the Turkmen government decided to replace the names of almost all of the streets of the capital with a four-digit number. Turkmenbashy Square in the heart of town was allocated the number 2000, the first year of Turkmenistan's 'Golden Century'. The numbers of other streets generally descend to the east of this central square, and ascend to the west of it, though there seems to be little clear logic in the assignation of numbers to streets. Only the largest thoroughfares have retained their names alongside the new numbers. Few Ashgabat residents have learnt the new numbers, and most navigate by a mix of Soviet street name, the initial post-independence one, micro-district and landmark.

Ashgabat is the transport hub for Turkmenistan. All international flights originate here. It has a wide selection of accommodation and a good range of restaurants. Its main sights are the monuments, fountains and statues of the post-independence era, several worthwhile museums (in which the cult of personality focused on President Niyazov is strongly apparent), and the sprawling and colourful Tolkuchka Bazaar to the north of the city. It is, in short, a city which the visitor to Turkmenistan is both likely to come to, and should.

HISTORY

A small mound, which was known affectionately as Gorka ('Little Hill'), behind the present-day Hotel Turkmenistan, appears to have been the site of the original settlement here, and offered much information about the early history of Ashgabat. Gorka was, however, flattened as part of the post-independence redevelopment of the city.

There seems to have been a fortified settlement at Ashgabat during the Parthian period, when Ashgabat was probably a satellite of Nisa. Parthian ceramic tiles were found at Gorka. One theory as to the origin of Ashgabat's name links this to the Parthian king Arsakh, founder of the Arsakhid Dynasty, whose name in medieval Persian literature is, according to Professor Ovez Gundogdiyev of the Turkmen State Institute of Cultural Heritage, spelt 'Ashk'. Professor Gundogdiyev suggests that Ashgabat may thus mean the 'city of Ashk', or 'city of Arsakh', and proposes that Ashgabat's date of foundation be commemorated as the middle of the 3rd century BC, rather than 1881, the date used in the Soviet period.

A more popularly diffused version of the origin of the name Ashgabat is that it means 'city of love'. A well-known legend linked to this meaning runs roughly as follows. The children of the rulers of Nisa and Anau fell in love. They fled into the mountains, but their god disapproved of their romance, and caused all springs and rivers to run dry as they approached them. The lovers were on the point of dying of thirst, and the angel of death was sent to them. But the angel was so enraptured by the beauty of the young woman that he forgot all about his task. At this, a spring of clear water suddenly appeared from the ground, the young couple were saved, and decided to settle on that spot. Ashgabat was born.

The archaeological evidence suggests that the settlement here during the Seljuk period was relatively important, with evidence of defensive walls and towers of fired bricks, and utensils of good quality. But Ashgabat was unable to bounce back from destruction by the Mongols. A Tekke Turkmen settlement was founded here in the early 19th century. However, when the tsarist Russian forces arrived here on 18 January 1881, less than a week after the fall of Geok Depe, they found a settlement characterised by the *Daily News* journalist Edmund O'Donovan, who reached here a day ahead of the Russians, as a decayed place. It was also deserted; its inhabitants having temporarily evacuated to Persia in fear of the advancing Russians.

When the tsar established the Transcaspian Region in May 1881, Ashgabat was chosen as its administrative centre. Gorka became the site of a Russian fortress, and an expanse of ground nearby was used for military parades. This acquired the name of Skobelev Square, after the victor of Geok Depe. The place remains a central square, whose name has changed with regime, to Karl Marx and now Turkmenbashy. The arrival of the railway in 1885 gave a further impetus to the growth of the town. The Honourable George Curzon, future Viceroy of India, was rather impressed by the place when he visited in the late 1880s. He described it as a town of whitewashed single-storey houses, with 'European shops and hotels'.

Following the Russian Revolution, power in Ashgabat passed to the Social Revolutionary Party. This mainly comprised railway workers, who had gradually formed a disaffected Russian urban underclass in Ashgabat. But the ascendancy of the Social Revolutionaries was unwelcome not just to the former municipal powers, but also to their revolutionary rivals, the Bolsheviks. The Bolshevik administration in Tashkent determined to take control of Ashgabat, and despatched a thug named Fralov, together with a bodyguard of former Austro-Hungarian prisoners. Fralov removed the Social Revolutionary government with considerable brutality, installing in its place a Bolshevik administration. He then moved on to Gyzylarbat, intending to take that town too from the railway workers. But when news filtered back to Ashgabat of Fralov's excesses in Gyzylarbat, including indiscriminate shootings into a protesting crowd, the railway workers of Ashgabat were spurred to rise up again against the new Ashgabat administration. They hanged nine of the Bolshevik Ashgabat Commissars (see page 124), and then sent forces to Gyzylarbat in support of their colleagues there, quickly killing Fralov and his guards, who had been suffering the effects of hangovers when the train carrying the Social Revolutionary forces had pulled in.

The Social Revolutionary government sought the help of the British in fighting off the Tashkent Bolsheviks. The British, seeing the Ashgabat administration as an ally against Turco-German advances, potentially threatening to India, gave what limited help they could (see page 126). But following the end of World War I, and the ensuing British withdrawal, Ashgabat was quickly retaken by the Bolsheviks, and the Social Revolutionary leaders shot. Ashgabat was in 1920 renamed Poltoratsk, after the most prominent of the Commissars hanged by the Social Revolutionaries. But this name never really stuck, and the city reverted to Ashgabat in 1927. It was by then the capital of the new Turkmen Soviet Socialist Republic.

At 01.17 on 6 October 1948, as the people of Ashgabat slept, the city was hit by a devastating earthquake which flattened most of it, killing well over 100,000 people. Hardly a building was salvageable. Karl Marx Square was turned into a huge open-air hospital. The Soviet press of the day, which was not prone to admit major disasters, even natural ones, gave little prominence to the earthquake, and fewer details of it. Suggestions that the Turkmen capital might be rebuilt elsewhere were considered but quickly rejected, and a new Ashgabat emerged from the rubble of the old. Until the mid-1950s, the designs of the most prestigious buildings attempted to identify a specifically Turkmen architectural style. The buildings of the Mollanepes Theatre and the former Academy of Sciences complex are good examples. But from the later 1950s, construction took on a more standardised Soviet design. Independence in 1991 was to change all that.

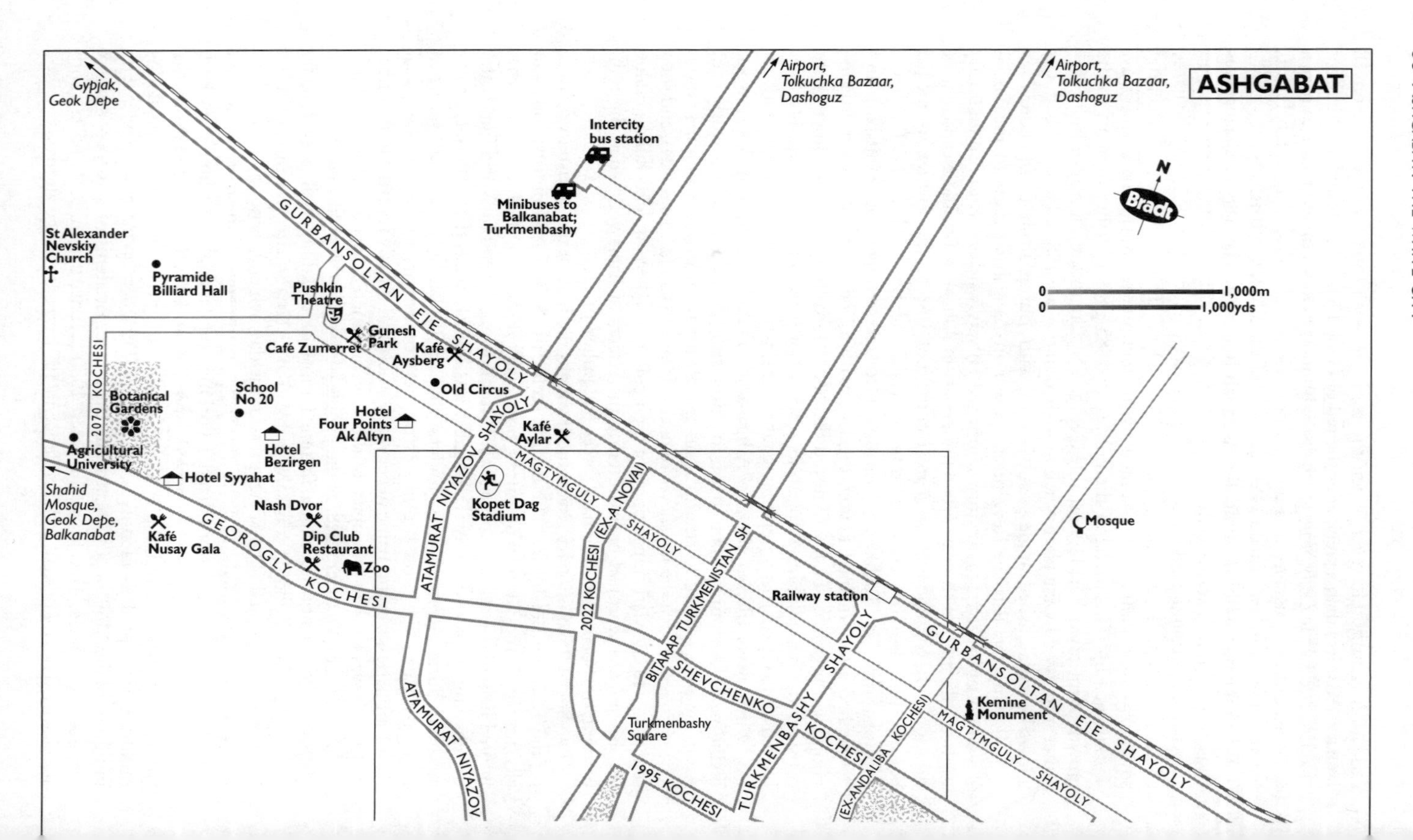
ASHGABAT
N
Bradt
0
1,000m
0
1,000yds
Gypjak, Geok Depe
Airport, Tolkuchka Bazaar, Dashoguz
Airport, Tolkuchka Bazaar, Dashoguz
Intercity bus station
Minibuses to Balkanabat; Turkmenbashy
St Alexander Nevskiy Church
Pyramide Billiard Hall
Pushkin Theatre
GURBANSOLTAN EJE SHAYOLY
Gunesh Park
Café Zumerret
Kafé Aysberg
Old Circus
2070 KOCHESI
Botanical Gardens
School No 20
Hotel Four Points Ak Altyn
SHAYOLY
Kafé Aylar
Agricultural University
Hotel Bezirgen
Hotel Syyahat
MAGTYMGULY
Kopet Dag Stadium
ATAMURAT NIYAZOV
Shahid Mosque, Geok Depe, Balkanabat
Nash Dvor
Kafé Nusay Gala
GEOROGLY KOCHESI
Dip Club Restaurant
Zoo
2022 KOCHESI (EX-A.NOVAI)
SHAYOLY
BITARAP TURKMENISTAN SH
Railway station
Mosque
SHAYOLY
GURBANSOLTAN EJE SHAYOLY
SHEVCHENKO
Kemine Monument
Turkmenbashy Square
TURKMENBASHY KOCHESI
(EX-ANDALIBA KOCHESI)
MAGTYMGULY SHAYOLY
ATAMURAT NIYAZOV
1995 KOCHESI

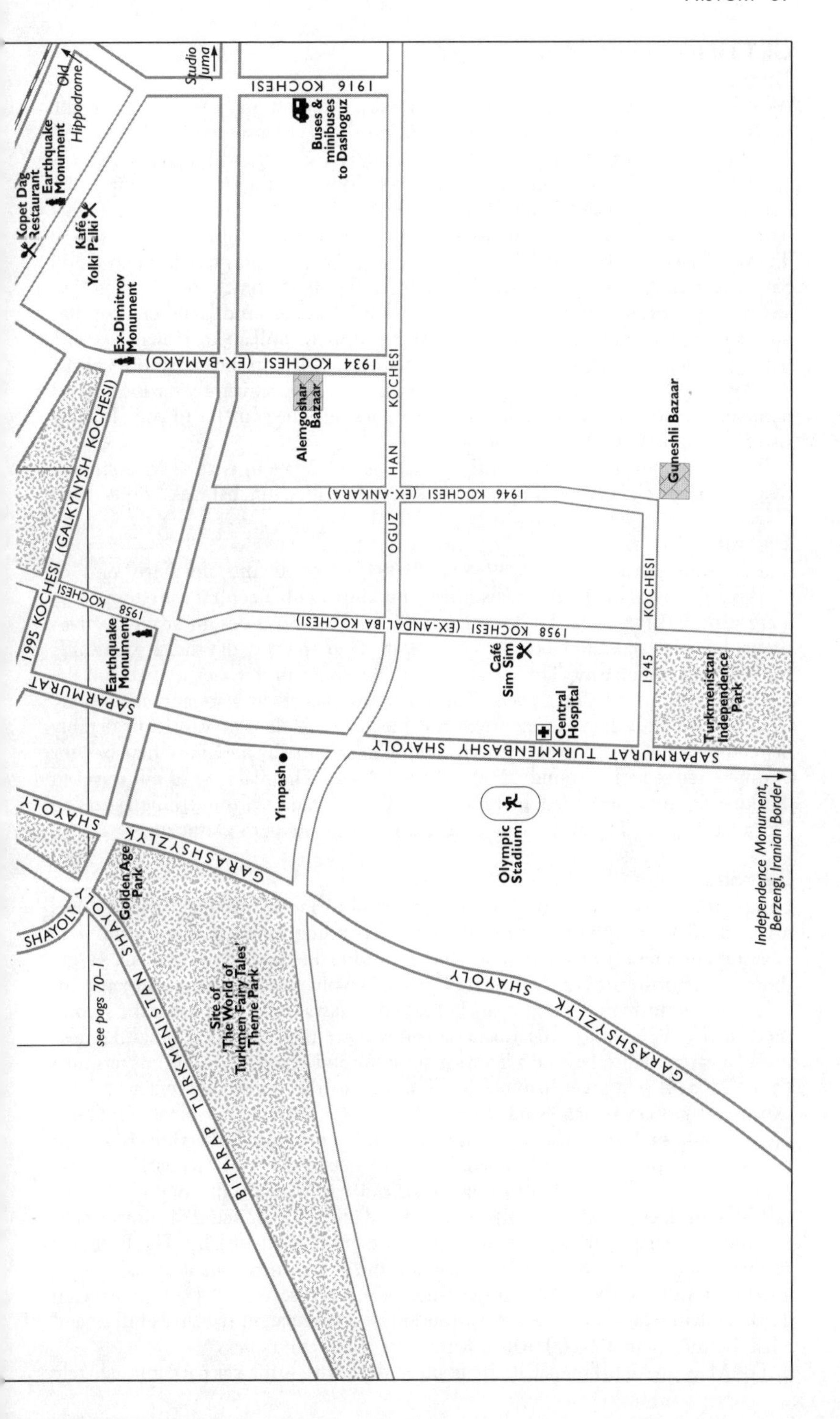
Kopet Dag Restaurant
Earthquake Monument
Old Hippodrome
Kafé Yolki Palki
Ex-Dimitrov Monument
Studio Juma
1916 KOCHESI
Buses & minibuses to Dashoguz
1934 KOCHESI (EX-BAMAKO)
Alemgoshar Bazaar
OGUZ HAN KOCHESI
1946 KOCHESI (EX-ANKARA)
Guneshli Bazaar
1995 KOCHESI (GALKYNYSH KOCHESI)
1958 KOCHESI
Earthquake Monument
1958 KOCHESI (EX-ANDALIBA KOCHESI)
Café Sim Sim
Central Hospital
1945 KOCHESI
Turkmenistan Independence Park
SAPARMURAT TURKMENBASHY SHAYOLY
Yimpash
Olympic Stadium
Independence Monument, Berzengi, Iranian Border
GARASHSYZLYK SHAYOLY
Golden Age Park
SHAYOLY
BITARAP TURKMENISTAN SHAYOLY
Site of 'The World of Turkmen Fairy Tales' Theme Park
see pags 70–1

GETTING THERE AND AWAY

By air

Ashgabat's airport, Saparmurat Turkmenbashy International Airport, lies at the northwest edge of the city, some 5km north of Magtymguly Shayoly. All international flights to Turkmenistan arrive here (see page 31), and Ashgabat is also the point of arrival/departure for every domestic flight, except one route between Dashoguz and Turkmenbashy. From Ashgabat, there are five flights daily to Dashoguz, two to Mary, four to Turkmenabat and three to Turkmenbashy. There is also a thrice weekly (Tuesdays, Thursdays and Saturdays) flight to Balkanabat. All internal flights currently use Boeing 717 aircraft. A taxi into town from the airport should cost around 50,000 manat, but taxi drivers may well try to charge a larger sum in dollars to manat-less and baggage-laden foreigners arriving on international flights in the early hours of the morning. If you are arriving on a tourist visa, a representative of your local travel company is required to meet you at the airport, and the transfer to your hotel is usually included in the arrangements.

The Turkmenistan Airlines office (☎ 12 354857, 393900) is at 82 Magtymguly Shayoly, in the city centre. It is open 08.00–20.00, with a lunch-break 14.00–15.00.

By rail

The railway station (☎ 12 393804, 383045) sits at the northern end of Turkmenbashy Shayoly. It is a distinctive building, with a central spire topped by a crescent and five stars. Its domed central hall features a design heavy on five-pointed Soviet stars and bunches of wheat. Two trains a day head westwards towards Turkmenbashy. Three trains head east: to Atamurat, Serhetabat, and the long journey to Dashoguz via Turkmenabat. There is also a twice-weekly departure to Serakhs. Ticket prices are inexpensive, though vary considerably depending on class of travel. Prices to both Turkmenbashy and Turkmenabat, for example, range from around 12,000–55,000 manat. The real cost of rail travel in Turkmenistan is measured in time more than distance: around nine hours to Balkanabat, 13 to Turkmenbashy or Turkmenabat, and 24 to Dashoguz.

By road

Long-distance taxis, minivans (known as *marshrutkas*) and less frequent private buses leave from several points around the city, depending on their destination. The government intercity bus station however is outside the old airport terminal. To get there, head northwards on Atamurat Niyazov Shayoly, towards the modern airport. After passing through the underpass beneath the railway line, turn left at the second set of traffic lights onto 2103 Kochesi. You will see the old airport building, now used for cargo flights, beyond a large square at the end of the road. The bus terminal (☎ 12 230544) is a green-painted building just to the north, adjacent to a large expanse of tarmac, which stands mostly devoid of buses. The terminal building is open 06.30–14.00, and most departures are in the mornings. Tickets are cheap, but buses are far from plentiful. There are three departures daily to Mary (21,000 manat), four to Tejen (15,000), one to Balkanabat (31,000) and one to Serakhs (20,000). In an enclosed area at the southern end of the square stand the private taxis and minibuses taking passengers to Balkanabat and Turkmenbashy. The liveliness of this area as against the deserted aspect of the government bus terminal gives a good indication of the relative importance of the two sectors. A place in a taxi to Turkmenbashy (at least six hours) is around 150,000 manat; to Balkanabat (four and a half hours) about 100,000 manat. Minibuses charge a little less.

For Mary and Turkmenabat, the point of departure is the car park immediately to the west of the railway station. A minibus will get you to Mary in around four and a half hours for 70,000 manat. A place in a taxi ranges from around 100,000 manat for a Russian make to 150,000 for a Japanese or German one. The journey to Turkmenabat takes around eight hours. Prices range from about 150,000 manat for a seat in a minibus to 250,000 manat for a place in an air-conditioned car.

For Dashoguz Region, the place of departure is currently a bazaar in the eastern part of town, known officially as Bazaar number 6, or the Azatlyk Bazaar, but more widely as Dashoguz Bazaar, since this is the place at which traders from Dashoguz Region concentrate. The future of this bazaar is, however, currently uncertain, so arrangements for departures to Dashoguz may change. Dashoguz Bazaar is located on 1916 Kochesi, about 300m south of the intersection with Atamurat Niyazov Shayoly. A place in a taxi to Dashoguz will cost around 200,000 manat, for a journey of about 12 hours. In a minibus, the fare is about 150,000 manat, and the journey time some two hours longer. Buses are considerably slower still, and cost about 100,000 manat. There are also departures available to other towns in Dashoguz Region.

To get to towns just to the west of Ashgabat, the departure point is the western side of the Tekke Bazaar. The main destinations served from here are Bagyr (for Old Nisa – a place in a minibus is around 3,000 manat), Abadan (about 4,000) and Geok Depe (5,000). For Anew, buses leave from a remote spot known as the Awtokombinat at the eastern end of Atamurat Niyazov Shayoly, close to the Coca Cola bottling plant. This place is also the terminus for several municipal bus routes, including trolleybus number 1, which will bring you here from Magtymguly Shayoly in the city centre. The bus fare to Anew is around 1,000–2,000 manat.

GETTING AROUND

The green-and-white buses and trolleybuses of the Ashgabat public transport system are modern and astoundingly cheap, though can get crowded. The fare is 50 manat, placed in a collection box in the driver's cabin as you get off. The fare for a taxi hailed in the street is 5,000 manat for a short trip; 10,000 manat for a journey across town. Fares rise considerably after 23.00. Ashgabat also has a bookable taxi service (☎ 12 353406). This is more expensive, but reasonably reliable, and particularly useful at night. The charge is 35,000 manat per call-out.

WHERE TO STAY

There is a considerable over-provision of hotel accommodation in Ashgabat, as a succession of new hotels, each more prestigious than the last, has been ordered by President Niyazov as part of his plan to make Ashgabat a capital fit to stand alongside the great cities of the world. The flow of visitors to Turkmenistan has not kept up with the pace of these new constructions, meaning that tourists who do make it here are spoilt for choice. During the annual oil and gas conference (usually in the autumn), and major government celebrations, such as Independence Day at the end of October, you may find that your first-choice hotel is booked, but even then there will be something available. The main choice lies between accommodation in or around the city centre, and staying in the southern suburb of Berzengi, where a whole line of hotels was constructed by presidential order in the mid-1990s, and which have now been joined by the Hotel President, currently the fanciest place to stay in town. Large discounts on the published room prices are often available, particularly if you are booking through a local travel company. But even when you are booking direct, asking about discounts will often net a saving.

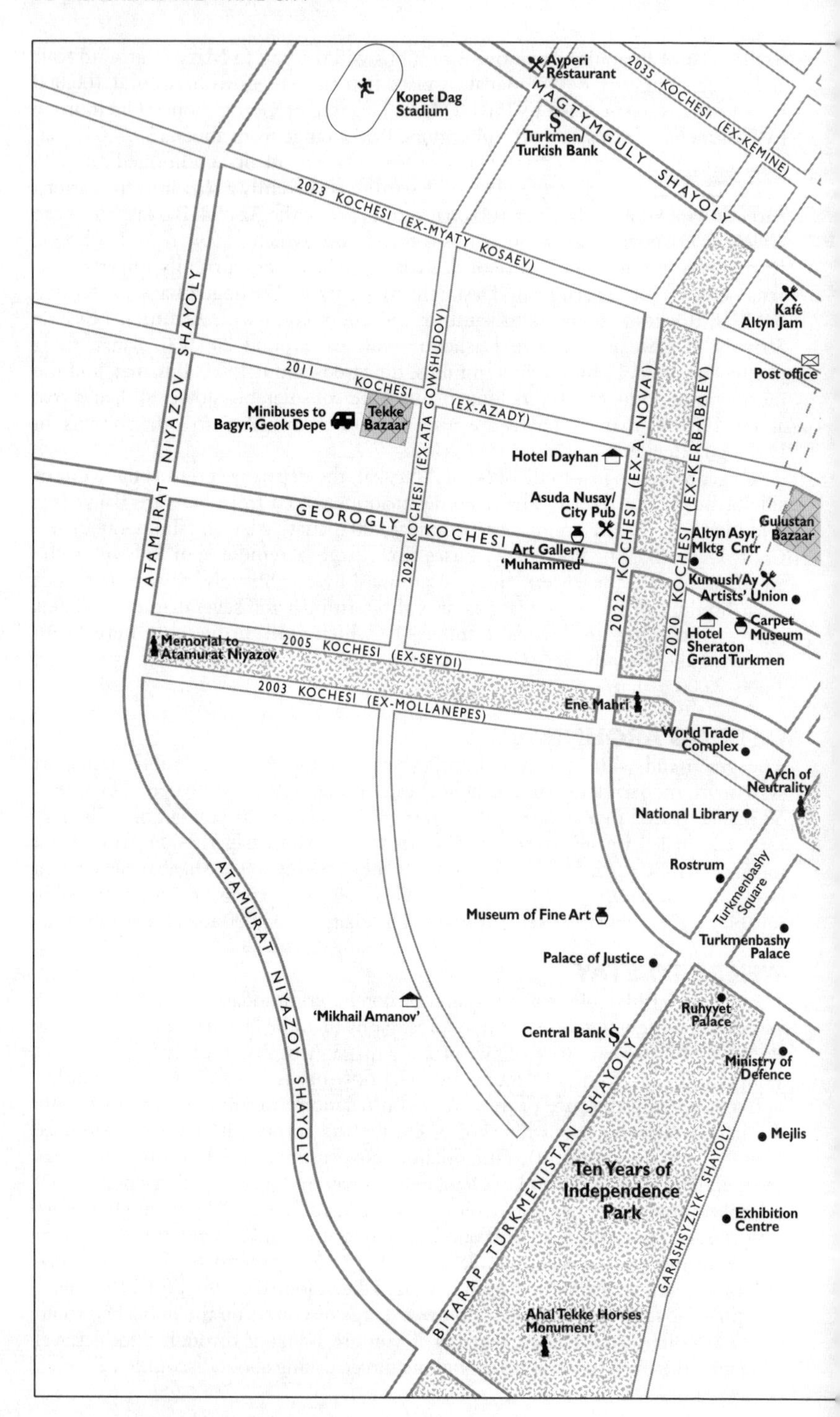
Kopet Dag Stadium
Ayperi Restaurant
2035 KOCHESI (EX-KEMINE)
MAGTYMGULY SHAYOLY
Turkmen/ Turkish Bank
2023 KOCHESI (EX-MYATY KOSAEV)
Kafé Altyn Jam
Post office
ATAMURAT NIYAZOV SHAYOLY
2011 KOCHESI (EX-AZADY)
2028 KOCHESI (EX-ATA GOWSHUDOV)
Minibuses to Bagyr, Geok Depe
Tekke Bazaar
Hotel Dayhan
2022 KOCHESI (EX-A. NOVAI)
2020 KOCHESI (EX-KERBABAEV)
Asuda Nusay/ City Pub
GEOROGLY KOCHESI
Art Gallery 'Muhammed'
Altyn Asyr Mktg Cntr
Gulustan Bazaar
Kumush Ay
Artists' Union
Hotel Sheraton Grand Turkmen
Carpet Museum
Memorial to Atamurat Niyazov
2005 KOCHESI (EX-SEYDI)
2003 KOCHESI (EX-MOLLANEPES)
Ene Mahri
World Trade Complex
Arch of Neutrality
National Library
Rostrum
Turkmenbashy Square
Museum of Fine Art
Turkmenbashy Palace
Palace of Justice
'Mikhail Amanov'
Ruhyyet Palace
Central Bank
Ministry of Defence
Mejlis
ATAMURAT NIYAZOV SHAYOLY
BITARAP TURKMENISTAN SHAYOLY
Ten Years of Independence Park
GARASHSYZLYK SHAYOLY
Exhibition Centre
Ahal Tekke Horses Monument

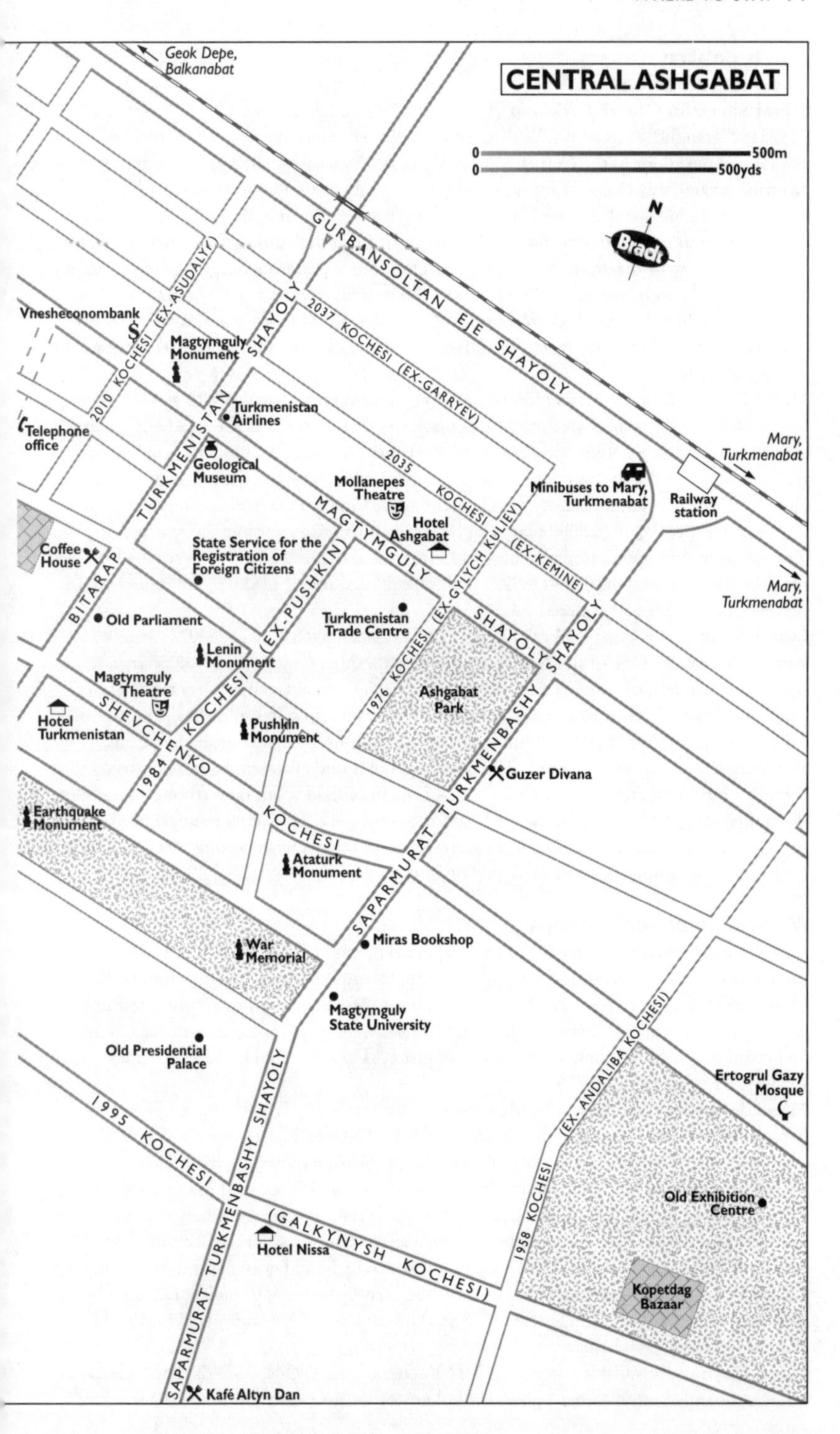
CENTRAL ASHGABAT
0 500m
0 500yds
N
Bradt
Geok Depe, Balkanabat
Mary, Turkmenabat
Mary, Turkmenabat
GURBANSOLTAN EJE SHAYOLY
2037 KOCHESI (EX-GARRYEV)
2035 KOCHESI (EX-KEMINE)
2010 KOCHESI (EX-ASUDALYF)
TURKMENISTAN SHAYOLY
MAGTYMGULY SHAYOLY
1976 KOCHESI (EX-GYLYCH KULIEV)
1984 KOCHESI (EX-PUSHKIN)
BITARAP
SHEVCHENKO KOCHESI
SAPARMURAT TURKMENBASHY SHAYOLY
1995 KOCHESI
(GALKYNYSH KOCHESI)
1958 KOCHESI (EX- ANDALIBA KOCHESI)
Vnesheconombank
Magtymguly Monument
Turkmenistan Airlines
Telephone office
Geological Museum
Mollanepes Theatre
Hotel Ashgabat
Minibuses to Mary, Turkmenabat
Railway station
Coffee House
State Service for the Registration of Foreign Citizens
Turkmenistan Trade Centre
Old Parliament
Lenin Monument
Magtymguly Theatre
Hotel Turkmenistan
Ashgabat Park
Pushkin Monument
Guzer Divana
Earthquake Monument
Ataturk Monument
Miras Bookshop
War Memorial
Magtymguly State University
Old Presidential Palace
Ertogrul Gazy Mosque
Old Exhibition Centre
Hotel Nissa
Kopetdag Bazaar
Kafé Altyn Dan

Town centre

Top-range options

Hotel Sheraton Grand Turkmen (120 rooms) 7 Georogly Kochesi; ☎ 12 510555; f 12 511251; e grandhtl@online.tm. With an unbeatably central location opposite the Russian Bazaar and next door to the Carpet Museum, Sheraton management and a pleasant outdoor swimming pool, this is a good top-range choice in many ways. However, some of the rooms are looking decidedly tired, and there have been complaints about the inadequacy of the hotel's centralised air-conditioning system at the height of summer. The management has responded with the creation of renovated 'club rooms', offering burgundy-toned luxury furnishings at a premium price. The business centre offers internet access at 52,000 manat per hour. Published room rates are US$130 for singles, US$145 for doubles, US$200 for club rooms and US$240 for suites, breakfast included. Large discounts on these rates are usually available.

Hotel Four Points Ak Altyn (136 rooms) 141 Magtymguly Shayoly; ☎ 12 363700–08; f 12 363494. *Ak Altyn* means 'white gold', cotton in other words, and the façade of the hotel is built to resemble a cotton boll. This is another hotel managed by the Sheraton and, like its sister, some of the rooms could do with refurbishment. The location, west of the centre close to the former circus, is not as convenient as the Grand Turkmen for the main sights. There is internet access (52,000 manat an hour) from its business centre, a gym and an outdoor swimming pool. Room rates, including breakfast, are US$100 for a single, US$115 for a double. 'Junior suites' are US$225 and 'presidential suites' US$400. Discounts of 50% on these rates are usually offered.

Hotel Nissa (141 rooms) 70 1995 Kochesi; ☎ 12 221025, 396838; f 12 221023, 353206; e ahal@online.tm. One of five hotels managed by the Ahal Group, the Nissa offers a reasonable standard of comfort at an attractive price. The Ahal Group's General Manager, Luigi Fontanabona, ensures that the restaurant serves authentic Italian dishes, with a good range of pasta options at prices around 100,000 manat, imported parmesan cheese and Parma ham, and expensive chianti. The outdoor pool is one of the nicest in Ashgabat, and there is a business centre with internet access. The published room rates (though ask about discounts) are US$100 for singles, US$120 for doubles, and US$180 for suites. For big spenders, a presidential suite is charged at US$240, and (somewhat mixing metaphors) a king presidential suite at US$400. Breakfast is included.

Mid-range/budget options

Hotel Turkmenistan (53 rooms) 19 Bitarap Turkmenistan Kochesi; ☎ 12 350544. This place has an excellent central location, close to the Neutrality Arch. The air-conditioned rooms are fine, though some tend towards pokiness. The lobby houses a store offering 'exclusive Turkmen handycrafts'. The adjacent restaurant is under separate management, and room prices do not include breakfast. Singles cost US$40, doubles US$50, suites US$60 and apartments US$70.

Hotel Ashgabat (150 rooms) 74 Magtymguly Shayoly; ☎ 12 357308. This hotel, perhaps because of its prime, central, location next to the Mollanepes Theatre, received a gleaming new white marble façade at the start of 2005, but at the time of writing the renovation programme had not penetrated to the bedrooms within, which retained the unmistakable flavour of Soviet hotel accommodation. Built in the 1960s, its exterior reliefs and the stained-glass panels in the restaurant were considered stylish in their day. But the bedrooms offer faded carpets, flimsy-looking wooden beds, and grimy en suites. Rooms are air conditioned, and those at the front of the hotel have balconies, though suffer the noise of Magtymguly Shayoly. Singles cost US$20, doubles US$30 and suites US$40. Breakfast is an additional 15,000 manat.

Hotel Dayhan (9 available rooms) 69 2011 Kochesi; ☎ 12 357344, 357372. The 'peasant' hotel is the only bottom-range option for holders of tourist visas right in the town centre.

Rooms have air conditioning and hot water, but the en suites are grotty and the mattresses look grim. Most of the rooms are currently rented out to Ukrainian construction companies, so there are few available to tourists. Singles cost US$10; doubles US$20. Suites seem to be charged at US$30 per person, which means that two people sharing a suite may be asked to pay an exorbitant US$60.

'Mikhail Amanov' (6 rooms) 106 2028 Kochesi (ex-Ata Gowshudov Kochesi); ↘ 12 393672. The closest Ashgabat offers to a private home-stay, this loquacious Azeri family offers 6 rooms, some air conditioned, with several beds in each and shared facilities. They charge US$5 per person per night, and will cook meals for US$5 more. There is a pleasant central courtyard, alive with the family's pigeons. As this is private accommodation, you cannot stay here if you have a tourist visa. The house is in a city-centre residential district, slated for possible redevelopment. It would be a shame if it disappears, as it offers a good bottom-end option for holders of transit visas.

Inner suburbs

Margiana Guesthouse (9 rooms) 67 Gurbansoltan Eje Shayoly; ↘/f 12 351323; e margiana-ashgabat@narod.ru. The Margiana is a great attempt to provide tourist accommodation which emphasises Turkmenistan's culture and traditions. Rooms are clean and air conditioned, with small but modern en-suite showers. Turkmen and international dishes are served in the carpet- and curio-covered restaurant, there is a *yurt* in the back yard, and *tapchans* on the first-floor terrace. A map of the Silk Road decorates the staircase, with a caravan of stuffed toy camels arriving at Merv. The only problem is that it is a private hotel, so you are not allowed to stay here if you have come to Turkmenistan on a tourist visa. Rooms cost US$30 for a single, US$40 for a double and US$50 for a suite, breakfast included.

Hotel Syyahat (130 rooms) 60A Georogly Kochesi; ↘ 12 344508; f 12 344071. A five-storey hotel close to the Botanical Gardens on the western side of town, the long wooden-panelled corridors of the Syyahat ('tourist') echo with the ghosts of the Soviet Union. The rooms are dark (brown seems to be the only colour favoured here) and the bathrooms fairly grim, but they do offer air conditioning and hot water. Singles cost US$25, doubles US$30, and triples US$33, breakfast included. A few rooms have been modernised, offering renovated bathrooms, small kitchenettes and, oddly, brass door-knockers. These rooms are charged at different rates, depending on their layouts, but are mostly around US$35 per person.

Hotel Bezirgen (20 rooms) 45 2060 Kochesi; ↘ 12 340644. Opposite the Azady World Languages Institute on the western side of town, this is one of the more palatable of Ashgabat's bottom-range places. It is run by the Ahal Region Consumers' Union. All rooms are air conditioned and have en suites of sorts with hot water. The Kafe Bezirgen under the hotel is under different management. Singles cost US$10, doubles US$20 and suites US$30.

Berzengi

A southern suburb of Ashgabat is emerging on a green-field site close to the Kopet Dag Mountains. Berzengi is one of the focal points for the Ashgabat redevelopment project of President Niyazov, and one of its major features is a line of more than 20 small hotels, built by various Turkmen government organisations on the president's instruction in the mid-1990s. The hotels are all designed in different styles; some exotic, others mundane. With more hotel rooms available here than there is possibly a market for, some of the hotels are now focused on providing rental accommodation for expatriates. Others are more geared up to Turkmen wedding parties than tourists wanting a bed. But many soldier on as hotels, offering some real bargains. There are, however, some downsides. Berzengi

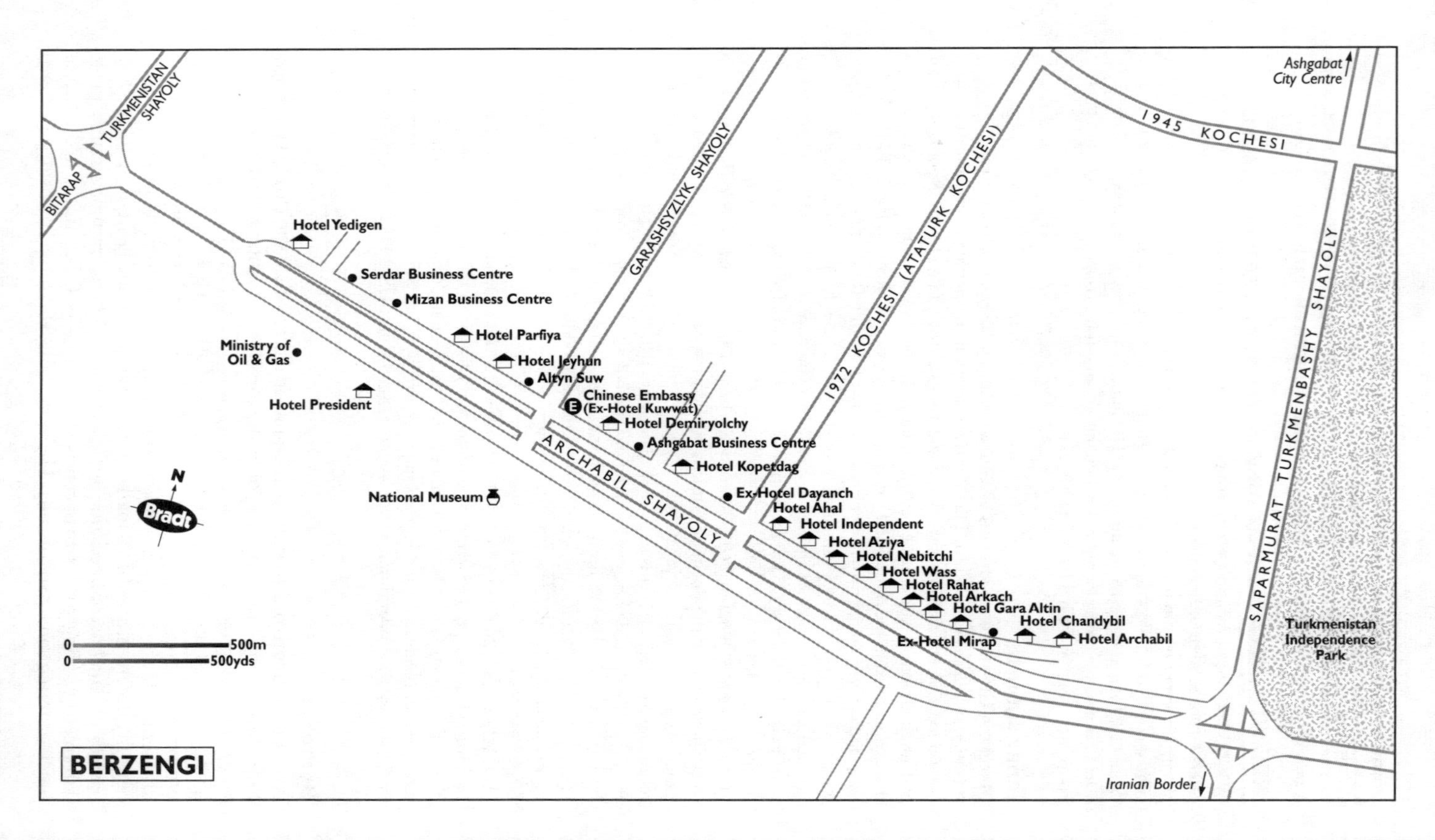
TURKMENISTAN SHAYOLY
BITARAP
Hotel Yedigen
Serdar Business Centre
Mizan Business Centre
Hotel Parfiya
Ministry of Oil & Gas
Hotel Jeyhun
Altyn Suw
Hotel President
Chinese Embassy (Ex-Hotel Kuwwat)
Hotel Demiryolchy
Ashgabat Business Centre
Hotel Kopetdag
GARASHSYZLYK SHAYOLY
ARCHABIL SHAYOLY
N
Bradt
National Museum
Ex-Hotel Dayanch
Hotel Ahal
Hotel Independent
Hotel Aziya
Hotel Nebitchi
Hotel Wass
Hotel Rahat
Hotel Arkach
Hotel Gara Altin
Hotel Chandybil
Ex-Hotel Mirap
Hotel Archabil
1972 KOCHESI (ATATURK KOCHESI)
1945 KOCHESI
Ashgabat City Centre
SAPARMURAT TURKMENBASHY SHAYOLY
Turkmenistan Independence Park
Iranian Border
0 500m
0 500yds
BERZENGI

is 4km from the centre of town. It has no shops, and its bars and restaurants are those of the hotels themselves, which tend to be either completely deserted or packed out by a noisy wedding party. Nonetheless, even if you are not staying here, the hotel strip of Berzengi is worth visiting as one of the more unusual sights of post-independence Ashgabat.

The list below gives details of every one of the hotels along the Berzengi strip, present and former, in geographical sequence from east to west. All lie on Archabil Shayoly.

Hotel Archabil (14 rooms) ☎ 12 488712, 488249. Managed by the Ministry of Tourism and Sport, this is outwardly one of the least attractive of the Berzengi hotels, consisting of two 4-storey pale blue boxes, prosaically titled 'A block' and 'B block'. Most of the somewhat run-down rooms are taken up by long-stay residents, but the hotel is good value at the bottom end of the range, with air-conditioned rooms, en suites, and even small kitchenettes in some of the rooms. Singles cost US$10, doubles US$15. There is no restaurant.

Hotel Chandybil (12 rooms) ☎ 12 488147. Offers spacious rooms, with separate bedrooms and living areas, which are, however, decidedly decrepit. Not all of the rooms have air conditioning, and hot water is available only for 2 hours in the morning and 3 in the evening. The rooms lead off of a balcony around a large central space, which provides the venue for frequent wedding parties. This could therefore prove a noisy choice. Rooms are charged at US$10.

Hotel Mirap. Now converted to office accommodation.

Hotel Gara Altin (18 rooms) ☎ 12 480322; **f** 12 480323. Like a sheikh's palace, with a green central dome, and little domed corner turrets, the Gara Altin ('Black Gold') is named in honour of oil, and built by the Ministry of Oil and Gas. It is a good mid-range option, with a restaurant, sauna, and outdoor pool in summer. Standard rooms, all of which are air conditioned, cost US$50, the more spacious 'semi-luxe' rooms are US$65, suites are US$80 and apartments US$125.

Hotel Arkach (10 rooms) ☎ 12 480351. The design hints at a medieval castle, and the hotel has a plumbing system to match. Both the receptionist and porter urged me to choose one of the more upmarket hotels along the strip, assuring me that the price difference was worth it. They have a point. If you do choose to stay here, the room prices, including breakfast, are US$25 for a 'semi-luxe' and US$30 for a suite. The place apparently has no standard rooms.

Hotel Rahat (11 rooms) ☎ 12 480325; **f** 12 480324. Entered through a semicircular columned arcade, this is a fair mid-range choice, with spacious rooms, central air conditioning, and breakfast included in the room rate. There is a bar and billiards in the basement. Singles cost US$25, doubles US$30, 'semi-luxe' US$45 and suites US$60. Simply enquiring about a discount will probably get you a 20% reduction on these prices.

Hotel Wass (12 rooms) ☎ 12 488156, 480336. Built by the Dashoguz regional administration, this place is set in pleasant gardens, and hosts frequent wedding parties. It does not, though, have a restaurant. Its rooms are air conditioned but basic. Standard rooms have en-suite showers; the suites have bathrooms. The published price is US$20 for a standard room, US$30 for a suite, though visitors booking through local travel agencies have reportedly been able to get rooms here for as little as US$5.

Hotel Nebitchi (18 rooms) ☎ 12 480261, 480262; **f** 12 480213. The oil workers' hotel features a waterless fountain centred around a 'nodding donkey' in the driveway. The interior is focused around a kitsch central hall, with mirrored arches and a modernist water feature. There is an outdoor swimming pool in summer. The rooms are pleasant, with tiled floors, en-suite bathrooms, central air conditioning and key-card entry system. With breakfast included, the standard room rate of US$45 is excellent value, especially as

discounts seem to be easily negotiable. Suites are US$100, and apartments US$290.
Hotel Aziya (10 rooms) ✆/f 12 480179, 480180. A small corner of China in Turkmenistan, the hotel is decked out in red lanterns and Chinese vases. The restaurant, too, is Chinese. The rooms, which have air conditioning and en-suite facilities, lead off from a balcony running around the barrel-vaulted entrance hall. The suite is room number 2006, which seems a somewhat inflationary figure for a 10-roomed hotel. The rates are US$25 for a single, US$30 for a double, US$45 for the 'semi-luxe' and US$50 for the suite.
Hotel Independent (10 available rooms) ✆/f 12 488155, 488700. The first international-standard hotel built in post-independence Turkmenistan, the Independent forms part of the Ahal Group, which also includes the Nissa and President hotels. The hotel is set around a barrel-vaulted central hall. Originally containing 22 rooms, the suites and apartments are all occupied by long-term residents. The 10 available standard rooms, all with en suites and air conditioning, offer either a balcony, a somewhat pointless 'closed balcony' (in effect a sparsely furnished extra room) or a kitchenette. There is no restaurant: guests are asked to use the restaurant in the Hotel Ahal next door, which is under the same management. The published room rate is US$80, including breakfast and use of the sauna. If a couple is sharing, there is an additional US$5 charge for the second breakfast.
Hotel Ahal (11 available rooms) ✆ 12 488737–9; **f** 12 480192. Sister hotel of the Independent, the Ahal has a distinctive exterior, with a rear tower resembling a space rocket, and a lattice design shrouding the walls. As at the Independent, around half of the original 22 rooms have been converted to offices, or let out on long-term rents, but the remaining rooms are comfortable, and the price includes breakfast, plus use of the swimming pool, fitness centre and sauna. The pool is indoor, a rare creature in Ashgabat, and run by the enthusiastic Svetlana, who also does massage at 100,000 manat for 30 minutes. (A notice reports that Lufthansa aircrews are entitled to 15 minutes free, for some reason.) The restaurant is Italian; the menu essentially the same as that at the Nissa. The published rates are US$80 for a single, US$100 for a double, though local travel agents should be able to get a 50% discount.
Hotel Dayanch No longer a hotel, this place now provides office accommodation and accommodates wedding parties.
Hotel Kopetdag (23 rooms) ✆ 12 480035, 480036; **f** 12 480037. A reasonable mid-range option, with air conditioning, satellite TV and en suites. The rooms lead off a balcony running around a glass-roofed central hall. The main hall also features a waterless fountain adorned with stuffed animals. There is a bar, where breakfast (included) is served. Standard rooms cost US$25, suites US$50.
Ashgabat Business Centre (ABC) Houses various offices and apartments. There is an open-air swimming pool here in summer, and a disco year-round.
Hotel Demiryolchy (12 rooms) ✆/f 12 480071, 480072. Built by a Turkish company on behalf of the Ministry of Railways, this is a good option in the upper-middle bracket. It is another hotel built around a large central hall, this time with a tinkling fountain, around which runs a first-floor balcony. The rooms are spacious, and decorated to a good standard. Some offer fine views across to the National Museum and the Kopet Dag Mountains beyond. There is a sauna (charged at US$2 per hour), a tennis court (US$8), and an outdoor pool in summer. The 2 apartments each have two bedrooms, both with en suites, around a central living room, and would make a good choice for 2 couples travelling together. Published rates, including breakfast, are US$50 for a standard room, US$60 for a 'semi-luxe', US$80 for a suite and US$100 for an apartment, but a 20% discount on these rates seems to be offered automatically.
Hotel Kuwwat Now houses the Chinese Embassy.
Altyn Suw Not a hotel: long-term rentals and wedding banquets only.
Hotel Jeyhun (18 rooms) ✆ 12 489010. A bulky, rather formless building, enlivened only by decoration on the façade based around the design of Turkmen carpets, the Jeyhun offers

grubby rooms, run-down bathrooms, and no bar or restaurant. The rooms are at least air conditioned, though in the 'semi-luxe' rooms the conditioners are unhelpfully located in the lounge rather than adjacent bedroom. Standard rooms are charged at US$20. The 'semi-luxe' rooms, at US$50, represent one of the worst deals in Berzengi.

Hotel Parfiya ☎ 12 488191, 488332. A green-painted fortress-like building, reached across a concrete footbridge, the rooms are air conditioned but run down, and there is no restaurant. There are rarely any rooms available here, as they are usually rented out to a Ukrainian construction company. Even if there are free rooms, I would not recommend the place, and the published rates are no bargain at US$25 for a standard room, US$35 for a suite and US$50 for an apartment.

Mizan Business Centre (43 rooms) ☎ 12 488641–3; f 12 488631. A complex of buildings, centred around a large hall, with a flat yellow roof, used mainly for large wedding parties and incorporating some office space. To the east of this is the business centre, which includes some reasonable mid-range accommodation. The bedrooms are clean, functional and centrally air conditioned. Behind the main hall are 2 blocks of apartments, which offer a potentially good choice for longer-stay visitors to Ashgabat, providing more freedom than a hotel can offer. Single apartments have a lounge with small kitchen area, a bedroom and en-suite bathroom. Double apartments have 2 bedrooms, lounge and separate kitchen. Standard rooms in the business centre are good value at US$20, and there is a suite for US$30. The single apartments are also priced at US$30; double apartments at US$45.

Serdar Business Centre A glitzy complex, run by the Ministry of Oil and Gas, opened in 2001 and the usual venue for Turkmenistan's annual oil and gas conference.

Hotel Yedigen (22 rooms) ☎ 12 480093; f 12 481011. The 'great bear' is another acceptable mid-range option, with rooms furnished to a reasonable standard, en suites and central air conditioning. The bar and restaurant are perhaps the most soulless in Berzengi – a hard-fought accolade. Singles cost US$25, doubles US$30 and 'semi-luxe' rooms US$40.

Hotel President (152 rooms) 54 Archabil Shayoly; ☎ 12 400000; f 12 400222, 400041; e presidenthotel@online.tm. Across the road from the small hotels of the Berzengi strip, the 80m tall President is the most luxurious of Ashgabat's hotels. Built by the French construction company Bouygues, it was opened by President Niyazov in July 2004 as part of the celebrations to mark the wheat harvest. Its exterior is faced with white marble; the interior offers chandeliered and columned opulence. Its restaurant is Italian, with the same management and menu as those of the Nissa and Ahal, though only this restaurant offers a mural of stampeding Ahal Tekke horses. It has indoor and outdoor pools, a tennis court and an internet centre (90,000 manat per hour). A minibus service ferries guests to the centre of town. The bedrooms feature imported French furniture in classical style. Standard rooms are US$110, suites US$180, and the lavish Presidential suites US$450. With large discounts usually available by booking through a local travel agent, a stay here will not prove outrageously expensive, though the standard of service here does not always match the glitziness of the décor.

WHERE TO EAT

The top-range places to eat in Ashgabat tend to be the restaurants of the major hotels. The Italian restaurants in the Nissa, Ahal and President hotels are certainly worth bearing in mind, with their extensive use of ingredients imported from Italy. The menu is basically the same at all three restaurants, but the main kitchen, from which the other hotels are supplied, is at the Nissa, which makes this probably the best choice. The Silk Road Restaurant at the Sheraton Grand Turkmen offers a reliable if unexciting lunchtime buffet, and periodic themed food weeks. The Chinese restaurant at the Hotel Aziya offers a change from the usual Ashgabat fare, but gets mixed reports.

At the other end of the scale, the main bazaars are the best places to head for cheap snacks, including savoury pastries such as *somsas* and *fitchi*, as well as Central Asian staples like *plov*. On the western side of the Gulustan Bazaar, several open-air places cluster around the entrance to the Gulustan Restaurant, serving *shashlik* and beer at plastic tables, on *tapchans* and even in a *yurt*.

Most restaurants in Ashgabat are open seven days a week, and almost all close at 23.00.

City centre

Turkmenistan Restaurant 19 Bitarap Turkmenistan Shayoly; ☎ 12 354673. Located within the Hotel Turkmenistan, but under separate management, this place has been through several changes of name, including the Diamond and Altyn Turkmenistan. With a liveried doorman and an extensive menu particularly strong on seafood, this is one of the smarter places to eat in Ashgabat. Main courses are mostly around 100,000 manat, though the brave can try frogs' legs at 250,000. It offers live music most evenings.

Asuda Nusay 110 2022 Kochesi (A Novai Kochesi); ☎ 12 350088; f 12 350250. The 'Peaceful Nisa', formerly known as the Nissa Truva, is a reliable if unspectacular mid-range place, with an international menu, including pizzas at around 50,000 manat. Next door, though with its entrance on Georogly Kochesi, and under the same management, is the **City Pub** (☎ 12 352288). A magnet for the expatriate community in Ashgabat, this friendly place is decorated with football scarves, from Arsenal to Zenit. It offers free (heavily salted) peanuts and popcorn, and opens daily 09.00–23.00. The live music (Tue–Sat) can on occasion be rather too loud for the modestly proportioned venue. The food is a basic selection of international favourites, including burgers at 50,000 manat, English fish and chips at 80,000, and a full English breakfast for 100,000. 'Juicy hot pork for gourmets' turns out to be a gammon steak.

Kumush Ay 73 Georogly Kochesi; ☎ 12 393351, 393352. The 'silver moon', right in the centre of town opposite the Sheraton Grand Turkmen, is still mostly known locally by its pre-Turkmenisation name, Florida. The place is a complex of several different venues. There is a Turkish restaurant on the ground floor (open: 12.00–23.00), with smart but antiseptic décor, and a good range of Turkish staples, including kebabs at around 75,000–85,000 manat, Turkish-style *manty* at 50,000 and, for the fearless, brain salad at 75,000. Next to this is the 'British Pub' (open: 09.00–02.00), another expatriate favourite. There is also a disco, held indoors on the first floor during the cooler months and outside in the courtyard in summer.

Guzer Divana 15/A Beyik Saparmurat Turkmenbashy Shayoly; ☎ 12 396006; f 12 395588. Formerly an expatriate pub named Mr John's, this place has been given a somewhat unsettling orange makeover. It serves basic international dishes like pizzas (50,000 manat), baked potatoes (40,000), burgers (45,000) and fish and chips (68,000). Live music Fri and Sat.

Coffee House 22B Bitarap Turkmenistan Shayoly; ☎ 12 350153, 353217. Soothingly decorated in natural shades, this small and somewhat quirky place arrived as a welcome addition to the Ashgabat restaurant scene. It is also known as Ak Maya, to meet the requirement that Ashgabat restaurants should bear a Turkmen name. A mostly unremarkable menu (pizzas for 40,000–55,000 manat, burgers 45,000) heads off into occasionally unexpected territory, including, as the English-language menu puts it, 'baked shark from chief' (130,000 manat), 'quail's nest' (100,000) and 'beanie stuffed fish' (100,000). There are also extensive lists of teas and coffees, with plenty of funky blends, including a coffee apparently called 'Costa Rican SHB (Tarzan Type)', and a tea named 'Jasmine Monkey King'. There is occasional live music.

Kafe Altyn Jam 101 Magtymguly Shayoly; ☎ 12 396850. A popular, central place, offering a reliable range of mainly international and Russian dishes. It has an outdoor terrace with large, shading umbrellas. Inside, plastic ivy trails from the ceiling. Mains cost from 40,000 manat up, *shashlik* is around 65,000–80,000 manat, and salads are priced at 20,000–30,000 manat. In front of the main restaurant is an 'ekspress kafé', under the same management, offering burgers, lasagne and slices of pie.

West of the centre

Kafe Aylar 9 2028 Kochesi; ☎ 12 354763. This is an imaginatively decorated place, not far from the Kopet Dag Stadium. The main room has murals depicting Turkmen village life, handicrafts and even a model desert monitor lizard patrolling the floor. Outside around the back is a courtyard, around which are tables set in open halved-*yurt* arrangements as well as reed-roofed cabins. There is a *tamdyr* oven and a bookable *yurt* for the traditional Turkmen dining experience. The menu has a good range of Turkmen dishes, but most of the more interesting items must be ordered in advance. These include dishes rarely found in restaurants, such as *tamdyrlama* for 120,000 manat and *gazanlama* for 230,000. There is also *dograma* and *yarma*, each at 50,000 manat. A more standard list of Central Asian and international dishes is available without pre-ordering.

Ayperi Restaurant 112 Magtymguly Shayoly; ☎ 12 395069; **f** 12 352916. The name may be Turkmen, but the red lanterns hanging outside betray this as a Chinese restaurant. Main courses, relatively expensive for Ashgabat, include a good range of beef, mutton, pork, chicken and fish dishes, mostly priced at around 100,000 manat. There is also a tofu-centred 'healthy menu', and medicinal Chinese vodka at 50,000 manat a shot in a range of flavours including, alarmingly, deer penis. 'It is health giving very much!' promises the menu.

Dip Club Restaurant 117 Georogly Kochesi; ☎ 12 345270; **f** 12 345271. This place offers a menu with a strong Middle Eastern flavour. The starters are a strong point, including *tabouleh*, *falafel* and a good lentil soup. The mains are expensive at around 120,000–130,000 manat, but portions are large. There is often live music, especially at weekends.

Kafe Nusay Gala 96 Georogly Kochesi; ☎ 12 342929. Almost opposite the Hotel Syyahat, this hard-to-find place is reached by taking the side road immediately to the west of the Nusay shop. The unmarked restaurant stands behind the shop, on your left. The interior of the 'Nisa Fortress' is decorated with a mosaic of the fortified walls. The yard out the back contains three *yurts* (book in advance), though two of them are furnished with tables and chairs, which somewhat diminishes the traditional dining experience. Mains are around 35,000–50,000 manat, *shashlik* 20,000–40,000, and the place offers a selection of Turkmen dishes, including *ciorba*, *dograma* and *plov* (all at 15,000 manat).

Café Zumerret 140 Magtymguly Shayoly; ☎ 12 364230. The Zumerret was formerly known as the Safari, before the Turkmenisation of restaurant names in the city took this place in an unexpectedly close direction to English West Country bucolic. The name actually means 'emerald'. It sits on the western edge of the Gunesh Park, and offers a pleasant terrace. The interior is decorated like a forest grove, with an artificial waterfall at the back of the room and stuffed ducks on the mantelpiece. Mounted heads of wild boar and urial look down from the walls, and the menu includes (pricey) game dishes, according to season, as well as a more standard international menu, at prices around 45,000–65,000 manat. The salads bear such immodest titles as 'delicious' and 'masterpiece', as well as the mysterious 'woodpecker's nest'.

Kafe Aysberg 10 2050 Kochesi; ☎ 12 361808. Ashgabat in the summer months offers a large number of places to eat *shashlik* and drink beer on pavement terraces outside simple cafés. The Aysberg, behind the old circus building, is one of the nicest. Its wooden tables are shaded beneath canopies and trees, and there are rose bushes around the entrance. Berk beer on draft is 9,000 manat a glass, *shashlik* is 20,000 manat, and *lyulya* kebabs 10,000. This is a popular and busy place.

Nash Dvor 90 2013 Kochesi; ☎ 12 344149. West of the town centre, and not advertised from the street, this is an Armenian restaurant specialising in *shashlik*, served with spicy tomato sauce and thin *lavash* bread. The *shashlik* costs around 25,000 manat a portion. Tables are mostly outside, in a large courtyard (the *dvor* of the title), each table enclosed by bamboo fencing for privacy.

South and east of the centre

Minara Restaurant Altyn Asyr Shopping Centre, Independence Park; ☎ 12 454601. Located on the fifth floor of the curious five-legged monument in Independence Park, the Minara offers some of the best restaurant views in Ashgabat. The interior is pleasing too, with murals of the archaeological treasures of Turkmenistan, and separate dining cabins designed to resemble traditional village houses. There is a broad international menu, with mains mostly around 40–50,000 manat. Unusually for Turkmenistan, Indian dishes are particularly well represented. The Minara also offers a good range of (more expensive) fish dishes, and an extensive wine list, at prices ranging from 100,000 manat for a bottle of Turkmen wine to 1.5 million for the best French wine on offer. Live music Fri–Sun evenings.

Café Sim-Sim 50/1 1958 Kochesi (ex Andaliba Kochesi); ☎ 12 453343, 451333. The 'open sesame' is located in a side street well out of the centre, but is a popular venue with a young, relatively well-heeled, Turkmen crowd. It offers a long menu of Russian and international dishes, including a wide choice of salads, with intriguing names such as Jakki, Breeze and Daring. To get here, head south along 1958 Kochesi. Turn right onto 1951 Kochesi (the former Yunus Emre Kochesi), and take the first right-hand turning, down a small side road. The restaurant is on your right.

Kopet Dag Restaurant 10 Magtymguly Shayoly; ☎ 12 272109. This large white marble-faced building on the eastern side of town has two large dining rooms indoors, and a pleasant terrace outside, where the bar has been built to resemble a large beer barrel. The main selling point is Austrian-recipe Salm Brau beer, brewed on the premises and sold for 10,000 manat a glass. The menu promises: 'Salm Brau. Das ist fantastisch'. Mains are around 50,000–60,000 manat, and the place does good *shashlik*. A floor show with belly dancers is offered outside, Wed–Sun.

Kafé Yolki Palki Asia Planet funfair; ☎ 12 287673; **f** 12 425561; **e** servettm@online.tm. Located in the small funfair near the eastern end of Magtymguly Shayoly, Yolki Palki means, in Russian, something like 'crikey!' It is an unpretentious place, decorated rather like a large wooden shack, with Russian pop music on tape and a young clientele. The Russian menu offers a good range of salads, *shashlik* and a standard selection of meat dishes. The toilet is in the games arcade next door.

Kafé Altyn Dan 49 Turkmenbashy Shayoly; ☎ 12 223711. Also known by its earlier Russian name, Rasswet ('Dawn'), the Altyn Dan has black-and-white checkerboard flooring and reasonably smart décor, though with an odd taste in model axes and crossbows on the walls. It offers a mid-priced range of Russian and international dishes, and a cocktail list featuring the inadvertently funny 'comicadze', the 'mudy water' and the alarming 'tegula bum'.

Payane Restaurant Ashgabat truck terminal, 458 Turkmenbashy Shayoly; ☎ 12 488770. Known among Ashgabat's expatriate community as the 'Iranian truck stop', this place, outside town, serves excellent and good-value Iranian food in a somewhat quirky location, within the truck terminal serving lorry drivers heading from and to the Iranian border, a few kilometres to the south. To get here, head south along Turkmenbashy Shayoly. Leaving Independence Park to your left, and passing beneath the underpass, turn left after a further 3km into a fenced compound signposted 'Ashikhabad Trucks Terminal'. The restaurant is at the rear of the compound. Alcohol is not served.

ENTERTAINMENT

Ashgabat is not the liveliest of cities as regards evening entertainment. Restaurants and bars are required to close at 23.00, and nightlife beyond that time is confined to discos and billiard halls. Since independence, the state has focused its efforts on the encouragement of Turkmen-language theatres and other forms of 'traditional' entertainment. Cinemas, the circus, and the opera and ballet theatre have all closed. There is nonetheless plenty of interest, from Sunday morning horse racing at the Hippodrome to the Turkmen Puppet Theatre, whose shows can be enjoyed even without a knowledge of the language. A theme park to be titled 'The World of Turkmen Fairy Tales' was under construction in the southern part of town during the period of research of this book.

Theatres

With their programmes focused around plays reinforcing the messages of national identity emphasised by President Niyazov, the construction of gleaming modern theatres is an important part of the president's redevelopment programme for Ashgabat. Even if you do not understand Turkmen, a trip to the theatre is worth considering, as plays are cheap, the costumes often visually arresting, and the performances offer an insight into the nation-building work of the government.

Magtymguly National Theatre of Musical Drama Shevchenko Kochesi; ↘ 12 350564. Opened in 2004, this white marble-faced building has a yellow central dome and two smaller domes flanking the main entrance. Its interior is opulent, with a gleaming white foyer and a wooden-panelled auditorium offering plush seats and pink carpets. Performances are usually at 19.00, Fri–Sun, for 8,000 manat. No performances Jul–Oct. The Saz Chamber Orchestra also puts on occasional programmes of Turkmen and Western classical music here.

Mollanepes National Drama Theatre 79 2035 Kochesi; ↘ 12 357463. The eastern part of this building is a pleasing 1950s construction, with a façade dominated by 3 tall arches and topped by a 5-pointed Soviet star. In 2005, the French construction company Bouygues added a western block, in the marble-faced, domed, independence style on the site of what was the Palace of Young Pioneers during the Soviet period. Performances (not Mon) usually start at 19.00, and cost around 5,000–10,000 manat. There is no programme Jul–Oct.

Pushkin Russian Drama Theatre 142 Magtymguly Shayoly; ↘ 12 364193. This was housed in a classical-styled 1950s building, fronted by 6 Corinthian columns, on the western side of the Sheraton Grand Turkmen Hotel. But the building was demolished, its place now occupied by an artificial waterfall in a small piece of parkland, and the theatre moved to a less central location on Magtymguly Shayoly, where it reopened in October 2004. A bust of Pushkin keeps watch outside. One of the first plays performed at the new location was called 'Sorry', though it was unclear quite who was apologising for what. It offers a mainstream Russian-language programme. Performances usually start at 19.00 Sat and Sun. Tickets cost 8,000–10,000 manat.

Turkmen State Puppet Theatre Atamurat Niyazov Shayoly; ↘ 12 418003. Currently housed in a somewhat dilapidated building, close to the '100 Fountains' Bazaar on the eastern side of town, the Puppet Theatre is due to move into an ornate fantasy of a home, the work of the Turkish construction company Polimeks, in the forthcoming 'world of Turkmen fairy tales' entertainment complex. Directed by Jeren Durdiyeva, a popular comic actress, the Puppet Theatre offers a visually attractive performance to a packed crowd. Most of the plays are based around traditional Turkmen folk tales, and often have a village setting. Performances are usually at 19.00 Sat and Sun, with additional shows at 11.00 and 13.00 in school holidays. Tickets cost 5,000 manat.

Cinema

The Soviet cinemas dotting the city, with names such as Peace, Spring and Motherland, have been either closed or converted to cultural centres, where they host occasional Turkmen-language musical and drama events. The only regular opportunities to watch films in Ashgabat are at a few privately run 'DVD Centres'. The smartest of these is **Yimpash Cinema Club** (54 Turkmenbashy Shayoly; ☎ 12 454266), based on the top floor of the Yimpash supermarket. It has three screenings daily (at 13.00, 17.00 and 20.00), plush cinema-style seats, and a kiosk serving popcorn, ice-cream and soft drinks. Most screenings are in Russian, though English-language films may be shown on Thursday evenings. Tickets cost 35,000 manat.

Discos

There are discos in several of the main hotels (the Ak Altyn, Sheraton Grand Turkmen and Nissa) as well as at the Kumush Ay (Florida) complex in the centre of town and the ABC Business Centre in Berzengi. Most of these places are frequented by prostitutes. The Florida, which is based outside in summer around a central courtyard/dance floor, is probably the most wholesome.

Horse racing

This is a popular spectator sport, and a great opportunity to see Turkmenistan's fine Ahal Tekke horses in action. Races are usually held on Sunday mornings, between late March and late May, and again for a few weeks in the autumn, at the **Old Hippodrome** on the eastern edge of the city. Before each race, the mostly male audience huddles in groups on the stands, as private betting transactions are carried out. The races are accompanied with a great deal of enthusiastic shouting, and then applause as the winning jockey receives the prize of a fridge, or video recorder. For Horse Day, the last Sunday in April, the race programme is combined with concerts, and the race-track decorated in multicoloured flags. To reach the Hippodrome, head eastwards along Magtymguly Shayoly, turning left when you reach the end of this street. Take the bridge over the railway line; on the northern side of the bridge you will see the Hippodrome on your right. At its entrance stands a golden monument of a cloaked President Niyazov, stroking an Ahal Tekke horse.

The **Ahal Tekke Horse Complex of the President of Turkmenistan**, built by the Turkish company Polimeks, was opened in 2004 to the southeast of the city. To reach it, head south along Turkmenbashy Shayoly, turning left onto the main highway as it crosses over the road, just beyond Independence Park. The horse complex is on your left, an artificially watered oasis of luxuriant green amid the arid surrounding landscape. The complex includes stabling for the president's many Ahal Tekke horses, white marble-fronted stands and a racetrack which features a modern starting gate, an electronic scoreboard and photo-finish technology. At the time of writing, all that these expensive facilities currently lack is regular horse racing.

Indoor games

Russian billiards remains a highly popular (mainly male) pastime, and there are billiard clubs across the city, usually in airless basements, at which the game is played into the small hours. Since other bars are mostly required to shut at 23.00, the billiard halls double as late-night drinking dens.

Luxor Altyn Asyr Shopping Centre, Independence Park; ☎ 12 454602. Located on the ground floor of the monument known across Ashgabat as 'five legs', the Egyptian-themed Luxor is Ashgabat's funkiest billiard hall. Pool and Russian billiard tables (a relatively pricey

80,000 manat per hour) sit amidst columns inscribed with hieroglyphics and statues of assorted pharaohs. The waitresses are dressed to match the theme.
Pyramide 29 2060/10 Kochesi (ex Kurban Durdy Kochesi). On the western side of town, this place also has an Egyptian name, but doesn't carry the theme through. It offers both Russian and American billiards, and a bar.
Yimpash 54 Turkmenbashy Shayoly; ☎ 12 454266. The third floor of Ashgabat's main supermarket offers billiards (55,000 manat an hour), table tennis (25,000 manat an hour), and 4 somewhat unreliable lanes of 10-pin bowling (45,000 manat a game). There are several eating options here, but no alcohol is served. Yimpash closes at 23.00.

SHOPPING
Tolkuchka Bazaar
Ashgabat's largest bazaar, and one of Turkmenistan's major sights, Tolkuchka is an out-of-town market which runs from around 08.00–14.00 on Thursdays, Saturdays and is particularly animated on Sundays. It is officially known as the Number 4 Bazaar, and also carries the Turkmen name 'Jygyldyk', but it is the Russian name which has stuck. Tolkuchka means, roughly, 'Little Push', and this is an apt description for the market which, unlike almost everywhere else in low-density Turkmenistan, gets decidedly crowded. It is a colourful, chaotic place, offering wildly contrasting sights: the indignant newly purchased camel which, while being winched onto its new owner's truck, sensibly tucks its legs under its body; the vendor of beautiful Turkmen embroidery who rubs breadcrumbs across her wares as a means, apparently, of adding lustre to them; the ethnic Korean ladies who run stalls covered with small mountains of pickled carrot; stalls selling Chinese clothing and shoes with names like 'Dafeeboys' and 'Jo's Love Fashionable'; and the Turkmen *telpeks*, unfeasibly shaggy white sheepskin hats, displayed on metal pegs stuck into the ground, so that they look like giant dandelion clocks. Most foreign visitors head straight for the carpets, but Tolkuchka offers a great deal more.

To get here, head north out of Ashgabat on the Dashoguz road (Atamurat Niyazov Shayoly in town). You pass over a bridge across the Kara Kum Canal some 4km north of the town centre. Three kilometres further on, the edge of the market runs adjacent to the road, on the left-hand side. To get to Tolkuchka's large parking area, keep on the Dashoguz road for another 800m, before taking the left turn being used by most of the other traffic on the road. You reach the car park after another 500m or so. Large numbers of battered buses run between Ashgabat and Tolkuchka on market days. They depart from several places in the city, but the Tekke Bazaar is a good place to head. The fare is 2,000 manat.

On the eastern side of the car park is a flat expanse of ground devoted to the selling of automobiles. The walled market proper is to the south of here, with large numbers of fruit and vegetable stalls spilled out in front of it. Having passed into the bazaar through the main brick entrance arch, a sharp turn to your left will take you to the large area devoted to carpets and handicrafts. Haggling is expected here. The deep red Tekke carpets, laid on the ground or hung across metal poles, make for an exotic sight. Note though that carpets bought here will need to be certified at the 'Expert Commission' behind the Carpet Museum before they can be taken out of the country (see page 53). Carpets more than 50 years old cannot be exported at all. There are many stalls in this part of the bazaar selling *telpeks* and the embroidered skull-caps known as *takhyas*, carpet bags, Soviet memorabilia, Turkmen jewellery, toy *yurts* and talismans to ward off the evil eye.

To the south of here are several rows of clothing stalls. One that should not be missed is a lane of stalls devoted to beautiful pieces of Turkmen embroidery, destined to adorn silk dresses, which are sold individually wrapped in plastic.

Further south are fabrics, and then a large expanse of containers, from which consumer goods are sold. A covered fruit and vegetable market is reached by turning right rather than left from the main entrance into the bazaar.

To the west of the walled area is an impoverished part of the market, where poor residents of Ashgabat try to make a little income from the sale of a few personal belongings, placed on cloths laid directly onto the ground. A large area near here is devoted to stalls selling odd bits and pieces from motors and engines. The most distant area of the market to the south is devoted to white goods and electrical equipment, while across to the west is the area reserved for the sale of livestock, including camels. This is a fascinating part of the market, though a particularly muddy one after rain. My favourite sight here is of a sheep being driven off in a motorcycle side-car.

Tolkuchka leaves the visitor grappling with thorny questions. Questions like why do so many of the plastic bags on sale at the market advertise something called 'Dezzy Bubble Gum'? Which is the more attractive perfume: 'Blue Lady' or 'Lady in Blue'? What does the product contained in a large cardboard box labelled 'sixty dozen flower bugle' actually look like, and do? Is anyone really going to buy, ever, the battered, rusty object that might once have been a cooker, and which is priced at 750,000 manat?

City bazaars

The **Gulustan Bazaar** in the centre of Ashgabat, usually referred to as the Russian Bazaar, is the main daily market. It is housed in a concrete Soviet structure, based around ten pillars, each supporting a section of roof. Fruit, vegetables and groceries fill the space beneath. Meat and milk products are kept cool in glass-fronted refrigerated cabinets bearing cheerful but odd English-language logos: 'Fanta Fan Club'; 'Thanks for your shoping'. The space is decorated with a large white sculpture of indeterminate subject. Around this central area is a line of shops, offering more expensive imported goods, alcohol, CDs and videos. Clothes stalls surround the main market space to the south and east.

The **Tekke Bazaar**, on the western edge of the town centre, is focused on fruit and vegetables. In the summer months melons are piled high into little hills along one side of the market.

The **Kopetdag Bazaar** lies along 1995 Kochesi, east of the Hotel Nissa. It is popularly known as the 'Old Fair', or often simply as the *domiki* ('little houses'), since the stalls comprise chalets, in front of which are metal-framed tented spaces in which the wares are displayed. Most of the stalls sell imported clothing and footwear, though a couple of places offer Turkmen handicrafts and carpets. The vendors mostly seem thoroughly bored, and spend much of their day chewing at sunflower seeds. The market is open from 09.00–20.00.

The **Alemgoshar Bazaar** is a good suburban market. It sits in the southeastern part of the city, and is more widely known as the *Sto Fontanov* ('100 Fountains') Bazaar, after a fountain ensemble which lies close by, in the strip of parkland running beside the adjacent 1934 Kochesi. The 100 fountains themselves, built as part of the commemorations in 1981 to mark the 100th anniversary of the foundation of Ashgabat, are less than exciting: 100 little tiled circles, from the centres of which water presumably once spouted, sitting in a basin. Nearby, 100 plane trees are another product of what seem to have been celebrations by numbers. The bazaar is centred on a fruit and vegetable market, with several rows of clothes stores behind. It is in theory open 07.00–22.00, though winds down by mid-evening.

The **Guneshli Bazaar**, 'Sunny Market' is much better known by its Russian name, *Optovi*, the wholesale market. It is located on a scruffy plot at the southern edge of town, on the corner of 1945 Kochesi and 1946 Kochesi. Traders offer imported packet food, household goods, alcohol and boxes of cigarettes from stalls housed in metal containers. The place is open 08.00–20.00, except Mondays.

Stores

The **Turkmenistan Trade Centre**, across Magtymguly Shayoly from the Hotel Ashgabat, is still generally referred to by its Soviet title of Univermag, when it was the city's central department store. It is now mostly given over to boutiques, offering imported products at a price far beyond the pockets of most Turkmens. Customers here are rare.

Ashgabat's main supermarket is **Yimpash**, a three-storey Turkish-built affair at 54 Turkmenbashy Shayoly (☎ 12 454266). Its escalators, Turkmenistan's first, became something of a local tourist attraction when the place opened. The supermarket occupies the ground floor, offering a good range of products, especially imports from Turkey, though no alcohol. The first floor is chunky furniture and forgettable clothing. The top floor offers the DVD centre, billiards, bowling and a range of (mainly Turkish) food outlets. It is open daily, 07.00–23.00.

Art galleries

Artists' Union 33 Asudalyk Kochesi; ☎ 12 395439. The Artists' Union buildings are focused around a two-storey exhibition hall, which displays the work of the union members around major Turkmen holidays. There is a small shop selling paintings and handicrafts on the ground floor. The artists' workshops are based in neighbouring buildings (enquire at the exhibition hall): it is possible to buy work direct from the artists. Around the back of the hall is a courtyard displaying various pieces of sculpture, from Turkmen notables to a couple of *rhytons*.

Art Gallery 'Muhammed' 12A Georogly Kochesi; ☎ 12 395931; **f** 12 394385. Owned by Allamurat Muhammedov, Chairman of the Artists' Union, and named after his son, the gallery stands next door to the City Pub, and is easily identified by the two stained-glass horse-head designs on the gate. The first floor of the gallery is the artist's spacious studio, with his paintings around the walls. Downstairs in the basement is a two-room private museum containing Muhammedov's considerable collection of antiquities, including weapons, jewellery, carpets and samovars. Ring ahead for an appointment to visit.

Studio Juma Sculpture Town, Mir 8; ☎ 12 432567; **e** jumnat@mail.ru. Located in the eastern suburbs of the city, the Studio Juma is run by Natalya Jumadurdieva, widow of the sculptor Juma Jumadurdy, whose work fills the main room of the gallery. A side room is devoted to temporary exhibitions of contemporary Turkmen artists, especially painters from Mary. Telephone ahead for an appointment, and for details of forthcoming exhibitions. Natalya speaks English. 'Sculpture Town' is an interesting district of Ashgabat. The workshops of several sculptors are clustered together here. Their yards and gardens contain scattered pieces of sculpture, including busts of the president. To get here, take Atamurat Niyazov Shayoly east from the centre. After 4km or so, you reach a mosque on the left-hand side of the road with twin minarets, topped by gently tapering cones in the manner of Ottoman Turkish architecture. Turn left immediately after the mosque, and then take the first turning on the right, down a narrow side street. Sculptures soon start to appear on all sides. Studio Juma is on your right.

Carpets and textiles

The Turkmen state carpets concern, **Turkmenhaly** (☎ 12 356545, 354768), runs several carpet stores which offer newly woven carpets based around traditional Turkmen designs. The main central shop lies on Georogly Kochesi, immediately to the east of the Carpet Museum (open 10.00–19.00 Mon–Fri, and 10.00–15.00

Sat, with a lunch-break 13.00–14.00; closed Sun). Another Turkmenhaly store is at 110 Magtymguly Shayoly (open 09.00–19.00, except Sun, lunch-break 13.00–14.00). There are also carpets on sale in the souvenir shops of most of the top-range hotels, though if you buy at a hotel you may need to get your carpet certified at the Expert Commission (see page 53).

Across the road from the Sheraton Grand Turkmen Hotel, at 10 Georogly Kochesi, sits the **Altyn Asyr Marketing Centre**, in a marble-faced building. The large portrait of President Niyazov surrounded by doves which once decorated the façade of this place has, however, been removed. Run by the Ministry of Textiles, the centre sells products from Turkmenistan's textiles factories, including some designs based around traditional Turkmen styles as well as a large amount of cotton leisurewear from lines focused on the US market. It is open 09.00–19.00, except Sunday, with a lunch closure 14.00–15.00.

Bookshops

Ashgabat's bookshops are increasingly dominated by government publications, with a large proportion of the wall-space in every shop occupied by books by, or about, President Niyazov. English-language copies of *Ruhnama* retail for 50,000 manat. Postcard collections of the post-independence buildings of Ashgabat or the Independence Park statues may be available. The most central bookstore is **Miras**, next door to the Magtymguly State University at 29 Turkmenbashy Shayoly. It is open 10.00–19.00 daily, except Sunday, with a lunch-break 14.00–15.00. A sign in English outside announces that this is the 'book shop of spiritual legacy'.

OTHER PRACTICALITIES

Medical

Central Hospital 1951 Kochesi (ex Yunus Emre Kochesi); ↘ 12 450303; f 12 450331. A private, 42-bed, Turkish-built hospital in the International Business Centre, across Turkmenbashy Shayoly from the Olympic Stadium. It has a basic range of diagnostic support services, an intensive-care unit, and an emergency ambulance. The hospital pharmacy has a somewhat patchy stock. A Jordanian doctor working at the hospital, Yahya Shihadeh, speaks good English.

Saparmurat Niyazov International Medical Centre Berzengi; ↘ 12 519005, 519009. A modern hospital, provided with much German equipment, the centre is mainly focused on cardiology, though also offers a general outpatient unit and dental services. This hospital also has an emergency ambulance, equipped with a defibrillator. There is reportedly a shortage of well-trained staff at the centre. Another new hospital, the Centre of Internal Diseases, lies beside it.

Medical Diagnostic Centre Berzengi; ↘ 12 489203, 489009. Opened in 2004, this marble-faced building is the latest addition to the complex of new medical facilities in Berzengi. It, too, has a wide range of modern equipment, but a shortage of well-trained staff able to use it.

Banking

Vnesheconombank 22 2010 Kochesi (ex Asudalyk Kochesi); ↘ 12 350252. The State Bank for Foreign Economic Affairs is conveniently located in the centre of town, close to the Magtymguly Monument. They will be only too happy to change your US dollars into manat at the official rate, and will also cash travellers' cheques. The bank is open Mon–Fri 09.15–18.00 (with a break for lunch 13.00–14.00) and Sat 09.15–14.00.

National Bank of Pakistan World Trade Complex, 1 2005 Kochesi; ↘ 12 351204. Open 09.30–15.00 Mon–Fri, with a lunch-break 13.00–14.00. Cashes travellers' cheques.

Turkmen/Turkish Bank 111/2 Magtymguly Shayoly; ↘ 12 511013, 510577. Open 09.00–17.00 Mon–Fri, with a lunch-break 13.00–14.00. Does not cash travellers' cheques.

Above Cleansing a sweet stall with smoke from the burning *yuzaerlik* shrub, Turkmenabat

Left Making chorek, Badkyz

Below Serdar Vodka, honouring President Niyazov

Above Flag day concert at the Olympic stadium, Ashgabat

Left Actor dressed as President Niyazov's father, saluting his son. Flag day concert, Ashgabat

Below Flag day concert at the Old Hippodrome, Ashgabat

Communications

The **central post office** is at 16 2023 Kochesi, a block to the north of the Russian Bazaar. It is open 09.00–18.00, though shuts an hour earlier on Saturday, and is open mornings only on Sunday. The **central telephone office** is immediately to the south of here, along the pedestrian 2016 Kochesi (ex Karl Liebknecht Kochesi). This is a somewhat chaotic place: you first queue up to request the number you want and the approximate duration of the call. You will then be directed to one of 30 cabins to take the call once the operator has dialled the number. You can also send faxes from here. It is altogether easier, though not cheaper, to call IDD from the main hotels, and send faxes from the hotel business centres. The latter are also currently your best bet as regards **internet** access. One other possible option, newly opened at the time of research, is **Club Matrix** (World Trade Complex, 1 2005 Kochesi; ☎ 12 355459, 355547). This youth-oriented centre, open daily 09.00–20.00, offers internet access at 50,000 manat per hour, as well as a small café.

WHAT TO SEE

City centre

Turkmenbashy Square

The centre of political power in Ashgabat is focused on a large tarmac rectangle of ground in the centre of the city, surrounded by the glittering domes and shiny white-marble façades of its grandest buildings. The western side of the square is occupied by the gold-domed **Turkmenbashy Palace**, built by the French construction company Bouygues. Senior official visitors to Turkmenistan pass through the huge and opulently furnished entrance hall beneath the dome on their way to meetings with President Niyazov here. Approaching the fence surrounding the palace to take a closer look will probably earn you a stern rebuke from one of the many uniformed officials on guard.

The smaller golden-domed structure opposite the Turkmenbashy Palace is the **rostrum**, in front of which processions of troops and military hardware, industrial workers, students, dancers and Ahal Tekke horses parade during major government celebrations. The president watches proceedings from the first-floor balcony, while diplomats and officials sit below. On the northern side of this is the only Soviet-era building remaining on the square. The **national library**, now named in honour of Saparmurat Turkmenbashy but once dedicated to Karl Marx, is a concrete square, completed in 1974, its interior walls enlivened by intriguing hieroglyphic designs. On the ceiling of the second floor, staring down over a flight of concrete steps below, is a wooden relief by sculptor Ernst Neisvestniy, modelled on the marble sculpture of the Parthian Princess Rodogon, now in the National Museum (see page 101).

The southern side of Turkmenbashy Square is occupied by the **Ruhyyet Palace**, with its pastel-blue central dome spawning four smaller domes. This is another marble-faced building of French design. Its auditorium, which seats 2,800 people, was designed to be large enough to accommodate the 2,500-member People's Council, ostensibly the highest decision-making body in Turkmenistan. This building is also used for concerts organised by the Turkmen government to commemorate the main public holidays, at which most of the songs are either about the president or written by him. The Ruhyyet Palace was also the venue for the summit of the five Caspian heads of state, held in Ashgabat in 2002, which aimed to give some impetus to negotiations on the delimitation of that body of water.

The buildings of two Turkmen ministries sit either side of the Ruhyyet Palace, in symmetrical marble-faced buildings with bevelled façades and shallow white domes. On the eastern side of the palace is the **Ministry of Defence**, with a statue of President Niyazov in front. Its sister structure to the west is the **Palace of**

Justice, which holds both Turkmenistan's Justice Ministry and Supreme Court. The statue in front of this building is an image of Niyazov's mother, Gurbansoltan Eje, holding the scales of justice in her right hand.

Arch of Neutrality

The northern side of Turkmenbashy Square is dominated by one of the most distinctive monuments of post-independence Turkmenistan. The 75m Arch of Neutrality was built by the Turkish construction company Polimeks to commemorate the United Nations General Assembly Resolution of 12 December 1995, approving Turkmenistan's status of 'permanent neutrality'. The white marble-faced monument resembles a comic-book space rocket, resting on three 'legs', which are intended to symbolise the trivet on which a Turkmen cooking pot traditionally sits. The monument is, predictably, nicknamed *trinozhka* (Russian: 'Three Legs') among the inhabitants of Ashgabat. It is topped by a 12m bronze statue of President Niyazov, arms outstretched in a gesture of welcome, standing in front of a fluttering Turkmen flag. Every day this presidential statue slowly revolves, so that it always faces the sun.

A curious lift ascends one of the sloping legs, for a charge of 1,000 manat (opening times: 08.00–22.00, with breaks 11.45–12.30 and 17.45–18.30). The lift brings visitors to a café which is usually shut, and has little on offer when it is open. From here, steps lead up to a viewing platform roughly halfway up the building. A lift (not always working) takes visitors to a higher viewing platform, not far below the president's feet. Both platforms offer excellent views across Ashgabat. You get a good sense of the clear demarcation of the city into strikingly different construction zones: the tall, marble-faced apartment blocks of the post-independence city, the four-storey blocks of the later Soviet period, and the single-storey detached dwellings around central courtyards which characterise many of the outer suburbs. Photography is not permitted from the viewing platforms.

Earthquake Monument

On the eastern side of the Arch of Neutrality is another meaning-laden composition of the post-independence period. This is a monument, completed in 1998, to the memory of those killed in the 1948 Ashgabat earthquake. A square building, faced with cream-coloured tiles, contains a small museum with sobering photographs of the destruction wrought by the earthquake. The museum is, however, almost always shut. On the southern side of the building, an eternal flame burns for those who died.

The most striking feature of the building is the sculpture which crowns, and dominates, it. A large bull has taken the world in its horns, and is proceeding to give the planet a good shake. The globe is covered with rubble, but a dying mother manages to lift a small child above the turmoil wrought by nature. Set starkly against the dark colour of the rest of the sculpture, the child is a shining gold. A child who will grow to be president. Another noteworthy feature of the sculpture is that the bull sports particularly large testicles.

Towards the university

Eastwards from the earthquake monument is a pleasant strip of parkland. On the southern side of this, behind the Turkmenbashy Palace, is a marble-faced rectangular building, used for state banquets in honour of visiting heads of state. East of here is the **Old Presidential Palace**, a 1950s building with a shallow dome atop a cylindrical drum. In the Soviet period this place housed the Central Committee of the Communist Party of Turkmenistan. It remains one of the buildings used by Turkmenistan's presidential apparatus, and uniformed officers discourage visitors from getting too close. But you should be able to get near enough to see the hammer-and-sickle motifs above the entrance.

Opposite the Old Presidential Palace, in the strip of park, is an elegant **war memorial**, built in the 1970s in honour of those who died in World War II. Four tall tapering columns of red marble surround an eternal flame, like petals shielding the heart of a flower. To the side of this composition is a red marble arch, beneath which kneel two combatants, watched over by a grieving female figure.

At the eastern end of the park, across Turkmenbashy Shayoly, stands the main building of the **Magtymguly State University**, built in 1960, when the university was named in honour of Gorky, rather than Turkmenistan's greatest poet. Golden statues of a male and female student stand hand-in-hand on the roof, looking worryingly as though they are preparing to jump.

Museum of Fine Art

Immediately to the west of the Palace of Justice, the Museum of Fine Art (☎ 12 351566) is housed in a grand Bouygues construction, a rectangular building with a white central dome, columned exterior, and four bronze lions guarding the corners. It is open 09.00–18.00, except Tuesdays. Admission costs US$10. There is a charge for taking photographs of 250,000 manat, a breathtaking US$50 at the official rate of exchange.

From the entrance, you first pass into a huge and largely empty central hall beneath the dome. A few post-independence canvases hang on the walls. *Abundance of the Harvest* depicts President Niyazov admiring a loaf of bread. A bunch of wheat in the foreground is tied together with a ribbon showing the annual harvest figure of 2,800,000 tonnes of wheat. Behind the central hall is the Independence Hall, centred around a bust of the president. The walls feature canvases of the heroic figures of the regime's nation-building texts: Oguz Han, Togrul Beg, Alp Arslan and the poet Seydi. President Niyazov is featured, in a canvas entitled *Ruhnama is my Soul*, in which the book, surrounded by a yellow light, is suspended above the president's head like a halo. The president's horse, Yanardag, gets a canvas too.

Behind the Independence Hall is a large area devoted to carpet work, with some colourful Soviet-era tapestries, as well as carpets featuring scenes ranging from melons to the monuments of Dekhistan. There is a selection of portrait carpets, including Nehru, Magtymguly and Pushkin. A carpet entitled *Eternal, Just, Magnanimous Serdar* features President Niyazov standing in front of a map of Turkmenistan, which in turn covers the Turkmen flag.

To the right of the central hall is an interesting display of Turkmen painting before 1950. Some canvases depict traditional Turkmen festivals, such as a 1923 work portraying a girl on a swing: part of the *Kurban Bayram* celebrations. Others reflect Soviet priorities, such as a Victory Day celebration scene from 1946, with the tea-drinking former combatants proudly sporting their medals. But more overtly political canvases from the Soviet period are absent. There are some attractive, brightly coloured works from the 1920s by Olga Misgiryeva, featuring rather aloof-looking girls. Also on this side of the building is a space devoted to Turkmenistan's archaeological sites. Pride of place here goes to the attempt to reconstruct the dragon frieze which once adorned the façade of the mosque at Anau (see page 123), using fragments of the original, recovered from the site. Sadly it seems that most of this has been lost, and the result is more gap than frieze.

To the left of the central hall is displayed post-1950 Turkmen painting and sculpture. There are many highly colourful canvases, seeming to incorporate the warmth of the Turkmen sun. A large 1966 canvas by Mamed Mammedov of the Turkmen composer Nury Halmammedov depicts its subject leaning against a tree, with a tortured expression, against a bold backdrop of yellow and orange colour. Intricate canvases by Izzat Klichev borrow from the dense patterns characteristic of Turkmen embroidery. Kossek Nurmuradov's 2003 work *Turkmens* is a dizzying painting of bright colours. In this hall too are several canvases glorifying the heroes identified in *Ruhnama* and other nation-building works of the Turkmen government. In *Courage: Hero of Turkmenistan Atamurat Niyazov*, the face of Niyazov's father shines out against those of his war-weary comrades, after their capture by German forces. There is a large and busy painting of the heroic warrior Georogly, as he enters a bustling marketplace.

On the first floor is an eclectic mix of non-Turkmen work. The gallery to the right includes a missable collection of painting, ceramics, carpets and textiles from India, China, Japan and Iran. There is a more interesting selection of Russian art, mostly from the 19th century, including historical (*Capture of Kazan*, *Battle of Sebastopol*), rural and religious themes, and several portraits of Russian tsars. There is some pleasant 19th-century Russian porcelain too. The gallery to the left, devoted to western Europe, is an even more mixed bag. Most of the landscapes and portraits are ascribed to unknown Dutchmen, Englishmen, Germans or Spaniards, but there are some big names represented here, albeit with mostly minor works, including Poussin and Tiepolo. There are displays of 18th-century Sevres and Meissen porcelain, including Meissen figurines of a group of musicians and their conductor. The prints on display are stamped with the label of the 'State Museum of the Turkmen Soviet Socialist Republic', revealing something of the origins of the older items in the collection.

Monuments to Niyazov's family

The building to the west of the Arch of Neutrality is the optimistically titled **World Trade Complex**. Behind this, in a pleasant, tree-shaded concrete park is the monument known as ***Ene Mahri*** ('Maternal Love'), based around the love of Gurbansoltan Eje for her son, Saparmurat Niyazov. Gurbansoltan Eje holds her baby boy tenderly in her arms, while standing on what may be a small, fluffy cloud. This in turn rests on a cylindrical column of red marble, which emerges from an open flower in the middle of a pond. Turkmen officials lay bouquets of flowers at this monument during major state holidays.

A long strip of well-manicured parkland running westwards takes you from this monument to President Niyazov's mother towards one honouring his father. On the way, you pass a small **Monument to Niyazov's Brothers**, Niyazmurat and Mukhammetmurat, killed in childhood in the 1948 earthquake. The **war memorial** at the western end of the park commemorates those Turkmens killed during World War II through the person of Niyazov's father, Atamurat, here depicted in uniform, his cloak billowing in an imaginary breeze, resolutely grasping his rifle, which he holds like a staff. An eternal flame burns in front of him, while reliefs behind the statue of Atamurat portray soldiers anxiously watching to his left and right. The composition rests in a pool, framed inside a curving rear wall. Two slender obelisks flank the monument, which is another favoured venue for the laying of wreaths, especially during the 8 May day of remembrance for those killed in the war.

North of the Arch of Neutrality

The roughly symmetrical marble-faced buildings either side of Bitarap Turkmenistan Kochesi, to the north of the Arch of Neutrality, are the Ashgabat

Governor's office and the headquarters of the Democratic Party of Turkmenistan. Amongst the many government buildings in this area, one worthy of note is the building housing the headquarters of Turkmenistan Airlines, a couple of hundred metres east of the governor's office, for the model of a Boeing aeroplane which decorates its roof. One block to the north of here is the road named Georogly Kochesi heading west; Shevchenko Kochesi to the east. Walking westwards, you reach the Carpet Museum, next door to the Sheraton Grand Turkmen Hotel.

Turkmen Carpet Museum

The Turkmen Carpet Museum is at 5 Georogly Kochesi (☎ 12 398879; open Mon–Fri 10.00–18.00, with a lunchbreak 13.00–14.00, closed Sun). Admission costs 119,500 manat. The museum displays a good range of carpets from across Turkmenistan in its two floors of galleries, which splay out either side of the entrance hall. To the left on the ground floor are Yomud carpets from western Turkmenistan. On the first floor are many Tekke and Sarik carpets and carpet bags. The displays feature both antique pieces of the 18th and 19th centuries and modern designs, the latter sometimes making a political statement. A carpet from 1968, incorporating designs characteristic of different regions of Turkmenistan, is labelled 'the carpet of brotherhood of all Turkmen tribes'. Nearby is a carpet portraying the family of President Niyazov. The space between these galleries is occupied by a hall, whose back wall is covered by a huge Tekke carpet, covering an area of 193m². This was the work of 40 carpet-makers, who toiled during 1941–42 to produce a carpet apparently intended for use as a curtain at the Bolshoi Theatre in Moscow. It proved too heavy for that purpose, and so was returned to Turkmenistan. A small carpet at its base lists the names of the carpet-makers who worked on this great project.

This huge carpet is a minnow in comparison with the one lurking in an extension building at the end of the western gallery of the museum. This is a Tekke carpet, covering 301m², a prodigious 21.2m in length and 14m in width. It was woven in 2001 by 40 carpet-makers of the Baharly state carpet enterprise, who completed the task in time for the tenth anniversary of Turkmenistan's independence. The carpet is dedicated to the 'golden age of Saparmurat Turkmenbashy the Great', and includes President Niyazov's signature, in yellow lettering three fingers wide. Proudly attached to the carpet is a certificate from 'Guinness World Records', supporting the claim that this is indeed the largest hand-woven carpet in the world. The extension building was constructed specifically to house it.

Statues to past and foreign leaders

Opposite the Hotel Turkmenistan, on Shevchenko Kochesi, stands a small bust of the Ukrainian poet **Shevchenko**, on a square column. Taking Bitarap Turkmenistan Shayoly northwards from here brings you to the **Old Parliament** building, with its curved drive and façade dominated by chunky Corinthian columns. Plenty of Soviet imagery remains on show here, including hammers and sickles in the tile-work above the entrance, and five-pointed stars and Soviet medals in the reliefs. The building has been a centre of government administration in both the Soviet and post-independence periods.

A block to the east of here, in a small area of park behind the new Magtymguly Theatre, is an unexpected survival from the Soviet period, a **Monument to Lenin**. The foundation stone was laid on the day of Lenin's funeral in January 1924, but the statue was not completed until 1927. The three-tiered base is attractively decorated with tiles, using patterns inspired by the motifs of Turkmen carpets. Inscriptions on the monument suggest that Leninism is the way to the liberation of the peoples of the East and record that the monument is a gift to the leader from the workers and peasants of Turkmenistan. A small museum was once housed inside the monument. The bronze statue depicts Lenin addressing the people, his right arm outstretched, gesturing towards the east. He holds his cap in his left hand, and a rolled-up newspaper sticks out of his jacket pocket.

Opposite the Lenin statue is a concrete conference centre, the **Mekan Palace**, which now houses the headquarters of the World Turkmen Humanitarian Association. The building is an early 1970s construction, which features some striking exterior reliefs by sculptor Ernst Neisvestniy. Best of all is the abstract end wall, in which can be discerned two heads in the midst of an argument, an arm around someone's throat, a hammer, a woman in Turkmen dress and a large pair of lips.

Southeast of here, in parkland, is a **Monument to Pushkin**, a small bust resting on a large column. A plaque records that, on 6 June 1999, earth from Pushkin's grave was laid at the base of the monument to mark the 200th anniversary of the birth of the Russian poet. A block further south and east, back across Shevchenko Kochesi, is a **Monument to Ataturk**, standing in the centre of a park whose lamp-posts are decorated with the twin flags of Turkmenistan and Turkey. The park, which stands appropriately opposite the Turkish Embassy, was opened during the 1998 visit to Ashgabat of President Demirel.

Ashgabat Park

Shevchenko Kochesi crosses the main north–south artery of Turkmenbashy Shayoly. Heading north along the latter road, you pass on your right the pink-coloured building now housing the Russian Embassy, which was built for a visit to Ashgabat by Nehru, though apparently never used by the Indian leader. The two-storey building is dwarfed by a white-marble apartment block, constructed on the site of the old Hotel Oktyabrskaya, reached through a curving arcade of marble-faced columns typical of the designs favoured in post-independence Ashgabat.

Across the road, the energetic fountains signal the presence of the oldest park in Ashgabat. Now officially titled **Ashgabat Park**, this rectangle of greenery is more widely known by its Soviet name of First Park (the sinister-sounding *Perviy Park* in Russian). The park was laid out in 1887, using convict labour. The place was originally known as the Officers' Park, and entry was restricted to privileged sections of tsarist Ashgabat society. An odd little folly in the park, comprising a small hillock topped by a pavilion, dates from the tsarist period. The video rental store occupying the space inside the hillock is a more recent addition. The open-air auditorium here once housed the Philharmonic Society named after Milli Techmiradov. The *telpek*-ed bust of Techmiradov which stood outside it has been removed, though the plinth is still there. The park houses a small funfair, decaying basketball court and unwelcoming-looking concrete restaurant.

Along Magtymguly Shayoly

Heading west along the main thoroughfare of Magtymguly Shayoly from Ashgabat Park, you pass the Turkmenistan Trade Centre. Between the trade centre and the purpose-built US Embassy, the pastel green single-storey building is one of the very few structures in Ashgabat to survive the 1948 earthquake. It was built in 1902 to house the Ashgabat branch of the Russian State Bank.

A block further to the west, where Magtymguly Shayoly is crossed by Bitarap Turkmenistan Shayoly, the building on the corner whose entrance is flanked by two concrete *rhytons* is the **Ministry of Foreign Affairs**. Opposite this is the **Institute of Geology**. This is one of several institutes (others include buildings devoted to desert research, and seismology) clustered around the open space just to the south, on the east side of Bitarap Turkmenistan Shayoly. The complex was once the heart of the Academy of Sciences, dissolved by President Niyazov. The open space is flanked to the north and south by pleasant arched arcades, a good example of 1950s building in Ashgabat, when architects strove to create an identifiably local style.

The Institute of Geology houses an eight-roomed **Geological Museum**, many of whose exhibits were put together for the 1984 International Geological Congress in Moscow. The museum owes much to the efforts of its director, Anatoliy Bushmakin, who has assembled most of the collection from expeditions across Turkmenistan, and painted the scenes of prehistoric life and portraits of Soviet geologists which decorate the walls. The rooms are heavy on display cases packed with rock samples, much of which is of rather specialist interest. Among the more interesting exhibits are sharks' teeth found in the heart of the Kara Kum Desert, dating from the time in which Turkmenistan lay submerged beneath the ancient Sea of Tethys. There are gypsum casts of the dinosaur footprints found at Hojapil in the Lebap Region (see page 198), a display featuring fragments of meteorites falling on to Turkmen territory, and several rooms devoted to mineral resources of current or potential commercial value, including a cabinet full of teacups, made with the help of the bentonite of the Balkan Region.

One side room is almost a time capsule to the Soviet period, presenting the samples collected by the children of Ashgabat's young geologists' club during their expeditions to wild places across the USSR.

The museum has no admission charge or fixed opening times. Phone in advance (☎ 12 353798) to arrange a visit. The entrance is from the courtyard at the back of the Institute of Geology building.

Continuing westwards along Magtymguly Shayoly, a statue of the Turkmen poet after whom the avenue takes its name sits on a small rock in the middle of a concrete square of parkland. The **Monument to Magtymguly**, constructed in 1971, shows the poet in thoughtful mood, keeping his book open at the correct page with the aid of his index finger. White marble-faced government ministries line both sides of Magtymguly Shayoly just to the west of here. A particularly eye-catching monument on the south side of the road, marking the entrance to a pedestrian street leading to the Russian Bazaar, is a **triumphal arch**, in front of which strides a statue of President Niyazov.

West of the city centre

Zoo

Taking the street once named Azady Kochesi, now labouring under the name 2011 Kochesi, westwards from the city centre, you pass the Tekke Bazaar on your left, reaching Ashgabat Zoo after perhaps a further 15-minute walk. Entered through an archway decorated with a pleasing frieze of elephants, camels and flamingos, the zoo is a run-down place. Its star attractions include Misha, a bear given to Niyazov in 2002 by the then President of Georgia, Shevardnadze, and an ailing lion with a bad paw. Much of the rear of the zoo has been turned over to gardening, to provide food for the animals. The cages still occupied by wildlife are pretty decrepit, and the stench from the duck pond hangs over the whole place. The monkey cage is full of birds, and wolves and hyenas prowl disconsolately around the perimeters of their undersized cages. A sign on the partridge cage announces that these birds were a gift from the president. Niyazov has announced plans to build a new zoo, on a more spacious site on the edge of town. I hope they materialise. The zoo is open during the summer months 08.00–19.30, except Mondays. In winter it opens 09.00–17.30. Entry costs 2,000 manat, though children and soldiers get in half price.

Back on 2011 Kochesi, heading one block east, towards the city centre, take quiet 2048 Kochesi a few metres northwards, to reach an area of parkland cleared in 2005 after a Turkmen elder was said to have recalled in a dream that the site was linked to the family and childhood of President Niyazov. A marble plaque in the centre of the space reports that a monument is to be constructed here to mark Niyazov's birthplace'. A wizened mulberry tree nearby is linked in another plaque to Niyazov's youth.

School No 20

This suburban school is of note as the institute at which the future President Niyazov completed his secondary education. He studied here from 1954–1957. To reach it, head north along 2060 Kochesi, which meets 2011 Kochesi four blocks west of the zoo. You pass the Azady World Languages Institute on your right. A block further to the north turn left, and the school is on your right. A statue outside it shows the adult president helping a small girl with her lessons. If you can talk your way inside, the teachers may show you the wooden desk at which the future president studied, as well as a little museum exhibiting Niyazov's school reports.

Botanical Gardens

Further westwards, beyond the junction of 2011 Kochesi with Georogly Kochesi, sit Ashgabat's botanical gardens (☎ 12 341863, 341857), just beyond the Hotel Syyahat. Established in 1929, the gardens cover 18ha. They offer an antidote to the sterile 'parks' of the post-independence city, with their newly-planted conifers, tiled walkways, fountains and geometric precision. The botanical gardens are a mostly wild place, whose Russian language signs alerting you that you are now in the Central Asian zone, or the Mediterranean one, suggest an order which the passage of time has undermined. They are a favoured place for Turkmen courting couples, and also contain a place of shrine pilgrimage known as Borkut Baba. The municipal authorities attempted to level the tomb here, planting conifers across the site, apparently out of reluctance to see pilgrimage traditions practised in the heart of the Turkmen capital. But pilgrims have again marked out the outline of Borkut Baba's reputed grave with a line of stones, and continue to offer their prayers here. Borkut Baba is particularly associated with prayers for rain. The botanical gardens are open 09.00–18.00, except Wednesdays and Fridays. Admission costs 2,000 manat for adults, 1,000 for children.

Shahid Mosque

Across 2070 Kochesi from the Botanical Gardens lie the buildings of the **Agricultural University**, named after Kalinin in the Soviet period, but now renamed in honour of Saparmurat Niyazov. There is a golden statue of a seated Niyazov in front of the entrance, the president looking out across the road junction.

Driving westwards from here, along Georogly Kochesi, you pass the red-roofed buildings of the **Turkmen-Turkish University** on your right. Across the road is the **Shahid Mosque**, a cut-off, white marble-faced pyramid, topped by a dome patterned with green and blue hexagons. Two minarets, detached from the building, flank it. The mosque was built with support from the United Arab Emirates, in honour of those who died in the 1948 earthquake. On the eastern side of the mosque is a simple monument, a broken piece of rock on a concrete base, which just about retains a faded inscription to the victims of the earthquake.

Nearby is another monument, a white marble-faced cube featuring a design of a weeping woman and the year '1948'. Across the hillside behind the mosque is a large **cemetery**, its graves occupying hilltops and gullies. Graves of members of more well-to-do families are surrounded by fenced enclosures, and shaded with trees. Others are unmarked mounds. At the entrance to the cemetery, a short walk to the east of the Shahid Mosque, a simple memorial records that the cemetery is a place of burial of victims of the earthquake.

St Alexander Nevskiy Church

Magtymguly Shayoly heads westwards from the town centre, passing the concrete spaceship of the **Old Circus**, now used as the venue for occasional concerts. A couple of blocks further west is the **Gunesh Park**, still known by its Soviet name of Second Park, a pleasant place for a breather, with a large central fountain, wedding reception hall, rickety amusement park and some odd pieces of statuary. One of these features a silver Turkmen girl standing on a ball, holding her right arm out for balance, while in her left perches a small baby, to whom she appears to be lecturing. About the joy of standing on balls, perhaps.

Magtymguly Shayoly ends at the old Cosmos Cinema, now rebadged as the Alem Cultural Centre and looking decidedly run down. A plaque records that, during World War II, the 238th student infantry brigade was established here. Just to the left, the blue-domed mosque, decorated with attractive floral tiles, is part of the **Iranian Embassy** compound. Taking the footpath round the side of the old cinema, you will reach the **St Alexander Nevskiy Church**, one of the main Russian Orthodox places of worship in Ashgabat, and a rare survivor of the tsarist period. It is a yellow brick building, topped by a silver onion dome, with another smaller dome on top of the adjacent belltower. The brightly coloured interior is crowded with murals and paintings, including a doom-laden vision of hell, and a young George slaying the dragon. The church is almost surrounded by a barracks: the sound of Turkmen soldiers marching forms a backdrop to services.

East of the city centre

Ertogrul Gazy Mosque

Taking Shevchenko Kochesi eastwards from the city centre, you reach on the left-hand side the impressive Turkish-built Ertogrul Gazy Mosque, named in honour of the Turkic leader who, facing the Mongol advance into Central Asia, took his followers into Asia Minor in the 13th century. His son Osman founded there what would develop into the Ottoman Empire. The mosque takes its inspiration from Ottoman architecture, as a symbol of the ties between Turkmenistan and Turkey, and offers more than a nod towards the design of the Blue Mosque in Istanbul. It has a large central dome, around which four half-domes cluster. The corners of the mosque are marked by slender minarets 70m high, each with three encircling exterior galleries. On the northern side of the mosque is a courtyard surrounded by an arched portico, topped with a further series of small domes. The interior is a rich concoction of red and white marble arches, deep-red prayer mats, and a reddish-tinged light achieved through spot lighting and stained-glass windows. There is a striking *minbar*, or pulpit, with a sharply pointed conical roof decorated in blue and gold designs. The glass-fronted building in front of the mosque houses the Turkmen Council for Religious Affairs and the Turkish Cultural Centre.

Two blocks to the north, across Magytmguly Shayoly, is a large statue of the Turkmen poet **Kemine**, depicted with the fingers of one hand thrown up, as if grasping for an idea. His head is cocked slightly; another suggestion of a thoughtful, poetical mood.

Exhibition centre

Across Shevchenko Kochesi from the mosque is a large expanse of unkempt parkland, some of which has been turned over to fields. In the centre of this sits the square glass-sided pavilion which in the Soviet period housed the Exhibition of Economic Achievements, and is still widely known as VDNK after the related Russian-language acronym. Now the **Sergi Merkezi**, the building houses annual exhibitions devoted to the oil and gas industry of Turkmenistan and to the development of Ashgabat. The completion in 2005 of a glittering new white marble-faced exhibition centre in the heart of Ashgabat (see opposite) means, however, the eclipse of this place. A couple of hundred metres to the west, the inscription on a block of stone, resting on a concrete base, announces long-forgotten plans to build on that spot a memorial complex to those killed in the 1948 Ashgabat earthquake. Across Galkynysh (1995) Kochesi from the southeastern corner of this large open area is a curious monument, in which a large pile of bricks is kept aloft by two corrugated concrete panels. This is what remains of a structure erected in honour of the then Bulgarian Communist Party leader, **Dimitrov**. An embellishment ('Limp Bizkit Britney Spears') has been added by a graffiti artist with evidently eclectic musical taste.

Earthquake memorials

Two moving monuments lie in this part of town, marking the fields which became cemeteries following the 1948 earthquake. To reach the first, drive eastwards along Magtymguly Shayoly as far as the roundabout centred on an abstract concrete fountain, close to the Asia Planet amusement park. On the north side of the road here is an **earthquake memorial** depicting an open-sided cube, within which a mother and father are being tossed around by the tremor. Between them, though, their child stands proudly defiant, his arms outstretched above his head. The building across the road, which once housed the Chinese Embassy, has an interesting Soviet-era frieze on its end wall, depicting two enthusiastic youngsters running with arms aloft.

Another graveyard of victims of the earthquake is reached by driving eastwards along Atamurat Niyazov Shayoly from the intersection with Saparmurat Turkmenbashy Shayoly. A large field amidst blocks of Soviet housing is covered with the mostly unmarked mounds of 1948 burials. On the eastern side of the field is a simple but effective memorial featuring a seated woman, her head concealed in her grief, beneath an arch faced with red marble.

South of the city centre

Ten Years of Independence Park

To the south of the Ruhyyet Palace stretches a large expanse of grass, the Ten Years of Independence Park, which eventually rises to a mound on which stands a monument centred around ten Ahal Tekke horses. One for each year. The structure, built by the Turkish construction company Polimeks, has an eventful history: the first effort was rejected by President Niyazov as the horses were deemed not sufficiently to resemble Ahal Tekkes. The new version depicted more slender steeds, and passed scrutiny. Inevitably, the monument has been named 'forty legs' by the citizens of Ashgabat. South of the monument is a golden statue of President Niyazov.

The strip of parkland continues across Atamurat Niyazov Shayoly; this southern extension, opened in 2002, bearing the title **Golden Age Park of Saparmurat Turkmenbashy the Great**. It features a curved line of arches from which a curtain of water descends.

Several large government buildings, constructed by the French company Bouygues, surround the Ten Years of Independence Park. Immediately to the south of the Defence Ministry, the rectangular building with a square black dome and a line of white marble-faced columns around its exterior is the **Mejlis**, Turkmenistan's parliament. The next building to the south is the **exhibition centre**, completed in 2005; it has a huge portico which is reached by a large staircase. Opposite the park from the Mejlis is the building of the **Central Bank**, its function made clear by the imitation gold ingot, stamped with President Niyazov's head in silhouette, which dominates the façade. Next to this is the almost equally lavish building of the **Dayhan Bank**, the state-run agricultural bank.

Independence Park and Berzengi

Turkmenistan Independence Park

Taking Saparmurat Turkmenbashy Shayoly southwards from the city centre, beyond the Yimpash shopping centre and the Olympic Stadium, you eventually reach on your left the largest and most impressive of the parks which have been laid out during the post-independence period, the Turkmenistan Independence Park. Buses 16 or 34 will bring you here from the city centre. The park was first laid out in 1993 and forms a rectangle almost 2km long and just under a kilometre wide. Much of this area is covered by struggling plantings of coniferous trees, and the places of interest in the park form a series of set-pieces, which are not fully connected with each other. There is, though, a largely complete circuit around the edge of the park of fountains and assorted statuary, from dolphins to *rhytons*.

Altyn Asyr Shopping Centre

Reached from the northern side of the park, the Altyn Asyr shopping centre is housed in a decidedly unusual monument, a stepped, five-sided pyramid topped with a golden needle. Cascades of water run down each of the edges, into hexagonal pools. Between these cascades, across the sides of the pyramid, sheets of water occasionally flow down past the five-headed eagles resting on the steps, giving the birds a good shower in the process. The recurrence of the number five in the design of the monument is a reference to the five regions constituting Turkmenistan. The monument has acquired the nickname 'five legs'. The shopping centre inside the building is unimpressive, with many of the available units remaining empty.

Ruhnama Park

On the western side of the park is the *Ruhnama* Park which, according to the English-language inscription on the plaque at the entrance, was 'complited in February 2003'. The complited park is an homage to President Niyazov's book, and is centred on a huge statue of *Ruhnama* in the form of a giant-sized replica of the book's pink and green cover. On special occasions, the book opens up to create a double-paged 'screen' onto which are projected images of the achievements of post-independence Turkmenistan. The act of opening the book reportedly has a tendency to burn out the statue's motor, so the monument mostly remains closed. Around the base of the *Ruhnama* Monument is a golden frieze depicting the new buildings of Ashgabat. Around each of the eight columns at the entrance to the park is a metal ribbon, on which is inscribed a name. These represent President Niyazov's family tree, moving from the president himself on the southernmost column, back through seven generations.

Independence Monument

Occupying the highest ground in the park, at its southern end, is the Monument to the Independence of Turkmenistan. This has a domed base, from which rises a

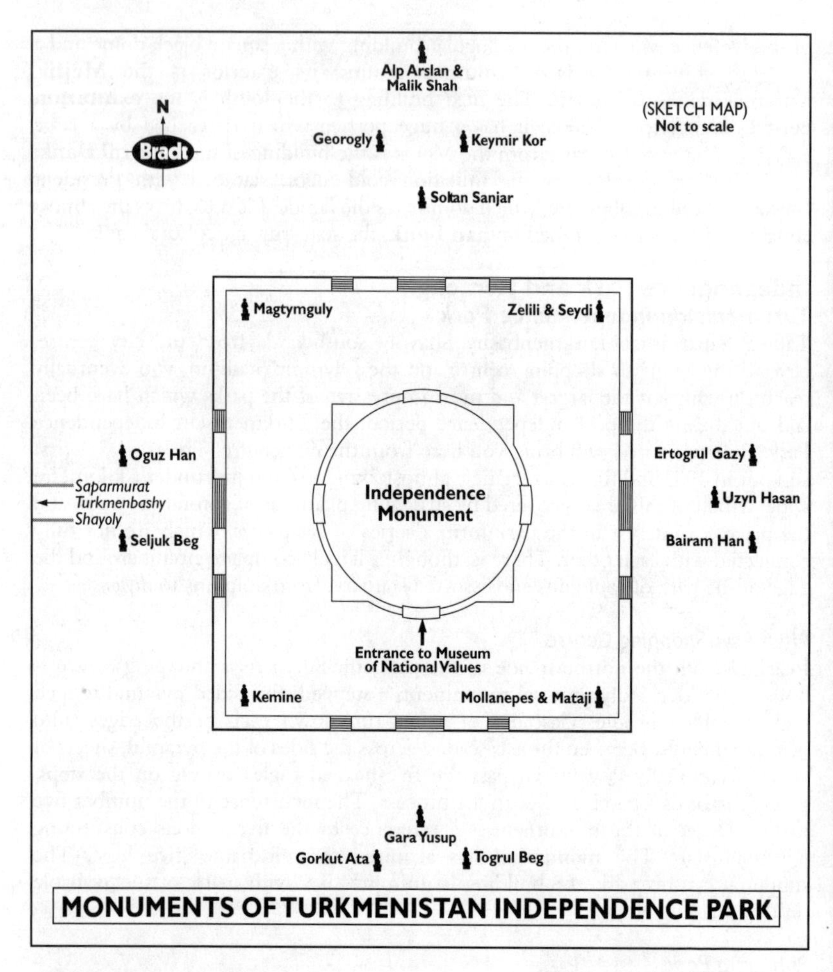

MONUMENTS OF TURKMENISTAN INDEPENDENCE PARK

central cylindrical column reaching a height of 118m. The figure 118 was chosen because of its significance to the independent state of Turkmenistan. If you are scratching your head over that one, note that Turkmenistan obtained its independence on 27 October 1991: 27 plus 91 equals 118. Obvious, really. The monument has been given the nickname 'eight legs', a reference to the eight struts across the domed base, down which flow channels of water. But another nickname gives a more accurate idea of the overall shape of the structure: 'the plunger'. In fact the form of the monument is supposedly a paean to an item of female headgear known as a *gupba*. The column is decorated with two huge motifs of five-headed eagles, symbols of the Turkmen president, and is topped by a golden crescent moon. There is a viewing platform at 91m, reached by a lift inside the column, though this is open only to members of official delegations, with prior permission.

A path leads to the Independence Monument from Saparmurat Turkmenbashy Shayoly. It is guarded by four large statues of Turkmen warriors. You are then greeted by a golden statue of President Niyazov, with a two-man guard of honour. The president's statue stands at the heart of a pentagonal fountain, which also includes five golden five-headed eagles, each in the process of crushing a two-

THE MONUMENTS OF TURKMENISTAN INDEPENDENCE PARK

Seljuk Beg The grandfather of Seljuk leaders Chagry Beg and Togrul Beg, identified in *Ruhnama* as the founder of the Seljuk Turkmen dynasty. Depicted as a wild-eyed figure, caressing his golden sword.

Oguz Han The legendary founder of the Turkmen people, here holding aloft a golden bow and three arrows.

Magtymguly The 18th-century Turkmen poet, wielding a quill pen.

Sultan Sanjar Seljuk leader, depicted holding a little model of his mausoleum in his right hand.

Georogly Legendary Turkmen warrior hero, here shown preparing to take his sword from its scabbard.

Alp Arslan and Malik Shah Seljuk rulers. The seated Alp Arslan is portrayed as a bellicose figure in chain mail, while the standing Malik Shah is more studious, his right hand clutching a rolled-up parchment.

Keymir Kor Legendary leader of the Ahal Tekkes in the first part of the 18th century, under whose guidance the Tekkes took control of the piedmont belt. Depicted as a proud man of noble bearing.

Zelili and Seydi Turkmen poets. Zelili is depicted as a rather emaciated figure, but Seydi is clearly made of stronger stuff.

Uzyn Hasan Leader of a tribal confederation known as Ak Goyunly ('White Sheep') which controlled in the 15th century large areas of present-day Turkey, Iran, Iraq and the South Caucasus. Here shown holding a standard featuring a sheep's head, portraying the alarm of an animal wondering where the rest of its body has gone.

Ertogrul Gazy Took his tribe from Khorasan to Asia Minor in the wake of the Mongol advances in Central Asia. His son Osman was to found what became the Ottoman Empire. Depicted as a chain-mailed man of action.

Bairam Han Ethnic Turkmen commander and poet of the Mughal Empire. Depicted as a thoughtful character, flicking through a book and perhaps pondering on his unusual taste in headgear, which looks like it belongs to the costume department of a 1970s' sci-fi series.

Mollanepes and Mataji 19th-century Turkmen poets. The seated Mollanepes looks up at the other poet, while patting the head of an invisible child with his right hand. Books and parchments piled on a table testify to the subjects' scholarliness.

Gara Yusup A leader of another tribal confederation of the 14th and 15th centuries, known as Gara Goyunly ('Black Sheep') whose lands were later to fall under the control of the Ak Goyunly, led by Uzyn Hasan. Gara Yusup too is depicted holding a banner bearing the head of a discomfited sheep.

Togrul Beg A Seljuk ruler, here depicted with crown and mitre.

Gorkut Ata Legendary spiritual leader, the subject of the epic *Book of Gorkut*, who is identified by President Niyazov as the central figure of the second Golden Age of the Turkmen people (after that of Oguz Han), around the 6th century. Depicted as a wise elder, with long beard and staff.

Kemine Turkmen poet of the late 18th and early 19th centuries.

headed snake. Jets of water spout from 35 of the possible 36 mouths in the composition. This statue is a favoured place for Turkmen newly-weds to be photographed. From here the path heads up the slope to the Independence Monument. Another guard of honour stands watch at the monument itself. The ceremony of the changing of the guard, which seems to take place at 11.00 and 16.00, is an occasion for much goose-stepping. Around the Independence Monument are a series of statues of the historical leaders, notable Turkmen poets and figures of legend whose lives and works are praised in *Ruhnama* and the other nation-building works of the Turkmen government.

Museum of Turkmen National Values

The Independence Monument is home to a Museum of Turkmen National Values (☎ 12 451954), open daily 09.00–17.30, with a lunch break 12.30–14.00. The admission fee is a heavy US$10, with another 25,000 manat fee to take photographs. The entrance is on the south side of the monument. The ground floor features elegant display cases offering Turkmen-language descriptions of the achievements of post-independence Turkmenistan, plus some displays on Turkmen history, focusing on the many states identified in *Ruhnama* as having been founded by Turkmens. The unlabelled displays of pottery from Margush are much less interesting than the exhibits at the National Museum. A display case of copies of *Ruhnama* features different language versions of the book, open at the page setting out the national oath. The only English-language labelling in the museum is the texts of various key pieces of post-independence legislation, such as a presidential resolution of February 14 1994 on the provision to the people of Turkmenistan of free salt.

A marble staircase with glass balustrades takes you to the first floor. There is a display of coins from ancient times to the present day. This is the only place you are likely to see the post-independence 1 tenne piece, its value 100th of a manat. A collection of coins of the world includes such rarities as a British 2p piece from 1979. There are displays of silver jewellery destined for women and horses, and actual-size replicas of the gold bull- and wolf-head sculptures found at Altyn Depe (see page 129). A display of modern jewellery features glittering jewelled Niyazov lapel badges and miniature models of the Neutrality Arch. There is a display case of watches decorated with the president's head in profile, and a collection of Turkmenistan's post-independence medals, which include the Orders of Neutrality, Turkmenbashy and Gurbansoltan Eje.

National Museum

Opened in 1998 during a visit to Turkmenistan of Turkish President Demirel, the National Museum (☎ 12 489018) is a sumptuous building in the southern suburb of Berzengi, its blue dome set attractively against the Kopet Dag Mountains behind. A path leads up to the museum from Archabil Shayoly, taking you past twin sculptures of winged horses and zig-zagging columned arcades, which trace a complex pattern around the central museum building. The museum is open 10.00–17.00, except Tuesdays.

The large space beneath the central dome is an area designed to awe rather than inform. Five clusters of columns, representing the five Turkmen regions, support the dome. In the centre of the space between them is a model of the Turkmen state emblem, on a golden plinth. Between the columns are display cases with copies of the texts of some of the key documents in the life of post-independence Turkmenistan, including the 1995 UN General Assembly resolution granting the country its neutrality. The permanent collection of the museum is laid out in eight halls on the ground and first floors. The second floor is used to house temporary exhibitions, usually coinciding with the main national holiday events.

Hall 1, to the left of the main entrance on the ground floor, is dedicated to post-independence Turkmenistan, centred on a large picture of President Niyazov. Display cases set out the achievements of independent Turkmenistan in education, medicine and sport. There are a number of gifts presented to the president, including an ornate silver sabre. The museum then continues upstairs. **Hall 2** focuses on ancient history, including offering a diorama of Mesolithic life in the cave of Dam Dam Chashma in Balkan Region. There are some fascinating exhibits from Bronze Age sites, including a charming smiley-faced toy clay chariot from Altyn Depe and a terracotta female statuette with sharply pointed breasts. There is an interesting range of artefacts from the Bronze Age Margiana sites in Mary Region too, including stamp seals, ivory items and a bronze mirror.

Hall 3 is based around artefacts found at the Parthian site of Nisa. There are some wonderful items, including a marble statue of Princess Rodogon, daughter of Mithradates II. According to a popular legend, the princess was caught washing her hair when the royal residence was suddenly attacked. She jumped onto her horse and, wet-haired, led the Parthian forces into battle. The range of items on display is nicely captured by the display-case label reading: 'Head of Aphrodita. Fragment of female statuette. Bulls.' But the star exhibits here are the *rhytons*, the exquisitely decorated ivory drinking horns found at Nisa in 1948, their bases decorated with creatures such as gryphons and centaurs.

Hall 4 focuses on the medieval period. A model of the Merv site in the centre of the room depicts the main surviving buildings, though not accurately placed in relation to each other. There are diorama scenes of Konye-Urgench and the mosque at Anau. Among the artefacts on display is the 'Merv vase', a beautifully decorated twin-handled jar, showing scenes depicting the stages of life, which was uncovered at the site of the Buddhist stupa in Merv. Other items include a range of glazed ceramics from Merv, and fragments of decoration from a mosque at Dandanakan, the site of the Seljuk victory over the Ghaznavids in the 11th century.

Hall 5 is devoted to ethnography, including displays of 18th- and 19th-century weaponry, a collection of Turkmen musical instruments, and a display focused on religion and belief, including a selection of amulets. The ethnography continues in **Hall 6**, which has a wide range of Turkmen silver jewellery and displays of female dress from different parts of Turkmenistan. The collection then continues back downstairs.

Hall 7 is dedicated to carpets, and is dominated by a real monster: 20.6m long, 12.9m wide, and weighing in at a tonne. Based around the Tekke design, and filling the rear wall of the hall, the carpet was the work of 38 carpet-makers, commissioned for the fifth anniversary of Turkmenistan's independence in 1996, and is named 'Turkmenbashy'. It has lines of 20 Tekke motifs, or *guls*, across its width, signifying the end of the 20th century, and a total of 480 *guls* in all, since the area of Turkmenistan is around 480,000km². At a total of 266m², it is a little over 30m² smaller than the Guinness World Records certificate-earning example in the Carpet Museum. Among the other carpets on display is one presented to President Niyazov for his 60th birthday in 2000, featuring the new medical facilities built since Turkmenistan's independence. The room also includes carpets characteristic of different Turkmen tribes, carpet bags and prayer rugs.

Hall 8 is devoted to the natural environment. A display case in the centre of the room houses an 820kg chunk of meteorite, which fell into a cotton field near Konye-Urgench in 1998, and was promptly named the Turkmenbashy Meteorite. There are numerous stuffed animals, most of which have unfortunately acquired peculiar grins, including a four-legged mutant eagle, and a Turan tiger, now extinct, which once prowled the forests of the Amu Darya.

Ministry of Oil and Gas

One other building in Berzengi worth a glance as you pass by is that housing the Oil and Gas Ministry, a stylish skyscraper built by the French construction company Bouygues in the form of a cigarette lighter. It lies on Archabil Shayoly, west of the museum.

AROUND ASHGABAT

Serdar Health Path

This is a concrete stepped path which snakes across the northernmost line of hills of the Kopet Dag, immediately to the south of Ashgabat. To get here, take the broad Archabil Shayoly from Berzengi. The health path meets the road where the hills begin. There is a car park. Infrequent buses make the trip for 500 manat.

The **Saparmurat Turkmenbashy Eternally Great Park** was opened here at the base of the health path in May 2005, and quickly became a favoured place for summer evening strolling for Ashgabat residents opting against the steep slopes of the health path. The park boasts manicured lawns, open-sided pavilions, vast cohorts of street lights and, on selected evenings, an illuminated artificial waterfall. In front of the arched entrance to the park, a stone ball rotates continuously atop a fountain. At the back of this park is a markedly less well-tended park dedicated to Turkmen-Turkish friendship, featuring 12,000 trees brought from Turkey.

The most heavily used part of the health path stretches westwards from here for 8km, ending close to the site of Old Nisa. The path is lined by metal balustrades and frequent lamps, providing a meandering line of light which can be clearly seen at night from planes flying into Ashgabat Airport. At roughly 1km intervals, small golden-domed pavilions provide a place to rest. The health path does not provide the pleasantest of walks – the initial stretch is a steep climb along a concrete stairway to reach the ridge of the hills. But the views from the top are good, down towards Ashgabat beyond large areas newly planted with straight rows of conifers: all part of President Niyazov's scheme to create a green belt around Ashgabat. The small complex of white marble-faced buildings between the path and Berzengi is the **Palace of Orphans**, a gift to Turkmenistan from the United Arab Emirates.

The highest point on the health path is marked by a large Turkmen flag. A helipad just beneath this was used by President Niyazov at the opening ceremony. The president flew to the top to greet his ministers and officials, who had made the journey the hard way. There is a much longer stretch of path heading eastwards from Archabil Shayoly, but this is less widely used, and is in a poor state of repair.

Turkmen television frequently extols the health-giving benefits of regular walks along the path. Niyazov held a Cabinet meeting there in March 2003, when he chided his ministers for taking the 8km stretch too slowly. They should be able to do the walk in 90 minutes, he said. It would set them up for a good day at the office.

Archabil

Some 35km west of Ashgabat, in a pleasant green valley within the Kopet Dag Mountains, Archabil, known as Firuza until 2001, is the traditional summer retreat for the citizens of Ashgabat. It offers temperatures a crucial few degrees cooler than those of the plains.

Practicalities

There is a scenic route out here from Ashgabat. Head westwards on the road which starts out in Ashgabat as Georogly Kochesi. Pass the village of Bagyr, and then at Julge, further west, turn to the south through an attractive canyon, the **Firuza Gorge**. The little Firuzinka River babbles attractively through woodland at the foot of the canyon. This is a favourite place for summer picnickers from Ashgabat. For those seeking a more formal place for lunch, the **Maral Restaurant** at the northern end of the canyon serves good *shashlik*. Just beyond the canyon is the small settlement of Vanovskiy, where the road forks. Take the left-hand fork for Archabil. The resort can also be reached, more quickly but less scenically, by the Archabil Highway from Berzengi.

Access to Archabil has, however, progressively become more limited, because President Niyazov's main residence lies here. It is now a restricted zone, for which permission to enter must be requested with your Letter of Invitation. Taxis from Ashgabat are not allowed into the settlement: they will take you as far as Vanovskiy, where local Archabil taxis are usually waiting to take you the last few kilometres. Many holiday *dachas* in Archabil have been demolished, and the government is building up nearby Geokdere as the main summer holiday centre in the Kopet Dag Mountains, in preference to Archabil.

There is however one good hotel in Archabil. The 68-roomed **Hotel Serdar** (☎ 12 312076, 312536; f 12 312102) is run by the Ahal Group, which also includes the President and Nissa hotels in Ashgabat. It has four accommodation blocks, imaginatively lettered A to D, air-conditioned rooms, and suites with mini kitchens. There is an outdoor swimming pool and a restaurant which, like all those of the Ahal Group, specialises in Italian dishes. The interior décor is heavy on pink, and the hotel is decorated with posters of tourist destinations in Turkey. Basic rooms cost 410,000 manat. Suites are 550,000.

What to see

The chief sight in Archabil is a tree. The **'Seven Brothers'** is a plane tree, with seven tall trunks rising from a central base some 4m wide. An eighth trunk was long ago cut back. Locals will tell you that blood was seen to flow at the site of the cut. A golden railing surrounds the tree, and an information board in Russian and Turkmen tells the legend associated with it.

Long ago, in the territory of present-day Iran, lived a sheikh, who had seven sons and a beautiful daughter named Firuza. These were troubled times, and the sheikh was forced to cross into the Kopet Dag Mountains to seek protection from rival tribes. He discovered this beautiful valley, and settled here. But his enemies found him, and killed all of his sons. Firuza then took up arms, and managed to defeat the aggressors, though she was herself fatally wounded in the battle. The grief-stricken sheikh buried his eight children close to each other, and planted a plane tree over each of their graves. As time passed, the plane trees gradually grew together into a single tree. The story of the 'Seven Brothers' is illustrated in a series of painted panels behind the tree. It stands in a military compound but free access is given.

To the north of here is a pleasant, if slightly run-down, park, which marks the centre of town. It offers cute statues of elephants, bears and panthers, a couple of *shashlik* options, with open-air dining on *tapchans* beneath the trees, and a summer disco. Much of the rest of town comprises government *dachas* and children's summer camps belonging to various ministries. The camps, decorated with slogans and paintings inspired by President Niyazov's works, are, however, being closed in favour of new sites in Geokdere. The small river flowing through town is tamed inside a concrete channel, which rather diminishes its romantic value.

The **presidential residence** on the north side of town is both invisible and unmistakable, as it is concealed by a long and high wall. An independence museum, being built nearby as a gift from the United Arab Emirates, was deemed to have occupied a site *too* close to the presidential residence, and construction was halted. The presence of the residence also means that attempts to walk in the hills around Archabil are likely to earn a rebuke from one of the many people in uniform around the town.

Geokdere

With the increased difficulties for foreigners and Turkmen citizens alike in getting to Archabil, the village of Geokdere, formerly Chuli, has become the preferred summer hill resort for Ashgabat. Some 45km from the Turkmen capital, it is reached by taking the right-hand fork from Vanovskiy settlement, rather than the left-hand route to Archabil. Alternatively, it can be reached from the main Ashgabat to Turkmenbashy road, via a marked turning 31km west of Ashgabat, beyond Abadan. The road reaches the line of the hills after 8km, and you reach the first of the children's summer camps 7km further on.

The tree-shaded streams of Geokdere offer popular picnic sites, which on pleasant weekends in late spring can get decidedly crowded. The cumulative litter effect of large numbers of picnickers can also somewhat diminish the natural beauty of the place. But there is some excellent walking in the hills and ravines to the south of the settlement. In spring, when the hills are covered in a carpet of poppies, tulips and other wild flowers, the scenery becomes spectacular.

The best-quality accommodation in Geokdere is provided by the 30-roomed **Central Bank Geokdere Training and Health Centre** (**`** 12 313166; **f** 12 313172). Notwithstanding the title of the place, it functions basically as a hotel, though you will probably find that your fellow guests are mostly Central Bank employees, who get a large discount. The hotel is Turkish built and, although it is starting to display the signs of poor maintenance, the air-conditioned rooms with en-suite facilities are good value at US$30. There is a swimming pool, with a dirty perspex roof, which is heated in winter and charged at 20,000 manat per hour. Tennis and billiards cost 30,000 manat an hour. Breakfast is not included in the room price.

Across a small stream from the Central Bank Centre lies a **holiday camp** (**`** 12 313111), offering small and basic cottages under the trees for 25,000 manat a bed. These are popular with Ashgabat families anxious to escape the summer heat of the capital.

Ahal Region: the Heart of Turkmenistan

4

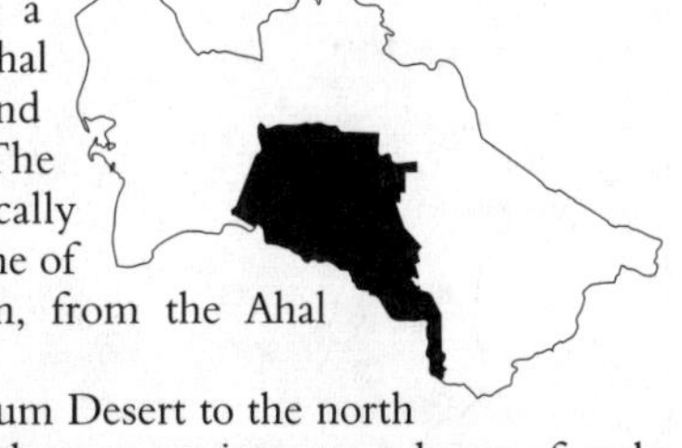

Centred on Ashgabat, which is, however, a separately administered capital territory, Ahal Region is geographically, politically and historically Turkmenistan's heartland. The region, and the Ahal branch of the locally dominant Tekke tribe, are the source of some of the best-known symbols of Turkmenistan, from the Ahal Tekke horse to the Tekke carpet design.

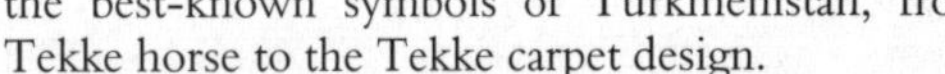

The piedmont lands between the Kara Kum Desert to the north and the Kopet Dag Mountains to the south were an important locus of early agricultural development, at sites such as Jeitun and Anau. This strip of land, the Ahal Oasis, later marked one of the main routes of the Silk Road. It was in this region, through the capture of the Turkmen stronghold of Geok Depe in 1881, that the Russians were able to consolidate their control over Central Asia. In the Soviet period, the construction of the Kara Kum Canal across the region brought a new phase of agricultural development, focused on cotton. President Niyazov's childhood home lay in this region, in the village of Gypjak, close to Ashgbat.

Ahal Region offers a wealth of interesting archaeological sights. Many of these, such as the Parthian site of Old Nisa, are easy day trips from Ashgabat. There are some superb places of natural beauty too. Some, such as the underground lake at Kow Ata, are straightforward excursions from Ashgabat. Others, such as the valleys and waterfalls around Nohur, require more planning. Close to the northern border of the region, in the depths of the Kara Kum Desert, a burning gas crater close to the settlement of Darvaza is a dramatic symbol of the results of man's interference with nature.

NISA

Some 15km west of Ashgabat, the village of Bagyr hosts one of the most popular destinations for a short excursion out of the capital: the Parthian site of Old Nisa, known as Konye Nusay in Turkmen. Old Nisa has a striking geographical location, on top of a small hill on the southeast side of the village, offering splendid views towards the Kopet Dag Mountains to the south. The western end of the Serdar Health Path is clearly visible at the foot of these hills. While most visitors see only Old Nisa, that site represents just a small part of the history of settlement here. A little over a kilometre to the northwest of the Old Nisa site, a series of ridges mark the walls of New Nisa (Taze Nusay), with the present-day village of Bagyr standing between the two. While Old Nisa, which seems to have been either a Parthian royal residence or temple complex, was abandoned at the end of the Parthian period, the main town of New Nisa was revived in the 5th century, and grew to become an important medieval Silk Road centre. It flourished under the Seljuks in the 11th and 12th centuries, and later fell under the domain of the

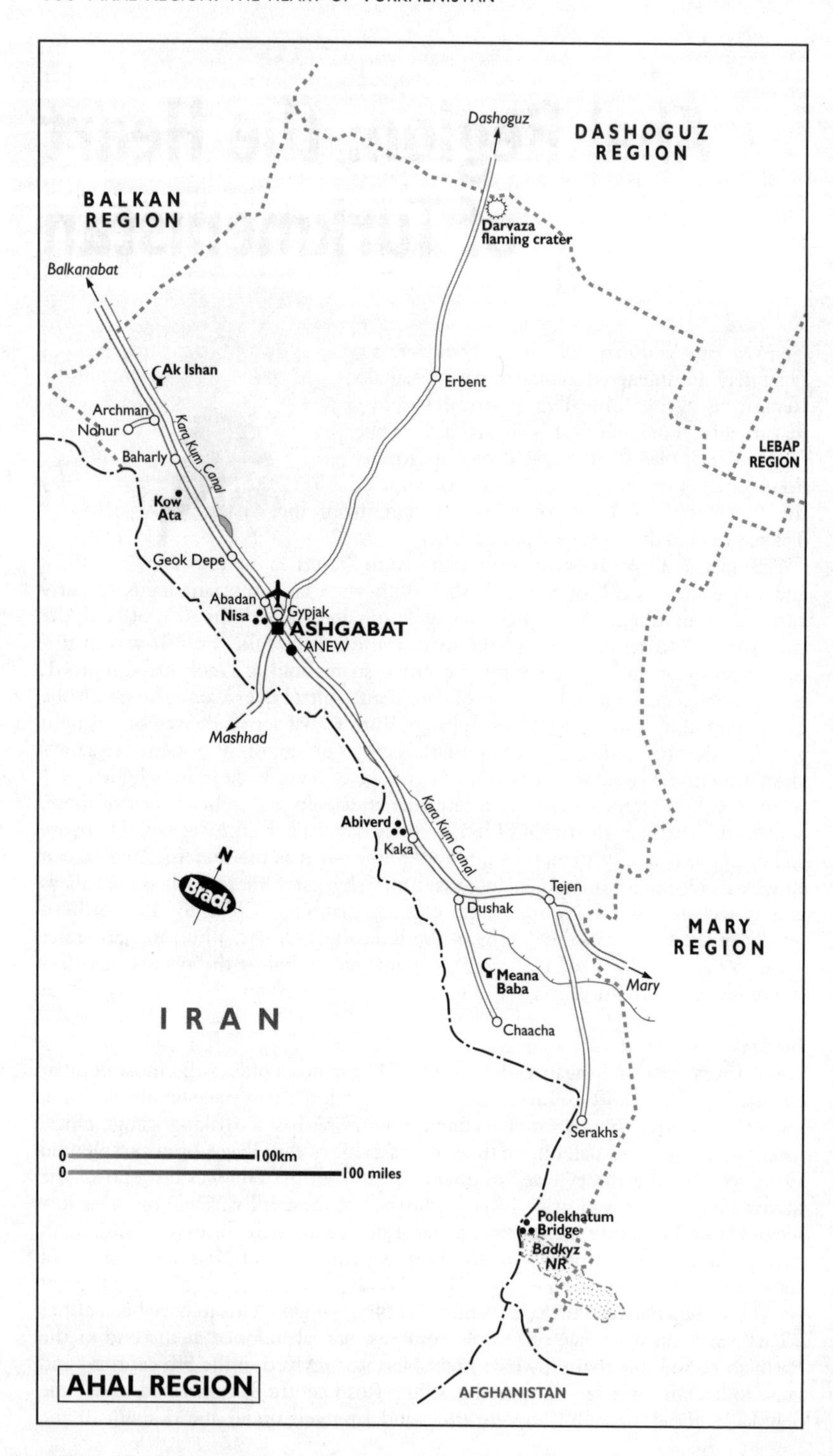
Dashoguz
DASHOGUZ REGION
BALKAN REGION
Darvaza flaming crater
Balkanabat
Ak Ishan
Erbent
Archman
Nohur
Kara Kum Canal
Baharly
LEBAP REGION
Kow Ata
Geok Depe
Abadan
Nisa
Gypjak
ASHGABAT
ANEW
Mashhad
Kara Kum Canal
Abiverd
Kaka
Tejen
Dushak
MARY REGION
Meana Baba
Mary
IRAN
Chaacha
Bradt
N
Serakhs
0 100km
0 100 miles
Polekhatum Bridge
Badkyz NR
AHAL REGION
AFGHANISTAN

Khorezmshahs. The Mongols sacked the town in 1220 with customary brutality, but it revived, to be finally abandoned in the early 19th century in favour of the adjacent new Tekke Turkmen settlement of Bagyr.

Practicalities

To reach Old Nisa from Ashgabat, take Georogly Kochesi westwards out of town, passing the ornate western gate into the city. Three kilometres further on, turn left at the roundabout, signposted to Bagyr, and then left again at another roundabout in the village. You will see a modern arch on your right welcoming you to Old Nisa. This is flanked with concrete models of the ivory drinking horns, *rhytons*, which are the best known of the artefacts uncovered at the site. There is a ticket office here (21,000 manat to visit), which also contains a useful relief model of Old Nisa. The site is through the arch and up the hill. Travel agencies in Ashgabat offer half-day tours to Nisa. A place in a minibus to Bagyr village costs around 3,000 manat, departing from the Tekke Bazaar in Ashgabat.

Immediately to the west of the arched entrance to the site, the **Nusay Restaurant** is a pleasant spot for a *shashlik* lunch. You can eat at plastic tables shaded by the trees or, if more privacy is desired, in bamboo wigwams. Water bubbles past along a concrete canal.

Another good, though sometimes over-popular, lunch spot lies between Bagyr and the village of Yanbash, back towards Ashgabat. Drive eastwards, past the entrance to the Old Nisa site, taking a right turn after a kilometre or so, just before the road crests the ridge. After 500m, take the unmetalled track to the right, leading down into the river valley. In the valley bottom you reach a collection of wooden platforms, *tapchans*, some built across the flowing stream itself, at which you are invited to lounge on cushions, and order *shashlik* and salad.

Old Nisa

The site of Old Nisa covers around 14ha, an irregular pentagon in plan, standing on a natural hill. The site is reached by way of a concrete staircase from the car park. A rather ugly viewing platform at the top was built for the visit here of an ailing President Mitterrand in 1994. Parthian inscriptions found during the course of excavations give the name of the fortress as Mithradatkirt. Some researchers have accordingly linked the construction of the site to the Parthian ruler Mithradates I. Others suggest that it was built earlier, possibly in the late 3rd century BC, and later renamed in honour of Mithradates. Archaeologists continue to debate the function of the complex. It has been described as either a royal residence or a religious complex. Or possibly both.

From the viewing platform, a concrete path leads across the site to the main complex of excavated buildings. Large depressions to your right probably mark the sites of water reservoirs. Continuing (currently Italian-led) excavations, some rather confusing conservation work and a reconstruction programme which has added a small museum in the heart of the excavated site all make it less than straightforward to get to grips with the plan of rooms and corridors, but there are some interesting structures to see here. In the southwestern corner of the main complex is a **round hall**, some 17m in diameter, its walls standing to a height of 4m or so. A row of statue-filled niches is believed to have run along the upper wall of this hall. Northwest of here lies the so-called **tower-like building**, the scene of recent conservation work which has controversially included the addition of a two-roomed **museum**, albeit using mud-brick construction and preserving the traces of plasterwork found on the original walls. The first room of the museum contains some delightful fragments of wall painting from Old Nisa and another

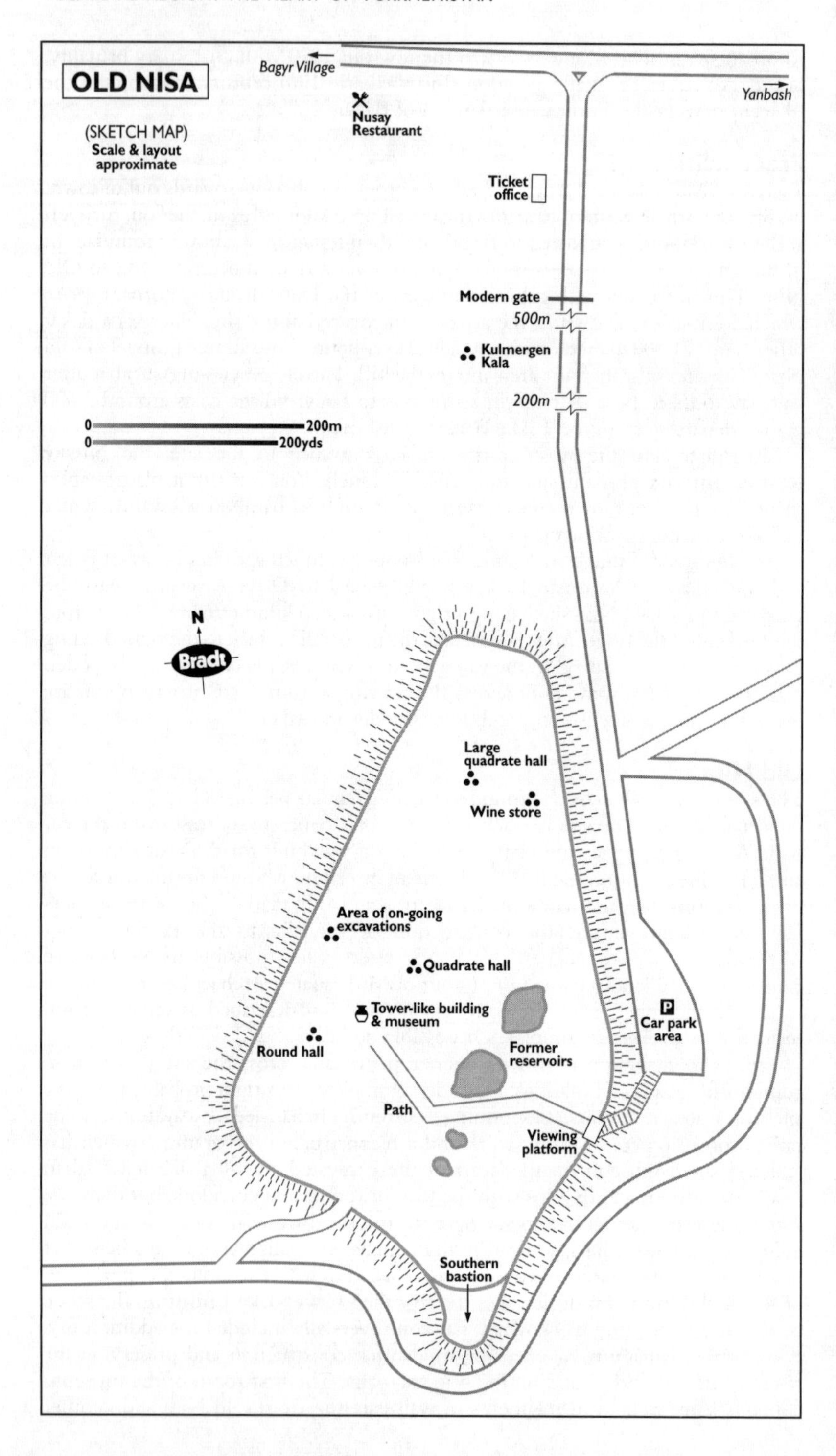
OLD NISA
(SKETCH MAP)
Scale & layout approximate
Bagyr Village
Yanbash
Nusay Restaurant
Ticket office
Modern gate
500m
Kulmergen Kala
200m
0 200m
0 200yds
N
Bradt
Large quadrate hall
Wine store
Area of on-going excavations
Quadrate hall
Tower-like building & museum
Round hall
Former reservoirs
P
Car park area
Path
Viewing platform
Southern bastion

Parthian site near by, Mansur Depe, as well as a large amphora. The second room is to be furnished to give the visitor a sense of life in the Parthian era. The museum is, however, frequently locked.

To the west side of the tower-like building lies the site of the latest excavations. To the northeast is the **quadrate hall**, with interior walls of roughly 20m, each wall containing six fired-brick columns. Where one of these columns is missing, an inverted semi-cylinder displays the horizontal marks once traced by ropes. Only one base survives of what were once four columns in the centre of the hall. It is an attractive survival – a sturdy-looking fired-brick column, its exterior presenting four semi-cylinders. All those fired-brick columns have led archaeologists to conclude that this was a tall structure, whose upper walls contained niches with large, brightly painted clay statues, fragments of which have been found. These depict both male and female figures. Archaeologists have proposed that the statues represented deified members of the Parthian dynastic leadership.

About 150m to the north of the quadrate hall is another assemblage of buildings. The structures remaining here are much less striking than those of the main complex, but it was from this northern complex that some of the most important artefacts found at Old Nisa were unearthed. The largest building here is the so-called **large quadrate hall**, square in plan with sides of 60m. Centred around a large courtyard, this building seems to have been a well-protected treasury. There was only one narrow entrance into the building, and the rectangular chambers around the yard seem to have been sealed with bricks as soon as they were filled. This did not stop the place falling later victim to robbers, but not everything was stolen. Archaeologists uncovered a collection of the beautiful ivory *rhytons* in 1948, carelessly thrown in a heap in one of the chambers. These drinking vessels have become one of the symbols of Turkmenistan, though some superstitiously recall that they were uncovered just before the 1948 earthquake devastated the area.

To the east of the treasury building, a **wine store** was identified, containing the large clay vessels which would have held the wine. This building proved particularly valuable to archaeologists because each of the vessels was accompanied by little clay shards, *ostraca*, on which mundane information was written about the origin and date of purchase of the wine. This information has allowed researchers to learn much about the economy and human geography of the region in Parthian times, and also to establish the Parthian name of the fortress itself.

Bagyr

The village of Bagyr has some further monuments worth a glance if you have time. To the west side of the access road leading to the Old Nisa site, you will see crumbling mud-brick walls. These are the ruins of **Kulmergen Kala**. These 19th-century defensive walls are rectangular in plan. Turkmen families would have lived in *yurts* and mud buildings within the courtyard protected by them.

On the far western side of the village is a mausoleum known as **Shikhalov**, a restored octagonal building with a domed roof. The tomb is said to be that of the 10th-century Sheikh Abu Ali Dakkak. A brick gate stands next to the mausoleum. Pilgrims say a prayer as they walk through it.

AROUND GYPJAK

After skirting to the north of Bagyr, the road to the west reaches the industrial town of **Abadan**, 25km from central Ashgabat. There is another road running between Ashgabat and Abadan. North of the Bagyr road, this is a smart highway, three broad lanes in each direction, which takes its name from the president's mother, Gurbansoltan Eje, and runs alongside the railway track. This route takes you to the heart of the iconography of the Turkmen government, passing through the model agricultural district of Ruhabat and Niyazov's birthplace of Gypjak.

Ruhabat

A police checkpoint marks the entrance to Ruhabat District, reached just 3km or so beyond the outskirts of Ashgabat. The district capital of Ruhabat is another kilometre on. President Niyazov has announced that Ruhabat is to be a model of a Turkmen village in the Golden Age. The concept appears to be that differences between village and city should disappear, with villagers accorded access to all facilities available to urban dwellers. At Ruhabat, a small settlement once known simply for its railway goods yard, large marble-faced buildings have appeared which do indeed seem to have been transplanted from the urban plan of Ashgabat.

Turn right across the railway line, and then left into the village, to get a closer look. Three white-marble buildings face the main road. The first reached is a shopping centre, semi-populated with a few state outlets, but usually lacking any customers. Next is a cultural centre named after Turkmenbashy the Great, with a columned façade. It is normally deserted. There is a little more life at the *Hyakimlik*, the office of the district governor, further on. This has a curved façade and palm trees out front. The road through the village then turns sharply to the right. A long two-storey marble-faced building just beyond is a school dedicated to the president's mother. A statue of Gurbansoltan Eje stands in front of it. She gestures hesitantly forward, her left arm protectively around her son, who holds up a copy of the book *Ruhnama*.

Gypjak

Another 7km on, the main road dips into an underpass. Turn right before entering it, and take the side road across the top of the underpass to reach the **Turkmenbashy Ruhy Mosque**, the largest in Central Asia. It stands on the edge of the village of Gypjak, where the terrible earthquake of October 6 1948 struck the Niyazov family, killing the president's mother and two brothers. The road takes you underground, to an elaborate subterranean car park, apparently able to hold 400 cars and 100 buses. Taking one of the staircases up to ground level, you emerge in the gardens of the mosque, with a view of the huge golden-domed building, flanked by four minarets, each reportedly 91m tall. Around each minaret are rings of Turkmen-language slogans, though the lowest ring in each case is comprised solely of exclamation marks. The mosque dominates the memorial complex for the victims of the 1948 earthquake, named after President Niyazov's mother Gurbansoltan Eje.

The mosque was built by the French construction company Bouygues, and opened to mark Earthquake Memorial Day in October 2004. The mosque is ringed by eight marble-faced arched entrances. Above the main arch, facing the road, an inscription reads, in Turkmen: '*Ruhnama* is a holy book; the Koran is Allah's book'. Two stone panels under the main arch carry the texts of the Turkmen national anthem and oath. Below the arches a cascade of water around the building runs into a long pool. The mosque building is octagonal in form, with seven heavy carved wooden doors. Above each of these is a circular stained-glass window, its design centred on the word 'Allah', in Arabic. The eighth wall houses the mihrab.

The spacious interior is marked out by a circle of 16 large columns. The dome is painted with a design of pastel lozenges, whose overall shape suggests a large flower. A line of latticed windows surrounds the base of the dome. Either side of these run two lines of Turkmen-language inscriptions in blue lettering, offering exhortatory quotations by President Niyazov. Immediately above the mihrab, the wording of both lines of lettering is the same: 'Saparmurat Turkmenbashy the Great'. A balcony, decorated with another line of Turkmen-language inscriptions, runs around the interior of the building. Small shelving units in the mosque offer copies of the Koran, and also books written by President Niyazov, including both volumes of *Ruhnama* and his books of poetry.

On the western side of the mosque is a place for the holding of the commemorative meal (*sadaka*) for those killed in the earthquake. This is a large open-sided columned area, with long, low marble tables behind which guests squat to dine. There is space here for 5,000 people. A large marble-covered head table is for the president and his senior ministers. The neighbouring kitchen area features a huge expanse of brick gas-fired *tamdyrs*, and circular brick receptacles in which cooking pots are placed for the making of *plov*. Bouguyes even built a pen for the sheep awaiting slaughter.

To the west of this complex is the original centre-piece of the **Gurbansoltan Eje Memorial Park**, a statue of an earthquake-tossed female figure protecting her son, which is dedicated to those killed in 1948. A flight of marble steps leading to this memorial is flanked by columns, designed to represent stylised female figures in Turkmen headgear, bowing their heads respectfully.

To the north side of the mosque, close to the road, is a golden-domed **mausoleum**. Inside are five tombs, the central one framed by an eight-pointed star design. An interior balcony rings the building. A female statue on the balcony, looking benevolently over the tombs below, is a replica of that of the memorial outside, an idealised representation of President Niyazov's mother. At a ceremony on 10 December 2004, the bodies of Niyazov's parents and two brothers were symbolically reburied in this mausoleum. The building, whose exterior is decorated by six granite eagles, is usually locked and guarded.

There is one more place to see, across the railway line in the village of Gypjak itself. This is a conifer-studded park, built by a Turkish construction company to mark President Niyazov's 60th birthday in 2000. The focus of the park is a semicircular arcade comprising a double row of marble-faced columns, framing a golden statue of the president, his right arm reaching forward. A book next to him rests on top of a squat Ionic column. Behind this statue a golden frieze depicts Niyazov's father heading off to war, his family bidding him farewell.

Abadan

The town of Abadan is 8km further on. Named Buzmeyin until 2002, President Niyazov proposed that the town be renamed, complaining that the name Buzmeyin did not mean anything, while Abadan ('Prosperous') was in his view one of the best Turkmen words. Niyazov worked at the power station here for three years, after graduating from the Leningrad Polytechnic Institute in 1967. His poem *Abadan* is printed on a large billboard at the entrance to the town. It is an autobiographical piece, telling of Sapar's happiness because the Golden Age has come and his country is prosperous.

GEOK DEPE

Continuing on the main road westwards from Abadan, you reach after another 23km the town of Geok Depe (telephone code 132), scene of a battle in 1881 which resulted in the subjugation of the Ahal Tekke Turkmens by the forces of the tsar. The thousands of Turkmen troops and civilians killed in that battle and the massacre which followed it are remembered every year on the anniversary of the battle.

THE SIEGE OF GEOK DEPE

The Tekke Turkmen tribes based around the Ahal Oasis refused to come to any accommodation with the Russians, who by the late 1860s had established themselves on the eastern shore of the Caspian. In particular, the Turkmens' slaving forays were becoming an increasing annoyance to the forces and interests of the tsar. Accordingly, in 1879 the local Russian commander, General Lomakin, was sent to take the key Turkmen camp at Geok Depe, in the centre of the oasis. The Turkmens routed the general's forces, severely denting Russian pride. The disgraced Lomakin was replaced as Commander-in-Chief of the Transcaspian Military District by General Mikhail Skobelev, a brilliant, brave and ruthless officer, whose moods swung violently between euphoria and depression. Skobelev had risen to prominence in Russia's Turkey campaign: he wore a white uniform into battle, replete with his medals, and rode on a white charger. He unsurprisingly acquired the nickname 'White General'. Skobelev had once authored a plan for the invasion of India, and his appointment worried the British, concerned at possible Russian designs on their empire.

Skobelev was detemined to avenge the defeat of 1879. With 7,000 troops and 60 artillery pieces, he reached Geok Depe at the end of 1880. Learning a lesson from Lomakin's experience, he decided to besiege the Turkmen fortifications, rather than make an immediate assault. But time was not on the Russians' side. They were far from their sources of supply, and fearful that the Tekke would be reinforced by their compatriots from Mary. In fact, the failure of the Mary Turkmens to come to the aid of the defenders echoes even today in the sometimes spiky relationship between Turkmens of Ahal and Mary regions. Skobelev's artillery was having an effect inside the fortress, but was making little impression on the walls. Skobelev therefore determined to tunnel beneath the wall, and mine it.

The mine, at the southeastern side of the fortress, was exploded on the morning of January 12, creating a 50m gap in the walls. Russian troops stormed the fortress, and by the early afternoon the Russian double-headed eagle was flying atop the hill of Dengil Depe in the heart of the Turkmen encampment. The Russians pursued the fleeing Turkmens with a brutality that would shock European public opinion. It is believed that around 6,500 Turkmens were buried in the fortress itself, and another 8,000 killed outside it, including many women and children. Skobelev admitted to the loss of only 268 Russian troops. Only one story of that day hints at compassion: Skobelev apparently spotted a three-year-old girl beside a pool of blood in the fortress. It being St Tatiana's Day, and the girl being a Tekke Turkmen, he named her Tatiana Tekhinskaya and sent her off to an orphanage in St Petersburg.

Skobelev was not to profit from his victory. The Russian authorities were concerned that Skobelev's military success and popularity were fuelling dangerous political ambition, and sent him off to a backwater job in Minsk. He was found dead, at the age of 38, in a bedroom of the Hotel Duseaux in Moscow, in somewhat compromising circumstances. After the fall of Geok Depe, the Ahal Tekkes were never again a source of trouble to the Russians. It is said that Turkmens present at the opening ceremony of the Transcaspian Railway fell to their knees when the military band started playing, having associated the sound of military music with the terrible carnage of January 12 1881.

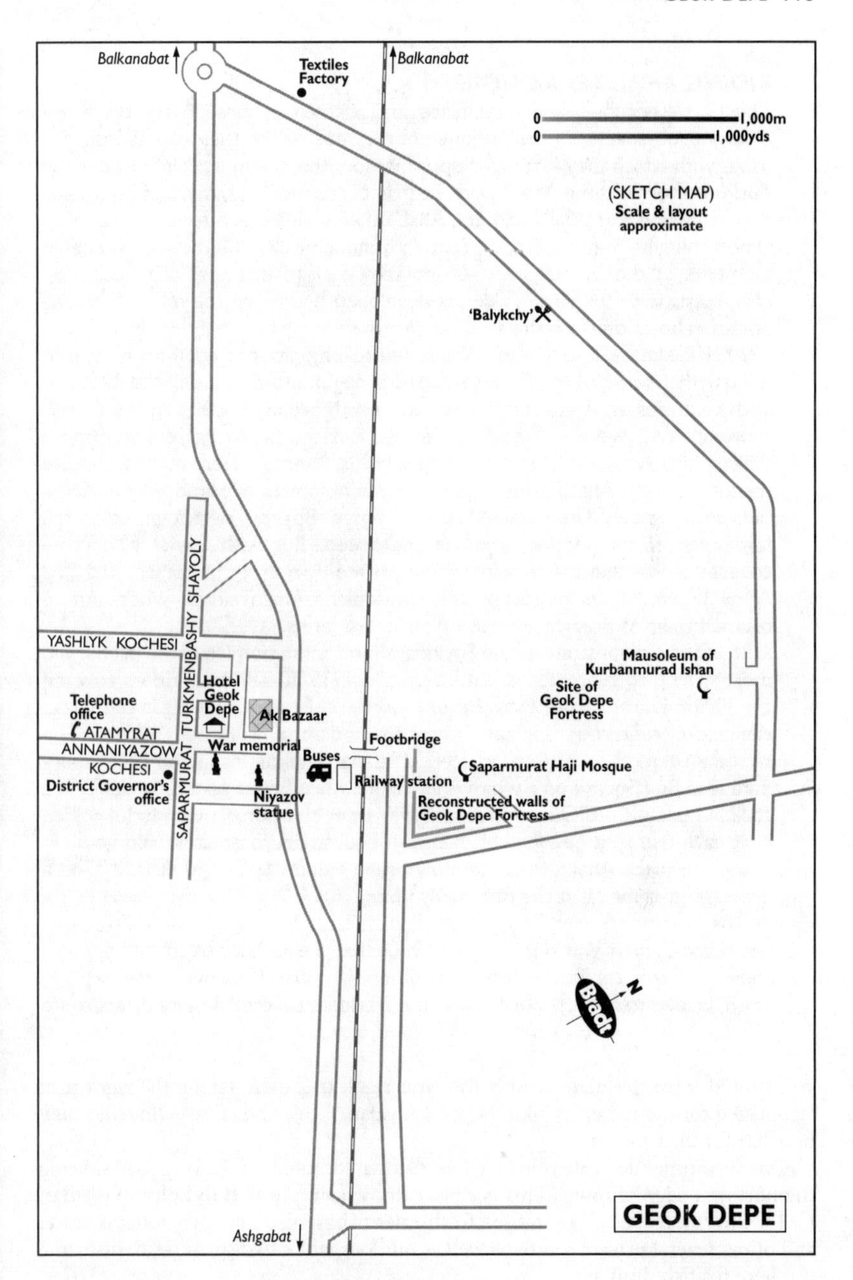

Practicalities

The train station is a single-storey building in the centre of town. Buses and minibuses leave in front of it. The bus fare to Ashgabat is around 2,000 manat; a place in a minibus will cost about 5,000 manat, and in a taxi 10,000. A footbridge takes you over the railway to the site of the Geok Depe fortress and the mosque. If you are coming from Ashgabat by private vehicle, to visit the mosque and fortress

RIDING AHAL TEKKE HORSES

The horse occupies a central place in Turkmen culture. While there are different sub-species of the Turkmen horse, most taking their names from the tribes with which they were traditionally associated, the most celebrated of the Turkmen horses is the Ahal Tekke. Lean in build, with long, thin legs, long ears, a sparse mane and small head, the Ahal Tekke is also characterised by a shiny, almost metallic coat, shown to particularly stunning effect in the golden-coated members of the breed. Turkmen horsemen claim that the long neck, also characteristic of the Ahal Tekke, is developed by placing the meals of young horses in holes dug into the sand, forcing them to stretch their necks to eat.

Ahal Tekkes are particularly well suited to long-distance endurance races. It is likely that some of the Eastern horses brought into England in the 17th and 18th centuries as 'Arabs' or 'Turks', and which helped to develop the English thoroughbred, were in fact Ahal Tekkes. But the breed has experienced a difficult history. Under tsarist rule in the 1890s, attempts were made to ensure the future of the Ahal Tekke through the establishment of a stud farm at Keshi, outside Ashgabat. The outstanding stud horse, Boynou, is recognised as the forefather of the modern lines of the breed. But with Soviet rule came collectivisation, and the banning of the private ownership of horses. The Red Army showed little interest in the thin-looking Ahal Tekkes, whose future seemed to lie as draught animals on collective farms.

It was to demonstrate to the Soviet authorities the stamina of the breed, and thereby help to guarantee its future, that in 1935 30 Turkmen riders covered a 4,300km journey from Ashgabat to Moscow in 84 days, arriving in the Soviet capital, to rapturous applause, wearing traditional Turkmen *telpeks*. The strategy seemed to pay off: in 1945, Marshal Zhukov inspected the Victory Parade in Red Square on a white Ahal Tekke. Khrushchev gave the Ahal Tekke stallion Melekush to Queen Elizabeth II in 1956; this horse's wonderful golden coat gave rise to a new colour in British equestrian vocabulary: 'old gold'. In 1960, the black Ahal Tekke stallion Absent, ridden by Sergei Filatov, won a dressage gold medal at the Rome Olympics.

The post-war Soviet focus on mechanisation of farming prioritised tractors, not horses, and it was not until the 1980s that the authorities started again to show real interest in the breed. Another Ashgabat–Moscow horse race, in 1988, helped to consolidate it. This time 28 riders covered a more direct route

you should leave the main road before you reach the town, taking the right turn signposted for the mosque 20km beyond Abadan. Cross the railway line and then bear left for the mosque.

One recommended café is in an edge-of-town location, on the ring road skirting the northern edge of town. This is a place known simply as **Balykchy**, 'Fish Bar' (☎ 132 20776). It specialises in fried freshwater fish, served in a spicy tomato sauce, and offers several private rooms as well as outdoor tables. Ashgabat residents come out here for fish dinners.

Geok Depe is so close to Ashgabat that there is little reason to stay here, and the one hotel in town certainly doesn't strengthen the case for doing so. The six-roomed **Hotel Geok Depe** (Atamyrat Annaniyazow Kochesi; ☎ 132 21448) at least enjoys a central location close to the bazaar, but its basic rooms are not air conditioned and the toilets are outside in the yeard. It is, however, cheap, at 15,000 manat a bed.

of 3,200km in 63 days. Following Turkmenistan's independence, the Ahal Tekke horse has been given a central place in the iconography of the new state. A Turkmen Horse Day has been celebrated each year since 1992 on the last Sunday of April. Yanardag, a golden Ahal Tekke stallion owned by the president, is depicted at the centre of the Turkmen national emblem. The state association Turkmen Atlary has been established to develop the breed, as well as the sport of horse racing.

There are good opportunities to ride Ahal Tekke horses. Some overseas travel companies bring tourists to Turkmenistan specifically for this purpose. Turkmen travel agencies can put together horse-trekking trips of varying lengths and degrees of difficulty. Two of the best-equipped private stables, both of which are used by travel agencies, lie in the Geok Depe area.

Shahmenguly Hemra Gulmedov runs a stable of 40 Ahal Tekke horses at this farm, 2km to the west of the village confusingly named Geok Depe, which lies northwest of Geok Depe town. Accommodation is available here, either in the form of *yurts*, decorated in traditional style with felt rug flooring, or in a motel block comprising six air-conditioned rooms with en-suite showers. Hemra does not accept direct bookings, but works through several local travel agencies, including Ayan and DN Tours. He can put together trekking programmes ranging from a few hours to long desert expeditions.

Alaja To reach these stables, turn southwards off the main Ashgabat to Geok Depe road, 8km west of Abadan. The turning is signposted for Geokdere. After another 8km, turn right at the base of the hills. A couple of kilometres further on, turn left onto a rough track, which heads a few hundred metres towards the clearly visible farm. Katya Kolestnikova has around 25 Ahal Tekke horses, amongst a menagerie of dogs, cats, doves and the occasional cow. Katya's stables stand at the foothills of the Kopet Dag Mountains, and her treks tend to focus on the hills, as opposed to the desert environments favoured by Hemra. While also working through local travel agencies, Katya can be contacted direct (m 800 663 30362), charging around US$10 an hour to ride one of her Ahal Tekke horses. She can provide helmets and basic riding equipment. Her husband Oleg will ferry visitors between Ashgabat and their farm for an additional charge. If you cannot get through to Katya's phone, try her colleague Gulya Yangebaeva (☎ 132 426358, or m 800 663 40198).

One accommodation option which is worth considering, though as an upland retreat rather than a means of seeing Geok Depe, lies in the Kopet Dag Mountains to the south of town. The tourist resort of **Sekiz Yap** (☎ 132 20844) is based around a meandering stream running through a steep, rocky valley. Four stone cottages have been built on the hillside, and offer a comfortable place to stay. The pair of two-storey cottages (bedroom upstairs, lounge below) have air conditioning, balconies and en-suite showers for 500,000 manat a night. The two single-storey cottages are cheaper, though more basic, and only one is air conditioned. The resort also has four *yurts*, where you can sleep more memorably but less comfortably for 25,000 manat per person. Meals of *plov* and *shashlik* are served to diners lounging on the platforms known as *tapchans* along the side of the stream. Sekiz Yap is a pleasant place to come for lunch, even if you do not plan on staying overnight.

To get to Sekiz Yap, take Atamyrat Annaniyazow Kochesi due south from Geok Depe town centre. After 9km the road reaches the base of the Kopet Dag

Mountains. Follow the road, which by now is just a track, another 4km into the hills, until you see a 'Sekiz Yap' sign and road barrier on your right. The youth manning the barrier will tell you in Turkmen to get a receipt from the resort management, confirming that you have stayed or dined there, before he will let you out on your departure from the place.

What to see

Across the footbridge from the railway station, the walls at the southeast corner of the **Geok Depe fortress** have been reconstructed, and offer a good sense of what an imposing defensive structure this must have been. The walls are built to a thickness of 11m at the base, tapering to 8m. You can climb a flight of steps to walk along the top. A museum, dedicated to the events of 1881, is scheduled to be built at the bottom of the walls here. Elsewhere, the unreconstructed fortress walls are discernible as degraded ridges. The hill of Dengil Depe is still prominent against the skyline, though is surrounded by vineyards and difficult to reach.

Dominating the complex, and indeed the town of Geok Depe, is the **Saparmurat Haji Mosque**. The mosque, named in honour of the *hajj* pilgrimage performed by President Niyazov in 1992, was the first major project in Turkmenistan of the French construction company Bouguyes, completed in 1995. The mosque can reportedly accommodate 8,000 worshippers. It has a central dome of deep green colour, surrounded by four green half-domes. The four minarets are each 63m in height, representing the age attained by the Prophet Mohammed. On the eastern side of the mosque is a square courtyard, centred around a star-shaped pool. Small white domes protrude from the roof around this courtyard like a row of eggs. This part of the complex includes both an area for ablutions on the ground floor and rooms originally intended to be a *madrasa* above. In a change of heart, the authorities have never allowed the latter to open.

The interior of the mosque features four pillars outlining a large central space into which hangs a huge French chandelier. It apparently weighs two tonnes and contains 260 lamps. The interior of the dome and half-domes are decorated with soothing pastel blue designs, and the interior walls feature pleasant tiled representations of the traditional patterns of Turkmen carpets. The mosque is the focus of the government's annual commemoration, on January 12, of those killed at Geok Depe.

In the graveyard at the northern side of the fortress complex is the simple **Mausoleum of Kurbanmurad Ishan**, a Naqshbandi sheikh who helped inspire the Turkmens to stand firm against the Russians. His tomb is a revered place of pilgrimage.

BAHARLY AND THE ROAD WEST

From Geok Depe, the main road continues northwestwards towards the coast, skirting the northern edge of the Kopet Dag Mountains. Some 30km west of Geok Depe, a road to the south runs to the cement factory of **Kelete**. By taking the track further southwards, beyond the factory, you will reach a good area for hiking, including a pleasant short walk along a stream bed which passes through a stone canyon etched with the graffiti of previous visitors. The area around Kelete was used for military training exercises for Soviet troops bound for Afghanistan, because of the similarity between the Kopet Dag Mountains and Afghan terrain.

Kow Ata underground lake

Nine kilometres further on, another turning to the south is signposted for Kow Ata. After 7km you reach the car park serving the underground lake. A popular weekend day trip for Ashgabat residents, the place is usually near deserted during the week. Ashgabat travel agents organise trips to the lake, or you can negotiate hire of a taxi. The lake is open daily 09.00–18.00.

Having paid the hefty 100,000 manat entry charge for foreigners, you descend from the cave entrance in the side of the hill into a gloom illuminated only by the orange glow of the electric lamps flanking the steep concrete staircase. The air is clammy. The sound of birds, keeping close to the light at the cave entrance, gives way to that of bathers below. There are some ramshackle changing rooms in the depths of the cave. Here too, bizarrely, is a subterranean coffee stall.

Just below, at a depth of 55m from the cave entrance, is the underground lake. With a length of 70m, and a depth of 10m or more, the lake is known for the warm temperature of its water, a year-round 35°C or so, giving a swim here a warm-bath feel. The water also has a high mineral content, prompting both claims about the health-giving properties of a swim and warnings that bathers should not stay in the water for too long. But the sulphurous smell from the lake, coupled with the half-sensed presence of bats overhead, also gives the place something of an underworld quality. The climb back towards the growing patch of light at the cave entrance can feel like the ascent towards salvation. Or at least towards a world less pungent.

Several legends surround the place. One of these is all about a peculiar cow, which every day for a month joined a shepherd's herd all day, before leaving at nightfall. The shepherd followed the cow, to claim the shepherding fee due to him from its owner. The cow arrived at the underground lake, where an old man was sitting. The man gave the shepherd a small bag as a shepherding fee. The shepherd left the cave, and opened the bag, to find it was full of fig leaves. He threw them away in disgust, but kept the bag as a gift for his wife. When he gave her the bag, another fig leaf fell out, and the shepherd and his wife noticed that it was made of gold. The shepherd therefore hastened back to the cave, to pick up the other leaves he had thrown away, presuming them to be golden too. When he returned, a garden of fig trees had sprung up at the mouth of the cave. Of the old man and his cow there was, however, no sign. This, the tale concludes, explains the origin of the name Kow Ata, as a contraction of the Turkmen phrase meaning 'The Old Man in the Cave'. Other sources suggest that the name just means 'Father of Caves'.

There are a couple of places serving *shashlik* around the car park, but past attempts to set up a tourist complex at Kow Ata have left no more than a legacy of various unused and decrepit concrete constructions.

Murche

Some 18km west of the turning to Kow Ata, the district capital, **Baharly**, is known for the fine quality of carpets made there, but contains little to detain the visitor. The town was named Baharden until a visit by Niyazov in October 2003, when the president determined that it should be renamed in order to restore a description deriving from the time of Oguz Han. Baharly, 'With Spring', reflected the spring seasons spent in the area by the ancestor of the Turkmen people.

Five kilometres west of Baharly, a track to the south is marked by a small, easily missable green sign pointing the way to the Mausoleum of Zengi Baba. The latter is visible from the road, surrounded by the crumbling earth walls of the abandoned village of Murche.

The **Mausoleum of Zengi Baba** is a heavily restored square-based building, topped with a dome. The transition between walls and dome is marked with four squinches, separated by niches. Researchers believe that the mausoleum dates either from the 13th or 14th centuries, when it was constructed using bricks taken from earlier buildings, or was built in the 10th or 11th centuries and then reconstructed two or three centuries later. The cenotaph is decorated with geometrically patterned tiles. Outside the mausoleum is a pile of what are popularly said to be the petrified eggs of dinosaurs. Or possibly cannonballs. Also collected here are ammonites and other stones whose unusual appearance has resulted in the ascription of sacred properties.

The mausoleum at Murche is the best-known of several across Turkmenistan dedicated to Zengi Baba, the patron of cattle breeders. The Turkmen traditions surrounding Zengi Baba combine Islamic beliefs with some decidedly pre-Islamic strands, including the Zoroastrian reverence for cattle. Many popular Turkmen tales depict the rivalry between Zengi Baba and Duldul Ata, the patron of horse breeders. One example is a hare-and-tortoise-style race, pitting horses against cows in a bid to get back to the village first. The canny Zengi Baba prayed for rain, which turned the ground to thick mud, impeding the horses but not the cows. And he summoned great clouds of mosquitoes, which troubled the horses dreadfully, but failed to deflect his cows from their steady progress to the village. The cows were, accordingly, the unlikely winners of the race.

The abandoned village of Murche is an atmospheric place. Its crumbling mud walls and doorways, and the overpowering silence of the place, give an impression of great antiquity. But the village was abandoned only in the early 1960s, when the construction of the Kara Kum Canal a few kilometres to the north prompted its relocation closer to the canal. University students working at the site have rebuilt a mud-brick round tower in the traditional style. Another reconstructed building features a fireplace crowned with an elaborate, stepped, mantelpiece.

If you have time, it is worth stopping briefly at the small village of **Sunche**, 12km west of Murche, where an ancient water-mill continues to grind flour as it has done for centuries.

Archman

A couple of kilometres beyond Sunche, a well-signposted turning to the left takes you, after another 10km, to the health resort of Archman, near a village of the same name. The place has long been known for its mineral springs. Local legend has it that the health-giving properties of the waters were discovered by a shepherd named Archman who, upon bathing in the warm waters of the pool at the spring head, discovered that his irritating rash was miraculously healed. A spa was established here as early as 1915. In 2001, a fully modernised resort was opened by President Niyazov, with white marble-faced accommodation and treatment blocks replacing the previous Soviet-era concrete buildings. A gold statue of the president, wearing a cape like that of a magician, welcomes visitors to the resort with outstretched arms. The resort is mainly geared to patients staying a week or more for the treatment of skin or intestinal complaints, but offers rooms on a short-stay basis too. They quote US$57.50 a night for foreign nationals. This price includes full board at the canteen-like restaurant and, ominously, 'treatment'. (☎ 12 511410.)

A steady stream of residents takes a regular evening walk just beyond the sanatorium complex to a run-down Soviet concrete building, dating from the early 1970s, around which a cluster of stalls sells beer, vodka, chocolate and other temptations. Café Bahar on the first floor of this block is a desolate place, but it is worth sticking your head around the door to see the Soviet mural depicting the taking of the waters.

A sulphurous-smelling spring sits just beyond the resort complex. It receives a steady flow of visitors, filling up plastic bottles or drinking direct from the source.

The small mausoleum nearby is, confusingly, not that in honour of the shepherd Archman (the site of which reportedly lies a few kilometres away, close to Archman village), but is dedicated to one Gochgar Ata.

Ak Ishan

One of the most popular shrine pilgrimage sites in Turkmenistan, Ak Ishan is reached by a signposted turning to the north of the main road, some 22km west of Sunche. Ak Ishan lies 13km north of the road. The complex includes a brick mosque, with a stubby minaret, and a second prayer hall. The grave of Ak Ishan lies close to the latter, within a walled enclosure. A small fenced enclosure nearby marks the grave of his wife. Ak Ishan, who lived in the 19th century, was highly respected for his piety. It is said that, on his death at the age of 90, local villagers were unable to bury him in his home village, as his grave collapsed whenever they came close to completing it. The villagers then placed the body on a white camel, which was left to wander free. The camel eventually ended its wanderings at this site, close to the grave of an unknown child. Here Ak Ishan was buried.

Three ram's horns rest on a wizened tree in front of the prayer hall. Turkmen women anxious for children will touch one of these horns to their forehead, and then tap it on the ground. If a large piece of dirt drops from the hollow interior of the horn, a boy is believed to be on the way. A small grain signifies a girl. From this area, a paved path runs a few metres to a circular enclosure, with a low brick wall. It is said that 40 followers of Ak Ishan are buried beneath the low earth mound inside the enclosure.

The Ak Ishan site also includes accommodation blocks for pilgrims visiting the place, as well as a large area for the holding of sacrificial meals. Behind these are sand dunes. A path leading into the dune area brings you to an odd sight: a blanket spread across the sandy ground, with legs (mainly female) protruding from beneath it. There is a round well here: pilgrims peer into the well for a sighting of the moon, which is supposedly visible to those whose wishes are to be fulfilled. The blanket is used to cut out external light sources. The circuit across the sand dunes continues to another well, this one a brick construction, whose water is considered to have particularly sacred properties.

NOHUR

High in the Kopet Dag Mountains, the village of Nohur and the neighbouring settlements occupying the terraced sides of the upland valleys are quite unlike other parts of Turkmenistan. The local Nohurli tribe retains conservative traditions protected by the remoteness of its settlements, and has a reputation for religious piety, hard work, and in-breeding. Claiming descent from the army of Alexander the Great, Nohurlis will show you a stone in the village said to bear a footprint of Alexander's horse. The porches of Nohur houses are indeed supported by wooden columns which recall the Ionic style. But the inspiration here perhaps draws less from Hellenism than from the horns of the local sheep. Combining fascinating villages, beautiful scenery, and excellent opportunities for guided trekking, Nohur repays a visit of several days.

Practicalities

Nohur is reached by a road heading south into the mountains from the village of Archman. A 4x4 is required, though the route can become all but impassable after heavy rains. Since 2004, visits to the Nohur area have required a special border zone permit, to be applied for when you request your letter of invitation for Turkmenistan. The border checkpoint lies 12km south of Archman. Nohur itself is another 10km further on, and up, at an altitude of around 1,000m.

There is one tourist complex in this area. The **Chandybil Tourist Centre** (☎ 131 51324) lies at 1,450m, midway between Nohur and the next village of Garawul, though off of the main track between the two villages. It offers 12 rooms, sleeping either two or four people in small cottages, with en-suite shower rooms and central heating. There are also five *yurts*, named after each of the regions of Turkmenistan. Foreigners are charged 400,000 manat per night, breakfast included. Otherwise, there are good opportunities for camping, and travel agencies may also be able to arrange a homestay in one of the villages in the area.

What to see

The graveyard at the eastern edge of Nohur village is striking, its carved wooden tombs decorated with the horns of rams. Visitors are asked not to enter the graveyard. Just beyond is the pilgrimage site of **Kyz Bibi**. A fat-trunked plane tree, surrounded by a small metal fence, is covered with small scraps of cloth representing wishes. From here, a flight of concrete steps leads up to a tiny cave, just a few centimetres across, in the side of the hill. The cave is surrounded by more pieces of material, some of which have been fashioned into tiny cribs, suggesting the nature of the wishes made here. The site is one of several in Turkmenistan dedicated to Kyz Bibi: the legends surrounding this female figure of great purity usually involve her being swallowed up by the mountainside to protect her from either heathen invaders or an unwanted marriage.

Beyond Nohur, the villages of **Garawul** and **Konyegummez** stand in fine upland settings. Unlike settlements of lowland Turkmenistan, whose houses focus inwards around family courtyards, the buildings here look out, with large glass-panelled verandas facing south, to capture the warming sunlight in this frequently chilly environment. Among the natural attractions around which to base walks is the **Khur-Khuri Waterfall**, 5km from the Chandybil Tourist Centre, below which lies an attractive tree-filled gorge. The **Ai Dere Canyon**, 7km from Chandybil, is punctuated with small waterfalls, some of which offer fine bathing opportunities in their plunge pools. The stream at the base of this canyon is a tributary of the Sumbar River, its waters making a long westward journey to the Caspian. Abandoned water-mills in the Ai Dere Canyon are evidence that this valley once supported a thriving rural population.

ANEW

If the Parthian site of Nisa makes for a good half-day trip to the west of Ashgabat, the remains of ancient and medieval setlements near the village of Anew provide a similarly straightforward short excursion to the east of the capital. Anew lies just 12km from Ashgabat, on the main road heading east towards Mary. The main sites of interest to the visitor lie among fields to the east of the village. A word about spellings. The modern village is spelt 'Anew' in this book, following the current usage of the Turkmen government. The spelling 'Anau' is the prevalent version in the archaeological literature, and this spelling has been retained to refer to the ancient and medieval sites.

Practicalities

Frequent buses ply the short route between Ashgabat and Anew, at a cost of 1,000–2,000 manat. But they depart from the inconveniently peripheral east end of Atamurat Niyazov Shayoly in Ashgabat and, unless you are on a really tight budget, it would make for a much pleasanter trip to negotiate a price with an Ashgabat taxi driver. Travel agencies in Ashgabat will also happily organise a half-day programme. If you do come by bus, the terminus in Anew lies on Azatlyk Kochesi, a couple of kilometres south of the centre of the village. The railway station sits on the main road between Ashgabat and Mary, officially known in town as Gurbansoltan Eje Shayoly. There is little point in using the train to get to Ashgabat, but Anew is also a stop for the daily departures from Ashgabat eastwards to Dashoguz, Atamurat and Serhetabat, and for the twice weekly departure to Serakhs.

The best of the uninspiring food options in Anew is probably the **Dovlet Restaurant** (☎ 137 36468), which occupies a deceptively grand-looking three-storey brick building on the main road through town. It offers *shashlik*, basic Russian staples, and dried fish hanging from the bar.

The ancient settlement

Two large mounds, 300m apart, are not hugely exciting to look at, but have proved greatly significant in uncovering information about early agricultural settlement in Turkmenistan. The north mound was first excavated by the Russian General Komarov in 1886. Komarov cut a trench straight through it, uncovering evidence of ancient civilisation. More systematic research was undertaken by the American geologist Raphael Pumpelly, who excavated here in 1904. This work led to the identification of four cultural layers: the Eneolithic Anau I and II cultures, in the north mound, and Bronze Age (Anau III) and Iron Age (Anau IV) cultures of the later south mound, to which the Anau settlement seems to have shifted around 4,500 years ago.

Pumpelly did not have an easy time at Anau. A plague of locusts filled up his trenches, and made further digging impossible, prompting him to shift his attentions to Merv. But one find in particular from the Pumpelly expedition has been highlighted by the present-day Turkmen government: the evidence of the cultivation of cereals, including wheat and barley, found even in some of the lowest layers at Anau. In his book *Ruhnama*, President Niyazov talks of the discovery of grains of 5,000-year-old white wheat, as evidence that Turkmenistan is the place of origin of cultivated white wheat. In 2003, Niyazov decreed that Gawers District, in which Anau stands, be renamed Ak Bugday ('White Wheat') District, to mark the fact that 'the ancient soil of Anau is the motherland of white wheat.' In 2004, the Turkmen government organised an international conference to commemorate the centenary of the Pumpelly expedition. It was called 'Turkmenistan is the native land of the Anau Culture and white wheat'.

The medieval settlement

To the east of the two mounds of the ancient settlement lie the ruins of a later one. Its origins seem to lie in Parthian times, when it may have been the settlement of Gatar, mentioned by Greek sources. The place later became known as Bagabad, centred on a fortress some 300m in diameter. The name Anau seems to have been used from the 18th century, and derives from the Persian, meaning 'New Water'. The major sight remaining for the visitor today is that of the ruins of the 15th-century **Seyit Jamal-ad-Din Mosque**. To get here, take the turning to the south, 5km east of Anew, passing under an archway inscribed with the name of the mosque, which lies a few hundred metres further on.

The mosque was built in 1456 through the finance of one Mohammed Khudaiot, the representative of the Timurid governor of Khorasan, who chose to site the building at the grave of his father, Sheikh Jamal-ad-Din. The mosque, which lies in the southern part of the old fortress of Bagabad, included an extensive religious complex, with a *madrasa* and accommodation for pilgrims. Its most distinctive feature, however, was the depiction of two great mosaic dragons high on the portal, as if guarding the central arch. The beauty of this mosaic, the slender

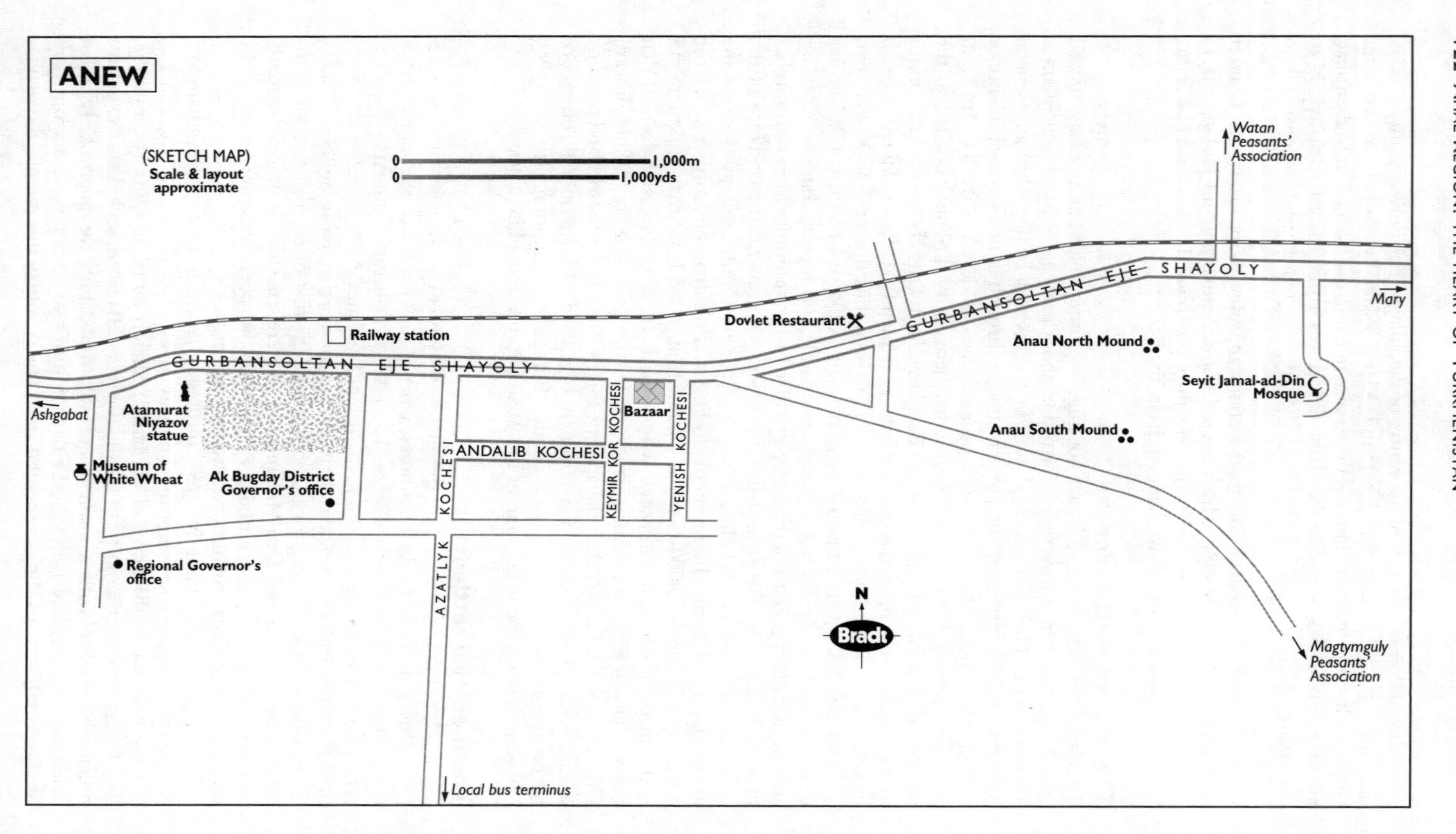
ANEW
(SKETCH MAP)
Scale & layout approximate
0
1,000m
0
1,000yds
Watan Peasants' Association
Mary
GURBANSOLTAN EJE SHAYOLY
Dovlet Restaurant
Railway station
Anau North Mound
Seyit Jamal-ad-Din Mosque
Anau South Mound
Ashgabat
Atamurat Niyazov statue
Bazaar
ANDALIB KOCHESI
KEYMIR KOR KOCHESI
YENISH KOCHESI
Museum of White Wheat
Ak Bugday District Governor's office
AZATLYK KOCHESI
Regional Governor's office
N
Bradt
Magtymguly Peasants' Association
Local bus terminus

THE DRAGONS OF ANAU

A local legend explaining the background to the highly unusual depiction of creatures on the portal of a mosque runs roughly as follows. In days of yore, the town here suffered greatly from the predations of a pair of dragons, who consumed livestock and harvests. The town had a bell, to be rung only in times of distress. One day, the people of the town were mightily surprised to see their bell being furiously rung by one of the dragons. The dragon managed to convey with gestures that they should follow him, and took the townspeople to his mate. She had swallowed a ram, whose horns had become lodged in her throat. She was finding it difficult to breathe, much less to set fire to anything.

The townspeople managed to extract the sheep from the throat of the ailing dragon. She was cured instantly. In gratitude, the dragons took the townspeople on their backs, and flew them to a mountain cave, which sparkled with diamonds. With their treasure, the people of the town built a wonderful mosque, with mosaic pictures on the portal of the two dragons which had made its construction possible.

dragons winding almost like snakes above the central arch, is well captured by photographs taken by the Soviet archaeological expedition led by Galina Pugachenkova in 1947. But on 6 October 1948 the mosque collapsed in the earthquake which destroyed Ashgabat, taking the mosaic dragons with it. Turkmen researchers have recently attempted to piece together the mosaic from the fragments uncovered at the site. The results of their work are on display at the Museum of Fine Art in Ashgabat. (See page 89.)

The main survivals of the mosque are the bases of the two columns of the portal. These retain some blue and turquoise tiles in geometric designs. Behind these columns, the once great mosque has been reduced to a pile of rubble. The courtyard in front of the portal has been cleared. Here stands a reconstructed brick cenotaph, considered to mark the grave of Seyit Jamal-ad-Din and an important shrine pilgrimage site. Another tomb nearby, more colourfully decorated with blue and turquoise tiles, is dedicated to Kyz Bibi. Facing the portal, the small, domed building to your right is said to offer the faithful relief from their heart disorders. The requirement is to crouch inside the tiny room beneath the dome.

Little pats of mud on the walls derive from the belief that mud from this holy place, applied at the site of joint pain or an ailment of the skin, can then take the pain away if slapped onto the walls here. Cribs fashioned from pieces of material are representations of wishes for children found at many shrine pilgrimage sites in Turkmenistan. A less common symbol, which you may see here, is an open pair of scissors, representing the cutting of the umbilical cord. Ears of wheat placed on top of the tomb of Seyit Jamal-ad-Din are considered symbols of fruitfulness, and seem to hark back to the discovery made by Pumpelly.

The modern settlement

Anew is basically a large village, strung out along the Mary road not far from the encroaching eastern suburbs of the city of Ashgabat. But it is also formally the capital of Ahal Region. While in practice the region centres around Ashgabat, Anew's administrative role has given the village a few oversized public buildings. The regional branch of the Senagat Bank, for example, in front of which stands a statue depicting Saparmurat Niyazov's father Atamurat, working his abacus. A large but uninviting park nearby, planted with rows of conifers, is also dedicated to Atamurat Niyazov.

The most interesting public building in Anew is the flamboyant **Museum of White Wheat**, built by the Turkish construction company Polimeks in commemoration of Pumpelly's discoveries. The museum was opened by President Niyazov in June 2005 as part of celebrations marking the reported fulfilment of the annual wheat harvest quota of 3,100,000 tonnes. The design of the building is striking: a circular, white marble-faced structure, topped by two golden crowns of giant ears of wheat. There are wheat-oriented decorations everywhere, including on the street maps and benches around the museum. In front of the museum stands a golden statue of a suited President Niyazov, depicted parting a field of wheat. Ten columns decorated with wheat motifs stand sentinel around the statue.

Following the grand opening of the museum, most of the exhibits were promptly withdrawn, reportedly pending the appointment of a museum director, and at the time of writing the museum was not properly open, though employees of the construction company working on site were happy to show visitors around. The ground floor displays focus on archaeology, including pottery found at Anau, and a handful of blackened grains of the celebrated ancient Anau wheat. Photographs of Raphael Pumpelly interest mainly for the length of the archaeologist's beard, which reaches comfortably to his stomach. There are photographs too of President Niyazov, brandishing a scythe in a field of wheat to signal the start of the harvest. Display cases promising treasures from Merv and Margiana stood empty at the time of research. The basement features displays on grain production in post-independence Turkmenistan. A display case features a Heinz-equalling 57 varieties of wheat, from Tejen-5 to Neutrality. A variety named Turkmenbashy is, we are told, capable of yields of an impressive 70kg per hectare. The Golden Age variety has particularly bushy ears. There is a display on the baking of bread, centred around a model of a traditional clay oven, or *tamdyr*, more empty display cases, and some toy tractors. A chart depicts the remarkable reported growth in the wheat harvet since independence, from 70,000 tonnes back in 1989 to a target of 5,000,000 tonnes by 2020.

A forgotten monument to Soviet icons lies to the east of Anew. Nine kilometres out of town, on the road to Mary, take the unmarked asphalt road to the left, heading off at roughly a 45° angle from the main road. After about a kilometre, you reach a long-abandoned car park. From here, walk across the adjacent railway line to reach a once smart pathway between now wild conifers. This takes you to a short flight of steps, above which stands a stone obelisk. This is the **Monument to the Nine Ashgabat Commissars**, members of the Bolshevik leadership in Ashgabat, who were hanged in 1918 following a coup in the town during the Civil War. The inscription has long since gone from the obelisk: the ghostly shadow of a hammer and sickle now makes its imprint on the stone. During the Soviet period, trains would respectfully sound their horns when passing this place. Now, it is silent.

KAKA AND AROUND

Kaka

The small town of Kaka is a district capital some 130km east of Ashgabat, close to the foothills of the Kopet Dag Mountains and lying immediately to the south of the main road to Mary. From the tsarist-era railway station, three trains daily head to Ashgabat, and one each to the three easterly destinations of Atamurat, Dashoguz and Serhetabat. The statue base standing in the small square of park in front of the station once supported Lenin. Across the road from here is the headquarters of the Abiverd Archaeological Park (☎ 133 21232), whose Director, Ahmed Halmurat, is a fount of information on the 200 sites under the jurisdiction of the park, including Eneolithic (Copper Age) and Bronze Age *depes* and medieval city sites.

Just to the east of town, on the north side of the main road, stands the rectangular **Konye Kaka Fortress**. Signs here tell you that this is a site of great archaeological significance, and that there is a 500,000 manat fine for grazing your sheep over it. An ancient settlement, the fortress was restored in the 14th century, in support of Timur's campaign to bring the lands to the east of the Caspian under his control. A large raised area within the walls marks the site of the citadel.

Abiverd

Eight kilometres to the west of Kaka, the ruins of the town of Abiverd lie just to the south of the Ashgabat road, and are clearly visible from it. Abiverd was once an important trading town of North Khorasan. It was a key link on the Silk Route between Nisa and Merv, and also enjoyed ties with Nishapur, across the Kopet Dag Mountains to the south. Taxes collected from Abiverd at one point in the 9th century were almost double those of Serakhs. But Abiverd never seems to have recovered its status following its sacking by the Mongols in 1221. Abiverd in its heyday had a sophisticated system of water supply, produced highly regarded pottery, and minted its own coins. The present-day site offers only a hint of these past glories. The eastern part of the site is a citadel, with earth ramparts topped in a few places by surviving stretches of mud-brick walls. The whole is surrounded by a dry moat. To the west are the crumbling mud walls of houses probably abandoned in the 18th century.

Namazga Depe

The largest of the proto-urban communities in southern Turkmenistan, Namazga Depe was occupied continuously from the end of the fifth millennium until the second millennium BC. It is notable not just for its size but for the degree of cultural development displayed here during the Bronze Age, including elegant pottery, developed metallurgy, and an urban plan characterised by multi-roomed dwellings, with adjacent open courtyards separated by narrow streets.

To reach the site, head west from the centre of Kaka along the road running to the south of the railway track. After 5km, turn to the right onto a rough track, which brings you to Namazga Depe after a further 2km. The site is a large irregular hill, reaching a height of around 20m and covering an area of some 70ha. A cemetery covers a large part of the site, whose associations with holiness are linked to its name (Namaz meaning 'Prayer'). The cemetery was initially used for burials by the residents of Abiverd, which lies just a couple of kilometres away, across the railway track to the north and clearly visible from the top of Namazga Depe. The presence of the cemetery has served as a block to archaeological investigation of much of the site, and the most rewarding place to head for is the highest point of the *depe*, at its northwest corner furthest from the cemetery area. This is an area known as the 'bastion', its height formed by the debris of late period occupation, and which seems to represent the residual settlement remaining through a period of cultural decline during the 2nd millennium BC. Rectangular kilns can be made out here.

The small hill next to the turning onto the track for Namazga Depe is named **Tekkem Depe**. This was excavated by Soviet archaeologists in the 1980s and is worth a stop on the way back from its larger neighbour as several mud-brick walls have been uncovered. Tekkem Depe seems to have been a village satellite of Namazga Depe.

Khusrau Kala

The citadel at this settlement is believed by some researchers to have been the summer residence of the Sasanian king, Khusrau. It lies just to the west of the village of Kaushut, a halt on the railway line some 25km west of Kaka. The citadel is a large platform of irregular plan. Below this, to the west, lies the walled settlement. Khusrau Kala seems to have been abandoned following the arrival of the Arabs to the area.

Nadir Shah Fortress

Just over 20km south of Kaka, close to the village of Khivabad, lies an 18th-century fortress, built during the rule of Nadir Shah, founder of the Afsharid Dynasty in Iran. Set in an attractive location at the foot of the Kopet Dag Mountains, the rectangular fortress walls retain a good sense of the original structure. Fluvial erosion has destroyed most of the southern wall of the fortress, but elsewhere towers and battlements survive. From gates in the north and east walls, roads run to the remains of a large walled building in the centre of the complex. A mound reaching a height of 10m in the north wall of the fortress offers an excellent vantage point across the site. The fortress is also known as Old Khivabad: it is said that Nadir Shah, held in slavery in Khiva in his youth, vowed that one day he would move Khiva to his homeland. When he became a powerful leader, he conquered Khiva. The tale runs that he took thousands of prisoners, ordering each of them to take with them soil from Khiva. With this he constructed the fortress of Khivabad near the Kopet Dag Mountains.

THE BATTLE OF DUSHAK

In the dying months of World War I, a little-remembered series of engagements took place in this part of what is now Turkmenistan, pitching British forces against those of Bolshevik Russia. Britain's chief concern in the region was the threat of an invasion of Transcaspia by Turkey, which was allied to Germany. This, it feared, would mark a stepping stone to India for the Turco-German alliance. Britain was accordingly backing the newly formed Transcaspian Government, although the immediate threat to the latter was less that of Turkish forces landing on the eastern shore of the Caspian than of the Bolshevik force advancing westwards from Tashkent. The British mission, led by Sir Wilfrid Malleson, based in Mashad, accordingly found itself caught up in the defence of the Transcaspian Government against the Bolsheviks.

The military campaign was focused almost entirely on the single-track line of the Transcaspian Railway, along which both sides moved in armoured trains. The Anglo-Indian forces comprised the 1/19th Punjabi Infantry, the 28th Light Cavalry, and elements of the 44th Battery, Royal Field Artillery, together with a disparate coalition of anti-Bolshevik forces, including Russians, Armenians and Turkmen horsemen. The Bolshevik ranks had been supplemented by German and Austro-Hungarian former prisoners of war, who had been promised that they would finally be allowed to return home once the counter-revolution had been defeated.

In August 1918, the Punjabis repelled an attack by Bolshevik troops on Kaka railway station, through an effective infantry charge with fixed bayonets. The British commander on the ground, Colonel Denis Knollys, decided to try to move onto the offensive, and take the Merv Oasis, whose food-stocks were desperately needed by a hungry Ashgabat. The first objective en route to Merv

AROUND DUSHAK

Some 37km to the east of Kaka, the main road and railway track both veer away from the line of the Kopet Dag Mountains close to the small town of Dushak, taking a route to the northeast which will bring the visitor to Tejen and then Mary. But southeast from Dushak, a minor road continues to run along the base of the hills, before fizzling out near the village of Chaacha. There are several worthwhile places to visit along this route, including Bronze Age settlements, shrine pilgrimage sites and, especially, the Mausoleum of Abu Said Meikhene.

Ulug Depe

To the east of Dushak, turn right off of the main road, at a turning signposted to the shrine pilgrimage site of Malik Baba. Turn to the south after another 4km, heading towards a large mound, about 30m high, and some 3km on. This is Ulug Depe, one of the early agricultural settlements of the fertile belt along the foothills of the Kopet Dag Mountains. Ulug Depe was a thriving settlement during the early Bronze Age. While smaller and less important than proto-towns such as Altyn Depe, it is currently one of the more interesting of the many ancient *depe* sites in this region for the casual visitor, as it is the object of an ongoing research programme being carried out by the French archaeologist Olivier Lecomte. The French excavations reveal a fortified mud-brick building of the late Iron Age, including a buttressed outer wall and paved corridor. A sign here does little to facilitate an understanding of the site, informing the visitor only that this is an important historical monument, over which it is not permitted to graze livestock or leave rubbish.

was the Bolshevik-held railway town of Dushak. Knollys resolved to capture this by circumventing the Bolshevik armoured train.

On the night of 12 October, the 1/19th Punjabis, Transcaspian infantrymen and light artillery circled north of the railway. The Indian Light Cavalry rode into the hills to the south, and Turkmen horsemen made a wide sweep, to cut off the line to the east of Dushak. The element of surprise was, however, lost when two Punjabi patrols opened fire on each other in the darkness, and the battle for Dushak became a bloody affair. The 1/19th Punjabis were particularly badly hit. Many of the accompanying Transcaspian troops went to ground in ditches at the start of the battle. A Bolshevik ammunition dump at the station was exploded by a British shell, and the Bolsheviks fled the town. Looting by the Transcaspian forces was, however, to cost the coalition its victory. The scattered Bolshevik units were able to regroup, and take reinforcements from Tejen. With only the Anglo-Indian troops and a few Russians left trying to defend Dushak, they had no alternative but to retreat. The Bolsheviks claimed victory, explaining away their own heavy losses by inventing the presence of a Scottish regiment.

However, the Bolsheviks, possibly fearing rumoured Anglo-Indian reinforcements, were to pull back from Dushak, Tejen and then Merv. The British and Transcaspian forces were able to occupy Merv on 1 November without further bloodshed. But then came the end of the First World War. With the Turco-German threat to India now gone, the British authorities had no wish to see Malleson get further embroiled in fighting against the Bolsheviks. In February 1919 he received orders to recall his Transcaspian mission. The Transcaspian Government was now abandoned to the Bolsheviks, who had secured the whole region by February 1920 under the able command of General Frunze.

Malik Baba

A visit to the popular shrine pilgrimage site of Malik Baba is easily combinable with Ulug Depe, which lies just 1km to the north. There is a guesthouse for pilgrims and an area for ceremonial meals around the car park. From here, a path leads to the tomb, identified as that of Malik Ajdar Palwan, which surprises by its great size. The sword, shield and arrows depicted on the recently reconstructed tomb of greyish-green marble identify its occupant as a warrior, whose greatness is reflected in the fact that the tomb is comfortably large enough to accommodate a giant. Behind the tomb runs an arcade of tiled columns topped with five turquoise domes. Nearby stands a tombless mausoleum, square in plan with a domed roof. As at Ak Ishan, there is a well at the site covered with a large blanket. Lie beneath the blanket and try to see the moon reflected in the water of the well.

Mausoleum of Abu Said Meikhene

This mausoleum, usually referred to as Meana Baba, is one of the most unjustly neglected sites of Turkmenistan, as it lies an inconvenient distance from the main Ashgabat to Mary road to make for a straightforward stop. It is nonetheless well worth the detour. From Malik Baba, return to the road running southeastwards from Dushak, along the line of the hills. Turn right onto it. After 40km, a gravel road to the north is signposted to Meana Baba. The mausoleum is reached after 5km, standing alone amid a wide expanse of pastureland.

Abu Said was born in 967 in the town of Meikhene, which lay on the trade route between Abiverd and Serakhs. His father was a herbalist and spice trader, who was able to give his son a fine education. Abu Said was known for his asceticism, reportedly reciting verses from the Koran while suspended head-first in a well. After spells in various cities, including Merv, Serakhs and Nishapur, Abu Said was to return to Meikhene, where he died in 1049. By the time of his death, he had become a widely respected Sufi authority, who played an important role in the political and spiritual life of the region. The Seljuk leaders Chagry Beg and Togrul Beg reportedly sought his blessing for their bid to overturn the Ghaznavids. Some criticised the use of elements of poetry, music and dance in his teachings, but he was a highly popular figure, such that it is said that a piece of watermelon, accidentally dropped by him, changed hands for the sum of 20 gold dinars. It is thus no surprise that a great mausoleum should have been built at the place of his death.

The mausoleum dates from the 11th century. It has a square base, with sides a little more than 10m in length, above which is a double dome, a feature typical of the buildings constructed in this period by the craftsmen of Serakhs. The transition between walls and dome is marked with four squinches, separated by four niches, each containing a small window. The entrance to the mausoleum is framed by a tall, arched portal. A major reconstruction in the 14th century added much colour to the building, including beautiful blue, turquoise and white mosaic tilework around the portal, based around geometric designs and Arabic inscriptions. The interior painting features geometric and stylised floral designs on a white background, plus a repeated water-jug motif. The decoration on the interior of the dome is based around a central eight-pointed star.

This attractive building is not however in the best of health. Part of the external wall in the northwest corner has collapsed. There are many cracks through the building, and the interior contains much rickety-looking scaffolding. Abu Said's tomb, surrounded by ten square-based columns, was covered by a dust sheet when I last visited.

Altyn Depe

Easily combined with a visit to the Mausoleum of Abu Said Meikhene, Altyn Depe ('Golden Hill') is a settlement of the Eneolithic and Bronze Ages. Extensive archaeological research was carried out here during the Soviet period. The site also lies off of the road running southeastwards from Dushak. Stay on this road beyond the turning for Meana Baba. You will reach the village of Meana after 7km. Two kilometres further on, turn left onto a gravel track, whose quality rapidly deteriorates. Make for the low, flattish hill, around 20m in height. This is Altyn Depe. It is somewhat smaller than Namazga Depe (see page 125), but has been more extensively excavated.

The settlement contains many features suggestive of an emergent town, including a specialised potters' quarter, across which much pottery and remnants of kilns were found, the evidence of separation of living quarters into districts differentiated by the wealth and status of their inhabitants, and indications of external trade networks. The discovery here of ivory objects such as gaming counters has led some researchers to identify links between Altyn Depe and the Harappan civilisation of the Indus Valley. A major discovery here was that of a monumental cult complex, centred around a stepped *ziggurat* structure, topped with a small shrine. Among the items found here were two to justify the name of the hill: a small gold head of a wolf, and a larger golden head of a bull, more than 7cm in height, with a turquoise crescent inlaid on its forehead. The Russian archaeologist V M Masson has suggested that the cult complex may have been dedicated to the Moon God, which in the mythology of Mesopotamia is often linked to the figure of a bull. Altyn Depe was abandoned by the middle of the second millennium BC, possibly as a result of over-exploitation of the land, its inhabitants moving eastwards to the Merv Oasis.

The site today is not easy to interpret. There have been no excavations here for several years, and the results of earlier digs have softened into depressions and mounds across the pottery-strewn hill.

TEJEN

Back on the main road between Ashgabat and Mary, the town of Tejen (telephone code 135) lies 50km to the northeast of Dushak. It is the administrative centre of the Tejen Oasis, but offers nothing to detain the tourist. It has fertiliser and textiles factories, a reputation for producing the most flavoursome melons in Turkmenistan, and a less welcome one for narcotics ('Tejen tea' is a slang term for opium). The caretaker of the newly constructed Charman Ahun Mosque may let you climb the tall brick minaret for a view across the whole town. Unfortunately, there is nothing to see.

The tsarist-era railway station handles three trains daily to Ashgabat; three to destinations to the east. The ticket office is open 11.00–14.30 and 19.00–03.30, reflecting the fact that many of the departures fall in the early hours. The bus station is near the western end of Hyakimlik Kochesi. There are three government buses daily to Ashgabat; two to Mary. Much more frequent minibuses and taxis to both towns depart from the same place. If you need a place to stay here, the 20-roomed **Hotel Tejen** (Khivaly Babaeva Kochesi; ☎ 135 21105) offers accommodation of last resort. The rooms are heated in winter but have no air conditioning, the showers are communal and the toilets outside. The room charge is 60,000 manat a night.

Nine kilometres east of town, close to the Serakhs turning, a roadside melon bazaar is a worthwhile stop in the summer months. It lies close to a peasants' association named after one of the most prized varieties, the Waharman, which is

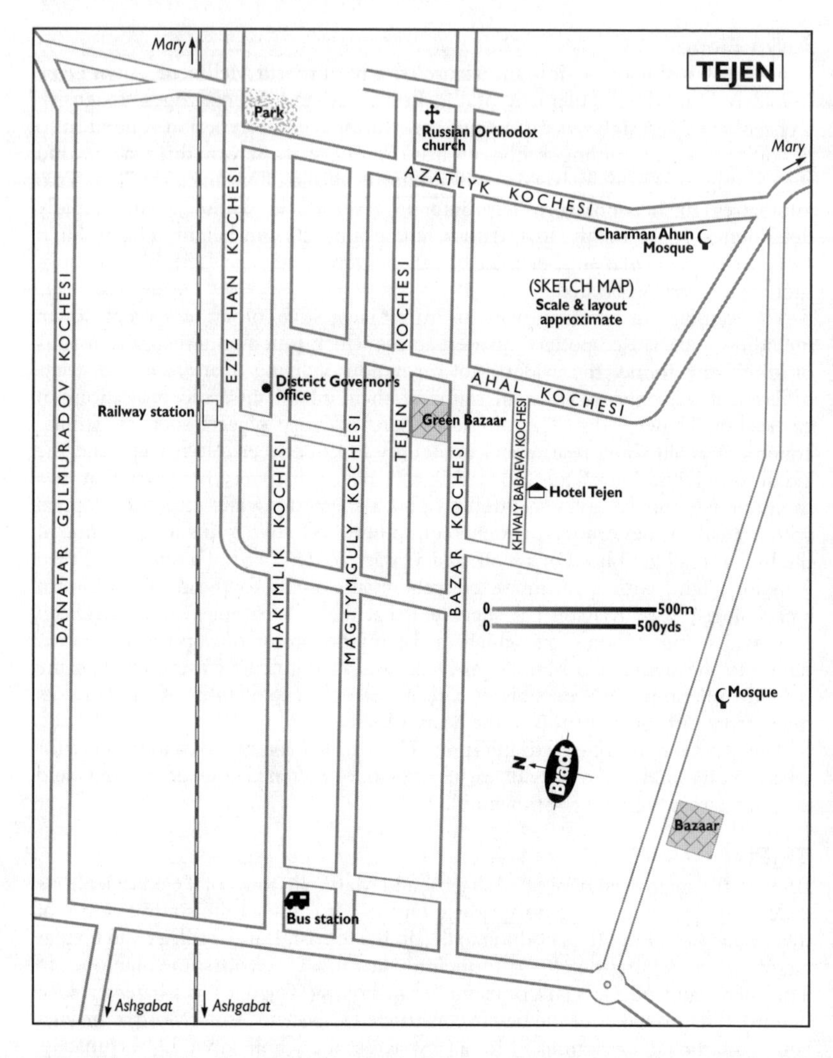

indeed the star product of the bazaar. You may also see strips of melon being dried here on lines. The strips are sold as *kak*, a sweet, sticky confection.

SERAKHS

A sleepy district capital close to the Iranian border at the eastern edge of Ahal Region, Serakhs is the border crossing point for a railway link (freight only) between Tejen and Mashhad in Iran, opened in 1996. The Turkmen authorities frequently depict this railway as a revival of the Silk Route links, and Serakhs in its heyday was indeed an important Silk Road town, owing its prosperity to its position along the route between Nishapur and Merv. Situated in an oasis along the Tejen River, Serakhs has been occupied since at least Achaemenid times, the town somewhat arbitrarily commemorating its 2,500th anniversary in 1993. Its major flowering came under the Seljuks, when the town occupied 120ha and was home to a renowned school of architects responsible for some of the finest constructions of the region, including the Mausoleum of Sultan Sanjar in Merv and the Ribat-i Sharaf Caravanseray on the road to Nishapur in present-day Iran.

The town fell into decline following the demise of the Seljuks, but a temporary recovery under the Khorezmshahs at the end of the 12th century was dramatically reversed by the Mongol invasion. After this, a minor rally under the Timurids notwithstanding, the once powerful trading town became an increasingly rural backwater. The Russians built their new administrative centre 2km to the north of Old Serakhs, which now has the status of a state historical reserve.

A special permit is required to visit Serakhs, which is reached by road from Tejen. Accommodation in the town is a problem, though Turkmen travel agents may be able to book a guesthouse of sorts, in a building constructed to house Romanian gas-industry specialists, now owned by Turkmen Gas.

Old Serakhs

The main attraction of the Serakhs historical reserve, to the south of the modern town, is the 11th-century **Mausoleum of Abul Fazl**. A highly respected Sufi sheikh, and mentor of Abu Said Meikhene, a mausoleum was built over the grave of Abul Fazl soon after his death in 1023. The mausoleum is a fine example of the skills of the architects of Serakhs during the Seljuk period. Known locally as Serakhs Baba, the mausoleum consists of a square chamber, its walls some 15m in length, above which is a double dome atop a 12-sided drum.

The external walls of the building, which was restored in the 1980s, each contain five blind-arched niches, with decoration provided by the alternations between vertically and horizontally placed bricks. The tall portal, with scalloped decoration beneath the arch, dates from a 15th-century reconstruction under the Timurids. In the interior, the transition between walls and dome is marked with four squinches, separated by niches. The cenotaph of Abul Fazl lies in the centre of the room, covered with sheets. It is possible to climb onto the roof of the mausoleum, via a steep spiral stairway. This offers a good view of the site, including the citadel to the north. Some of the tiles on the roof display a hand print; possibly simply to make the tiles easier to lay.

To the north of the mausoleum, the long low hill covered with pieces of pottery and red brick is the **citadel**. On the eastern side of this hill a section of wall, including a bastion, has been reconstructed. The main residential areas of Serakhs in its heyday stretched out east of the citadel, and were in turn surrounded by mud-brick walls, whose lines can be picked out from the vantage point of the citadel.

Yarty Gumbez

Leaving the historical reserve, head south, away from the modern centre of Serakhs. After 6km, turn left onto a gravel road, then left again after a further 4km towards the now visible ruined mausoleum known as Yarty Gumbez ('Half Dome'). The name is somewhat misleading, as none of the dome now survives. Another casualty of recent decay is an inscription on the east wall of the building, clearly visible in photos taken here in the 1970s, whose text dated the mausoleum to 1098. The north wall is almost entirely absent, and the only remnants of the drum beneath the dome are two elegant squinches, occupying the inside corners of the south wall. Scholars have suggested that this may be the mausoleum of one Sheikh Ahmed Al Khady, based on a 12th-century account which records that Al Khady was buried in one of the villages of the Serakhs Oasis.

Mele Hairam

At the village of Ashir Tekayev (formerly Ashgabat), 6km to the northeast of Serakhs on the road running towards the Hanhowuz Reservoir, take a rough track eastwards, leaving three small *depes* on your right. Fork to the right when the track divides beyond the last of these small hills, and head towards another *depe*, reached 5km after leaving the asphalted road. This small mound, Mele Hairam, has been comprehensively excavated by a Polish-led archaeological team, working at the site since 1997. They have discovered that the mound covered the remains of a Zoroastrian temple of fire.

The temple dates from the Sasanian period, which ran from the 3rd to the 7th centuries. The main entrance lay on the eastern side of the complex. A large table, whose longer faces were covered by stucco decoration, almost serves to block the door on the west side of the first room, suggesting to researchers that ordinary worshippers were not allowed beyond this point. A square room to the west, presumably therefore reserved for members of the priesthood, has the base of a fire altar at its centre, now protectively covered with a mound of earth. Small platforms, coated with plaster, were found in three of the corners of this room, and have also been protectively covered with earth. There is a large arched niche in the south wall of the altar room. The Polish team has speculated that the function of a small room to the north of the altar room may have been to store the embers of the sacred fire. To the west of the altar room, another room with an area of paved flooring also contains evidence of a hearth, and this room too was probably devoted to religious rituals.

Mele Hairam serves to demonstrate what fascinating secrets may lay beneath the hundreds of unexcavated mounds scattered across this part of Turkmenistan.

Polekhatum Bridge

Head south from Serakhs, beyond the turning for Yarty Gumbez. After 38km, turn to the right along a gravel track. After 25km, you reach a checkpoint along a fence marking the controlled border zone with Iran. Getting beyond here requires special permission from the Turkmen Border Guards, over and above the restricted zone permit needed for Serakhs District as a whole. This additional permission is rarely given. If you do get it, the track reaches the Tejen River, which marks the line of the border, after another 14km.

Across the river near this point is an attractive stone bridge of five arches, which gently slopes to a peak in the centre of its span. The bridge, now unused, is covered by grass. This is the Polekhatum Bridge, which was reconstructed in tsarist times. A popular local legend surrounding its origins is based around the bridge's name, meaning 'Wealthy Woman'. The woman is said to have made her fortune by taxing all those who wished to cross her bridge. One day, Alexander the Great arrived, at the head of his army. He refused to pay the toll, and to spite the woman forded the river just to the north of her bridge. It is indeed believed by historians that Alexander crossed the Tejen River somewhere near this point, in 350BC.

A couple of kilometres to the south of the Polekhatum Bridge is the **Dostluk Dam**. This earth dam, whose name means 'friendship', was a joint project of the Turkmen and Iranian governments, inaugurated by the two presidents in 2005. The dam aims to regulate the flow of the Tejen River, and provide irrigation and drinking water for both sides. The lake behind the dam is set to extend to a length of 37km.

INTO THE KARA KUM DESERT

North from Ashgabat, the long road to Dashoguz cuts through the heart of the Kara Kum Desert. The scattered villages along the way are favoured by Ashgabat travel companies as destinations for tours aiming to give the visitor a taste of desert life. The astonishing fiery crater near Darvaza is another good reason to come this way, even if you are not heading further north into Dashoguz Region.

Jeitun

This archaeological site north of Ashgabat, first excavated by the Russian archaeologist V M Masson in the 1950s, occupies an important place in the understanding of early prehistoric agriculture in the region. Masson's excavations revealed a series of small, single-roomed dwellings, each with an oven and adjacent yard. Artefacts and botanical evidence demonstrated that the economy of this settlement was based around a mixture of hunting, domestic sheep and goats, and the cultivation of cereals, including wheat and barley. The site has been dated to the 6th millennium BC. Other, less well preserved, roughly contemporary sites have also been identified along the foothills of the Kopet Dag Mountains, leading archaeologists to use the term Jeitun Culture to refer to this group of Neolithic sites, which represent the earliest known agricultural settlements in Central Asia.

To reach Jeitun, take the Dashoguz road from Ashgabat. Fifteen kilometres beyond the marble-faced northern city gate, take the turning to the left, over an unmanned level crossing, and then along a pot-holed asphalt road. The once good state of the rural roads in this area is apparently down to the fact that a former head of the local peasants' association, then called the Socialism Collective Farm, was a political figure of some influence. Three kilometres on, turn right at the T-junction, then immediately left, such that you are continuing in a westwards direction. Park a kilometre on, immediately beyond the irrigation channel. The site lies about 500m to the north. The most recent excavations here were carried out by a joint British, Russian and Turkmen team in the early 1990s, and the site is not immediately straightforward to spot. It is a mound, slightly less than a hectare in size, in an area of undulating sandy ground on the edge of the desert. It is in turn covered by many small mounds; the spoil heaps from Masson's excavations. There is not, frankly, anything much to see, though the site does impress for its solitude.

Erbent

The largest village on the road from Ashgabat to Dashoguz, Erbent lies 157km north of the Dashoguz Gate into Ashgabat. As with most of the desert settlements in the Kara Kum, Erbent is surrounded by sand dunes; the result of over-grazing. Some Turkmen travel agencies organise day trips here from Ashgabat, offering the visitor a packaged but still pretty authentic taste of desert life. Activities typically include displays of felt rug making, the baking of bread in a *tamdyr*, and camel-milking. Two-day visits, including an overnight stay in a *yurt*, are also sometimes available.

Erbent is a somewhat chaotic settlement of single-storey buildings, many with adjacent *yurts*, its economy focused on pastoralism. An obelisk in the centre of the village, featuring a relief of a Turkmen lady whose head is held low in grief, commemorates the deaths of 11 men in 1931 at the hands of the *basmachi*, Central Asian opponents of Soviet power. The inscription on the obelisk records that they made their sacrifice to secure the triumph of socialism, the realisation of the dictatorship of the proletariat and the collectivisation of agriculture.

Darvaza

Darvaza ('Gates') lies 110km north of Erbent, close to the border with Dashoguz Region, and the start of a special permit zone. The settlement was once the site of a sulphur works, which closed in the 1960s. Prospecting for gas during the Soviet period has resulted in a curious series of sights around the area: several large, circular craters, one of which is aflame.

To reach the **flaming crater**, a 4x4 is essential, as is a good driver who knows the route. The track heads east from the main road, immediately to the south of the road checkpoint. It then passes over a formidable sand dune (hence the importance of good off-road driving skills), reaching the crater after 7km. The crater is roughly circular in plan, some 60m in diameter. Its floor crackles with hundreds of small fires, the flames fiercest around the edge. The smell of gas and all those flames will take you back to school chemistry lessons, with every Bunsen burner in the classroom in action. This is a worthwhile sight in daytime, but truly remarkable at night, when the glow from the crater can be seen for miles around.

Another gas crater lies in the settlement of Darvaza itself, just off to the west of the main road. Another deep, circular hole, this somewhat smaller crater is surrounded by a metal barrier. There is no fire here, though it too offers a strong smell of gas. Another crater lies some 18km south of Darvaza, on the west side of the main road and just about visible from it. This crater has neither fire nor a particularly pungent smell. Instead it is partly filled with water, through which gas bubbles gently up.

Until 2004, Darvaza was the major halt on the drive between Ashgabat and Dashoguz. A series of cafés, mostly run by ethnic Uzbeks from Dashoguz Region, was spread out along the road north of the settlement, serving the buses and minibuses making the long journey between the two towns. Several of these places offered overnight accommodation in *yurts*, an option which Turkmen travel agents were wont to describe as the authentic desert experience, but which felt rather more like the authentic night-in-a-litter-strewn-truck-stop experience. Nonetheless, this was convenient accommodation for a nocturnal visit to the flaming crater. In 2004, the whole settlement was demolished, including the roadside cafés, for reasons which have not been made clear, but which may have been linked to the government's plans to upgrade the transport link between Ashgabat and Dashoguz. It is possible to visit the gas craters as a (long) day trip from Ashgabat, but in order to see the flaming crater at night the only current option seems to be to camp nearby.

Ahal Region carpet gul

Above Looking out across the Eroulanduz Depression, Badkyz
Below Detail of relief by Ernst Neisvestniy, Mekan Palace, Ashgabat

Above Abu Said Meikhene Mausoleum, Ahal Region

Right Tiles bearing hand prints. Roof of Abul Fazl Mausoleum, Serakhs

Below right Mausoleum of Il Arslan, Konye-Urgench

Below left Detail of portal to the Mausoleum of Nedjmeddin Kubra, Konye-Urgench

5 Balkan Region: the Caspian and the West

The westernmost region of Turkmenistan has a feel quite unlike the rest of the country. The reach of the Kara Kum Canal extends only to a small area in the eastern part of Balkan Region, which largely lacks the irrigated cotton and wheat fields typical of rural Turkmenistan further east. Camels amble across arid dunescapes. Rusting derricks and 'nodding donkeys' testify to the role of the region as the heart of Turkmenistan's oil industry. The main port, Turkmenbashy, was the point of departure for the tsarist Russian conquest of Transcaspia, and the town still houses a substantial ethnic Russian minority. The major Turkmen tribe of this region, the Yomud, is associated with a distinctive carpet design, displaying an anchor motif appropriate for a littoral tribe, and an energetic dance step involving much flailing of arms and deep chanting.

There is much of tourist interest in Balkan Region. The waters of the Caspian offer an obvious lure in the heat of the Turkmen summer, and Turkmenbashy, together with the adjacent village of Awaza, is being developed as a domestic tourist destination. Inland, worthwhile attractions include the remote ruins of the Silk Road site of Dekhistan, the orchards of the Sumbar Valley, the shrine pilgrimage site of Parau Bibi and the magnificent polychrome canyon of Yangykala. The region is the birthplace of Magtumguly, Turkmenistan's greatest poet, and the final resting place of the 26 Baku Commissars, icons of the Soviet era.

TURKMENBASHY

Turkmenistan's main port, the town of Turkmenbashy (telephone code 243), occupies a striking geographical location. Its houses nestle in a series of parcels of low ground along the shores of the Caspian. Steep, arid cliffs form a natural amphitheatre around the town. Turkmenbashy sits on the northern shore of a gulf, providing an obvious harbour which first drew the interest of tsarist Russia almost 300 years ago. Prince Alexander Bekovich, from an elite family of the Caucasus, arrived here in the early 18th century, to pursue the interests of Peter the Great in the trade routes of Central Asia and rumours of abundant gold along the banks of the Oxus. But Bekovich's attempts in 1717 to persuade the Khan of Khiva to accept Russian protection resulted in his murder, and the massacre of most of his troops.

Russian engagement in the region was therefore delayed. But in 1819 a young captain named Nikolai Muraviev arrived at this natural harbour, then known as Krasnovodsk, as part of another Russian expedition. Travelling eastwards across the desert to Khiva, Muraviev was able to deliver to the khan the message that the tsar was keen to develop his trading links, by way of a new port at Krasnovodsk. Muraviev was lucky that, unlike Bekovich, his mission to Khiva concluded with his head still attached to his body, not least because he had also been tasked with

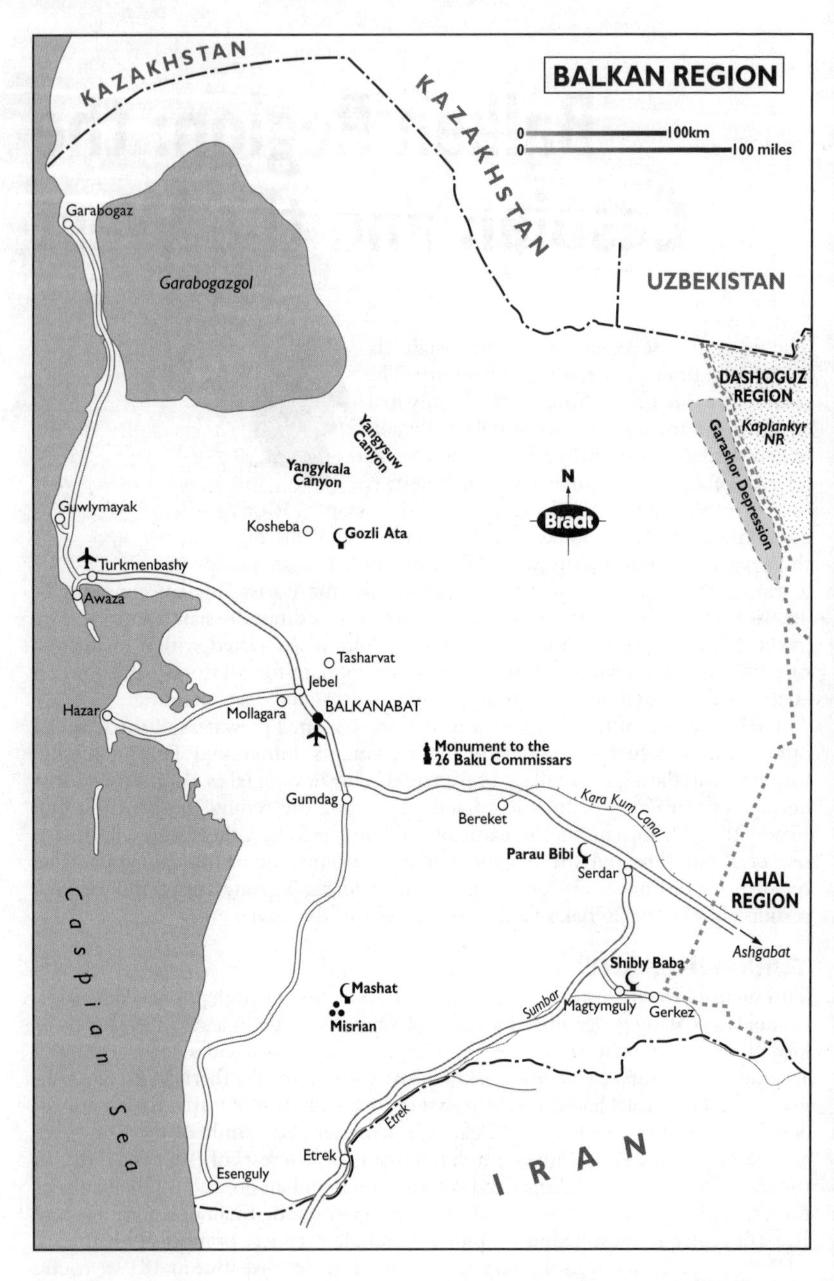

covertly gauging the state of Khiva's defences, with a view to possible Russian conquest, including to free the many Russian slaves held by the khan. But Russia was not yet ready to launch an attempt to bring the region under its control.

That moment was to come in the 1860s. Following the annexation of Tashkent, Samarkand and Bukhara, Russia found itself increasingly in need of a port on the eastern shore of the Caspian which could help serve as a launch-pad to bring

Transcaspia under its control and improve its lines of supply to its new domains. In 1869 a Russian force under the command of Nikolai Stoletov landed at Krasnovodsk, and established a permanent fort. By the end of the 19th century, the port of Krasnovodsk had become the western terminus of the Transcaspian Railway and a town of vital strategic importance. This was not reflected in any grandeur of urban planning. Its most impressive building was long its ebullient railway station, and Krasnovodsk acquired an out-of-the-way feel. Karlis Ulmanis, the first prime minister of independent Latvia, died here in detention in 1942. The main buildings in the town centre were the work of Japanese prisoners of war. In the Soviet period many people were sent here who had been deprived of Moscow residence permits.

With the break-up of the Soviet Union, Krasnovodsk has been renamed Turkmenbashy, 'leader of the Turkmen', the title now held by President Niyazov. The Turkmen government has made substantial investments in the modernisation of the oil refinery, the largest in Turkmenistan, which was moved here during World War II to keep it out of German reach. A redevelopment of the town's coastal strip has been launched too, bringing better hotel accommodation, but at the cost of some of the nicest single-storey brick buildings of the old town. The town's ethnic mix has been changing rapidly since independence, especially through the emigration of Russians and other non-Turkmen minorities.

Turkmenbashy is a pleasant place to while away a couple of days in summer, with some good accommodation options and an impressive natural setting. As the terminus of the Baku ferry route, it is also for some travellers the first point of contact with Turkmenistan, or the last.

Getting there and away

Turkmenbashy is served by three daily flights from Ashgabat. The flight time is one hour, and the fare around 35,000 manat. There is also a flight between Turkmenbashy and Dashoguz, currently operating on Monday, Wednesday, Friday and Sunday. The airport is some 8km outside the town centre, on the flat upland above the port. It is reached by a road which winds upwards, past the oil refinery. The airport terminal is small and rather run down. (Enquiry office ☎ 243 25092.) The Turkmenistan Airlines ticket office (☎ 243 25474) is in the centre of town, its entrance on the southern side of the Hotel Hazar. It is open daily 09.00–20.00, though closed for lunch 14.00–15.00.

The railway station, built at the end of the 19th century, is a playful piece of tsarist architecture, its exterior a confection of pink and white horizontal stripes, a lozenge-patterned rectangular-based domed roof, crenellations and miniature turrets. Its ticket hall and waiting rooms are walled with heavy relief tiles, the designs on some of which resemble corn on the cob. One of the rooms retains a fine painted ceiling, offering geometrical designs. There are two overnight trains in each direction between Turkmenbashy and Ashgabat. The railway station enquiry office is open 08.00–20.00, with a lunch break 12.00–13.00 (☎ 243 99462).

Long-distance taxis and minibuses leave from the open ground immediately to the west of the railway station. A place in a taxi to Ashgabat (about six hours) will cost from about 150,000 manat, depending on the type of vehicle. A seat in a minibus to Ashgabat costs around 100,000 manat, though these are infrequent. To Balkanabat, a seat in a minibus is around 20,000 manat; in a taxi 40,000. The station for local buses lies on Balkan Kochesi in the old town. It has three shelters, a couple of stalls selling fizzy drinks, and a rusted-metal timetable board recalling some long-abandoned service.

The ferry terminal (ticket office ☎ 243 24491) lies at the eastern end of the port. The entrance to this part of the port is 2.5km further on from the roundabout at

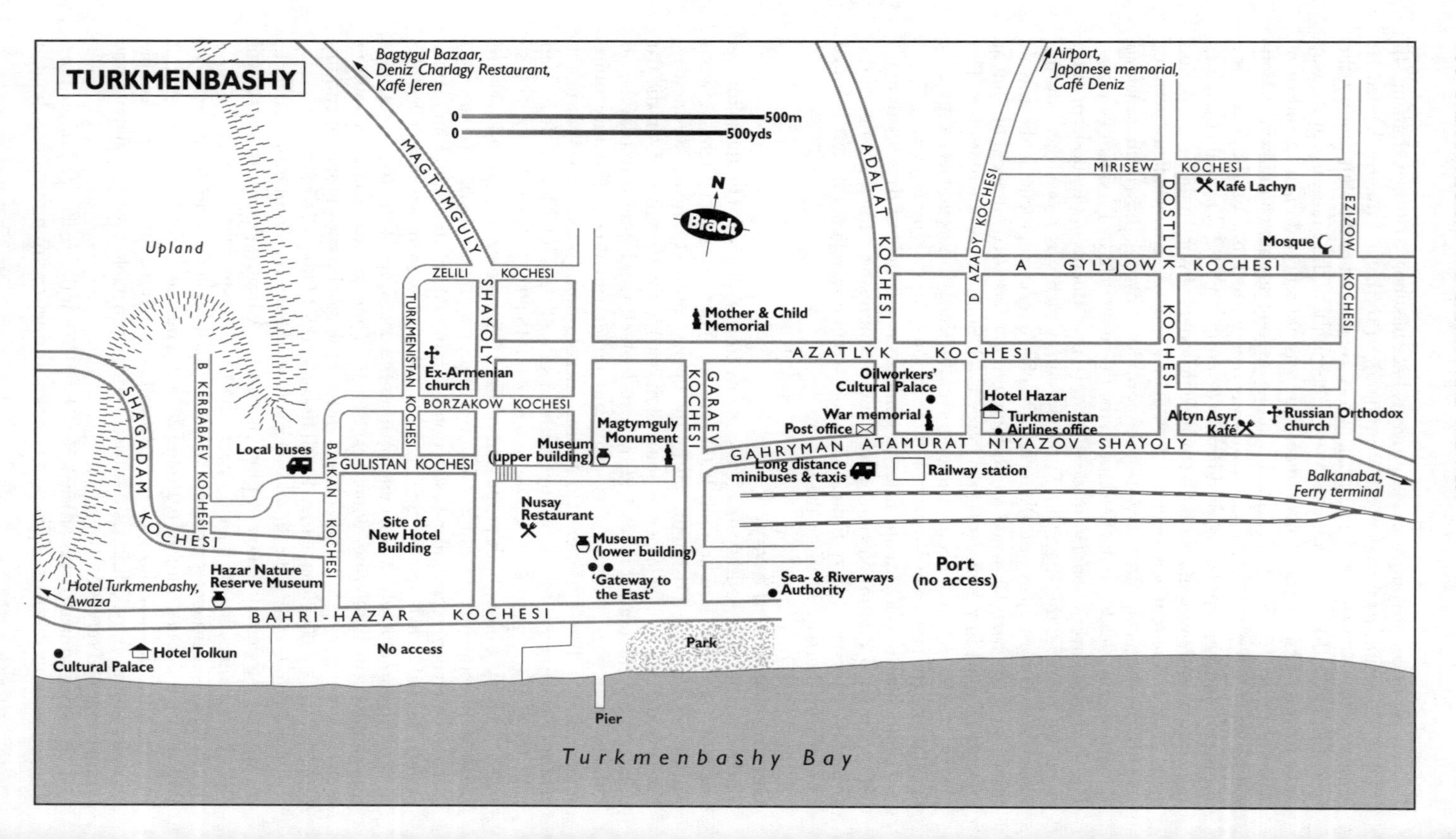
TURKMENBASHY
Bagtygul Bazaar, Deniz Charlagy Restaurant, Kafé Jeren
Airport, Japanese memorial, Café Deniz
0 500m
0 500yds
N
Bradt
Upland
MAGTYMGULY SHAYOLY
ZELILI KOCHESI
TURKMENISTAN KOCHESI
BORZAKOW KOCHESI
ADALAT KOCHESI
D AZADY KOCHESI
MIRISEW KOCHESI
DOSTLUK KOCHESI
EZIZOW KOCHESI
A GYLYJOW KOCHESI
AZATLYK KOCHESI
GARAEV KOCHESI
GAHRYMAN ATAMURAT NIYAZOV SHAYOLY
GULISTAN KOCHESI
BALKAN KOCHESI
B KERBABAEV KOCHESI
SHAGADAM KOCHESI
BAHRI-HAZAR KOCHESI
Kafé Lachyn
Mosque
Mother & Child Memorial
Ex-Armenian church
Oilworkers' Cultural Palace
Hotel Hazar
Turkmenistan Airlines office
War memorial
Post office
Altyn Asyr Kafé
Russian Orthodox church
Magtymguly Monument
Museum (upper building)
Local buses
Long distance minibuses & taxis
Railway station
Balkanabat, Ferry terminal
Nusay Restaurant
Site of New Hotel Building
Museum (lower building)
'Gateway to the East'
Hazar Nature Reserve Museum
Hotel Turkmenbashy, Awaza
Sea- & Riverways Authority
Port (no access)
Cultural Palace
Hotel Tolkun
No access
Park
Pier
Turkmenbashy Bay

the eastern end of Gahryman Atamurat Niyazov Shayoly. Inside the port complex, the road takes you back 2km towards town. (See page 32 for details of the ferry service to Baku.)

Where to stay

Turkmenbashy town

Hotel Turkmenbashy (90 rooms) Bahri-Hazar Kochesi; ☎/f 243 21308, 21314, 21317. To the west of the town centre, set back from the coastal promenade, this is a 10-storey white marble-faced block, with an indoor swimming pool and fitness centre (52,000 manat for 2 hours) in an adjacent building. Rooms are air conditioned and comfortable. The hotel looks out over the sea, but has no beach to speak of. During the summer season, which runs from 1 June to 31 August, the hotel charges a hefty US$100 for a single, US$120 for a double, and US$150 for a suite. Off-season, room rates drop by 50%.

Hotel Tolkun (7 rooms) Bahri-Hazar Kochesi; ☎ 243 23059, 23905. Well located, on the seafront close to the centre of town, this local authority-run hotel is a once-smart place which has somewhat gone downhill. There is no restaurant, but the rooms are air conditioned and have en-suite facilities. The price for a single is US$35, for a double US$45, and for a suite US$65. Unlike most places in Turkmenbashy and the nearby resort of Awaza, the prices do not change according to season, which makes the Tolkun a pretty good mid-range option during the summer months, but a poor bargain off-season.

Hotel Hazar (101 rooms) Azady Kochesi; ☎ 243 24633. A decrepit 4-storey concrete block close to the railway station, this hotel was named the Krasnovodsk during Soviet times. It then had a brief spell as the Turkmenbashy, before that title was appropriated by the altogether smarter hotel along the seafront. A frieze close to the entrance shows the good ship *Turkmenistan* at port, seagulls circling overhead. In the lobby, a copy of *Ruhnama* is lovingly preserved in a glass case. The bathrooms are unsavoury, bedrooms worn out, staff unfriendly, and not all the air conditioners work. Singles are around 135,000 manat, doubles 210,000 and suites 240,000. The hotel also has some cheaper beds available on the top floor, which is particularly rundown, with shared facilities. Beds here cost 60,000 manat in a twin-bedded room, 45,000 manat in a triple. Foreigners may be asked to provide a currency exchange certificate, to demonstrate that they have obtained their manat at the official rate of exchange. The restaurant, reached by a separate entrance, has an alarming pink-tiled décor and seems mostly to be given over to wedding parties.

Awaza

Eight kilometres west of town, facing out onto the open waters of the Caspian rather than the secluded bay, the village of Awaza is Turkmenistan's seaside holiday resort. The village comprises holiday complexes owned by various government organisations, plus many privately owned *dachas*. It is altogether fairly scruffy, with small parcels of sand sitting amidst concrete blocks and other detritus thrown up by the collision between coastal construction and maritime erosion. There are battered pedalos for hire, and a few outdoor bars offering plastic furniture and Turkmen pop music. The lure of the sea is somewhat tempered by the many water snakes, though the locals will assure you that these are not poisonous.

Many of the *dachas*, including cottages in some of the government-owned complexes, are available for rent. But demand is high in summer, and the prices are accordingly steep. In winter, most of the places are locked up. Some of the better places can be booked through local travel agencies. A decent cottage, sleeping four people, at the complex owned by the State Bank for Foreign Economic Relations, costs around 3.6 million manat per week in summer, plus 100,000 manat per person per day for food, on full-board terms served at the canteen in the complex.

Alternatively, you can simply look out for the many '*dachas* to rent' and 'rooms to rent' signs around the village. There is an enormous variation in the quality of accommodation on offer, from pleasant air-conditioned chalets to bare, airless rooms, so make sure you are clear exactly what is being offered before you agree the deal. Most Turkmen holidaymakers either cater for themselves or eat at their holiday complexes, so there is not a strong range of places to eat in Awaza.

Hotel Serdar (106 rooms) ↘ 243 21581, 51208; **f** 243 20750, 20751. This tall, marble-clad hotel dominates Awaza. All rooms are centrally air conditioned, with satellite TV, en suites and good views. The hotel is filled in summer by well-to-do Turkmen families. In winter it is mostly empty. Prices from mid-June to mid-September are US$100 for singles, US$140 doubles, US$200 suites, and US$350 if you insist on a Presidential Suite. The price does, however, drop considerably off-season. Use of the outdoor swimming pool is included in the room rent, but the indoor pool and health centre incur an extra US$6 per hour. The hotel offers internet access, but at a steep US$10 per hour. Various games are available for hire at expensive hourly rates. The restaurant is priced more reasonably (main courses around 45,000 manat), but the menu offers little choice, and service is poor.
Hotel Awaza (18 rooms) ↘ 243 24121, 24149; **f** 243 24375. Once the smartest hotel in the village, the 2-storey Hotel Awaza now finds itself quite literally in the shadow of the Serdar next door. Its rooms have central air conditioning and en-suite showers, but are markedly less plush than those of its neighbour. The 5 stars claimed in the faded sign on the front gate are seriously overstating the place, but it is worth considering as a less expensive option to the Serdar. A double here costs US$80 in summer. There is an additional charge of 26,000 manat per hour for the use of the swimming pool, housed in an adjacent circular building.

Where to eat

Nusay Restaurant Formerly known as the Korsar, this restaurant near the seaward end of Magtymguly Shayoly was long the best, though also priciest, place to eat in town, with a particularly good range of sturgeon dishes. It has, however, been knocked down as part of the redevelopment of the old town. A new Nusay is planned, to open a few hundred metres to the east of its predecessor, at the back of the marriage registry office. Which will be convenient for wedding receptions, presumably. There will also be a disco here.
Altyn Asyr Kafé Gahryman Atamurat Niyazov Shayoly; ↘ 243 20752. A single-storey lavender-coloured building to the east of the railway station, this offers reliable food but little atmosphere. The *tefteli*, a meat and onion dumpling in a mint-flavoured soup, is a good option at 20,000 manat. The *shashlik* here also enjoys a positive local reputation.
Kafé Lachyn 34 Mirisew Kochesi; ↘ 243 21888. With a basic, *shashlik*-oriented menu, this place offers models of jolly jack tars, fish nets strung over the drinking booths, loud pop music, tables out the front in summer and a billiard hall at the back.
Café Deniz 54 Azady Kochesi; ↘ 243 28851; **f** 243 28099; **e** denizcatering@mynet.com. Out of the town centre, not far from the football stadium (home to the Turkmen league side Shagadam), this place offers a mainstream Russian/international menu, with mains for around 50,000 manat. It opens much earlier than most of the town's cafés, at 08.00, and offers a set breakfast for 50,000 manat. It has a good range of cakes and pastries too, and Turkish coffee for 15,000 manat.
Deniz Charlagy Discobar Restaurant Magtymguly Shayoly; ↘ 243 25653. A large blue cube to the west of the town centre, everyone refers to this place by the Russian name *Chayka* ('Seagull'). It is a restaurant from 14.00–23.00, offering an uninspiring selection of pizzas, salads, *shashlik* and main courses, and then runs as a disco from 24.00–04.00. Its décor is maritime, with the bar decked out like a galleon, plying the seven seas with a cargo of beer-filled fridges. The waitresses are dressed in sailor suits, and the walls covered with paintings of rather voluptuous mermaids. Expect loud music.

Kafé Jeren 80 Magtymguly Shayoly; ☎ 243 14111; f 243 14549. West of the Cheryomushki Bazaar, this offers a large room, decorated a sterile white, with an open space in the middle where evening diners may get up and dance. There is a pleasant outdoor dining area in summer, with tables beneath straw umbrellas. The menu is a familiar mix of *shashlik*, Russian and international dishes, with mains around 35,000 manat.

Shopping

Bagtygul Bazaar, universally known as Cheryomushki after the local suburb, is now the main market, the Old Bazaar in the town centre having fallen victim to the ongoing redevelopment of the old town. Bagtygul Bazaar lies on Magtymguly Shayoly, west of the town centre. This is the place to buy sturgeon. Caviar is also sold here in plastic bags, though not always legally, at prices upwards of 3 million manat a kilo.

The main **post office** is close to the railway station, on the corner of Gahryman Atamurat Niyazov Shayoly and Adalat Kochesi. It is worth peering inside, as the building contains some unexpected abstract-patterned stained glass.

What to see

Around the railway station

Opposite the railway station is a bulky **Oilworkers' Cultural Palace**, built by Japanese prisoners of war in the late 1940s. The windows are marked out by arches, and geometrical patterns around the entrance also help add life to the building. The Japanese also constructed the apartment blocks facing the cultural palace to the north and west, topped with little obelisks.

There are several pieces of statuary around the cultural palace. On the northeast side of the building sits a gold President Niyazov in front of a row of concrete arches. On the seaward side is a **war memorial**. The main statue here is of Atamurat Niyazov, President Niyazov's father, in military uniform, right hand over his breast. This was installed in 2004, replacing a Soviet composition which depicted three bereaved Turkmen ladies (mother, wife and sister, perhaps). The eternal flame at the foot of the statue now burns at the centre of an eight-pointed star, rather than a five-pointed Soviet one. A memorial to the Bolsheviks who died during the Civil War stood until 2004 immediately to the west of the main war memorial, but has now been removed.

The main street running east–west here was formerly named in honour of Valeriy Rilov, Hero of the Soviet Union, native of Garabogaz, and defender of Stalingrad, who was killed in action in 1944. It has been renamed to honour the war hero favoured by the post-independence regime, Atamurat Niyazov. Walking east from the station, along this street, you soon catch sight of the eight-sided dome of the **Russian Orthodox Church**, one street landward, almost directly behind the Altyn Asyr Kafé. A tsarist-era building, the church has been heavily battered during its lifetime, suffering removal from an earlier site and use during the Soviet period for meetings of the Young Pioneers. At the western end of Gahryman Atamurat Niyazov Shayoly is a golden statue of the poet **Magtymguly**, stroking his beard.

Heading landward from the Magtymguly statue, along Garaev Kochesi, you come to an unmistakably Soviet **Mother and Child Memorial**, reached by a double flight of steps. The mother, arms outstretched above her, balances her child on her head, the poor infant taking on the role of a gymnastics prop.

Regional history museum

The museum is housed in two separate buildings, a couple of hundred metres apart. The higher of the two buildings, part of the old fort, lies one block to the west of the Magtymguly statue. Near its entrance stands a tall and ugly concrete monument, '100' written on it in white lettering, built in 1969 to commemorate the centenary of the birth of the town. The museum (☎ 243 59904) is open 09.00–18.00 daily except Mondays, with a lunch-break 13.00–14.00. Foreigners pay 2,000 manat. The lower building is a whitewashed bungalow, reached by walking directly towards the sea. It is, however, frequently shut, which is a shame, as it houses the more interesting exhibits.

Beyond a display relating to President Niyazov in the lobby, visitors to the **upper building** are then confronted with a natural history room. It has walls decorated like artificial cliff-faces, with stuffed birds of prey preparing to swoop down onto the parquet flooring. There are stuffed-animal-heavy displays of local maritime and desert environments, a relief map of the Caspian, and a large wall map on which light switches allow you to illuminate the geographical whereabouts of your favourite mineral deposits. Immediately beyond is an ethnography room, focused on the shell of half a *yurt*, in which are arranged various carpet bags, a *dutar*, a *samovar* and assorted pots. There are small displays too of Turkmen jewellery and clothing. Off this room is one devoted to carpets, featuring some prayer rugs, a large carpet of Yomud design, and a colourful tapestry of swimming sturgeon which was apparently exhibited at a Communist Party conference in 1988.

The strangest exhibits in the upper building are found in a small side room off the natural history hall. These are a display of ten holograms, mostly of Christian religious themes, and apparently the work of one Y N Denisuk. They are 'complete replicas of rare masterpieces', according to a brochure attached to the display, produced by the Minsk Art and Production Association and the Institute of Physics named after B I Stepanov of the Academy of Science of the Belarus Soviet Socialist Republic.

In Soviet times, the **lower building** was a museum dedicated to the 26 Baku Commissars (see box). This is the former courthouse in which the commissars were held while their fate was decided on by the authorities in Ashgabat. In the corridor running beyond the entrance to the building are two heavy doors, with metal grilles. The commissars were held behind these. The museum guides get flustered if you ask questions about the commissars, who have been excised from the displays in the museum. The busts of the leading commissars have been removed from the four concrete plinths which still remain in front of the building, and the eternal flame which once burned in the courtyard has been snuffed out.

The first room in the lower building today focuses on the development of the town since independence in 1991, with photographs of new marble-faced buildings, and samples of the products of local enterprises, from motor oil to tinned sardines. This leads on to a room devoted to the history of the town during the tsarist period. This includes some interesting early photographs and postcards of the town, a painting of Stoletov, and two large 1980s' canvases by one V A Artikov. One of these depicts the Turkmen merchant Hodjanepes meeting Peter the Great in St Petersburg, the right hand of the Turkmen placed across his chest in a show of respect to the somewhat windswept emperor. Hodjanepes' tales of the gold of the Oxus River, and of its former course to the Caspian, to which the river might perhaps be redirected again to facilitate Russian trade, helped persuade Peter to despatch the ultimately ill-fated expeditions of Prince Alexander Bekovich. The second canvas, entitled *Handshake*, features that act being performed by a Russian commander and a Turkmen tribal leader. The two paintings together offer a political message of the late Soviet period, depicting the Russian annexation of the region as an act welcomed by the local Turkmen leadership.

The next room offers an eclectic mix of items from the Soviet period, including

THE 26 BAKU COMMISSARS

In early 1918, the port city of Baku was under Bolshevik control, led by Stepan Shaumian, an ethnic Armenian friend of Lenin. The ruling group was a disparate one, with a large Armenian component. At the end of July, with the Baku Soviet in increasing panic about the imminent arrival of Turkish forces, Shaumian was overthrown, and the authorities turned instead to the British for support. A small force under Major General Lionel Dunsterville, which had been waiting anxiously in northern Persia for permission to help defend Baku against the Turks, was immediately despatched.

Dunsterville's forces were too few, and were evacuated from Baku in the face of an overpowering Turkish onslaught on September 14. Among the many others attempting to leave Baku were Shaumian and his colleagues, who had been released from their Baku jail to save them from the predicted bloodshed to come. Shaumian and his associates left Baku on the night of September 14, on a refugee boat bound for the safety of Bolshevik-controlled Astrakhan. But the boat altered its course, making instead for Krasnovodsk, which was under the control of the anti-Bolshevik Transcaspian Government. Soviet historians were later to see a British hand behind that fateful change of course, but it may have been down to an anti-Bolshevik ship's captain. Shaumian and his colleagues were arrested on arrival in Krasnovodsk, and placed in a temporary jail in the town's courthouse, while the local commandant telephoned his bosses in Ashgabat to ask what to do with the prominent prisoners.

President Funtikov, the former train driver at the helm of the Transcaspian Government, convened a meeting on September 18 to decide the fate of Shaumian and the other Baku Commissars. Captain Reginald Teague-Jones, the local representative of the British General Malleson, based in Mashhad, was also invited to the meeting though, recovering from an injury, reportedly did not stay until the end. The meeting concluded that the prisoners would be shot.

In the early hours of September 20, Shaumian and his colleagues were awoken, and bundled into a railway goods wagon, with the explanation that they were being taken to a jail in Ashgabat. The train set off from Krasnovodsk, but came to a halt in the desert, just before dawn. The prisoners were marched into the desert, lined up, and shot.

The murder of the 26 Baku Commissars became part of the iconography of the Soviet Union, with a central role ascribed to the British in ordering the action. A painting by Isaac Brodsky shows uniformed British officers personally directing the execution. Held responsible by Soviet writers for the order to kill the commissars, Captain Teague-Jones was forced to conceal his identity, changing his name to Ronald Sinclair. Following the death of Teague-Jones/Sinclair at the age of 99, his diary of the events of the period was finally published, with the help of the Great Game authority Peter Hopkirk, as *The Spy Who Disappeared*.

five golden busts of war heroes and an interesting range of items commemorating a journey made in 1936 by an intrepid group of Krasnovodsk fishermen. Setting off on 5 July, they took their small fishing boats 4,653km across the Caspian and along the Russian river system, reaching Moscow on 6 October. They were welcomed by thousands of Muscovites assembled in Gorky Park. Items on display include one of the little wooden boats which made the journey, press clippings marking the 60th anniversary of the event, and a romanticised painting.

Two further visitable rooms on the other side of the building offer little of interest. A regional industry room has more canned fish, plus photographs of the town's oil refinery and power station. Beyond this is a room devoted to the writers of the town, with photographs, books and prizes.

Around the seafront

To the seaward side of the lower building of the regional history museum are two towers resembling large syringes, their needles topped with crescent moons and barrels decorated with motifs inspired by the designs of Turkmen carpets. These are known as the 'Gateway to the East'. A small pier with a basic café on the end juts out into the harbour immediately beyond here. To the east of this is a run-down park, with some ancient-looking rides and assorted statuary, including one of a moustachioed military man battling a many-headed sea serpent. The task is made no easier by the fact that the good soldier's hands have fallen off. A MiG fighter, once installed here for use as a climbing frame, was removed in 2004, but the authorities have reportedly simply parked it in a new location, away from public access in the port complex which takes up the rest of the coastal strip east of here. On the landward side of the park, the gleaming modern building shaped like a ship is the headquarters of the Turkmen Sea and Riverways Authority. A golden statue of President Niyazov, cloak billowing in the coastal breeze, stands outside.

To the west of the small pier is a murky scrap of beach. In summer, boys leap into the water from the rusting wreckage of old boats. Immediately to the west, the coast is again inaccessible, behind the walls of a decrepit industrial area and then a naval base. Inland of here are the single-storey buildings of the old town, decorated with half-columns and painted in pastel colours. Much of this area is, however, undergoing redevelopment, with a new multi-storey hotel building under construction. A couple of blocks further inland, along Turkmenistan Kochesi, the former **Armenian Church** sits around the back of the city mayor's office. The building has suffered badly from damage and neglect over the years, and is not open to visitors.

West of the naval base is an outdoor concert venue which has seen better days, and then a white marble-clad cultural palace, built to host the 14th session of Turkmenistan's People's Council in 2003.

On Bahri-Hazar Kochesi, immediately opposite the outdoor concert venue, sits the headquarters of the **Hazar Nature Reserve**. This originated in 1932 as the Esenguly Nature Reserve, covering the coastal environment of the far southwest of Turkmenistan. Its emblem was the flamingo, one of the showiest of the species found in the area. The Krasnovodsk Gulf was added to the reserve in 1968, bringing a new emblem, the coot. The reserve includes the offshore sanctuary of Ogurchinsky Island, to which permission to visit is not usually given to non-specialists. This is home to thousands of Caspian seals as well as a protected population of goitred gazelle, established on the island in the 1980s. The Hazar Reserve is particularly celebrated for its diverse population of wintering birds: Turkmenbashy Gulf and the coast to the south offer excellent opportunities for ornithologists.

The reserve headquarters building includes a small **nature museum**, opened in 1982. The museum (☎ 243 22318, 25058) is in theory open 09.00–18.00 weekdays only, with a break for lunch. In practice it is usually locked unless you call ahead, or go round to the back of the building and ask someone to open up.

The museum appears to be little changed since its opening. The entrance lobby features some tacky furniture, a large wall map of the nature reserves of the Soviet

Union, and a stained-glass window decorated with swan designs. There is one large room, offering relief maps of the two main parts of the reserve and tableaux of various maritime environments comprising stuffed birds in front of painted backgrounds. A swan flies out of one of these scenes in an apparent escape bid. Also on display is a miscellaneous collection of elderly publications, including a Nature Conservancy Council brochure from 1978 entitled 'Nature Conservation in the United Kingdom'. A corridor running behind the main room offers more stuffed animals, from hare to hoopoe, and some display panels describing, in Turkmen, the work of the reserve. The visitors' book in the lobby includes an upbeat write-up from July 2000, signed 'Kylie and Jason'. Hadn't they split up by then?

Japanese memorial

The road from the town to the airport passes through a sheer-walled cutting, reportedly built by Japanese prisoners of war. On reaching the plateau at the top of this cutting, you come to a road junction. On the seaward side of this is a graveyard, which houses a simple monument. The melancholy inscription on this, in Russian and Japanese, talks of the Japanese prisoners of war who died in captivity, while thinking only of their homeland. With the aims of peace on Earth and the building of friendship between Japan and Turkmenistan, this monument, concludes the inscription, was built here on 'Homesickness Hill' in 1995.

GARABOGAZGOL

Midway between Turkmenbashy and Awaza, a turning to the right marks the start of the long, lonely road heading north to the Kazakh border. This part of the country is well off even Turkmenistan's modest tourist track: a checkpoint 19km to the north marks the start of a restricted border zone for which a special permit is required.

Immediately beyond the checkpoint, a turning to the left heads to the coastal village of **Guwlymayak** ('Swan Lighthouse'), 9km away. There are two lighthouses here; a decaying metal one flanked by a more modern concrete version. But the main business of the village is salt. This is collected from a large salt lake, dry in summer, on the edge of the village, and brought to the Guwlyduz Salt Factory, where it is processed and packaged for the domestic market. The glistening white salt pan, crossed by railway tracks along which the salt is collected and transported, is a simultaneously beautiful and bleak sight.

North of the Guwlymayak checkpoint, the road passes along an arid and scarcely inhabited coastal belt. North of the hamlet of Garshi, reached after a further 60km, the road quality sharply deteriorates. Another 40km on, the road passes over a bridge, where the waters of the Caspian flow into the gulf of **Garabogazgol**. There is another checkpoint here. The gulf is a remarkable natural feature: save for this one narrow channel it is almost completely enclosed. A narrow causeway, along which the road now takes you, separates it from the Caspian. Since the gulf is large, shallow, and supplied only through one small channel, the outcome is a particularly salty body of water. Away from the channel, the shores of Garabogazgol are an eerily lifeless landscape. Calcified plants and sea creatures lie amongst the rocks. There are dead fish. Dead mice. What appears to be a brown stain along the shoreline proves to be comprised of thousands of dead insects. The whole place suggests death.

Some 49km north of the checkpoint, at the top of a small hill, is a shrine known as **Duldul Ata**, the fenced-off area said to be the burial place of a legendary winged horse. Thirteen kilometres north of here you reach the town of **Garabogaz**, formerly Bekdash. Probably the bleakest settlement in Turkmenistan, the livelihood of the town is based around sodium sulphate. This is a long-standing industry, developed in the late 1920s, which depends on the concentration of salts in Garabogazgol. Waters from this are then led into a series of natural depressions around the town, relying on the power of the Turkmen sun progressively to increase further the salt concentration. The outcome of the process is sodium sulphate and other salts which can be shovelled up into 500kg sacks. The workers who carried out this tough labour under the burning sun were praised as heroes in the Soviet period; a sign at the entrance to the town features one masked sulphate collector proudly bearing his spade like a rifle. But the industry is facing difficult times. Sacks of sodium sulphate fill warehouses and railway wagons around the town for want of markets, the workforce has reduced, and many of the apartment blocks of the town stand half-empty.

The **Hotel Jennet** (18 rooms), in a building which once housed the local Procurator-General's office, offers a just-about-passable place to eat and sleep and a lobby tiled in a loud shade of pink. It sits behind the war memorial, the latter now centred around a statue of President Niyazov's father. (☎ Garabogaz 446.)

THE ROAD TO HAZAR

The main road from Turkmenbashy to Ashgabat heads around the northern edge of the Turkmenbashy Gulf before commencing its long, arid, southeastwards journey. After 130km, at the village of Jebel, a turning to the southwest leads to the oil-industry town of Hazar.

Mollagara

Six kilometres past Jebel along the Hazar road, a turning to the south takes you to the salt lakes of Mollagara, 4km on. These are narrow lakes occupying the meandering bed of the former Uzboy River, which once acted as a spillway, taking Amu Darya waters accumulated in Sarygamysh Lake more than 500km to the Caspian. The most inviting of the salt lakes here has become a popular swimming spot. Only 24km from Balkanabat, it makes an easy trip out from that town by private car or taxi. There are also occasional buses.

There is a 1,000 manat entrance fee to get to the lakeside. Facilities include a shower block: vital for removing the salt in which you will be caked after a dip. It is possible to sleep overnight here, on one of four *tapchans* under a corrugated roof. The latter may help to keep off any rain, but will do nothing to protect you against mosquito attack. The overnight charge seems to be only 1,500 manat.

The lake is murky but great fun. In this salty water it is easy to float; much less straightforward to do anything else, as limbs are constantly propelled surface-wards. Groups of Turkmen women chat while lying in the water, still wearing their long dresses. Men cake themselves with lakeside mud, which is considered to have great therapeutic qualities. Families picnic on the banks of the lake. On summer weekends this is an altogether busy and festive place.

Three kilometres back to the north, the **Mollagara Sanatorium** lies just off of the road, on a patch of upland overlooking the Uzboy Valley below. Treatment here is focused on the medicinal qualities of the local mud and salt water. There is also a new complex, built in 1998, for the treatment of spinal damage. The sanatorium (☎ 222 42225) is geared more to 20-day treatment programmes than short-stay visitors. Its grounds are full of odd pieces of sculpture, such as a concrete pavilion resembling a piece of Turkmen female headgear, or possibly half an egg, and topped by an eagle. A plaque records that the pavilion was built in 1979 to commemorate the 1,300th anniversary of the foundation of the state of Bulgaria.

Hazar

Named Cheleken until 2000, Hazar (telephone code 240) is an oil town at the end of a peninsula running along the southern side of Turkmenbashy Gulf. It lies in a restricted border zone (the checkpoint is just to the east of town), slightly over 100km from Jebel. The road to the town passes through bleak but strangely compelling landscapes of blown sands punctuated by the rusting detritus of the oil industry.

Hazar town

The population of the town has declined rapidly since independence, mainly through emigration of the town's non-Turkmen communities. Many of the apartments in its three- and four-storey blocks now stand empty. A large open central square is overlooked by a cloaked statue of President Niyazov standing atop a podium. The Bar Jeyhun, to the side of the square (disco on the ground floor; bar above), is about it as regards evening entertainment in Hazar. Behind the statue of the president is a battered Oil Workers' Cultural Palace. To the side of this is a rusty monument depicting rockets heading off into the cosmos. The combined post and telephone office is next to this. Behind the cultural palace, the sea has reclaimed what was once part of the town.

Two tree-lined streets head off at 45° angles from the central square. The street to the east ends with a silver statue of a poor, barefoot man triumphantly holding aloft a bowl of oil. This monument, built to commemorate the first oil extracted in Cheleken, demonstrates the ease with which the early oil, simply seeping up out of the ground, could be collected. The street to the west ends at a war memorial. The inscription on a stone opposite this memorial promises, apparently forlornly, that a monument will be built in honour of Turkmens drowned by the White Forces in the Civil War in 1919.

The town's small airport was closed to passenger traffic in 2004, as the runway cannot accommodate a Boeing 717. But as you begin the journey back by road towards Jebel, a sign in English on the town's gate does at least urge you to 'hove a nice trip'.

Origins of the oil industry

The road out of Hazar to the northwest reaches after a kilometre or so the small village of **Geokbayur**, which was known in the Soviet period as Azizbekova, in honour of one of the Baku Commissars. The origins of this village, with its distinctive pitched-roofed chalets, date back to the beginnings of oil exploration in Turkmenistan, when the Nobel brothers established a community here to house their engineers. On the landward side of the road, just to the south of this village, is a **mud volcano**. Bubbles plop out of a mud lake, like a witch's brew.

Turning off the road at Geokbayur, a rough track towards the coast brings you after a few hundred metres to a monument constructed of drilling pipes to resemble a spout of gushing oil. This is a Soviet-era **monument to 100 years of oil exploitation** in Turkmenistan. In front of the monument is inscribed a rather prosaic quotation from Lenin: a telegram of February 1920 to Frunze, asking for an update on how things are going as regards Cheleken oil and the oil sector in general. The landscape around the monument is testimony to the environmental damage wrought by the extended period of oil extraction. There are abandoned buildings, 'nodding donkeys', and numerous rusting pipes. Oil seeps out of the ground at the sites of old wells which have not been properly plugged. The remnants of wooden structures here are another echo of early oil extraction, when the oil was run along wooden chutes. An even more curious piece of industrial archaeology lies on the coast, a couple of hundred metres further north. This is a rusting railway train, languishing in shallow waters on a small section of track. There was never a railway here. The train was apparently brought from Ukraine in the Soviet period to serve as an electricity generator.

BALKANABAT

The capital of Balkan Region is no longer Turkmenbashy, but the unassuming town of Balkanabat (telephone code 222), pleasantly situated at the foot of the steep-sided arid massif known as Big Balkan. Until 1999 the town was named Nebitdag ('Oil Mountain'), and it is to the oil industry that Balkanabat owes its foundation and development. The first Russian hydrocarbons prospectors came here in the 1870s. Bores were drilled in the following decade, but the area was eclipsed by the rapid development of the oilfields of Baku, and it was not until the 1930s that commercial oil production from the Nebitdag area really started in earnest. The settlement of Nebitdag, built around the railway station to service the oilfields, was given city status in 1946. The Turkmen press reported in 1999 a request from local residents to rename the city Serdarabat ('Leader City'), in honour of President Niyazov. The president suggested the name Balkanabat instead.

Balkanabat is laid out in a grid pattern, with Soviet-era apartment blocks dominating the western side of town, and Turkmen bungalows forming the eastern suburbs. Buildings are addressed not according to their street number, but by the block, or *kvartal*, in which they lie. Higher numbers usually suggest more northerly and westerly addresses. While not a town of great intrinsic tourist interest, the one good hotel and decent food options make this a useful base for exploring the southern and eastern parts of Balkan Region.

Getting there and away

Balkanabat Airport reopened for passenger flights in 2004, following modernisation, but there are currently just three flights a week between Balkanabat and Ashgabat, on Tuesdays, Thursdays and Saturdays. The flight time is one hour. Tickets cost around 30,000 manat. The tiny airport is 2km east of town, off the Ashgabat road. A taxi into town will cost around 10,000 manat. There is a Turkmenistan Airlines booking office (☎ 222 33525) in the railway station, open weekdays 09.00–17.00, though with a generous 13.00–15.00 lunch-break.

The railway station is an ugly brown block on the southern edge of town. Its main hall is enlivened by mosaics of oil workers in action. There are two trains daily to Ashgabat (7 hours), and two to Turkmenbashy (3 hours or so), although the latter both currently depart inconveniently in the early hours of the morning. The ticket office (☎ 222 41380) is open 09.00–20.00, with a lunch-break 13.00–15.00.

The bus station, just in front of the railway station, is a sleepy affair. A daily public bus makes the trip to Ashgabat in six and a half hours for 31,000 manat. The fare to Serdar is 15,000 manat. Private taxis cluster around the back of the bus station, anxious to take you to Ashgabat, Turkmenbashy or Hazar. A taxi to Ashgabat should take around four and a half hours, for around 100,000 manat a seat. Within town, a short ride by taxi should cost only 2,000 manat.

Travel agency

Balkansyyahat Kvartal 198; ☎/f 222 45338/40. A state-run agency, with its office behind the reception of the Nebitchi Hotel, which it manages. It can put together tours to the main sights of the region, including Dekhistan.

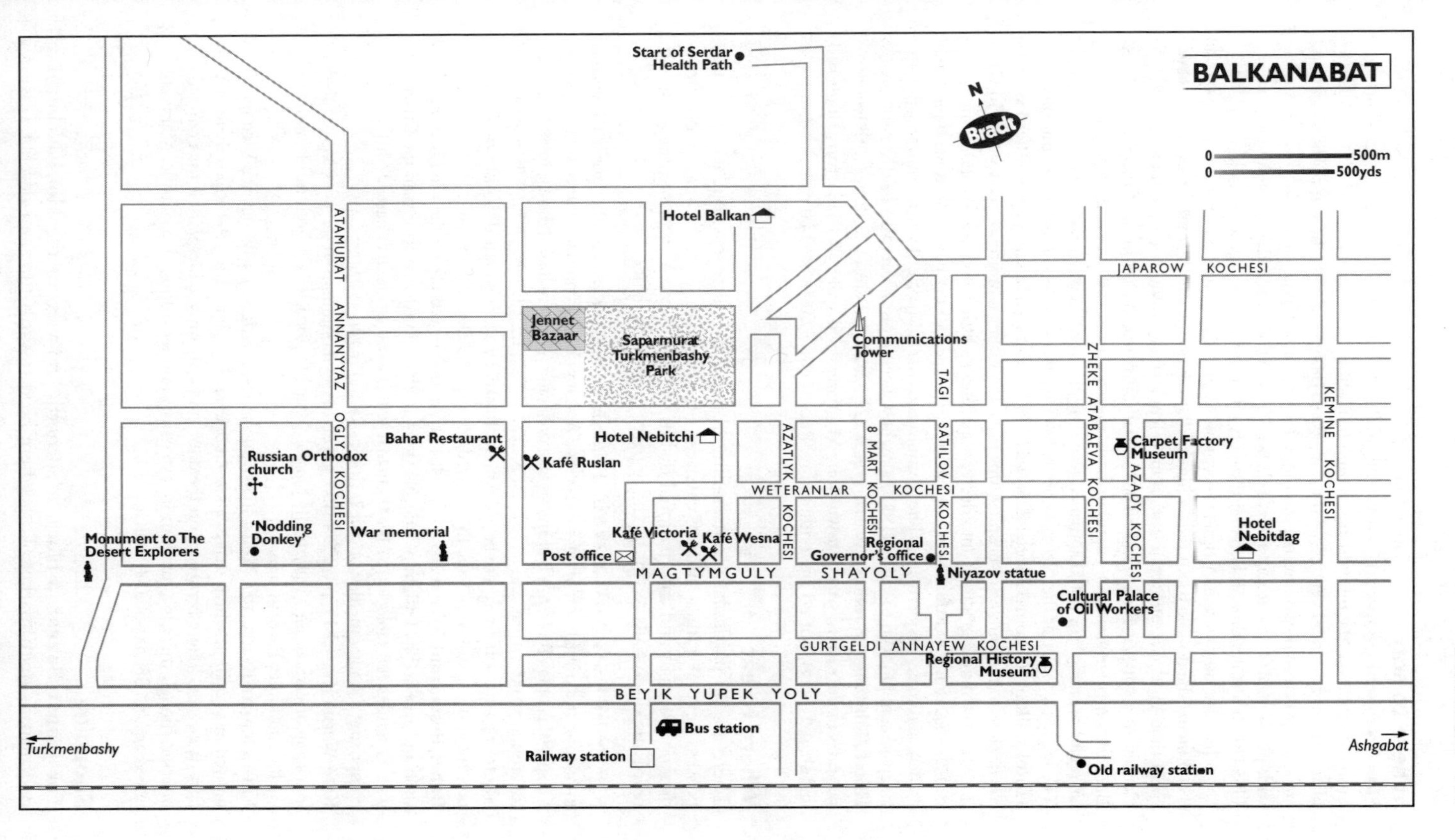
BALKANABAT
0 500m
0 500yds
Bradt
N
Start of Serdar Health Path
Hotel Balkan
JAPAROW KOCHESI
Jennet Bazaar
Saparmurat Turkmenbashy Park
Communications Tower
ATAMURAT ANNANYYAZ OGLY KOCHESI
TAGI SATILOV KOCHESI
ZHEKE ATABAEVA KOCHESI
KEMINE KOCHESI
Bahar Restaurant
Hotel Nebitchi
Kafé Ruslan
Russian Orthodox church
AZATLYK KOCHESI
8 MART KOCHESI
Carpet Factory Museum
AZADY KOCHESI
WETERANLAR KOCHESI
Hotel Nebitdag
Monument to The Desert Explorers
'Nodding Donkey'
War memorial
Kafé Victoria
Kafé Wesna
Post office
Regional Governor's office
Niyazov statue
MAGTYMGULY SHAYOLY
Cultural Palace of Oil Workers
GURTGELDI ANNAYEW KOCHESI
Regional History Museum
BEYIK YUPEK YOLY
Bus station
Turkmenbashy
Railway station
Old railway station
Ashgabat

Where to stay

Hotel Nebitchi (38 rooms) Kvartal 198; ☏/f 222 45335. This smart hotel, pitched at business visitors in the oil industry, is built to resemble a Turkmen *yurt*, with a circular plan and gently domed ceiling, whose corrugated design suggests the *yurt* poles. The rooms are arranged around two internal balconies, looking onto a large central lobby decorated with plastic palm trees. Room rates are US$100 for a single, US$150 for a double, and US$250 for a suite, though booking through a Turkmen travel agency should get you a large discount on this rate. A sign at reception warns that inviting guests between 23.00 and 09.00 incurs the double room rate; a hint perhaps at how some visiting oil executives have spent their time. The antiseptic restaurant offers a range of international, Russian and Central Asian dishes, for around 50,000 manat for mains, 30,000 manat for salads. Breakfasts involve various set combinations at prices from 55,000 manat, including a 'standard breakfast' for 200,000 manat, featuring chicken, caviar, eggs, salami and cheese. The business centre at the Nebitchi offers internet access, at 1,500 manat per minute.
Hotel Balkan (6 rooms) Kvartal 225; ☏ 222 43293. A guesthouse on the northern side of town, close to the children's hospital, this place is awaiting a promised renovation. In the interim, it is sliding gradually into decrepitude, and its little wooden beds and grim bathrooms are not worth the current rate of US$30 per person per night. It has a pleasant garden, and many resident cats. The administrator may also offer basic accommodation in an apartment block in town, at US$10 a night. Check it out before you pay.
Hotel Nebitdag (58 rooms) Kvartal 115; ☏ 222 52520. A 2-storey building with wooden verandas in the eastern part of town along Magtymguly Shayoly, this has scruffy single beds and shared toilets, but no air conditioning. Rooms cost 32,000–50,0000 manat. Grim.

Where to eat

There are no particularly outstanding options in Balkanabat, but the town does possess several rather similar eateries, offering a mixture of reasonably priced *shashlik*, Russian and international dishes in environments whose pop music and revolving disco balls tempt birthday party crowds to dance.

Kafé Ruslan Kvartal 200; ☏ 222 44007. Formerly the Kafé Evropa, this place has been renamed in honour of the small son of the manageress. A sign in English outside promises 'special food for special people'. It offers a Balkanabat take on a range of international dishes, including pizzas for around 50,000 manat, and teriyaki for 55,000. I was quite taken by an English-language flyer, advertising a one-off concert to be given in the Ruslan by a group named Benjamin. 'We promise that you not come!' the flyer vowed. Promise fulfilled: I didn't go.
Bahar Restaurant Kvartal 209; ☏ 222 46131. Across the road from the Kafé Ruslan, over a shop and accessed by a flight of external steps. It is fractionally smarter than the Ruslan, with tasteful green tablecloths. 10,000 manat will get you a side dish named 'difficult', comprising a stodgy medley of chips, rice, pasta and mash.
Kafé Wesna Kvartal 197; ☏ 222 48155. Close to the monument to the poet Magtymguly, in a scrap of park along Magtymguly Shayoly, this has plastic tables both inside and out, *shashlik*, and loud Russian music.
Kafé Victoria Kvartal 197; ☏ 222 40306. In the same park as the Wesna, the Victoria is housed in a pavilion which makes a low-budget attempt at creating the atmosphere of a fairy-tale castle. There is no sign on the door, and only three tables within the cramped interior, though there is a much more extensive summer seating area outside. Mains are priced around 35,000–50,000 manat.

Shopping

The **Jennet Bazaar**, a block or so north and west of the Hotel Nebitchi, is Balkanabat's main market. To get here head towards the semi-derelict 12-storey building, which stands at the side of the bazaar and serves as a useful landmark. There is also an out-of-town bazaar (Saturdays and Sundays only), reached along the road heading west out of the city close to the foot of Big Balkan. The main **post office** lies on Magtymguly Shayoly, the east–west thoroughfare which is the fulcrum of the town. There is a cluster of **banks** around the large expanse of asphalt, like a parade ground, immediately north of here.

What to see

Western side of town

A golden statue of President Niyazov stands atop a tribune on Magtymguly Shayoly, looking out across a pedestrianised central square. The offices of the city and regional authorities, and the headquarters of the state oil concern Turkmennebit, are all immediately to the west of here. Further west along Magtymguly Shayoly, beyond a statue to the poet, there are some nice Soviet mosaics on each end of one of the buildings of the oil and gas institute. The mosaic on the western side of the building depicts a blond oil worker, surrounded by derricks, a 'nodding donkey' and a helicopter. On the eastern wall, a Turkmen girl impressively manages to hold an ear of wheat, a bunch of cotton and an oil rig.

At the western end of Magtymguly Shayoly stands one of the most attractive statues in Turkmenistan: a **monument to the desert explorers** who first identified the oil wealth of the area. A camel strains forward amidst a fierce sandstorm, the men around it shielding their eyes from the harsh sand-laden wind. One block back along Magtymguly Shayoly, a now stationary 'nodding donkey' ('donkey which formerly nodded', perhaps) stands in a derelict plot of land behind a row of apartment blocks, as a reminder of the backbone of the town's economy. Not that this would be easy to forget. Oil rig symbols are everywhere, including in the design of some of the street lighting and the decoration of bus stops. The local football team is named Nebitchi ('Oil Workers'). The **Russian Orthodox Church** stands just to the north of the 'nodding donkey', its blue onion domes attractive under the Turkmen sun. The church is surrounded by a garden of neatly tended cypresses.

Eastern side of town

Two blocks to the east and one to the south of the central statue of President Niyazov is the Cultural Palace of Oil Workers named after Saparmurat Turkmenbashy the Great. It is faced with white marble and has a model oil rig out the front.

Over the road from here is a small **regional history museum** (☎ 222 49126). It is open 09.00–18.00, with a lunch-break 13.00–14.00, but closed on Mondays. Admission is 5,000 manat. You enter into a room devoted to the achievements of post-independence Turkmenistan, including photographs of President Niyazov's visits to Balkanabat. A hall to the left contains a mix of ethnography, archaeology and ecology. The former section includes a display focused around a segment of *yurt*, displays of jewellery worn by ladies and horses, a selection of carpets and assorted agricultural and domestic implements. There is a small display devoted to the early oil industry, when the precious liquid was extracted from shallow deposits just as water from a well, and then transported in barrels loaded onto camels. The underwhelming archaeology section manages a few pots, and a couple of models of the sights around Dekhistan. The ecology section involves numerous stuffed animals. The final room in the museum is a large hall displaying the paintings of local artists. These include some ideological works of the Soviet period, featuring oil workers, cotton pickers and a sulphate worker from Bekdash. There is a painting depicting the construction of the Kara Kum Canal, and another of a group of actors performing in remote pastureland to an audience of shepherds.

To the northeast of here, along Azady Kochesi, the **Balkanabat Carpet Factory** has a small museum (no fixed opening times), displaying some of the products of the factory, including entries to past competitions of carpet design. There is a set of decorations for a camel, a carpet design named *Unity*, combining the *guls* characteristic of different Turkmen tribes, and one called *Peace to the World*, whose *guls* incorporate numerous doves.

Northern side of town

Opposite the Hotel Nebitchi, in the northern part of town, is the **Saparmurat Turkmenbashy Park**, a large open space with a few pieces of independence-era statuary amongst rows of saplings. A tall marble obelisk in the centre of the park is part of a monument which also includes mosaic panels depicting scenes from Turkmen life: baking bread in the *tamdyr*, scything wheat, and playing the *dutar*. The central panel is a portrait of President Niyazov. To the east of this monument is a statue of the president, seated in a comfy armchair in front of a semicircular arcade. Immediately to the north of this somewhat sterile park is a cluster of three- and four-storey apartment blocks of the Soviet period, with murals on their end walls devoted to the 1980 Moscow Olympics. Some of these feature the cute bear mascot of those games.

The steep slopes of **Big Balkan** frame the town to the north. This dry massif rises to a height of 1,880m. Along its base, at the northern edge of town, a concrete **Serdar Health Path** was opened on Niyazov's birthday, 19 February, in 2004, aping the larger version in Ashgabat. A sign at the start of the path offers a presidential quotation to the effect that a healthy nation is a strong nation.

SOUTHWEST BALKAN REGION

Around Gumdag

The main road from Balkanabat to Ashgabat heads southeastwards for 30km or so towards the small desert oil town of Gumdag, before taking a more easterly direction en route to the Turkmen capital. A sign on the main road, just after the turning to Gumdag, informs drivers that Samarkand is 1,414km away. Taking the road to Gumdag, rather than that to Ashgabat and Samarkand, you pass a field of 'nodding donkeys' before reaching the town. A few kilometres to the south, you will see off to the east of the road a lone hill, some 130m high, with at its peak what appears to be a tower. The hill is called **Boyadag**. It is an ancient mud volcano; the tower comprised of solidified mud which once lay in the crater. There is a gas field near here, and a distinct smell of gas hangs over the place.

Dekhistan

The most important archaeological site of Balkan Region, the Dekhistan Oasis was inhabited for some 3,000 years, from the end of the 3rd millennium BC until the early 15th century. From the 9th century, its capital was the city of Misrian, which covered an area of some 200ha and was sustained by an extensive irrigation system. Misrian reached its peak under the Khorezmshahs, when it was an important centre along the Silk Route from Khorezm to the Caspian region of northern Iran and on to the Arabian Peninsula. Misrian was sacked by the Mongols, but managed to re-establish itself, only to be abandoned altogether around the start of the 15th century, probably due to the decline of its irrigation system, perhaps linked to excessive deforestation of the nearby slopes of the

Kopet Dag. The region today offers a flat, arid landscape. The names of villages such as Bugdayly ('Wheat Filled') hint at earlier agricultural riches, but there is now sand where once wheat grew.

Practicalities

Dekhistan is not really on the road to anywhere, and the easiest way to see the place is to book a one-day visit from Balkanabat through Balkansyyahat or one of the travel agencies in Ashgabat. From Gumdag, take the road south through Bugdayly. About 5km south of this village, turn east off the main road onto a track, passing the hamlet of Shahman. The track takes you southeastwards across large expanses of hard, flat *takyr*, over which it is possible to maintain a reasonable speed in dry weather. After rain, the route can become impassable. A 4x4 and a guide who knows the route well are both strongly recommended. The archaeological site of Misrian is visible to the south of the track, some 28km from the main road. The mausolea of Mashat lie just to the north of the track, at the foot of some gently sloping ground at the edge of the plain.

What to see

Misrian

The city of Misrian was protected by a double row of walls, punctuated by semicircular towers. Within these walls, only a few monuments survive. One of the most attractive comprises the two sides of the portal of the **Mosque of the Khorezmshah Mohammed**. These twin columns, reaching a height of 18m, are beautifully decorated with brickwork and turquoise glaze in fine geometrical and floral designs, with calligraphic work identifying the names of the architects and the Khorezmshah, who ruled at the start of the 13th century. The area around the mosque has been excavated and restored, presenting numerous fired-brick column bases both in the mosque and surrounding the courtyard in front. A somewhat incongruous sight in the centre of the courtyard is the presence of three evergreen trees, surrounded by a metal fence. An inscription reports that the trees were planted in 1993 on the instruction of the president. In the corner of the courtyard stands the remains of a minaret, now reaching a height of around 20m, and with a diameter of 7m at the base.

This minaret appears something of an ugly duckling when compared with the **Abu-Jafar Ahmed Minaret**, which stands about 120m away, and is preserved to a similar height. This minaret features two rings of Arabic inscriptions, a third, higher, ring offering pleasant geometric designs, and a spiral staircase snaking up inside the structure. The inscriptions confirm that this minaret is considerably older than that of the Mosque of the Khorezmshah Mohammed, and was built at the start of the 11th century on the design of an architect named Abu Bini Ziyad. A trench dug by archaeologists nearby has uncovered a fired-brick well. A ghoulishly large quantity of bones protrude from the trench walls. Archaeological excavations have also uncovered the foundations of several **caravansarays**, testimony to the importance of the trade routes on which Misrian stood.

Mashat

A few kilometres to the north of Misrian lies the medieval graveyard of Mashat. Five ruined mausolea stand in a line here. Circular or octagonal in plan, and all now lacking their domes, these date from the 11th or 12th centuries. They have notably deteriorated as compared with photographs taken at the site during the Soviet period. In the 19th century there were reportedly around 20 mausolea here, most long disintegrated.

The most important monument at Mashat lies on a mound, off of this line of mausolea. This is the **Shir Kabir Mosque-Mausoleum**. This dates from the 9th or 10th centuries, making it the oldest surviving mosque in Turkmenistan, though it has been restored and extended several times. Its interior is square in plan, with a domed roof. There are three niches in each wall, with the mihrab at the centre of the southern wall. This is a beautiful feature, comprising three arched recesses, one inside the other. It is intricately carved with Arabic inscriptions and swirling, floral designs. The mihrab has been boarded up for protection, but gaps between the boards offer a reasonably good view of the decoration. A carved panel in the central niche on the eastern wall is another riot of inscriptions and geometric designs. Above this lower line of niches, and immediately below the dome, are four squinches, separated by niches. The interior of the building is full of scaffolding poles, from which hang strips of cloth, marking wishes made at the site, some fashioned into elaborate cloth cribs, making clear the nature of the wishes.

Etrek and Esenguly

The Etrek River, which flows westwards into the Caspian, marks for a long stretch Turkmenistan's southern border with Iran. The two district capitals of Etrek and Esenguly lie in restricted border zones of little touristic interest, and the only real reason to come this way is to cross into Iran via the Gudurolum checkpoint, which lies just over 20km southwest of Etrek.

The 19th-century Hungarian traveller Arminius Vambery wrote that a Persian curse ran 'may you be driven to **Etrek**!' Today the place once associated in Persian minds with slavery at the hands of the local Turkmen tribes has a more peaceful existence, its dry subtropical climate helping it to serve as the centre of Turkmenistan's olive industry. Many of the houses here, and across the districts of Etrek and Esenguly, are built in a distinctive style, their walls of irregular flat stones cemented together like crazy paving. Some houses have one signature stone, cut to a careful design, such as a heart. On a few older buildings this stone is a five-pointed red star.

The town of **Esenguly**, near the Caspian coast, is one of several littoral settlements noted for its wooden houses standing on brick pillars, these 'stilts' offering protection from marine inundation. A carpet factory sits just off the main square. The latter is covered, not with gravel but with myriad tiny shells.

EAST TOWARDS ASHGABAT

Monument to the 26 Baku Commissars

From the Gumdag turning, the main road from Turkmenbashy to Ashgabat bypasses the district capital of **Bereket**, formerly Gazandjyk, some 125km east of Balkanabat. Ten kilometres west of Bereket, the main road crosses over the railway. A kilometre west of this railway bridge, an asphalt road to the north is unpromisingly marked with a no entry sign. The purpose of the sign appears to be simply to warn of the pot-holed character of the road, and this is certainly not a side trip to attempt after dusk. But it is nonetheless an interesting detour, to the place of execution of the 26 Baku Commissars (see box, page 143).

The road heads towards the eastern foothills of the massif known as Little Balkan, passing on the right a railway halt which still bears the name of Shaumian, the most prominent of the commissars. After reaching a small village of livestock farmers, continue for 6km, before taking a turning to the right which runs a few hundred metres down to a derelict railway station. Here stands a rectangular monument in gradually disintegrating pink-and-white tiling. Most of the lettering, which once spelled out the names of the commissars, has gone, but it is still possible to make out the main inscription, which records that the blood of the 26 Baku Commissars was shed for the happiness and freedom of the people, and was not given in vain. Once carefully tended flower beds around the monument are now full of dead bushes.

A couple of hundred metres up the line in the Balkanabat direction, on the other side of the track, stands a smaller metal monument, erected by factory workers in 1935 in memory of the commissars, 'shot by bandits'. This is a silent spot, the railway line snaking through an undulating desert scrub.

Parau Bibi

Some 54km east of the Bereket turning, 19km west of the town of Serdar, a turning to the south is signposted for Parau Bibi. The asphalt road heads towards the Kopet Dag Mountains. Passing after 6km through the village of Parau, the road then crosses the site of the medieval settlement of **Ferava**. This started out as a fortress, lying between Khorasan and Dekhistan, but was enlarged somewhat under the Seljuks, when it became a notable Silk Route staging post, covering an area of around 35ha. A square-based but now roofless mausoleum, known as Parau Ata, is the main structure standing at the town site.

But the building of most interest lies on the steep hillside to the south. This is the **Mausoleum of Parau Bibi**, which dates perhaps to the 11th century. It is now one of the most important centres of shrine pilgrimage in Turkmenistan. A legend surrounding the place, similar to the tales governing several other mountain shrines across Turkmenistan, is that Parau Bibi was a maiden of great virtue. When faced with the prospect of capture by an approaching enemy raiding party, Parau Bibi prayed that the mountainside should open up and take her, in order to preserve her honour. It did so, and the local people, so the story runs, built the mausoleum on that very spot.

At the base of the hillside stands a large complex comprising a guesthouse, an area for meals and a large car park. There is also a war memorial here, topped by an artillery piece. A flight of concrete steps leads up to the whitewashed mausoleum. On the way up, pilgrims walk three times anticlockwise around various natural features, including a clump of trees and a large rock, considered to be sacred places associated with the legend of Parau Bibi. The mausoleum contains many votive offerings, including model cribs and plastic rattles. In one corner of the mausoleum is a small cave: it is believed that this is the spot at which Parau Bibi entered the mountainside. Immediately to the left of the mausoleum, steps lead down to a little side room. This contains a large collection of hair-related objects, including mirrors, combs and hair-grips. Female pilgrims often brush their hair in this chamber, since it is believed that Parau Bibi herself often visits this place to comb hers.

Serdar

Formerly Gyzylarbat, the town named Serdar ('Leader') in honour of President Niyazov lies roughly midway between Balkanabat and Ashgabat. The centre of town lies roughly a kilometre to the south of the main road. A gold statue of the president stands on a podium overlooking the central square. Off to the east of this is the central bazaar. A couple of cafés along Georogly Kochesi at the northern edge of the bazaar offer basic lunch options to break the car journey between the two regional capitals. On the northern side of the central square is the former Russian Orthodox Church. It now houses a small museum, which rarely seems to be open. Immediately to the west of the church lies the railway wagon repair yard, whose origins lay in tsarist times, when for a while Gyzylarbat was the industrial motor of the Transcaspian Railway. A plaque on one of the walls of the repair yard records a visit here by the Russian opera singer Chaliapin in 1891.

THE SUMBAR VALLEY

One of the most picturesque districts of Turkmenistan, the Sumbar Valley runs on an east–west axis close to the border with Iran, taking the waters of the River Sumbar westwards to join the Etrek, and thence to the Caspian. The Kopet Dag Mountains help to protect the Sumbar Valley from the worst of the cold air from the north in the winter, and from the dessicating air from the Kara Kum Desert in summer. The floor of this mountain valley is covered with orchards, and the area is renowned within Turkmenistan for its fruit production, especially of pomegranates.

The Sumbar Valley is reached by turning south off the main Turkmenbashy to Ashgabat road at Serdar. The main town in the valley, Magtymguly, is 75km from the turning. The valley lies in a restricted border zone, for which special permission (request 'Magtymguly') is required. The checkpoint lies 11km to the west of Magtymguly town. Between checkpoint and town is a fascinating 'lunar' landscape of bare, rounded hillocks, corrugated with little dry rivulets.

Magtymguly

Named Garrygala until 2004, President Niyazov proposed that the local district and its main town be renamed Magtymguly to honour the 18th-century Turkmen poet who was a native of this area. The small town is full of monuments to and other reminders of the district's famous son, from a statue near the district mayor's office to the name of the main street.

MAGTYMGULY

Turkmenistan's hugely popular national poet, who wrote on a wide range of themes, may have been born in 1733, possibly in the village of Hajy Gowshan, but uncertainty surrounds almost every aspect of his life. Magtymguly Fyragy was a member of the Gerkez group of the Goklen tribe, which lived in the area around Garrygala and adjacent districts of present-day northern Iran. His father, Dowletmamet Azady, was himself a noted poet and author, and acted as the young Magtymguly's early mentor. Magtymguly studied at the *madrasa* of Idris Baba in Lebap Region (see page 195), then in Bukhara and Khiva. Returning to his home district, he worked as a silversmith and teacher.

Magtymguly's life seems to have been one of much sadness. His one true love, a cousin named Mengli, married another while he was away at his studies. According to some accounts, Magtymguly married his brother's widow. His marriage seems to have been an unhappy one, and his two sons died in childhood.

Turkmen tribes in the 18th century were engaged in wearying internecine conflict, enhancing their vulnerability to external aggression, and Magtymguly himself seems to have been captured in more than one raid. According to one popular tale, Magtymguly was once taken hostage together with his mother, Arazgul, and other relatives and neighbours, and held in Mashhad. She was suffering from a crippling illness, and the ruler agreed to release her, together with one male relative. Arazgul chose her son-in-law over her son. The ruler was much surprised, and asked Magtymguly why his mother had foresaken him.

Where to stay

The **guesthouse** (☎ 31461) next to the plant research station has 21 beds. The best room in the place has two beds, and an en-suite bathroom with intermittent water. The other rooms lack working plumbing. There is no air conditioning. When I stayed there my bed collapsed when I sat on it. They charge US$10 per night. If the weather is good, camping further up the valley is an altogether more pleasant option.

What to see

Plant research station

The plant research station is the southernmost of a network established across the Soviet Union by the St Petersburg-based plant research institute known as VIR, which was run by the celebrated plant geneticist Nikolai Vavilov. Vavilov came to a sad end during the Stalinist era, when his theories were briefly discredited in favour of those of Stalinist favourite Trofim Lysenco, and he died in Saratov Prison in 1943. But he was rehabilitated in the later Soviet period, and the St Petersburg institute came to bear his name. Its Garrygala station started out life in 1925, for the experimental trialling of a rubber-bearing plant, brought back by Vavilov from one of his plant-gathering expeditions to Mexico. The climate of Garrygala offered one of the closest approximations to that of Mexico found across the Soviet Union. Interest in rubber-bearing plants declined when the Soviet Union started to focus on the production of synthetic rubber, and the Garrygala station changed its attention to other plants, and to the natural flora of the western Kopet Dag.

The station today is attempting to preserve its important collection of subtropical fruit trees, and the gardens surrounding its buildings remain luxuriant. But there is little scientific work being done, and the place, which now falls under the purview of the Turkmen Ministry of Agriculture, seems to be mainly focused on selling saplings, and fruit jam.

He replied that he was a poet, and his mother had been confident that he would be able to recite his way out of captivity. The ruler decided to test him out. Magtymguly recited a poem about the Twelve Imams, in which he asked for forgiveness in the name of the virtues of each of the Imams. The ruler was so moved by the poem that he freed not only Magtymguly but all of the captured Gerkez people.

The date of Magtymguly's death is even less certain than that of his birth. Some scholars believe that he died in 1782; others that he survived until the late 1790s. Cenotaphs to Magtymguly and his father lie in the village of Ak Tokay in northern Iran, visited each year by an official Turkmen government delegation on 18 May, celebrated as the Day of Revival, Unity and the Poems of Magtymguly.

His poems are comprised of quatrains, with lines usually of eight or eleven syllables. The final stanza of each poem includes his own name, as an identification of authorship. The poems were taken up enthusiastically by Turkmen folk singers. Magtymguly, whose work has always remained popular, has been given a major place among the icons of independent Turkmenistan. The nation-building aspects of his poetry have been accorded particular prominence by President Niyazov, especially his call to the fractious Turkmen tribes to unify into a single, proud nation. Magtymguly gives his name to a major thoroughfare in most Turkmen towns. The state-run national youth union bears his name, and there are many statues to the poet across the country.

Syunt-Hasardag Nature Reserve

Just west of town is the head office of the Syunt-Hasardag Nature Reserve, set up in 1978 to protect the threatened landscapes of the western Kopet Dag. Among the rare flora of this area is the Turkmen mandrake, discovered in 1938 by the research station's scientists on the southern slopes of the hills. The reserve is also home to a few leopard, the subject of a conservation programme organised by the WWF. This features an imaginative scheme to compensate farmers for livestock killed by the leopards, to dissuade the farmers from trying to hunt these rare animals. Entry to the reserve requires the permission of the Ministry of Nature Protection (see page 28).

Shibly Baba

This shrine pilgrimage site lies at the base of the hills, close to the town of Magtymguly. Just beyond the eastern outskirts of the town, take the asphalt road to the north, signposted for Shibly Baba. After a kilometre or so, turn left onto a rougher road, which heads towards the hills, reaching the Shibly Baba Mausoleum complex after about 11km. Shibly Baba, who is said to have been a wise and educated man from Baghdad, is the protector of the insane, and it is believed that a night here will cure the pilgrim of disorders of the mind. The long cloth-covered tomb of Shibly Baba lies in a recently reconstructed mausoleum; the caretaker told me that the tomb was lengthened after local people were told in a dream that the tall Shibly Baba was cramped and uncomfortable in his original grave.

The versatile Shibly Baba is also considered to offer protection against lightning and fires. One of the artefacts in the complex suggests a further set of demands placed upon him. This is a stone shaped like a rather stumpy phallus. It has a small hole in the top: women wanting a child reportedly pour yoghurt into this, and then spend the night next to the stone. Close by is a small area in which mandrake is cultivated. I asked the caretaker what this was used for. Nothing, he claimed: they grew it here because mandrake was known to have been one of the components of the sacred narcotic drink of Zoroastrian priests. It was therefore considered to be a sacred plant. But it was not, he said, put to similar purposes today – adding, plaintively, 'we don't know the recipe'. A twin-trunked tree on the edge of the complex is another focus of pilgrims' attention. It is said that the tree will physically prevent sinners from walking between the trunks.

Gerkez

About 20km west of the town of Magtymguly, the village of Gerkez, in an attractive location along the Sumbar, is closely associated with the Turkmen classical poet. There is a three-room **Magtymguly Museum** in the village. The first room contains display cases full of books about the poet, and collections of his works, mixed with a few apparently unrelated items, such as a United Nations Environment Programme report entitled *Principles and Methods of Shifting Sands Fixation* and a tourist map of Turkey. There are carpets depicting the poet, a map showing his extensive travels, and two, somewhat conflicting, family trees. The second room is devoted to ethnography, including a display of Turkmen silver jewellery, as a reminder of Magtymguly's skill as a jeweller. Museum staff claim that an ornate teapot, with a dragon motif, was a gift from Magtymguly to his sister Zubeida. A third room offers a jumbled mix of more ethnography and paintings of celebrated poets. Lettering in white stones in the hills around here to 'Magtymguly 270' refer to the commemoration celebrations of the 270th anniversary of the poet's birth in 2003.

At the eastern edge of the village, take an unmetalled track to the south, crossing the Sumbar by way of a treacherous-looking bridge constructed of metal pipes. Just beyond the last house of the village, you reach the 15th-century **Sheikh Ovezberdy Mausoleum**. Standing in an overgrown meadow, this is an attractive domed building, constructed of fired bricks, with a square base with sides some 9m long.

Makhtumkala

This riverside village lies 9km east of Gerkez. Standing in a meadow, visible from the road, at the western edge of the village is the **Mausoleum of Makhtum**. This rectangular building, dating from the 14th or 15th century, suffers from the modern addition of a tin domed roof, and is usually locked up, but it is nonetheless worth a glance. The portal on the east side of the building, flanked by niches, is attractive.

Some 14km east of the village, take the rough track to the north, which brings you after a kilometre or so to the small but scenic **Kozhdemir Waterfall**. This is a good place to camp.

THE DESERT OF BALKAN REGION

Tasharvat

Heading westwards from Balkanabat along the main road to Turkmenbashy, the small town of Jebel is reached after 18km. The southwest turning from here runs to Mollagara and Hazar. But for journeys into the western part of the Kara Kum Desert, take instead the turning to the northeast, signposted 'Gozli Ata 130km'. Head along this road for 20km, the massif of Big Balkan to your right. Amidst arid, undulating terrain, you will reach a spring on the right-hand side of the road, supporting a verdant grove. This is Tasharvat. A little concrete area has been built here, with a somewhat incoherent Soviet-era sculpture and an inscription reporting that the place was constructed in 1978 by Bulgarian builders. A lever brings forth water from a metal pipe. Another inscription resolves that, through this spring, the roots of Bulgarian–Soviet friendship will never dry up. Three stone benches allow the weary traveller to sit and contemplate Bulgarian–Soviet friendship.

Behind the spring, a ravine is the subject of a sign in Russian warning of a 50 rouble fine for trespassing. On the hillside beyond this stand the ruins of a **caravansaray**, hinting that this place once lay on one of the branches of the Silk Road.

Gozli Ata

The road runs north of Tasharvat, gradually deteriorating in quality, for some 80km, before it hits a road running eastwards from Turkmenbashy (by which route you can reach this point with approximately the same degree of difficulty and distance). Turning east, you get to the small village of **Kosheba** after 13km. The main attraction of this place is its petrol pump, tied to a rusty metal fence. The 'petrol station' is open from 08.00–17.00, though you would be unwise to rely on the availability of petrol here. The road is frequently engulfed by blown sand around here, and 4x4 is advised. Some 15km further on, a turning to the right is signposted for Gozli Ata, 9km away.

Gozli Ata is one of the remotest shrine pilgrimage destinations in Turkmenistan. Its setting is also among the most beautiful. It lies in the centre of a natural bowl, surrounded by escarpments of bands of pink and white rock. Gozli Ata was reportedly a respected Sufi who lived in the early part of the 14th century. His mausoleum is a brick building with twin white domes, standing in an old graveyard containing many nicely carved stone tombs. The twin-domed structure of the mausoleum is necessary to accommodate the length of the tomb: a triangular prism perhaps three ordinary graves long.

LAKE TURKMEN

This grand but controversial project, launched by President Niyazov in 2000, involves turning the Garashor Depression into the largest artificial lake in Central Asia, with a projected surface area of around 3,500km2. This will be achieved by collecting the run-off waters from irrigated lands across Turkmenistan, and channelling them to the lake by means of a purpose-built network of 'collector' canals. Some 2,600km of drainage channels are planned, with the largest single channel, the Golden Age Collector, to run for 1,152km across the country. The project is due to take 20 years to complete, at a projected cost of US$4.5 billion. The goal is to create a large area of new farmland in what is now desert, allowing, the Turkmen government forecasts, the production of an extra 450,000 tonnes of cotton and 300,000 tonnes of grain annually.

The Turkmen government argues that the project will bring many environmental benefits, including a reduction in the pollution of the Amu Darya, by reducing the flow of run-off waters returning to it from Turkmen fields. It is hoped that the lake will also help to moderate Turkmenistan's harsh continental climate. But many commentators are more sceptical, arguing that a reduction in the quantities of run-off returning to the Amu Darya will reduce the water supplies available to that river and exacerbate the problem of the drying of the Aral Sea. The unlined drainage channels passing across sandy soils will, it is feared, be highly water-inefficient, and there are concerns about the likely water quality of Lake Turkmen and the levels of evaporation from it.

The government continues to put much energy into the project. Small construction teams, using top of the range Japanese and American excavating machinery to dig the new drainage channels, are a common sight across some of the remotest stretches of the Kara Kum Desert.

Yangykala Canyon

Continuing eastwards beyond the turning to Gozli Ata, the road passes through some highly attractive canyon country, its polychrome escarpments a riot of bands of greenish, white and pink rocks. Around 40km from the Gozli Ata turning, the road climbs an escarpment. At the top, take the left hand of the tracks heading northwards from the road, the escarpment to your left. After 6km a stunning pink-floored canyon suddenly opens up on the right. The track passes along a narrow strip of high ground between escarpment and canyon, ending shortly beyond at a promontory. The view from here is one of the best in Turkmenistan. The ravine-dissected pink floor of Yangykala Canyon gives way to corrugated greenish-white walls, topped by a hard brown cap. The promontory on which you are standing ends at a rock resembling the jaws of a crocodile, snapping shut on air. For this, and all routes involving off-road driving in the desert, at least two 4x4 vehicles, experienced off-road drivers and plenty of spare petrol and water are important measures.

Taking the right hand of the two tracks heading north from the main road atop the escarpment will bring you to another local beauty spot, the **Yangysuw Canyon**, 25km away. An experienced guide is needed to navigate the right route, as there are many competing tracks here. The top of the canyon appears suddenly, its walls and floor sculpted out of bright white rock, rather than the pinks and greens predominating at Yangykala. The track descends steeply into the canyon, towards the eastern shores of Garabogazgol, a few kilometres away along dismal tracks.

Garashor Depression

Back on the tarmac but pot-holed road, the village of **Gyzyl Gaya** lies 75km east of the turnings to Yangykala/Yangysuw. The village is a bleak place, full of the detritus of an abandoned mining industry. There is, though, a petrol pump here. There is also a restricted zone checkpoint just to the west of the village. Expect the process of registering documents and checking on the validity of permits to take an hour at the very least. The Garashor Depression is some 150km east of here, across rough tracks. An experienced guide is essential. The depression is an impressive sight. With a flat floor and in many places sheer sides, it runs from northwest to southeast for 100km, though is nowhere more than about 20km wide. The Turkmen government plans to fill the depression with water, to construct Lake Turkmen (see box opposite). If you are making the cross-desert transit from Balkan to Dashoguz Regions, the main track runs around the north side of the Garashor Depression. There is another checkpoint here, at **Dahly**, an outpost which offers perhaps the remotest gold bust of President Niyazov in Turkmenistan.

Balkan Region carpet gul

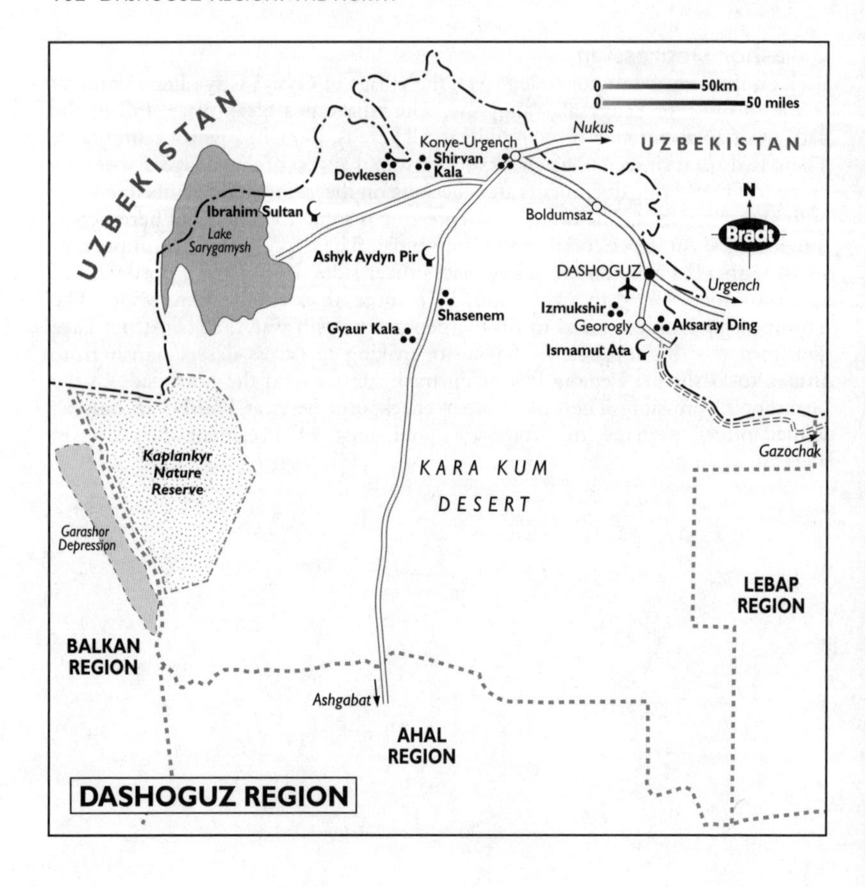
UZBEKISTAN
0 50km
0 50 miles
Konye-Urgench
Nukus
UZBEKISTAN
Devkesen
Shirvan Kala
N
Ibrahim Sultan
Lake Sarygamysh
Boldumsaz
Bradt
Ashyk Aydyn Pir
DASHOGUZ
Urgench
Shasenem
Izmukshir
Georogly
Aksaray Ding
Gyaur Kala
Ismamut Ata
Gazochak
Kaplankyr Nature Reserve
KARA KUM DESERT
Garashor Depression
LEBAP REGION
BALKAN REGION
Ashgabat
AHAL REGION
DASHOGUZ REGION

6 Dashoguz Region: the North

The Khorezm Oasis, fed by the waters of the Amu Darya, sits astride the border between Turkmenistan and Uzbekistan, a frontier defined in the 20th century serving to divide the lands of what was for many centuries a single civilisation, based around the geographical territory of the oasis. The area of agricultural land under cultivation expanded and contracted as the powers of the ruling regimes here rose and fell: building new irrigation channels or letting existing ones fall into disuse. Even today, the complex pattern of irrigation canals bringing water to the fields from the Amu Darya, and of deep 'collectors' drawing run-off waters away, is testimony to the crucial role of water in the economy of the region. The evidence presented by the many abandoned fields, their soils encrusted with salt, hints at the major environmental problems wrought by a focus on short-term yields of cotton.

Dashoguz Region feels remote from Ashgabat, far to the south across the unforgiving Kara Kum Desert. Ethnic Uzbeks are a sizeable minority. In common with adjacent areas of Uzbekistan, the region has felt the environmental consequences of the dessication of the Aral Sea, to the north. This is one of the poorest parts of Turkmenistan. The settled areas lie in the Khorezm Oasis, close to the Uzbek border, and the government is concerned about cross-border smuggling of petrol and other products subsidised in Turkmenistan. All of these factors have helped prompt Niyazov's government to try to integrate Dashoguz Region more closely with the rest of Turkmenistan. A railway is under construction, running audaciously straight across the desert from Ashgabat, to remove reliance on the current roundabout route via Turkmenabat, which both takes an eternity and crosses a stretch of Uzbek territory. The direct road from Ashgabat is also being upgraded. Controversially, Niyazov has announced plans to resettle families from certain border areas deemed 'overpopulated' to new sites in the interior of the country, on the margins of the Kara Kum.

For the tourist, Dashoguz is not the most straightforward region to visit. Travellers on tourist visas need the appropriate border permit to get almost anywhere of interest here. You cannot fly to Dashoguz Airport without such a permit. The amount of time currently eaten up by road or rail options in getting here also means that demand for the domestic flights between Ashgabat and Dashoguz is high, and seats correspondingly difficult to get. But this is nonetheless a rewarding region. The most important site is the former Khorezm capital of Konye-Urgench, whose attractions mix archaeology with shrine pilgrimage. There are also many other, less well-known historical sites around the Khorezm Oasis. The region is also the natural point of departure for onward visits to the Uzbekistan side of the oasis, including Khiva. The regional capital, Dashoguz, provides a good accommodation base for exploring the region. Temperatures are often a few degrees cooler than other parts of Turkmenistan, and Dashoguz has a deserved reputation for bleak winters.

DASHOGUZ

The name of the regional capital (telephone code 322) has undergone a number of changes of spelling. Once known as Tashauz, the name Dashhovuz briefly held sway until a presidential decree in 1999 announced that city and region would both be named Dashoguz. The new spelling draws on one version of the origins of the name: that it refers to an Oguz clan living 'far' ('*dash*') from their compatriots. The presidential decree refers to the importance of correcting the 'distortion' of historical names, in this case to help young people develop the 'spirit of patriotism' associated with the Oguz Turkmen. But there is a quite different version of the name's origins: '*dash*' can also mean 'stone', and under this interpretation the town draws its name from a stone-clad spring, which provided an important water supply for travellers passing through.

The first references to a settlement here date from the early 19th century. Later, as part of the Khanate of Khiva, its role included that of ensuring that local Turkmen tribes remained in line. The modern town dates from the Soviet period: construction began in earnest along the southern side of the Shabat Canal in the 1920s. The place serves as a transport hub, and base for exploring the region, rather than as a tourist destination in its own right. With wide and rather empty streets, and expanses of run-down Soviet apartment blocks in the town centre, Dashoguz can feel a somewhat desolate place. But it has a reasonable range of accommodation and food options, and a good central bazaar.

Getting there and away

Dashoguz is served by five daily **flights** from Ashgabat. The flight time is 50 minutes, and tickets cost around 30,000 manat. Despite the relatively large number of flights, all on Boeing 717 aircraft, it can be fiendishly difficult to get a ticket. Arrive early for your flight: there are many stories of overbookings. There is also one flight, four days a week, to Turkmenbashy. As you enter the terminal building from your plane, your passport will be checked by border guards for the appropriate restricted zone permit. The airport is 14km south of town. Taxis meet the flights, and shouldn't charge more than 10,000 manat for the trip into town. The Turkmenistan Airlines booking office is in the town centre, adjacent to the Hotel Dashoguz.

The **railway station** (☎ 322 46875) sits at the north edge of town, at the end of Turkmenistan Kochesi. One train a day makes the epic journey to Ashgabat, at a cost of less than 60,000 manat but around 24 hours of your time. There is also one train daily heading on to Konye-Urgench. The display boards at the station list prices to all manner of destinations, such as Tashkent and Moscow, to which there no longer seem to be any passenger trains.

Buses, **minibuses** and **taxis** depart from an expanse of open ground just to the west of the Bai Bazaar. There are no timetables. The buses are mostly battered-looking, and indicate their destinations with a piece of card behind the windscreen. One announced 'October', which I hope referred to a place rather than the likely departure time. There are reasonably frequent departures to all district capitals in Dashoguz Region. For trips to Ashgabat, a place in a taxi is likely to cost around 200,000 manat for a journey of about 12 hours (less following one of the periodic attempts by the authorities to tackle the pot-holes in the road across the desert). Minibuses charge around 150,000, and (infrequent) buses 100,000. The cost of a taxi around town in Dashoguz should be 3,000–5,000 manat.

Travel agency

Dashoguzsyyahat 88 Azatlyk Kochesi; ☎ 322 57294, 36797; f 322 36485; email soitur@tashauz.ngo-tm.org, tourism@tashauz.ngo-tm.org. A state-run agency, Dashoguzsyyahat manages the Hotel Uzboy, organises trips to Konye-Urgench and other historical sites in the region, and is able to provide a full range of services for foreign tourists, including obtaining letters of invitation. The main private agencies in Ashgabat are, however, more efficient as regards the latter.

Where to stay

Hotel Diyarbekir (15 rooms) Saparmurat Turkmenbashy Shayoly; ☎ 322 59037. Built by a Turkish construction company for the Dashoguz oil and gas organisation, the Diyarbekir features vast, cream-coloured rooms, a central location, a reasonable level of comfort and dismal service from the bored staff. Rooms cost US$60, with the 1 suite charged at US$100. There is an additional (and apparently unavoidable) reservation fee of US$5 for the rooms and US$10 for the suite. Breakfast is not included in the room price.

Hotel Uzboy (26 rooms) 19/1 Saparmurat Turkmenbashy Shayoly; ☎ 322 59738, 56016; fax and email contact through Dashoguzsyyahat (see above). This relatively new hotel, run by Dashoguzsyyahat, is on the western side of town, less conveniently located than the Diyarbekir, but a good option nonetheless. Rooms all have air conditioning, though some are pokey and the en suites feature shower attachments but no cubicles. Breakfast is included in the room rate: a reasonable US$30 for singles, US$50 for doubles. There are 3 'semi-luxe' rooms available at US$75. If you feel like splashing out, the best room in town is the apartment, at US$120, for which, as well as your bedroom, you get a dining room, lounge, sauna and plunge pool.

Hotel Dashoguz 44/1 Saparmurat Turkmenbashy Shayoly; ☎ 322 53785, 55206. This is a run-down legacy of Soviet times, with air conditioning but tatty rooms and grotty en suites. The management were unable to specify how many bedrooms the hotel possessed, a sure sign that some are now too decrepit to be used. The bedrooms still display stickers on their doors, recording that the delegates to the eighth session of Turkmenistan's People's Council were accommodated here in 1998. The hotel charges US$30 a night for ordinary rooms, US$60 a night for suites. The rooms are not worth this.

Hotel Shahabad (6 rooms) 35A Al Khorezmi Kochesi; ☎/f 322 50110, 53852; e eric@tashauz.ngo-tm.org. A small private hotel run by an energetic ethnic Uzbek entrepreneur, and located above his print shop in a convenient central location. This is a clean and comfortable place, offering 4 rooms with en-suite facilities, 2 with a shared shower room, and a large kitchen for the use of guests. Rooms are charged at US$25 per person for double occupancy, US$40 for single occupancy.

Where to eat

Shatugy Restaurant 6 Al Khorezmi Kochesi; ☎ 322 59742. Located at the end of an expanse of concrete park, just around the corner from the Hotel Diyarbekir, the Shatugy qualifies as the smartest restaurant in Dashoguz. The menu comprises an eclectic mix of inexpensive Central Asian and international dishes, from *plov* to spaghetti.

Nadira Restaurant Andalyp Kochesi; ☎ 322 52005. A bright-blue-painted pavilion, in an area of scrubby parkland south of the Dashoguz Hotel, this place offers Uzbek music, small rooms off the main dining area if a more intimate meal is required, and draught beer at 12,000 manat a glass. The Russian/international menu is inexpensive, including pizzas for 20,000–35,000 manat and cheeseburgers at just 12,000 manat.

Café Marat Saparmurat Turkmenbashy Shayoly; ☎ 322 50600. Just south of the roundabout on Turkmenbashy Shayoly, this place offers a similar deal to the Nadira, including an almost identical menu and prices, and the same taste in Uzbek pop music. The interior décor is bland, but there is a pleasant terrace in summer.

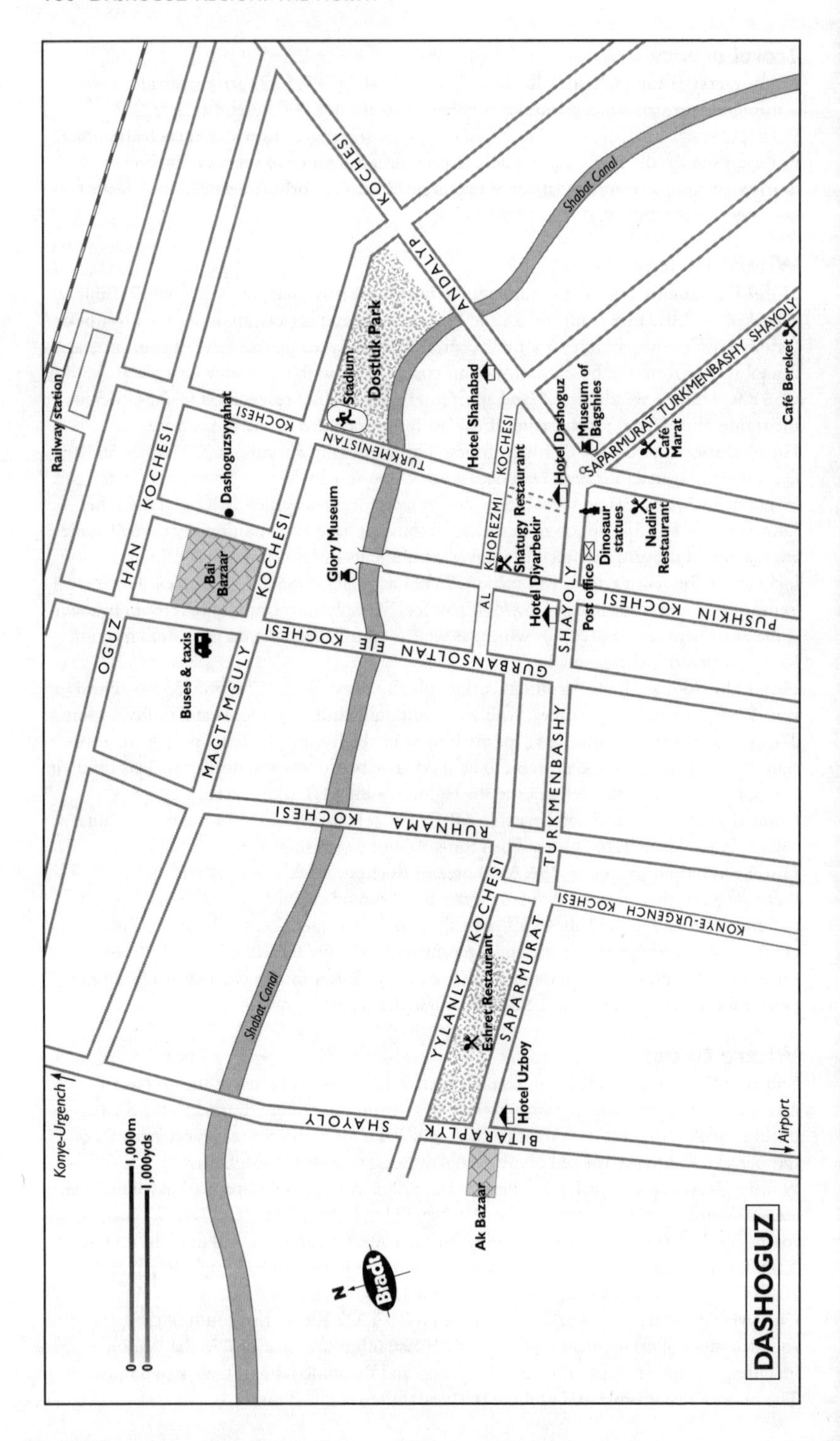
DASHOGUZ
Railway station
Dashoguzsyyahat
Bai Bazaar
Buses & taxis
OGUZ HAN KOCHESI
MAGTYMGULY KOCHESI
Stadium
Dostluk Park
Glory Museum
KOCHESI
ANDALYP
Shabat Canal
TURKMENISTAN KOCHESI
Hotel Shahabad
AL KHOREZMI KOCHESI
Shatugy Restaurant
Hotel Diyarbekir
Hotel Dashoguz
Museum of Bagshies
SAPARMURAT TURKMENBASHY SHAYOLY
Café Marat
Café Bereket
Dinosaur statues
Nadira Restaurant
Post office
PUSHKIN KOCHESI
GURBANSOLTAN EJE KOCHESI
RUHNAMA KOCHESI
KONYE-URGENCH KOCHESI
YYLANLY KOCHESI
Eshret Restaurant
SAPARMURAT TURKMENBASHY SHAYOLY
Hotel Uzboy
BITARAPLYK SHAYOLY
Ak Bazaar
Konye-Urgench
Airport
0 1,000m
0 1,000yds
N
Bradt

Café Bereket Saparmurat Turkmenbashy Shayoly; ☎ 322 52559. Further south from the Marat, heading out of the town centre, this is a cheap Uzbek café serving *somsa*, *pelmeni*, and lamb kebabs. The place has 2 rooms, allowing diners to sit on plastic chairs or lounge on cushions. The mostly male clientele usually features several representatives of the local law-enforcement agencies, contentedly gnawing at lumps of meat.
Eshret Restaurant Saparmurat Turkmenbashy Shayoly; ☎ 322 37805. Located in the park close to the Hotel Uzboy, this is the most atmospheric place to eat in Dashoguz. The restaurant is located inside a monument to President Niyazov: the 5-sided pyramid in the centre of the park, topped by a golden statue of the president. You reach the dining area across a causeway over a usually dry pool, and then up some twisting stairs. The restaurant itself has 2 floors: chairs and tables on the lower level, intimate dining higher up, including 1 room offering floor cushions around a low table. The place is decorated throughout in a mix of traditional Turkmen items, such as carpet bags and wooden ornaments, and symbols of independent Turkmenistan, including a large Turkmen flag. Prices are reasonable (12,000–15,000 manat for a portion of *shashlik*), but watch hidden extras on the bill. Grazing from the fruit bowl on the table incurred a 50,000 manat charge.

Shopping

The **Bai Bazaar**, officially known as the Dayhan (Peasant) Bazaar, offers everything that a good central bazaar should. It is located off Gurbansoltan Eje Kochesi, a couple of blocks north of the Shabat Canal. Entering the bazaar through the nicely carved wooden doors on the western side, the small bar on your left sells locally produced Concord beer. This remarkable liquid is produced by a Dashoguz entrepreneur using home-brew kits imported from Britain.

If you are staying at the Hotel Uzboy, you might glance at the **Ak Bazaar** over the road. The main, domed building is virtually deserted, save for a shop making wedding dresses. The bazaar itself is round the back: a shrine to car parts, with rows of radial tyres, headlights and shock absorbers. There is an out-of-town market, the **Shor Bazaar**, just to the east of the town gate on the Konye-Urgench road, but it is not really worth the trip out.

What to see

Town centre statues

The hotels and major administrative buildings of Dashoguz cluster along Saparmurat Turkmenbashy Shayoly, which runs from east to west through the town centre. This road was formerly named Andalyp Shayoly, in honour of the 18th-century Turkmen poet who was a native of this region. A statue of **Andalyp** sits atop a pile of rocks in a rather bleak park to the west of the Dashoguz Hotel, surveying the road that used to be his. Andalyp does, however, get another road to his name: the former Turkmenbashy Shayoly, a less central thoroughfare running northeastwards from the roundabout close to the Dashoguz Hotel, is now Andalyp Kochesi, completing the swap. In the same park is a golden bust of the 9th-century scientist, **Al Khorezmi**, a corruption of whose name gave us the mathematical term 'algorithm'.

On the other side of the Dashoguz Hotel, a statue centred around President Niyazov's book ***Ruhnama*** groups together many of the symbols favoured by the Turkmen government. A seated golden President Niyazov, looking nothing like the man, holds a copy of *Ruhnama*. Behind is a large concrete mock-up of the cover of *Ruhnama*. To either side stand statues of the four leaders heralded by Niyazov as responsible for the past Golden Ages of the Turkmen people: Oguz Han, Georogly, Gorkut Ata and Magtymguly. Across the road from here is a particularly quirky sculpture: a pair of **dinosaurs**. A stegosaurus snarls at a looming tyrannosaurus, the latter evidently discomfited by its oversized tail.

Museums

Just beyond the eastern side of the roundabout along Turkmenbashy Shayoly, on the ground floor of a residential apartment block, sits the **Museum of *Bagshies*** (traditional Turkmen singers, who accompany their sung and spoken tales with *dutar* playing; open Mon–Fri 09.00–18.00, with a 13.00–14.00 closure for lunch; ☎ 322 56042). It has two main rooms, offering photo-based displays of the most renowned 20th-century singers of Dashoguz Region, including detailed 'family trees' linking the *bagshies* of different generations by their teacher–pupil relationships. There is a display of Turkmen musical instruments, and a bright mural of Ashyk Aydyn Pir, patron of singers and musicians, who is depicted wearing a long pink coat. A small room to the side features a display of the back pages of the Soviet entertainment magazine *Krygozor* ('Prospect'), with smiling pictures of the singing stars of the 1960s and 1970s. Among the rows of Soviet stars are a few Western acts who were obviously big in the USSR, such as Abba and a young Julio Iglesias.

At the north end of Pushkin Kochesi, which runs off Turkmenbashy Shayoly just to the east of the Diyarbekir Hotel, take the footbridge across the Shabat Canal. The single-storey detached building on your left is the **Glory Museum**, opened on Victory Day in 1984 to honour the veterans of the Great Patriotic War. The museum (☎ 322 58776) is open Monday–Saturday 09.00–18.00. Admission costs 1,000 manat. The main gallery of the museum is devoted to local war heroes, centred around busts of four such Heroes of the Soviet Union. One of them, Saparmurat Hojayev, survived the war to become a teacher. His civilian suit, replete with dozens of medals, is preserved in a glass case. His wheelchair is also on display – the fighting claimed one of his legs. Other rooms focus on Labour Veterans, honoured during the Soviet period for the excellence of their work. There are two rooms of paintings, including a lino-cut in the realist style titled *Hot Day 1962*, depicting a thirsty agricultural worker. In the museum's entrance hall rests, for some reason, a broken car-rally game.

Behind the Glory Museum stands a tiled obelisk topped with a Soviet star. An eternal flame burns in front. There is a dedication to those killed in the building of Soviet power, and inscriptions recording the names of some of those on the Bolshevik side who lost their lives during the Civil War.

GEOROGLY DISTRICT

The southern flank of the Khorezm Oasis, to the south of Dashoguz, is an agricultural area with several interesting monuments. The district was named Tagta ('Wooden Plank') until 2002, when President Niyazov, visiting Dashoguz, asked local officials whether any of them could tell him why the district bore such an unusual name. All kept silent, and Niyazov therefore proposed renaming the place in honour of the legendary Turkmen hero Georogly, since 'it is quite possible that Georogly's roots came from Tagta's soil'.

Izmukshir

Some 25km southwest of Dashoguz, beyond the airport, sit the ruins of the town of Zamakhshar, now known locally as Izmukshir. The place was probably settled from ancient times, and became a significant regional town of medieval Khorezm. The site is roughly oval in form, its longest diameter some 650m. The walls are degraded, but a number of towers can be discerned. The main southern gate remains impressive, with a tall round mud-brick tower still attempting to stand menacingly against would-be invaders. There is another gate in the north wall: the main street of Zamakhshar would have run between them. But of the buildings inside the walls, their location is simply suggested by elevated areas of ground. The large number of pieces of human skeleton all too visibly protruding from the external walls have given rise to many sinister tales about the place, which many locals believe to be haunted.

Zamakhshar is best known by virtue of its most famous son: the scholar Az Zamakhshari, who wrote more than 50 works on a prodigious range of subjects, though less than half have survived. Az Zamakhshari was born here in 1074, though he spent much of his working life in more cosmopolitan Gurganj. His reputation as a great man of learning was such that he received the nickname 'Fakhri Khorezm' ('Pride of Khorezm'). In the cemetery abutting the walled city is a recently rebuilt brick mausoleum, with two low domes. A plaque identifies the occupant as Az Zamakhshari. The long cenotaph lies in the second of the two rooms within. Outside the mausoleum, trees display the small strips of material representing the prayers that have been made here.

Ismamut Ata

This complex of religious buildings at the southern edge of the oasis is one of the most atmospheric places of shrine pilgrimage in Turkmenistan, and deserves to be much better known. It lies 13km south of the district capital of Georogly, a couple of kilometres beyond the main settlement of the Zaman Peasants' Association. The complex, which is surrounded by a large graveyard, has been constructed on the ruins of the medieval Khorezm settlement of Eshretkala. 'Eshret' means 'pleasure', probably reflecting the feelings of those travellers on Silk Road caravans upon reaching the first settlement of the Khorezm Oasis after their wearying journey across the Kara Kum Desert.

There is a modern brick-built gate, alongside which are rooms offering basic overnight accommodation for pilgrims. The historic complex is a little way beyond, a whitewashed ensemble of buildings of different periods, the oldest built no earlier than the 16th century. Pass through a carved wooden door to enter an attractive courtyard, around which lie a series of small rooms, each bearing an old door of carved wood. These rooms have domed ceilings, fireplaces with blackened walls, and wooden second floors, looking rather like bunk beds. This part of the complex appears to be a *madrasa* or a hostel for pilgrims. At the far side of this courtyard, climb five steps, passing through a wooden screen, to reach the summer mosque. This features a covered rectangular space to your left, dominated by two beautifully carved wooden pillars, tapering to narrow bases in the Khivan style. To the right is a kitchen, with circular brick constructions in which cooking pots would have been placed.

Beyond the summer mosque lies the winter one, a domed building with four large arched spaces giving a cruciform design. Stairs in the corner lead up to the roof, from which the call to prayer once sounded, and which now offers an excellent view across the roofs of the complex to the desert beyond. Latticed windows beneath the dome give the building a tranquil light.

On the left side of the mosque complex is a long, narrow building topped by a line of seven white domes, and leading to a domed mausoleum at the far end. This long building is known as the *dashkeche* ('stone street'). It is an enclosed corridor, along which runs a green carpet. Pilgrims visiting the mausoleum walk the corridor backwards on their return, so that the most sacred place remains always in sight. Arched niches along the sides of the corridor may represent places of burial. There is a four-domed lateral corridor to the right, close to the eastern entrance of the *dashkeche*. This leads to the western side of the winter mosque, though the connecting door is often kept locked.

The mausoleum is entered by a small anteroom, behind which lies the cloth-covered cenotaph of Ismamut Ata, in a locked chamber. A prayer chamber leads off to the left, from which an internal window offers pilgrims a sight of the cenotaph. So who was Ismamut Ata? Legend has it that he was actually two people. The story runs roughly as follows, though there are several versions. A young man named Isim was a contemporary and follower of the Prophet Mohammed, and volunteered to set off for Khorezm, to convert the peoples of the oasis to Islam. Accompanied by just 40 men, Isim reached Eshretkala, where he had little difficulty in persuading the local sultan, named Mahmut, to take up the Islamic faith. Isim then died, and Mahmut organised lavish burial arrangements for him, reasoning that, by so doing, successor generations would remember his name alongside that of Isim. So it proved, and the name Ismamut is said to be a shortened form of the two names: Isim and Mahmut. Scholars, however, have been unable to find record of a historical figure called Isim, and point out that 'Isim' is simply a word meaning 'name'. There have been suggestions that 'Isim' may be a figure named Said ibn Musaib, but there is no record of the latter ever having been involved in the Islamisation of Khorezm, and the identity of Ismamut Ata remains a mystery.

A few hundred metres away, legend has it that Duldul, the fabled winged horse of Imam Ali, was pastured in the woodland here. The faithful used to bring their horses to a certain tree, considered sacred, and circle the horses three times around the tree to receive protection. The practice continues today, but now with motor vehicles rather than horses. Around a dry tree, marked with a couple of white flags, a large number of car tracks, drawing a tight circle, attests to the continued popularity of the tradition.

East of Georogly Town

The district capital of **Georogly** itself is a quiet agricultural town. When heading out of town to the east, take a glance at the Soviet monument depicting a rocket zooming off into the cosmos between two elderly tractors. The monument honours the local organisation providing agricultural machinery to the rural communities. The road east heads towards the Uzbek border. Some 10km beyond Georogly town, a turn to the right is marked with a sign for the Balysh Ovezov Peasants' Association. After 7km you reach the ruins of the fortress of **Bedirkent**, its ridges of earth topped with substantial chunks of mud-brick walls. Bedirkent was the headquarters of Juneid Khan, a Turkmen ruler of the early 20th century who attempted to resist the Bolsheviks.

An interesting monument lies some 6km north of the road running eastwards to the Uzbek border, close to the Peasants' Association of Aksaray. This is **Aksaray Ding**, a highly unusual fired-brick structure. A passageway runs through a stepped base. On top of this stands a tower, roughly square in form, with arched entrances on each of its sides. A cylindrical drum on top of the tower supports a double dome, though the latter is now badly damaged. Archaeologists believe that the building dates from the 11th or 12th century. The overall form of the ensemble vaguely resembles a *kejebe*, the traditional elaborate saddle structure, placed on a camel, in which the Turkmen bride would travel to her wedding. This has given rise to a local legend that the building was the work of a rich man, whose beloved daughter died young. One night she came to her father in a dream, and asked him to build a *kejebe* over her grave, since she had not been given the opportunity to ride to her wedding when she had been alive. More probably the building was the elaborate entrance to a rural estate or even a forgotten town.

WEST OF DASHOGUZ

Taking the main road northwestwards from Dashoguz to Konye-Urgench, you pass through the town gates of Dashoguz after around 6km, an English-language inscription on the tiled gate rather charmingly wishing you a 'nice trip'. Immediately after the gate, the well-kept fields and smart buildings signal that you have reached the Sadullah Rozmetov Peasants' Association, headed by a veteran farm director frequently held up by President Niyazov as a model of hard-working rural leadership.

Around 28km from Dashoguz, you pass through a gate into Boldumsaz District, this gate too offering you a cheery English-language 'welcome'. Two kilometres further on, to the north of the road and clearly visible from it, the fortress of **Boldumsaz** makes a square plateau, standing proud above the surrounding fields. Some historians identify this place with the medieval town of Nyzvar, though this attribution is disputed. Destroyed by the Mongols, the place was later resettled, now known by its present name, which scholars believe to mean 'Fortress in a Marshy Place'.

A local legend offers a more colourful explanation of how the fortress received its name. A khan of Khiva determined to build the tallest and most beautiful minaret in the world (different versions of the legend place this at Khiva or Konye-Urgench). The khan engaged a fine architect to build it. The minaret duly took shape, the architect remaining at the top of this growing structure day and night as he toiled on his masterpiece. The khan, however, was not a nice man, and decided that, on completion of the minaret, he would have the architect killed, so that he would be unable to build so beautiful a structure for anyone else. The architect's assistant overheard the khan's plotting, and etched a message of warning to the architect on a brick. The resourceful architect sent down for the materials he needed to fashion a pair of wings and, on completion of the minaret, flew from the top to evade the khan's men. The architect landed at this fortress, exclaiming as he touched the ground: 'Safe and sound!' The name 'Boldumsaz' is apparently an approximation of the latter expression in Turkmen, and the fortress has been so named ever since. Locals say that an owl seen flying over the ruins of the fortress in the evening is the architect's ghost.

KONYE-URGENCH

Konye-Urgench (telephone code 347) is today a quiet agricultural town some 100km to the northwest of Dashoguz, but this place was for long periods the capital of Khorezm. In the 11th century it was one of the most important cities in the Islamic world. It certainly has not had the easiest of histories, destroyed both by the Mongols and by Timur, but enough monuments of strong architectural and historical interest remain to make Konye-Urgench one of Turkmenistan's most important tourist sights.

History

Our knowledge of the early history of settlement here is sketchy. Following the Arab invasion of Khorezm in 712 the town, known as Gurganj, gradually developed in importance thanks to its favourable position on trading routes between China and the Volga. It became the capital of Khorezm in 995, taking over from the city of Kath, following the triumph of the Emir of Gurganj against the last ruler of the Afrighid dynasty. The latter was murdered, the Emir of Gurganj took over his title of Khorezmshah, and Kath was destroyed by the capricious waters of the Amu Darya. Gurganj, in contrast, thrived. In the first part of the 11th century, under the reign of Ma'mun II, it became one of the major centres of learning and culture in the Islamic world, the home to scholars such as Avicenna and Al-Biruni. Gurganj then briefly fell under the control of the Ghaznavids, but, following the latter's defeat at the hands of the Seljuks in 1040, became a remote outpost of the Seljuk Empire. It again grew in importance as the capital city of the Khorezmshahs, a dynasty which gradually broke free from the shackles of the Seljuk Empire, and which by the end of the 12th century had eclipsed it. Indeed, in a reversal of fortunes, Gurganj now controlled Merv. This was a golden age for the city, known by the Turkic peoples as Urgench, with trade routes flourishing, especially the western route to the Volga. The Khorezmshah, Mohammed II, saw himself as a latter-day Alexander the Great, and set about further expanding the boundaries of his empire.

This period of prosperity came to an abrupt end at the hands of the Mongols. Genghiz Khan reportedly began with some ostensibly favourable gestures towards Mohammed II, including by sending to him a lump of gold said to be the size of a camel's hump. But Mohammed took offence at Genghiz Khan's reported comment that he was ready to treat the Khorezmshah 'as he would his sons', since this seemed to imply a relationship of subordination. When the Khorezmshahs intercepted a caravan sent by Genghiz Khan at the frontier settlement of Otrar, they murdered the merchants. This was not, perhaps, tactically wise. Genghiz Khan launched an assault against Mohammed II in 1219, first razing Otrar to the ground. In 1221, after a siege of seven months, the Mongols took Urgench, destroying the buildings, slaughtering male occupants and enslaving the young women and children.

Thanks to its favourable geographical location, Urgench recovered importance relatively quickly, becoming the capital of the eastern province of the Golden Horde. The Arab traveller Ibn Battuta, visiting in the 1330s, found it again a great city. But history was to repeat itself. The ascendant Timur, known in the West as Tamerlane, was concerned about the challenge posed by the Sufi dynasty which now controlled Urgench. He pillaged the city in 1379, and then completed the job in 1388, razing Urgench to the ground and ordering that barley be sown over the site. The city was never to recover. Subsequent centuries brought unfavourable shifts in the course of the Amu Darya. In the 17th century the Uzbek Khan Abulghazi shifted the water-starved population to a new location in the east of the oasis, close to Khiva. Thus was born the new town of Urgench, in present-day Uzbekistan. The old capital became known as Konye-Urgench ('Old Urgench').

Konye-Urgench made a minor rally in the 19th century, thanks to the construction of the Khan Yap irrigation canal by the Khans of Khiva, and gradually settled into the agricultural centre it is today.

Getting there and away

The place to catch buses, minibuses and inter-urban taxis in Konye-Urgench lies on the northern side of the Dashoguz road, named Gurgench Shayoly in town, just to the east of the Gurgench Hotel. A place in a minibus to Dashoguz will cost around 15,000 manat, a seat in a taxi about 25,000. There are also frequent departures to Ashgabat. The railway station is south of town, just beyond the main archaeological park on the Ashgabat road. Since it offers just one slow train daily to each of Dashoguz and the agricultural town of Saparmurat Turkmenbashy, it is unlikely to be of use. The Uzbek border crossing point between Konye-Urgench and Hodjeyli is 13km to the north of town.

Where to stay

Hotel Gurgench (16 rooms) Gurgench Shayoly; ☎ 347 22465. Naked light bulbs in the rooms, no air conditioning, and the bathroom doors all seem to be nailed shut. For this the hotel charges 120,000 manat per person. There are suites available at 468,000 manat, which basically offer larger versions of the same grimness. The price for Turkmen citizens to stay

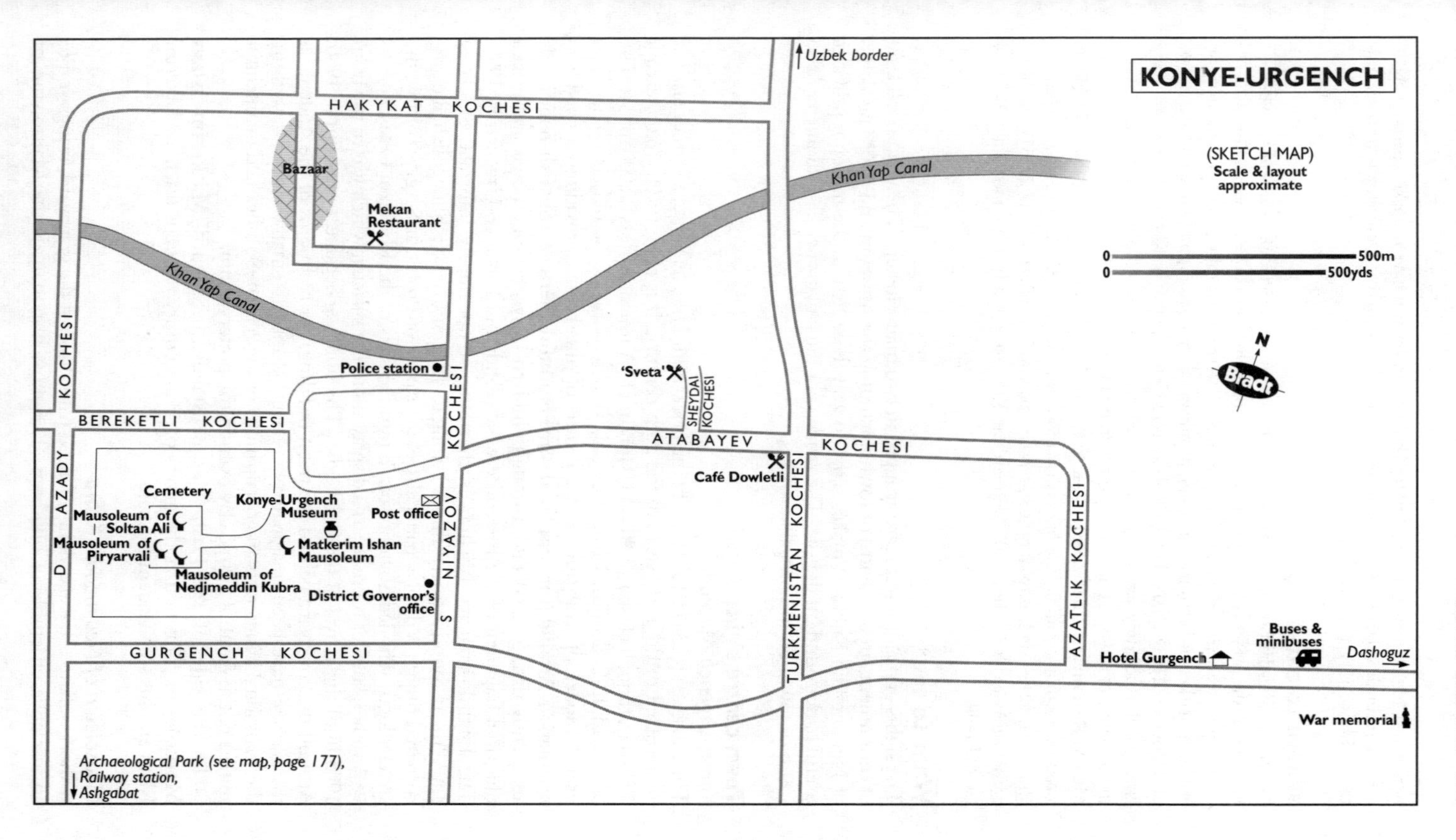

KONYE-URGENCH
(SKETCH MAP)
Scale & layout approximate
0
500m
0
500yds
N
Bradt
Uzbek border
HAKYKAT KOCHESI
Bazaar
Mekan Restaurant
Khan Yap Canal
Khan Yap Canal
Police station
KOCHESI
BEREKETLI KOCHESI
'Sveta'
SHEYDAI KOCHESI
ATABAYEV KOCHESI
Café Dowletli
AZADY
D
Cemetery
Konye-Urgench Museum
Post office
Mausoleum of Soltan Ali
Mausoleum of Piryarvali
Matkerim Ishan Mausoleum
Mausoleum of Nedjmeddin Kubra
District Governor's office
NIYAZOV
S
KOCHESI
TURKMENISTAN KOCHESI
AZATLIK KOCHESI
GURGENCH KOCHESI
Buses & minibuses
Hotel Gurgench
Dashoguz
War memorial
Archaeological Park (see map, page 177), Railway station, Ashgabat

here is just 10,000 manat. There is no restaurant. Unless you have to make a particularly early start for the Uzbek border, you would be better off making Dashoguz your base, and seeing Konye-Urgench as a day trip.

Where to eat

'Sveta' 3A Sheydai Kochesi; ☎ 347 22526. One of the unexpected pleasures of Konye-Urgench is the presence of several restaurants run by members of the town's Korean community, who arrived here in Stalinist times. These are basically private houses, usually either unmarked or bearing a small sign promising 'Korean food', and known by the name of the owner. These establishments will prepare Central Asian or Korean food to order, the latter usually including a good range of pickled salads, and puffy Korean dumplings. 'Sveta', in the centre of town, is one of the most highly regarded.

Mekan Restaurant ☎ 347 22681. Close to the bazaar, this offers plastic chairs and tables in a cavernous room, with private booths for more intimate dining. The menu offers cheap and filling dishes such as *golubtsy* and *pelmeni*. The **Café Dowletli** (☎ 347 22251), on the corner of Atabayev Kochesi and Turkmenistan Kochesi, is run by the same family and does good *shashlik*.

What to see

The sights of major interest are grouped in two main clusters. There is a small knot of monuments in the centre of town, including the museum and the Mausoleum of Nedjmeddin Kubra. It makes sense to visit these first, as the museum provides useful background on the site. The remains of the city proper lie a kilometre or so south of town, on the Ashgabat road.

Town centre sights

Konye-Urgench Museum

The museum (☎ 347 21571) lies in the brick-built Dash Mosque, a former *madrasa* constructed in the early years of the 20th century. It is open 08.00–16.00, except Tuesday, though closed 13.00–14.00 for lunch. Admission costs 22,000 manat. The largest room is dedicated to the history and treasures of the old city. There is a useful model of Gurganj in the centre of the room, providing a good site orientation. Around it are displayed some beautiful artefacts, from fish-bone beads apparently dating to 6000BC, through children's toys, ceramic bowls and glazed tiles, to a fragment of the meteorite which landed near Konye-Urgench in 1998. The English-language labelling is charming, if not hugely informative: 'clayey cup'; 'many found artificial things belong to 4th century AD'; 'blue polished eight-cornered thing'. A display panel charts the career of Professor Sergey Tolstov, the archaeologist who led Soviet research into the sites of the Khorezm Oasis.

Another, smaller room offers a display about the *madrasa*, which was in use from 1905 until the arrival of the Bolsheviks. The building became a museum in 1980. Around the courtyard behind the main building, the bedrooms of the students at the *madrasa* have been imaginatively converted into 19 small displays, describing the traditional handicrafts and occupations of the region. So a bearded mannequin spins a pot in front of a large clay oven in the pottery room.

To the side of the Dash Mosque stands the domed **Matkerim Ishan Mausoleum**. This houses the graves of 19th-century religious teacher Matkerim Ishan and his son Madamin Ishan.

Mausoleum of Nedjmeddin Kubra

A short walk to the west, along a fenced path through the graveyard, brings you to an attractive ensemble of buildings. The most important is the Mausoleum of

Nedjmeddin Kubra, the founder of the Kubravid school of Sufism, who was born in Khiva in 1145, and died here at the hands of the Mongols in 1221. The 14th-century mausoleum has a delightful portal, with blue and turquoise tiles in geometric, floral and calligraphic designs. Local guides will tell you that the outward lean of the portal is not a sign of future collapse, but a deliberate architectural feature, to symbolise the building bowing down in prayer. Let us hope they are right. Nedjmeddin Kubra's tomb itself is in two parts: the larger for his body, the smaller one for his head, which was separated by the Mongols. The tombs are covered with fine majolica tile-work, but this is covered over by velvet cloths. The mausoleum is a major place of pilgrimage: visitors circle it three times, touching the walls and then their foreheads while reciting prayers, before entering.

Mausoleum of Soltan Ali

Standing opposite the Mausoleum of Nedjmeddin Kubra, and forming a harmonious composition with it, is the Mausoleum of Soltan Ali. This domed building, with cracks in its exterior walls and an altogether rather parlous appearance, is one of the most puzzling of Konye-Urgench. Some researchers date it to the 14th century, others to the 16th. Soltan Ali himself, to whom the building may, or may not, have been dedicated, was a local governor who died in 1565. The building was never completed: the wooden beams protruding from the façade may have been required for decorative tiling, which was not in the event applied. One theory runs that the building was commissioned by Soltan Ali's successor, one Haji Mohammed Khan, who was forced to flee Urgench in the 1580s by the advance of the forces of the Khan of Bukhara. The building is usually kept locked. The portals of the Mausolea of Nedjmeddin Kubra and Soltan Ali suggest two elderly gentlemen, politely bowing to each other.

Mausoleum of Piryarvali

Immediately to the west of the Mausoleum of Nedjmeddin Kubra stands the heavily restored Mausoleum of Piryarvali, a brick-built domed structure with the large portal typical of the Konye-Urgench mausolea. The building is often kept locked but, if you are able to get inside, you will be confronted with four adjacent cenotaphs, one of which is said to mark the grave of Piryarvali, a disciple of Nedjmeddin Kubra and the father of a well-known Khorezm poet and wrestler named Pakhlavan-Ata. The others are by local tradition ascribed to three sheikhs; Attar Vali, Duyar Vali and Daniyar Vali. A grave along the northern wall of the mausoleum is said to be that of Piryarvali's brother, Pir Attar Vali, the patron of confectioners. A series of burial vaults were found close to the Piryarvali Mausoleum during its reconstruction in 1989.

Around the main mausolea are various other graves, many linked popularly to the names of disciples of Nedjmeddin Kubra or to local rulers. This graveyard, locally known as the '360', a reference to the membership of the Kubravid school of Sufism, is the nucleus of the more modern cemetery which surrounds the site. Several of the older graves are associated with rites of shrine pilgrimage. For example, next to the two conical graves just to the north of the path running to the Nedjmeddin Kubra Mausoleum stands a tree, bent by the wind in the direction of the tombs. The tree is said to have special powers in the treatment of children's ailments: you may see parents splashing into the faces of their children water from the little pool at its base.

Main historical site

Take the Ashgabat road south of the modern town of Konye-Urgench to reach the old-city site. There is a small car park. The monuments of the old city stand rather forlornly across a grave-studded wasteland, a testimony to the destructive power of Timur's forces. Pay your entrance fee to the site at the wooden ticket office: 22,000 manat, with another 11,000 manat charged if you wish to take photographs.

Mausoleum of Turabeg Khanum

Across the road from the car park stands one of the most impressive monuments in Turkmenistan. The Mausoleum of Turabeg Khanum has an imposing south-facing portal, some 25m high. Behind this is a domed lobby, with a spiral staircase (locked to visitors) to the right. The main chamber beyond is hexagonal in plan, with tall arched niches on each wall. The mosaic on the underside of the dome is stunning, its design apparently involving 365 interlocking geometric figures, one for each day of the year. The preponderance of dark blue in the design, and the fact that most of the figures are star shapes, give the viewer the impression of looking up at a stylised night sky. There are 24 arches running along the drum below the dome, one for each hour of the day. A line of 12 larger arches running around the chamber below suggests the number of months in the year. The overall message seems to be of the insignificance of humans when set against the great natural order.

The building has a 12-sided external plan, its outside walls enlivened by tall niches. Little remains of the exterior dome, which some researchers believe may have been conical in shape, save for a small corner of turquoise tiling, offering a tantalising hint of the beauty of the original roof.

Turabeg Khanum was the daughter of Uzbek Khan, under whose rule the Golden Horde converted to Islam, and the wife of Gutlug Timur, a governor of Urgench in the early 14th century. There is speculation among researchers as to whether the building had in fact anything to do with her. Some researchers believe that it was a mausoleum of the rulers of the Sufi dynasty, dating from the second half of the 14th century. Others point to the unusually well-illuminated interior, the presence of structures with a possible defence function (such as a small room opposite the staircase which has been described as a guard room), and the absence of cenotaphs to argue that the building may have been a palace, not a mausoleum.

Mausoleum of Seyit Ahmet

Many of the key monuments are grouped along a path which runs southeast from the car park. The first building you come to, south of the path, is the Mausoleum of Seyit Ahmet. A modern reconstruction of a 19th-century mausoleum, this is a twin-domed brick building, the cenotaph lying in the second and larger of the two chambers. It is linked by popular tradition to Sheikh Seyit Ahmet, who died around 1308 and played a major role in the Islamisation of the Mongol Khans of the Golden Horde.

Gutlug Timur Minaret

The next monument reached is the Gutlug Timur Minaret, which at almost 60m is the tallest medieval structure in Central Asia, apparently. It was even taller before recent reconstruction work, aimed at stabilising the still somewhat unsafe-looking structure, had the effect of reducing the height by a couple of metres. The minaret is an attractive, tapering column, some 12m in diameter at the base, but just 2m wide at the top, on which a long-vanished wooden balcony would once have stood. There are 18 horizontal bands of decoration, some incorporating blue majolica tiles. There are three bands of inscriptions in Kufic script, one of which links the

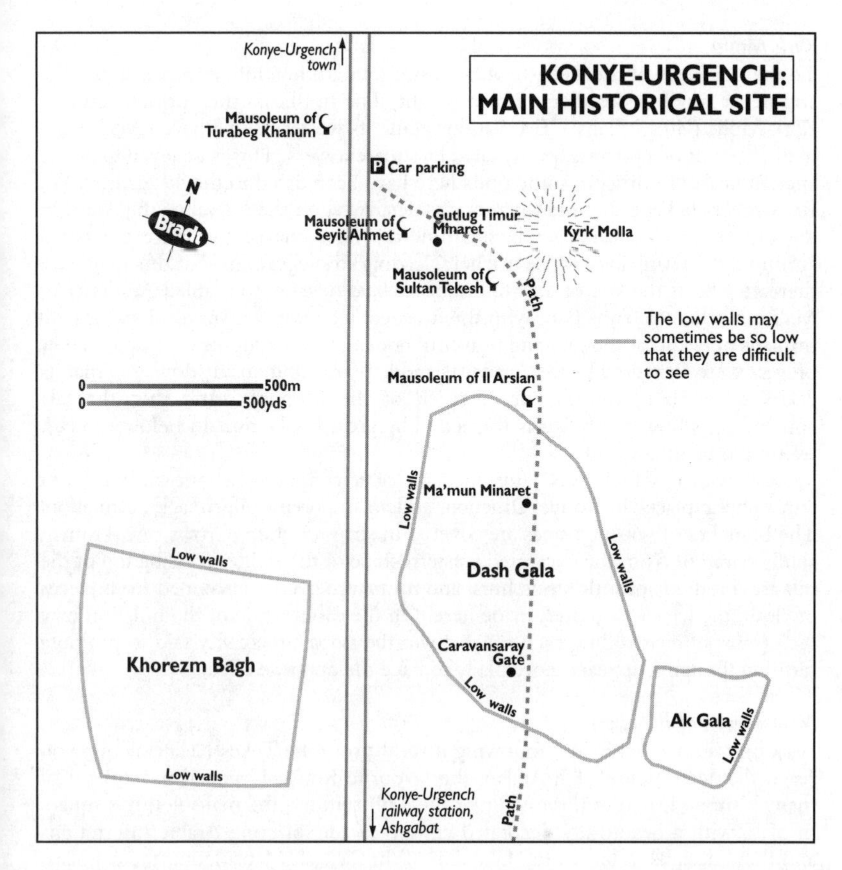

minaret with Gutlug Timur and his father-in-law Uzbek Khan. This led researchers to date the monument to 1320–30. But it is now believed that the minaret is much older, probably dating to the 11th or 12th century, and that Gutlug Timur's role was limited to ordering its reconstruction.

Mausoleum of Sultan Tekesh

Some 200m further on sits the Mausoleum of Sultan Tekesh, which dates from the end of the 12th century, or the beginning of the following one. Tekesh, who ruled from 1172–1200, turned the Khorezmshahs into a major power, his conquests including Khorasan in present-day northern Iran. The building, which has been recently restored, is square in plan, with a distinctive conical dome above a 24-sided drum. The beautiful turquoise tile-work that still adorns the dome explains one local name for the building, Gok Gummez ('Blue Dome'). The 'stalactite' decoration adorning the arch above the main doorway is also particularly fine. The building is sometimes known as the Mausoleum of Sheikh Sheref, following a local tradition as to its occupant. The absence of a cenotaph here has led some researchers to speculate that it was not a mausoleum at all, but a temple complex or palace of the Khorezmshahs. But architectural and written evidence mostly supports the attribution of the building as the Mausoleum of Sultan Tekesh, which according to one contemporary source formed part of a large complex built by Tekesh, including a *madrasa* and a library.

Kyrk Molla

To the northeast of the Tekesh Mausoleum stands a low hill, covering some 3ha and never much more than 12m in height. The hill bears the curious name of Kyrk Molla ('40 Mullahs'). Excavations along its western slope have revealed the inclined walls of a fortress, punctuated by square towers. This is believed to be the ancient heart of Gurganj: some finds here have been dated to the 5th century BC. Researchers believe that the fortress was destroyed on the arrival of the Arabs in the 8th century. Local legends surrounding the name of the place are based around the 40 mullahs as wise teachers, leading to suggestions that this may have thereafter been the site of an important *madrasa* or even the fabled Academy of Ma'mun. One tale runs that, with the dreaded Mongols fast approaching, the 40 mullahs prayed that the rare and beautiful books of the Academy be spared. Their prayers were answered by the Academy suddenly turning upside down, so that its doors were underground, out of reach of the Mongols. And this, the tale concludes, is how the hill was formed. The great books remain below ground, waiting to be uncovered.

Kyrk Molla, which was later the site of a cemetery, is one of the most atmospheric places in Konye-Urgench, and an important pilgrimage destination. The branches of wizened trees are covered in strips of cloth. Crows caw. Human skulls stare out from the excavated western slope of the hill. Across the top of the hill are hundreds of little stone huts, and miniature cradles fashioned from pieces of cloth, the legacy of wishes made here. On the eastern side of the hill, you may see groups of girls rolling each other down the slope, an activity said to promote fertility, though it appears more likely to have the opposite effect.

Mausoleum of Il Arslan

Back on the main path, and following it south from the Tekesh Mausoleum, you reach the Mausoleum of Il Arslan, the favourite Konye-Urgench monument of many visitors. Dated to the middle of the 12th century, the mausoleum is square in plan, with a beautifully decorated eastern façade, offering Arabic inscriptions and floral designs in terracotta. Like that of the Tekesh Mausoleum, the cupola is conical in form, but unusually that of the Il Arslan Mausoleum retains the 12-sided structure of the drum below. The cupola is decorated with turquoise tiles, set in a playful zig-zag design. The mausoleum is identified locally as that of Fahr ad-Din Razi, a well-known scientist of the 12th century, but he is known to have died in Herat around 1209. The building might nonetheless have been built in honour of Fahr ad-Din Razi, but some historians, looking for a suitably important person who actually died in Gurganj at the right time, have suggested that the tomb may be that of the Khorezmshah Il Arslan, father of Tekesh, who ruled 1156–1172. The scholar Az Zamakhshari has also been suggested as a possible occupant.

Dash Gala

The above itinerary covers the most impressive sights of Konye-Urgench. But if you have the time, and Khorezm fatigue has not set in, the path continues southwards to more monuments of interest. The remains of moated walls here enclose Dash Gala, the pre-Mongol settlement which may later have formed the citadel of the larger city of Urgench. Inside Dash Gala, not far from the site of its north gate, is the stump of the **Ma'mun Minaret**. It was built in 1011, making it the oldest structure in Gurganj of which anything is standing, but probably collapsed during an earthquake at the start of the 13th century. A new, taller minaret, believed to have been some 55m high, was built around the remains of the old one, but this in turn was brought down by an earthquake, although not until 1895. Archaeologists in the 1950s unearthed around the site evidence of the Friday Mosque of which the minaret would have been part. According to tradition, the mosque in its heyday could accommodate 40,000 worshippers.

Continuing further south along the main path, you reach the most substantial standing monument within the Dash Gala site. This is a heavily restored arched gate, leading nowhere. Traditionally known as the **Caravansaray Gate**, the structure, with elegant blue and turquoise tile-work decorating the underside of the arch, seems rather too grand to have been built as the entrance to a caravansaray. Researchers have suggested that it might have formed part of an important *madrasa*, or a palace of the Khorezmshahs.

Ak Gala

To the east of the Caravansaray Gate, just outside the confines of Dash Gala, is the fortress known as Ak Gala. Its southern wall ran alongside the old channel of the Amu Darya, making a formidable defensive barrier. The fragments of mud-brick wall which survive along its 1km perimeter reach a height of up to 8m. These probably date to no earlier than the 16th century, but are built on top of earlier walls, destroyed by Timur. Researchers have speculated that this fortress may have been the Keshk-i-Ahchak mentioned by a 13th-century scholar as one of two monuments of Urgench (the other being the Tekesh Mausoleum) not destroyed by the Mongols.

Khorezm Bagh

The rectangular fortress of Khorezm Bagh lies in the southwest corner of the archaeological site, west of the Ashgabat road. It is a relatively recent monument, though built on the site of a citadel which probably dates to the time of the Golden Horde. It was built on the order of a khan of Khiva named Mohammed Emin, who decided in 1846 that he would make Konye-Urgench his place of residence. This plan was terminated abruptly by Mohammed Emin's death in battle in 1855, and that was it for Khorezm Bagh.

WEST OF KONYE-URGENCH

Westwards from here, Saparmurat Turkmenbashy District contains the final area of irrigated farmland of the Khorezm Oasis, before hitting the escarpment of the Ust Urt Plateau and the Uzbek border. There are several places of interest along routes skirting south of the border, although for forays around Lake Sarygamysh and into the desert terrain of the Kaplankyr Nature Reserve 4x4 vehicles and good pre-planning are necessary.

Around Shirvan Kala

From Konye-Urgench, take the main road west towards the district capital of Saparmurat Turkmenbashy. After 18km, you pass the sign welcoming you to the district, featuring a silhouette of President Niyazov. Turn left after 3km, along a more minor asphalt road. After a further 26km you reach on the right-hand side of the road the remains of the fortress of **Shirvan Kala**, on the side of a plateau. Taking the track up the hill here brings you to a modern graveyard, where burials range from modest heaps of earth to elaborate mausolea. Wooden ladders are lain on or beside many of the graves. A metal sign in Russian and Cyrillic Turkmen near the entrance to the graveyard records a rather plaintive instruction of 1984 by the local authorities, banning the erection in the graveyard of the Gyzyl Baydak ('Red Flag') Collective Farm funerary monuments larger than 2.5m square or taller than 40cm. An instruction that clearly had little effect. At the southern edge of the graveyard, the **Mausoleum of Nalach Baba**, a site of local shrine pilgrimage, stands among some older ruins on the edge of the plateau. A cave dwelling has been built into the side of the hill below, even featuring little windows. The hum in the air comes from the nearby Deryalyk Compressor Station, through which much of Turkmenistan's gas passes on its journey to export markets in Russia and Ukraine.

Devkesen

Due west from here, along a difficult track requiring a 4x4, lie the atmospheric ruins of Devkesen. This place features in the publicity handouts of several Turkmen travel agents, and tourists were certainly visiting the site until late 2003, but more recent would-be visitors report being turned back by Turkmen border guards at one of the checkpoints along the way, with the explanation that the track crosses Uzbek territory, and is out of bounds for tourists. If you are interested in visiting the site, you should check the current position with a Turkmen travel agent when applying for your tourist visa.

Devkesen seems to have first been settled around the 4th century BC. The site is almost certainly the medieval settlement of Vazir, visited by the Elizabethan merchant Anthony Jenkinson in 1558. Jenkinson was particularly impressed by the melons of Vazir, reporting that here grew 'many good fruites among which there is one called a Dynie of great bignesse and full of moysture'. But Jenkinson also reported that the river waters on which the town depended were failing, and Vazir was soon to be abandoned, the victim of changes in the course of the Amu Darya. Soltan Ali, the Khorezm Khan whose mausoleum (possibly) lies in Konye-Urgench (see page 175), was based here, but his successor moved to Urgench around 1573.

The site of Devkesen is dramatic. The city stands at the edge of a 30m escarpment, on a southern tip of the Ust Urt Plateau, protected by a moat and walls on the sides facing the plateau. A citadel, overlooking the escarpment, has distinctive corrugated walls. Within the city site are three ruined mausolea, dating to around the 15th century, and the remains of a mosque. One of these mausolea is popularly believed to be the final resting place of Farhad and Shirin, the doomed young lovers who were the subject of a popular poem by the 15th-century Timurid writer Navoi.

Butentau

Ibrahim Sultan

Continuing on the road south beyond Shirvan Kala, you immediately cross the Deryalyk Collector, a deep channel which takes run-off water from the irrigated fields to the Sarygamysh Lake. Turn right at the crossroads reached after another couple of kilometres, to join the road heading lakewards. A checkpoint signals the Druzhba ('Friendship') Collector, another channel taking irrigation waters to the lake. Druzhba is crossed by means of a nervousness-inducing bridge of metal pipes. This channel also marks the end of the area under irrigation: from here, the pot-holed road draws a straight line across a wide expanse of arid scrub. Some 65 apparently unending kilometres from the crossroads at which you joined the road, take the signposted turning to the right towards the shrine pilgrimage site of Ibrahim Sultan, which lies 7km to the north, close to the village of Bent.

The Ibrahim Sultan site has a stunning geographical location. Three recently reconstructed domed mausolea stand at the top of the 25m escarpment of the Butentau Heights, the path up to which is flanked by a metal fence. The caretaker described Ibrahim Sultan as a holy man from far Arabia, who came here to help the local people. The mausolea, and adjacent tombs, are said to mark the graves of Ibrahim Sultan and various members of his family and followers. A square-based signal tower stands nearby. In the graveyard behind the mausolea are tombs labelled with the names of such figures as 'Imam Hussein', as well as one huge cloth-covered grave, perhaps 20m in length. This, said the caretaker, was the grave of one Shilgiz Baba who was, he added, very tall. At the bottom of the escarpment, an enclosure of stones several metres long is said to mark the burial place of Shilgiz Baba's lower right leg.

A little brick bowl to the side of one of the tombs contains some sheep vertebrae. The caretaker explained that these should be tossed five times. Every time one of the vertebrae landed 'upright' during the course of those five throws, the greater would be the good fortune bestowed upon the thrower. At the base of the escarpment, a complex of buildings includes accommodation for visiting pilgrims both indoors and in a *yurt*. They are happy to put up tourists, and, camping aside, there are no other accommodation options in the area.

Butentau Cave Settlement

Drive eastwards from the guesthouse at Ibrahim Sultan, along an earth track at the base of the escarpment. After 5km, you will see about two-thirds of the way up the escarpment a line of artificial caves, cut into the soft limestone. The Butentau Cave Settlement extends for some 2km northeastwards. Several hundred caves have been identified, probably occupied in early medieval times. Cave settlements have also been uncovered in several other escarpments in the region. The caves cannot be reached without climbing equipment, with a few possible exceptions where there have been rock falls, which may be accessible through a hard scramble, depending on your fitness and perception of risk.

Ak Kala

A few hundred metres in front of the Butentau Cave Settlement stand the mud-brick walls of Ak Kala, once the late medieval town of Adak. The walls are roughly square in plan, with five semi-circular towers along each side and a round tower at each corner. There is a walled rectangular 'suburban' space on the north side of the settlement. The proximity of the three very different attractions of Ibrahim Sultan, the Butentau caves and Ak Kala make the Butentau area a worthwhile destination for an excursion, overnighting at Ibrahim Sultan, into a little-known area of Turkmenistan.

Lake Sarygamysh

The road you followed to reach Ibrahim Sultan continues southwestwards to Lake Sarygamysh, reaching the lake-shore at the former collective fishery of Dashoguzskiy Rybhoz. However, there have been reports of visitors being turned back by border guards here (the lake sits on the border between Turkmenistan and Uzbekistan), and there is more reliable access to the lake by turning off the road early, on one of the tracks to the south, then following the lake round to the southern shore. This requires both 4x4 and a guide who has been here before. There is good camping here, mosquitoes apart. Lake Sarygamysh forms the northern limit of the large area under the protection of the Kaplankyr Nature Reserve, and access therefore requires the appropriate permit from the Ministry of Nature Protection.

Lake Sarygamysh is a natural depression, in which a lake has formed on several occasions. Lake formation began again in the early 1960s, collecting the run-off from the irrigated lands of the Khorezm Oasis. The lake is now a considerable size, and its waters seem almost magical after a long drive across the parched surrounding terrain. But they are particularly salty, and quite polluted. The lake does, however, support a flourishing migratory birdlife.

Kaplankyr Nature Reserve

The Kaplankyr Nature Reserve, established in 1979, is the largest in Turkmenistan, covering a vast expanse of escarpment-fringed plateau in the western part of Dashoguz Region. Kaplankyr, a southern spur of the Ust Urt Plateau, means 'Plateau of Cheetahs', but cheetahs have not been sighted here for years. You may, however, be lucky enough to see a herd of goitred gazelle (*jieran*) or Central Asian wild ass (*kulan*), the latter reintroduced here in the 1980s. The intrepid Hungarian traveller Arminius Vambery, crossing the Kara Kum by caravan in the 1860s, found the ascent to the plateau wearying. But from it he was greeted with 'an extraordinary spectacle; the land on which we stand, as far as the eye can reach, seems to raise itself like an island out of the sea of sand'.

SHASENEM AND THE ROAD SOUTH

From Konye-Urgench, a road heads south to Ashgabat across the very centre of the Kara Kum Desert. There are several sights of interest along or close to the road in its northern journey across Dashoguz Region. There are, however, few opportunities en route to refuel or to eat. One welcome café lies 67km south of Konye-Urgench, a modest brick building on the western side of the road, easiest spotted by the cluster of lorries usually parked outside. It offers loud music, eccentric interior décor focused around murals of waterfalls and beach resorts, and cheap meat and onion pies known as *fitchi*.

Mausoleum of Ashyk Aydyn Pir

Two kilometres further on, a turning to the west is highlighted by a monument featuring an upright *dutar*, on which stands a bird, and a slim arch over the road. The tree-lined side road leads to the Mausoleum of Ashyk Aydyn Pir. The patron of singers and musicians, the character of Ashyk Aydyn Pir appears in many Turkmen legendary tales, often helping the young hero attain great musicianship. An overnight pilgrimage to this symbolic double-domed mausoleum is believed to help the faithful in their quest to master the musician's craft. What looks like an upturned colander is set in concrete behind the mausoleum: peer into the well beneath this, visitors are told, and behold your future. The well stands in a graveyard. A statue of Ashyk Aydyn Pir in prayer dominates the car park, which is also decorated by quotations from President Niyazov, praising Ashyk Aydyn Pir as a symbol of song, talent and justice.

Diyarbekir Fortress

Just to the north of Ashyk Aydyn Pir, and visible from the side road leading to it, stands the ruined fortress of Diyarbekir. Rectangular in plan, the medieval walls preserve semicircular towers and battlements. The walls of one interior building are still standing, and the ground inside the fortress is studded with so many fragments of brick as to take on a reddish hue. Diyarbekir is believed to have been first settled as early as the 4th century BC. It was later abandoned, but seems to have been resettled around the 10th century, before being abandoned for good by the 15th.

Shasenem Fortress

The rectangular fortress on sloping ground sighted 6km further south along the main road is **Akdzhagelin Kala**. After another 22km, a side road to the east is marked with a sign for the village of Tuniderya. Drive through the village and turn right onto an unmetalled track after a kilometre. This requires a 4x4, and the track may nonetheless be impassable following rain. You reach the fortress of Shasenem some 9km on. The fortress, which stands among low-lying ground, makes a fine sight from the upland to the north traversed by the track. Shasenem, which stood at

Above Russian Orthodox church, Turkmenabat
Above right Saparmurat Haji Mosque, Geok Depe
Below Turkmenbashy Ruhy Mosque, Gypjak

Above Earthquake Monument, Ashgabat

Right Statue of President Niyazov. Independence Park, Ashgabat

Below right Statue of Oguz Han. Independence Park, Ashgabat

Below left Arch of Neutrality, Ashgabat

the southern limit of the areas irrigated from the Amu Darya, was probably occupied from around the 4th century BC. Known as Suburna in medieval times, it was sacked by the Mongols and again by the Timurids, and eventually abandoned to the encroaching desert. The present name probably derives from a later association of the ruined settlement with the popular Turkmen legend of Shasenem and Garip, a Romeo and Juliet-style tale of doomed young love.

The fortress itself lies on an artificial mound, its mud-brick walls standing like scattered teeth in a rough L-shaped plan. Some of these still preserve crenellations, slit holes and battlements. Running water has exposed a slice through the walls, demonstrating how they were gradually built up into increasingly elaborate defensive structures in response to advances in military technology. This section also reveals an alarming number of pieces of human bone. A few hundred metres to the south of the fortress stand four outbuildings, believed to have formed part of an extensive park complex of the 12th and 13th centuries. The northernmost of these buildings is focused on an octagonal corner tower, preserved to a height of around 4m and constructed of large mud bricks. An intact mud-brick arch straddles an adjacent room. A rusted metal sign, which has been used in the past as target practice, now succeeds in informing the visitor only that this is an 'archaeological monument'. Taking a line southwestwards from this corner tower, you reach first a gate building and then another corner tower, almost a mirror-image of the first. Making a line with the gate building, to its southeast, is a further structure, with four large rooms each opening to the exterior of the building, which would have stood at the centre of the park complex.

Gyaur Kala

Back on the main road, 25km south of the Tuniderya turning a road checkpoint straddles the bridge over the southernmost of the canals of the Khorezm system. South of here is open desert. A few hundred metres to the north of the checkpoint is a turning to the west, along a road which eventually reaches Sarygamysh Lake. Taking this side road, you will see after 5km the ruins of the fortress of Gyaur Kala on the promontory just to the north of the road. Gyaur Kala is an unusual settlement. The small fortress is roughly square in plan, preserving sections of mud-brick walls and corner towers. From this citadel, two ridges representing the remains of further exterior walls head off southeastwards towards the crest of the hill. They disappear beneath a large barchan sand dune, but then reappear again on the other side of the dune, running down the side of the hill to enclose an area never more than 150m wide, and almost 0.5km in length. The undulations of the external walls reflect the sites of the many towers which would have stood along them. The unusual form of the site has led some researchers to speculate that this may have been a Zoroastrian sanctuary, centred on a ceremonial staircase rising up the hill.

Dashoguz Region carpet gul

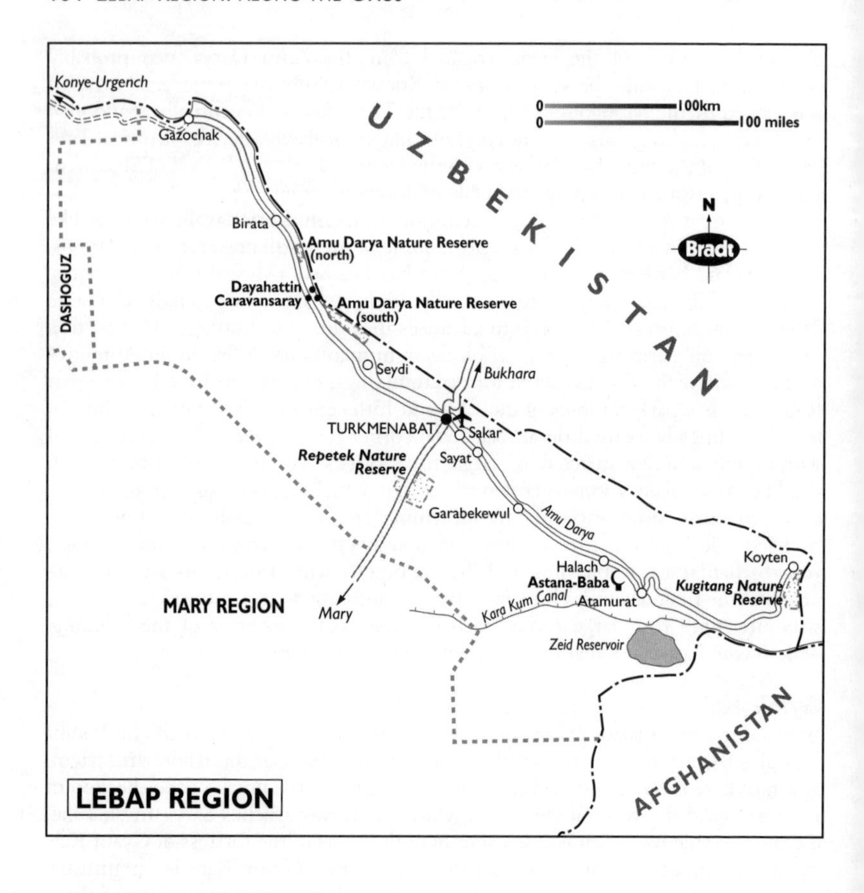
Konye-Urgench
Gazochak
UZBEKISTAN
0 100km
0 100 miles
N
Bradt
Birata
Amu Darya Nature Reserve (north)
Dayahattin Caravansaray
Amu Darya Nature Reserve (south)
DASHOGUZ
Seydi
Bukhara
TURKMENABAT
Sakar
Sayat
Repetek Nature Reserve
Garabekewul
Amu Darya
Halach
Astana-Baba
Atamurat
Koyten
Kugitang Nature Reserve
MARY REGION
Mary
Kara Kum Canal
Zeid Reservoir
AFGHANISTAN
LEBAP REGION

7

Lebap Region: along the Oxus

The Amu Darya River, known as the Oxus to the ancient Greeks and the Jeihun in medieval times, flows 2,400km from its headwaters in the Pamir Mountains, through Tajikistan, Turkmenistan and Uzbekistan, before reaching the Aral Sea. It has always been a vital bestower of life to Central Asia, and today supplies more than 90% of the irrigation water in Turkmenistan; much of this through the Kara Kum Canal, which begins its long journey westward from the southern part of Lebap Region. The Amu Darya is an impressive sight, broad and muddy, its volumes swollen following the winter rains, and again in summer, when it carries the snowmelt from the Pamirs.

The name Lebap, 'riverbank', was chosen in 1992 to replace the earlier designation of Charjou Region for Turkmenistan's easternmost region, a broad strip of land running from southeast to northwest along the border with Uzbekistan, through which the Amu Darya snakes. It is a region with a mixed population of ethnic Uzbeks and Turkmens of the Ersari tribe, some of the former still sporting traditional square black skullcaps, with white embroidery, and long brightly coloured gowns. Many tourists, hurrying to Bukhara, see nothing more of this region than the main road from Mary to the Uzbek border at Farap, perhaps with an unmemorable overnight stop in Turkmenabat on the way. But there are some worthwhile tourist destinations here. Pride of place goes to the Kugitang Nature Reserve in the far southeast, which offers dinosaur footprints, a vast network of caves, and Turkmenistan's highest peak. But the region has some fine historical monuments too, including the Dayahattin Caravansaray, which offers a strong feel of life along the Silk Road, and the impressive restored mausoleum of Astana-Baba.

TURKMENABAT

Turkmenistan's second city, Turkmenabat (telephone code 422) is, however, a sleepier, impoverished distant cousin of Ashgabat rather than an energetic sibling rival to the capital. It has a long history, based around its geographical position as a suitable crossing point of the broad and treacherous Amu Darya. Initially named Amul, it was first settled more than 2,000 years ago, and gradually became a prosperous crossroads for Silk Road routes heading east to China, south to India and north to Khorezm. Amul was razed by the Mongols in 1221, but the city re-emerged, now called Charjou ('Four Channels'). It fell under the control of the Khanate of Khiva and then the Emirate of Bukhara in the 18th and 19th centuries. The construction of a railway bridge over the Amu Darya in 1886 marked a new stage in the development of the town. Following the Ashgabat earthquake of 1948, some suggested that the capital of the Turkmen Soviet Socialist Republic be moved to Charjou, as it was less earthquake-prone than Ashgabat, but nothing came of the idea, and the town has slipped into an increasingly provincial existence. By a decree of President Niyazov issued in July 1999, Charjou was renamed Turkmenabat, the city of Turkmens, in order to reflect the 'great ideas of unity and stability of the country … as well as taking into consideration the wishes of the population of Lebap region'. Many local people still refer to the place as Charjou.

Like Turkmenistan's other regional capitals, Turkmenabat serves as a base from which to explore its region. The shortage of accommodation options towards the top end of the market, however, makes it less than ideal in fulfilling that function. Its sights, which include a regional museum and the unexcavated ruins of the town of Amul, are by no means unmissable, but Turkmenabat is a friendly place, if not a particularly dynamic one.

Getting there and away

Turkmenabat is served by four flights daily (flight time 50 minutes) from Ashgabat. Flights cost around 35,000 manat. The airport, at the eastern end of Magtumguly Shayoly, is so close to the centre of town that if so inclined you can walk it. Fortunately, you don't have to: there are taxis waiting outside the airport terminal to meet every arriving flight. Don't miss the cosmonaut-themed Soviet-era frieze in the departure hall of the airport.

The railway station is a modern building in the centre of town with a sloping, tiled marble frontage (inquiry office ☎ 422 46959). There are two trains daily to Ashgabat (about 13 hours), one to Atamurat and one to Dashoguz, the last departing in the small hours of the morning. There is an additional train between Mary and Turkmenabat on Tuesdays only.

As in Ashgabat, inter-urban buses and minibuses go from different places depending on the destination. Minibuses, shared taxis and (rare) buses to Mary and Ashgabat leave from outside the railway station. By minibus, the trip to Mary should cost about 50,000 manat; to Ashgabat 125,000. For destinations south of Turkmenabat, transport leaves from the Dunya Bazaar, 9km south of the town centre. A place in a minibus to Garabekewul will cost you around 10,000 manat; to Atamurat 30,000.

Getting around the city is easiest by taxi: expect to pay 5,000 manat for a short journey, or 10,000 manat for one of more than a couple of kilometres or so. There is no urban public bus service, but frequent private buses ply the north–south route between the railway station and the Dunya Bazaar. The fare is 1,000 manat.

Travel agency

Lebapsyyahat 12 Altyn Kok Kochesi; ☎/f 422 61051, 61486. The one state travel agency based in Turkmenabat is by no means the most dynamic in Turkmenistan. They can, however, organise letters of invitation and visa registrations, and put together tours within Lebap Region and more widely. They charge around US$320 per person for a three-day trip from Turkmenabat to the Kugitang Nature Reserve, including an English-speaking guide. They can also arrange boat trips on the Amu Darya.

Where to stay

There are few accommodation options in (or anywhere close to) the upper end of the market, but if you are not too fussy there should be no problems in getting a bed for the night.

Hotel Turkmenabat (45 rooms) Magtumguly Shayoly; ☎ 422 60226. This new hotel was still under construction at the time of research, but the hope of every travel agency in

Turkmenistan is that this place will finally offer the reasonably smart hotel option that has always been sorely missed here. En-suite bathrooms and air conditioning in every room are promised at a price likely to be around US$35–40.

Hotel Amu Darya (42 rooms) 14 Niyazov Shayoly; ☎ 422 22434. This 3-storey building has a good, central location, right opposite the railway station, but is decidedly run down, with tired bathrooms and reports of cockroaches. In summer, make sure that the air conditioner is working in the room you are offered. Single rooms cost US$20, doubles US$30. The 8 suites are poor value for money at US$60, the extra money getting you a lounge full of elderly furniture.

Lebapgurlushyk Hotel (17 rooms) 51A Magtymguly Shayoly; ☎ 422 44420, 44104. In a secluded central spot away from the street, just behind the Hotel Turkmenabat, this hotel is owned by the regional construction organisation. It is a passable option, providing you can cope with the remarkably bright décor: some rooms are painted to an *Arabian Nights* theme, with murals heavy on elephants. The place is managed by the cheerful 'Auntie Sonia'. The rooms are suites with different numbers and configurations of beds: foreigners are charged 160,000 manat per bed. Air conditioners tend to be located in the lounge areas of the bedroom suites rather than in the bedrooms themselves, which can result in hot nights in summer.

Hotel Lukman (30 rooms) Bitarap Turkmenistan Shayoly; ☎ 422 52445. The 'Doctor Hotel' is owned by the regional health authority, and is not usually open to tourists, though they may agree to put you up if they are not busy. The place is south of the centre of town, its entrance marked by a sign, in English: 'Welayat Medical Training – Metchodical Centre'. Even more unpromisingly, taxi drivers know this place as the 'old gynaecology department'. The Lukman was opened to accommodate delegates to the People's Council meeting held in Turkmenabat in 2002, but has quickly become run-down. Rooms are twin-bedded, the beds are hard wooden cots, and air conditioners cool only the adjoining lounges. If you are allowed to stay, a room will cost you 200,000 manat. The inconvenient location, difficulty of booking and unfriendly staff more than outweigh the marginally better room quality than that offered by the Amu Darya.

Hotel Gunesh (34 rooms) 36 Kopet Dagh Kochesi; ☎ 422 61251, 21388. Formerly the Hotel Charjou, this central place is an option to consider only if you are on the tightest of budgets. Beds cost US$6 a night: single travellers may initially be charged US$12, on the grounds that since each room has at least 2 beds in it, you are deemed to be taking 2 places, but the hotel management is open to negotiation on this point. You get what you pay for: the toilets are communal, the showers are out in the yard and rely on the sun to heat the water, and there are plenty of cockroaches. Some of the air conditioners are broken. Turkmen citizens pay just 22,000 manat to stay here.

Gozel Restaurant Magtymguly Shayoly; ☎ 422 64755 (restaurant), 422 61436 (hotel). As a restaurant, this place near the airport is unexceptional, save for a colourful frieze of a Turkmen girl caressing a deer, which dominates the dining area. It offers potentially more interest as a place to stay, with 3 air-conditioned bedrooms at 350,000 manat per night. The **Café Tolkun** (see *Where to eat*, below) is another restaurant with an adjacent private hotel, its 3 large bedrooms available at 250,000 manat per night.

Where to eat

Lebap Restaurant Pushkin Kochesi; ☎ 422 45055, 63521. This state-owned place in the centre of town is the closest that Turkmenabat gets to fine dining. The interior décor is relentlessly pink, leavened by paintings of Alpine scenes, the food a mix of Russian and Central Asian dishes. Mains cost around 20,000–30,000 manat. The place is open ('the time of work', as its charming English-language sign puts it) 09.00–23.00 daily.

Traktir Restaurant 14 Arsarybaba Kochesi; ☎ 422 61438, 48148. Owned by a local entrepreneur who has made his money through the provision of large posters of President

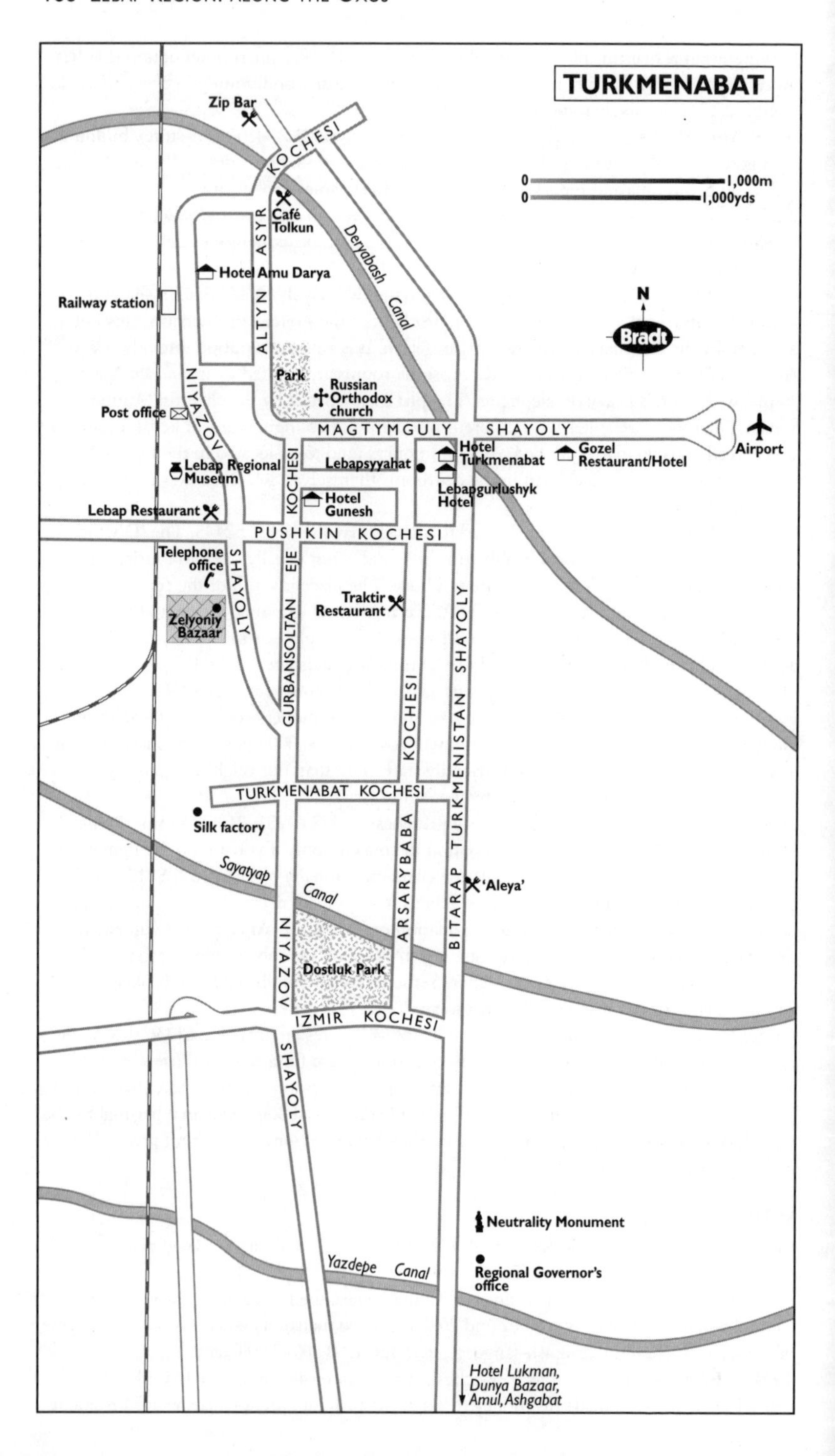

TURKMENABAT
0 1,000m
0 1,000yds
N
Bradt
Zip Bar
KOCHESI
Café Tolkun
Deryabash Canal
ALTYN ASYR
Hotel Amu Darya
Railway station
Park
Russian Orthodox church
NIYAZOV
Post office
MAGTYMGULY SHAYOLY
Airport
Hotel Turkmenabat
Gozel Restaurant/Hotel
Lebapsyyahat
Lebap Regional Museum
KOCHESI
Lebapgurlushyk Hotel
Hotel Gunesh
Lebap Restaurant
PUSHKIN KOCHESI
Telephone office
SHAYOLY
EJE
Traktir Restaurant
Zelyoniy Bazaar
GURBANSOLTAN
KOCHESI
BITARAP TURKMENISTAN SHAYOLY
TURKMENABAT KOCHESI
Silk factory
Sayatyap Canal
ARSARYBABA
'Aleya'
NIYAZOV
Dostluk Park
IZMIR KOCHESI
SHAYOLY
Neutrality Monument
Yazdepe Canal
Regional Governor's office
Hotel Lukman, Dunya Bazaar, Amul, Ashgabat

Niyazov, the Traktir is a livelier option than the Lebap Restaurant. The style is high-seas piracy, with dark wooden walls and tables, and a live budgie which flies about the room. An international menu offers pizzas, *shashlik* and cutlets, most dishes costing around 15–20,000 manat. The English-language menu confuses rather than illuminates. How about 'that tea – the tea with elephant' at 3,000 manat? It is open Mon–Sat 09.00–23.00, but opens only at 18.00 Sun.

Café Tolkun ☎ 422 60272. In the northern part of town close to a small canal, this friendly café run by an enterprising ethnic Uzbek family offers some excellent, cheap Uzbek cooking, including chicken soup with noodles (20,000 manat) and good *somsas* (3,000 manat a time). For more intimate dining, the place offers 2 reed cabins, their sides open onto the canal, one of them built in the style of a little oriental pagoda.

Zip Bar No phone. In a side street just beyond the Tolkun, this place, whose rough-hewn stone-walled décor gives it the feel of a cave, has an unexciting but inexpensive menu (most items 15,000–30,000 manat), and Zip beer on tap for 11,000 manat a glass. Diners here frequently dance along to the music, despite the fact there is no space in which to do so.

A good option on warm evenings is the fountain-studded concrete strip along Bitarap Turkmenistan Shayoly known as **Aleya**. Open-air *shashlik* places set up here, offering basic food around plastic tables. The food quality is generally pretty poor, but this is a popular summer spot for the people of the town, and provides an excellent place to meet the locals.

Shopping

There are two major bazaars, in both of which most of the stallholders are ethnic Uzbek women, in long colourful padded gowns. The **Zelyoniy (Green) Bazaar**, officially known as the Merkezi (Central) Bazaar, is in the centre of town, one block south of the Lebap Restaurant. Fishmongers here sell huge catfish from the Amu Darya. The **Dunya (World) Bazaar**, also known as the New Bazaar, is in Turkmenabat's distant southern suburbs, but offers the best selection of handicraft items and (albeit mostly uninspiring) carpets.

What to see

Town centre

The **Lebap Regional Museum** (☎ 422 43370) is housed in one of the most interesting buildings in Turkmenabat: a former Shia mosque, built around the turn of the 20th century by an Iranian merchant named Hajy Malik. The brick building, which stands in a small park just to the north of the Lebap Restaurant, has a rectangular central tower, topped by two small brick minarets, its sides opened by arches separated with fluted columns. The mosque was secularised during the Soviet period, and became a museum in 1967. But many older locals still regard it as a holy building, and say a prayer when they pass by. Admission costs 5,000 manat for foreigners. The museum is open 09.00–18.00 (with a lunch-time closure 13.00–14.00), daily except Sundays.

The ground floor of the museum is devoted to ethnography, archaeology and natural history. The ethnographic displays include a walk-through *yurt*, a life-sized model of a traditional Turkmen courtyard, complete with stuffed sheep, and collections of silver jewellery, musical instruments, and even 19th-century agricultural implements. The archaeological section is most useful in displaying models and photographs of some of the main sites of the region, such as the Astana-Baba and Darganata mausolea, and the *madrasa* of Idris Baba. Some artefacts from Amul are on display, but lack any proper labelling, and the museum guides

TUGAY

Along the banks of the Amu Darya River, the parched lands typical of Turkmenistan give way at certain points to patches of vivid green. This is the *tugay*, a dense forest of salt-resistant species. Beneath a canopy of poplar trees, a tightly packed undergrowth of reeds and branches makes for an almost impenetrable environment. The trees here, with their creaks and groans, almost seem to be talking to the visitor, perhaps to ward off further intrusions. Through the Soviet period, this unique environment came under considerable threat from the expansion of agricultural cultivation in the Amu Darya Basin. One of the casualties was the Turan tiger, lost from these woodlands in the 1960s. In response, the Amu Darya Nature Reserve was established in 1982. While some key species of the *tugay* remain vulnerable, the reserve authorities have reported some success in helping to raise the stocks of the prized Bukhara deer, a red deer whose numbers had reached dangerously low levels of a dozen or so in the 1980s.

One of the species of the *tugay* flora, liquorice, has long been exploited as an industrial crop. The liquorice-processing factory in Turkmenabat has its origins in the tsarist period. The press used to bale the liquorice roots, ready for export, is an ancient British machine, manufactured by H Bailey and Sons of Salford. It was brought to Charjou in 1906 from Azerbaijan, where it had apparently been in use since the 1870s. The factory did buy a more modern, automated press from the Ukraine, but this proved unable to cope with the heat of the Turkmen summers. So the employees of the Turkmenabat liquorice factory continue to work with their faithful Victorian machinery, calibrated in tons per inch.

As with every nature reserve, a visit to the Amu Darya Reserve involves first securing the appropriate permission from the Ministry of Nature Protection (see page 28). The most accessible location at which to see the *tugay* involves turning riverwards off the main road, just beyond the village of Gabakly, which lies roughly midway between Seydi and Dayahattin. This is the place to which the reserve rangers will probably take you. There is a small and very basic guesthouse here, with a room for visitors to sleep on the floor: a concrete platform outside serves as the bedroom in summer.

(who are more at home with the ethnographic parts of the museum) are unable to provide much illumination. The natural history displays are designed to give a flavour of the natural wealth of the three nature reserves lying within Lebap Region, but attempt to do this largely by means of stuffed animals. These include a Turan tiger, an animal now extinct. Also on display is the Amu Darya shovel-nosed sturgeon, a particularly rare species whose meat was, said the museum guide, a particular hit with Churchill when served to the British prime minister at a meal hosted by Stalin. And there is a diorama featuring plastic dinosaurs stomping across the hills of Kugitang, demonstrating their footprint-making skills.

The displays upstairs offer a presentation of the economic achievements of modern Turkmenabat. There are cases devoted to the main industries of the town, including the production of silk, cotton and liquorice. Other displays include samovars, modern banknotes from across the region, and tsarist coins.

In the **small park** outside the museum, a group of statues features the busts of seven prominent Turkmen classical poets, grouped around Magtymguly, as if for protection. The park also retains ten broken fizzy-water dispensers, a legacy of the Soviet era. Another Soviet relic is the **old cinema** beyond the western edge of the park. Built in 1948, it is now mostly used for displays of Turkmen dancing. The colourful foyer retains faded photographs of film stars dressed in 1970s styles. Among the mostly Russian stars on display is a photo of Jean-Paul Belmondo.

The **Russian Orthodox Church**, dedicated to St Nicholas Maker of Miracles, is nearby on Magtymguly Shayoly. This is a tsarist-era domeless brick building, with a plain white barrel-vaulted interior, decorated with icons around the walls. The entrance is beneath a white arch on the west side of the building. Another arched entrance on the side facing the road is kept locked. In the streets around the church are some interesting single-storey brick buildings of the late 19th and early 20th centuries.

South of the centre

The Soviet town, of four-storey apartment blocks, sprawls to the south of here along two main arteries, now called Niyazov Shayoly and Bitarap Turkmenistan Shayoly, the latter a broad highway offering at one point four lanes in each direction and no prospect, ever, of a traffic jam. Several canals running from east to west cross these thoroughfares. **Dostluk (Friendship) Park** sits to the south of the Sayatyap Canal. There is a war memorial here, honouring those who died in World War II and Afghanistan. The park also features some rusting fairground attractions, including a big wheel, and a boating lake with ancient pedalos for hire. A sign warns that 'ramming' incurs a 15,000 manat fine. Further to the south, along Bitarap Turkmenistan Shayoly, the small **park** opposite the offices of the *Hyakimlik* (regional government) features a choice example of post-independence statuary. The monument, dedicated to Turkmenistan's neutrality, involves a central column with a globe, around which four silvery birds are fluttering, and a ruffled flag, and is topped by two olive branches which look like wings.

The ruins of the old town of **Amul** lie on the southern outskirts of Turkmenabat, unromantically abutting a chemical plant. There is little to see at this unexcavated site beyond a raised fortress, with a higher citadel at the northwest corner of the mound. Take a taxi to get here.

EAST FROM TURKMENABAT

The main road to the Uzbek border crosses the Amu Darya around 5km north of Turkmenabat. The rickety-looking pontoon bridge is worth seeing even if you are not planning on crossing it. Buses disgorge their passengers before making the crossing, in order to lighten the load. The passengers make the journey on foot, before rejoining the bus on the other side. The tsarist-era railway bridge, a triumph of late 19th-century construction, is also visible from here. There is a toll to cross the pontoon bridge: a few thousand manat for Turkmen drivers, but several dollars (the exact amount depending on the type of vehicle) for foreigners. The district of Farap across the river is a designated border zone, and you will not be allowed to make the crossing without the correct permit, or Farap specified on your visa as your place of departure from Turkmenistan. The border is just 36km from Turkmenabat, the last few kilometres spent in the company of the Amu-Bukhara Canal, which takes waters from the Amu Darya to irrigate the fields of Uzbekistan.

NORTH FROM TURKMENABAT

The road and railway following the Amu Darya northwestwards from Turkmenabat to the northern capital of Dashoguz are tracing an important Silk Road route, which ran from Amul to Khorezm. This route is well off the usual tourist path, and the northern part of the journey requires you to obtain restricted zone permits, but there are some worthwhile sights here, especially the Dayahattin Caravansaray and the dense forest known as *tugay* along the banks of the river. Both can be seen as a day trip from Turkmenabat.

Seydi

The town of Seydi, an hour's drive to the north, was formerly known as Neftezavodsk ('oil factory'), a name which gives a rather clearer view of the town's economic base. The focus of the town is its oil refinery, built in the late Soviet period, in what was then a virgin desert site, to treat oil piped from Siberia. The collapse of the Soviet Union disrupted the supply network, and Seydi now receives oil only from the cross-border Kokdumalak field with Uzbekistan. But the Turkmen government has embarked on an ambitious programme to modernise the refinery here, and there have been periodic, though so far inconclusive, discussions about reviving the Siberian pipeline network.

For the tourist, this all means that Seydi, with its industrial chimneys and Soviet-era apartment blocks, is not promising terrain. But it does house the headquarters of the Amu Darya Nature Reserve, in a building on the edge of town

THE RICH WOMAN

Locals refer to the Dayahattin Caravansaray as Bayhattin, 'Rich Woman', and tell a legend about the place that runs roughly as follows. There lived a wealthy merchant, who had a beautiful wife, coveted by a friend of the merchant. The merchant departed on a trading trip, and the friend, seeing his opportunity, made advances to the wife. She was faithful to her husband, and rejected these. The amorous friend hooked up with an old lady. He secreted himself in a trunk, into which he had bored holes, enabling him to see out. The old lady told the wife that she needed to leave town for a few days, and could she leave the trunk containing her precious belongings in the wife's safe keeping? The wife agreed. The unfriendly friend was thereby able to spy on the object of his affections, noticing as she undressed a mole on her back. After a couple of days the old lady returned, and took back delivery of her trunk. When the merchant returned, his 'friend' reported that his wife had been unfaithful, citing as evidence his knowledge of her mole. The humiliated merchant left immediately, to begin a new life as an itinerant tramp.

The merchant's wife used her wealth to construct a glorious caravansaray, which would be able to give refuge to those, like her husband, who wandered the desert. Bricks were brought all the way from Merv for the new construction. By this time, the merchant, pining for his wife, had returned home. But he was still too proud to show himself, and so worked as a humble labourer on his wife's great project. One day the wife recognised her husband, but kept this fact a secret until the building was complete. On that day she held a great feast to mark the inauguration of the splendid new caravansaray, to which all those who had worked on its construction were invited. At the feast the wife told an allegorical tale, designed to demonstrate to her husband the facts of her faithfulness and his friend's trickery. Husband and wife were reunited. According to one more bloodthirsty version of the story, the couple then killed the merchant's erstwhile friend, whose body lies now in the graveyard next to the caravansaray.

identified by the golden statues of a Bukhara deer and a goitred gazelle. The reserve headquarters has a **museum**, open 10.00–12.00 and 15.00–17.00. The admission charge is 3,000 manat. The museum has just one large room, its walls decorated with lurid paintings of the wildlife you might see in the reserve, from desert monitor lizards to rabbits. Stuffed animals feature heavily in the list of items on display, including a Bukhara deer, a rare species which is one of the prides of the reserve. This one died naturally, the park director assures visitors. The museum also features a large display of Bukhara deer antlers, a collection which has prompted one or two visitors to add to it by sending in horns from their own lands, including one from Karelia. Other protected species found in the reserve are also represented in the museum, from goitred gazelle (*jieran*) to shovel-nosed sturgeon.

Dayahattin Caravansaray

The Dayahattin Caravansaray lies just off the main road, 170km to the north of Turkmenabat. To find the place, which is not signposted, turn onto the track heading riverwards a few metres south of the Halkabat checkpoint, marking the entrance to a restricted border zone. A few hundred metres along, turn right where another track crosses yours. You will see the caravansaray in front of you.

Dayahattin is by far the best preserved medieval caravansaray surviving in Turkmenistan. Dating from the 11th or 12th century, it was built to service the trade route between Amul and Khorezm, and probably remained in use until the 16th century. The caravansaray is square in plan, its walls 53m long. Around a central courtyard brick arches lead into a vaulted arcade, off which run various small rooms. The main gate, whose arched roof of fired bricks is still in place, lies on the eastern wall, facing the river. The geometrical patterned decorations in which the bricks have been laid on the external east wall are particularly fine. Around the caravansaray are degraded outer defensive walls. Pack animals would have overnighted in the area enclosed by these, which now accommodates a small graveyard.

Birata

To travel further north, you will need restricted zone permits specifying Birata and then Gazochak districts. North from the Halkabat checkpoint, and past another section of the Amu Darya Reserve, you reach the district capital of Birata, a town known as Darganata until 2003. The renaming of the place apparently came about because one interpretation of the meaning of 'Darganata' is 'The Divided Ata Tribe'. To emphasise the unity of modern Turkmenistan, the new name chosen suggests 'The Single, United Ata Tribe'. Birata is a sleepy place today, but its roots lie in the once significant Khorezm settlement of Dargan, a stopping-place on the Silk Road route north from Amul.

The ruins of Dargan lie about 3km to the south of modern Birata. A blue sign on the main road, marked 'Hezretli Abu Muslim', points out the side road, heading eastwards. This brings you to a modern shrine pilgrimage complex, including a recently constructed brick mosque, and places for pilgrims to sleep and hold sacrificial meals. Behind these modern buildings rise the mud-brick walls of Dargan. A concrete path leads past lovingly tended orchards to the 14th-century Darganata Mausoleum, with its ornately carved wooden door. Local tradition links this place with the tomb of Abu Muslim, the 8th-century leader of the Abbasid rebellion at Merv.

Gazochak

The northernmost town of Lebap Region, Gazochak comes as a surprise after a wearying journey across sparsely populated arid landscapes. You arrive at a Soviet-era town of four-storey apartment blocks, built to house employees working at the gas fields in the area. The Nayip field, 50km away, is one of the key sites in Turkmenistan's bid to develop a liquefied gas industry, with a modern Italian- and Canadian-built plant. Gazochak's airport was closed in 2004, and it is unclear if and when it will reopen to passenger traffic. There is, in short, little touristic reason to come here, but if you need to overnight (for example, if you are making the tough road journey from Turkmenabat to Dashoguz) the Jeihun Hotel in the centre of town, closed for renovation at the time of research, ought to provide an option.

REPETEK NATURE RESERVE

The main road to Mary runs southwestwards from Turkmenabat, across the desert. The only specific attraction along the Lebap segment of this road is the Repetek Nature Reserve and desert research institute, 70km from Turkmenabat. The origins of scientific research here date back to tsarist times and efforts to mitigate the damage wrought by the march of the barchan sand dunes across the tracks of the Transcaspian Railway. The Repetek State Reserve, Turkmenistan's oldest, was established in 1927. UNESCO awarded it the status of an International Biosphere Reserve in 1979.

The most important habitat in the Repetek Reserve is that offered by the groves of black and white saxauls; stumpy trees, whose twisted branches bear green stems rather than leaves, all the better for water conservation. The roots of the black saxaul probe deep in their search for groundwater: hence the interest of these trees to the tsarist engineers worried about sand on their railway line. In some areas, the excessive cutting-down of saxauls is a problem – its wood is considered by Turkmens as the best with which to fire up a *tamdyr* or to barbecue kebabs. In spring, these habitats are given a colourful carpet of poppies and other flowers, making this a wonderful time to drive through the area. There are some particularly large and venerable saxauls around the research institute buildings, with nicknames like 'Old Man' and 'Big Knight'.

The reserve headquarters offer faded reminders of the proud research past of this place. Black-and-white photographs on the walls portray Soviet scientists in straw hats and shirtsleeves. There are a couple of photographs of the British naturalist Gerald Durrell visiting Repetek in 1985. The bathroom built to make his wife's visit a little more pleasant is still standing but, like many of the former accommodation and scientific blocks, is in a stage of deep decay. There is a small **museum** on the site, whose exhibits consist mostly of stuffed animals and pickled reptiles. The reserve rangers delight in describing to you the quantities of poison packed by each of the latter. On reaching a display of the beetles found in the reserve, a ranger recalled that one Soviet-era experiment had involved sending a collection of beetles from around the world into space. 'Only the Repetek beetle returned alive'. The museum also contains a small collection of pottery, a reminder that Repetek, then known as Al-Akhsa, was once a staging point on the Silk Road route across the desert to Amul.

With the approval of the Ministry of Nature Protection, it is possible to stay overnight at Repetek for a few dollars, in one of the very basic guest rooms. This is an atmospheric place, though not a comfortable one at the height of summer.

SOUTH FROM TURKMENABAT

The main road heading southeastwards from Turkmenabat towards the town of Atamurat runs past fields of cotton and wheat along the west bank of the Amu Darya. There are several interesting monuments by the side of, or close to, this road, making for a series of worthwhile stops.

Garabekewul

The first two district capitals passed through, Sakar and Sayat, offer no compelling reason to break your journey, but Garabekewul District, known for its love of wrestling and its brandy distillery, has more to offer. This was the birthplace of the Turkmen classical poet and military leader Seyitnazar Seydi, to whom a large **statue** was erected in the early 1990s, a few kilometres north of Garabekewul town and easily visible from the main road. A line of conifers from the car park leads to the statue. Seydi is depicted standing in front of his horse. His sword in its scabbard and the poetry he holds portray the two careers on which his fame rests. This is a favourite place for local newly-weds to have themselves photographed. Immediately to the south of this statue are the mud-brick walls of **Soltaniyaz Beg Fortress**, which retains some reasonably well-preserved battlements. This place is closely linked with the struggle by local Turkmens, led by Soltaniyaz Beg and Seydi, against the ruling emirate of Bukhara in the 1820s.

Halach

The next district to the south, Halach, has a couple of sites of interest, also with connections to Turkmen classical poetry. A few kilometres northwest of Halach town, along the main road, a bus stop labelled 'Zynhary' on the east side of the road alerts you to the 19th-century *madrasa* of Aly Isha, best known as the place at which the poet **Abdirahim Zynhary** studied. Zynhary was a local man, who lived from 1791 to 1880, and combined his career as a poet with work as the village blacksmith. His golden bust stands in a rather lonely nearby site, in the middle of a large patch of asphalt. The main building of the *madrasa* has a square design, topped by a dome. Some of the adjacent blocks which once held the student cells have been recently restored; others stand derelict, their earth walls crumbling.

Two kilometres to the south, along the main road, is the village of Gyzylayak ('Red Leg'). Turn eastwards off the road here, and after 3.5km you reach the *madrasa* of **Idris Baba**. The main building here dates from the 18th century, a square design with walls 7m in length and a domed roof. It is popular with Turkmen school groups, who come here mainly because of the *madrasa's* association with the poet Magtymguly: he studied here in 1753. The caretaker will tell you that the dead-looking rotund tree nearby, covered in prayers offered in the form of strips of cloth and hair grips, is 350 years old and that the young Magtymguly composed poetry beneath it. The caretaker will also show you 'Idris Baba's fishing hole'. He keeps his own fish suppers in it.

Astana-Baba

Alamberdar Mausoleum

To head further south into Atamurat District, the appropriate restricted zone permit is required. Immediately into the district, you reach the village of Astana-Baba. Here, 12km northwest of the town of Atamurat, lies the Alamberdar Mausoleum at the side of the road as if placed there as a photo-stop for tour groups heading to the Kugitang Reserve. The mausoleum is one of the best examples of 11th-century architecture in Turkmenistan. Square in plan, its external walls feature three blind niches on each side. The decorative brickwork is particularly fine. Inside, a brick tomb near the door is covered with cloths. At one head of the tomb, a short column was, when I visited, topped with a few used matches and an ominously sticky substance to which a couple of feathers were clinging, all too suggestive of recent avian sacrifice. The tomb is apparently a false one: research has indicated that no-one was ever buried beneath it.

SEYDI

Born in 1775 in Garabekewul District, the Turkmen poet known as Seydi was educated locally in Halach, and then at *madrasas* in Bukhara and Khiva. Returning to his home district, he soon became known for his intellect, wisdom and fine poetry. Together with Soltaniyaz Beg, he was one of the leaders of the uprising of Turkmens in Lebap between 1821 and 1824 against the cruel ways of the Emir of Bukhara, in whose domain the region then fell. The uprising was unsuccessful, and Seydi then led a migration of a group of members of his Ersari tribe, to find sanctuary beyond the emir's grasp. After a crossing of the Kara Kum Desert, the group eventually settled close to the Caspian, in the Gorgan region of present-day Iran. But this area proved little more hospitable, and the group had to fight off the predations of Kurdish raiders. Seydi himself did not survive these skirmishes: he was probably either killed in battle or died a prisoner, though one version of his life story, for those who prefer happy endings, has him escaping his captors and returning to his family.

Seydi is one of the historical Turkmen figures celebrated with approval by the Niyazov government, who emphasise the patriotic aspects of his poetry; in particular his calls for the Turkmen tribes to show greater strength by uniting, and for the defence of the Turkmens' homeland against foreign aggressors. Seydi rests well below Magtymguly in the pantheon of Turkmen classical poets, but in compensation does have the distinction, shared by rather few poets worldwide, of having an oil refinery named in his honour.

Locals believe that the mausoleum is the place of burial of a standard bearer of the Prophet. While there is no definitive answer as to the figure for whom the mausoleum was built, written sources record that the last Samanid ruler, Abu Ibrahim Ismail Muntazir, was killed in this general area in 1004. Some historians suggest that Alamberdar might be the symbolic mausoleum of Muntazir.

Astana-Baba Mausoleum

A few hundred metres to the south, on the same side of the road, lies another interesting mausoleum, that of Astana-Baba. This is an unusual and attractive complex, consisting of four domed rooms, reached by way of a brick corridor beyond the portal, the corridor leading into a now roofless four-pillared hall before reaching the first of the domed rooms. The two westernmost domed rooms, those furthest from the entrance, each contain two tombs. The building has been progressively enlarged, and several times altered, over the centuries. The oldest part of the complex seems to comprise the two easternmost domed rooms, one of them a mosque, the other containing a single tomb, which probably date from the 12th century. The portal and the twin-tombed room known as the Kizlyar-Bibi Mausoleum are among the most recent additions, probably 19th century. The whole complex is a place of shrine pilgrimage.

'Astana' derives from the Farsi word meaning 'mausoleum', and it is unclear who is actually buried beneath the various tombs. One tale begins with the sudden death at this place of the beloved only daughter of the ruler of Balkh, Ibn Ali Nur Ogly Zuveida, just a week after her marriage to a local worthy. The distraught father ordered the construction of a magnificent mausoleum to his daughter. But no sooner was the building completed than it fell down. This happened a second time, and a third. One day a wise old man advised the grieving father to mix earth and water brought from Mecca to the building materials. This he did, and this time the building remained standing. On his death, the father was buried in the mausoleum alongside the daughter he had loved so much.

Atamurat

The town of Atamurat is the main urban centre of the southeast corner of Turkmenistan. Under its earlier name of Zemm it was an important medieval Silk Road settlement. A fortress mound on the west bank of the Amu Darya is testimony to the historical roots of the town. Later called Kerki, it now carries the name of President Niyazov's father, to commemorate the fact that Atamurat Niyazov once worked as a teacher here. The town has a statue of Atamurat Niyazov dressed in a suit rather than his familiar military uniform, and holding a book and pen. The main interest of the town lies in the single-storey brick buildings of the tsarist era which make up the old town centre, presenting one of the nicest surviving early 20th-century urban neighbourhoods in Turkmenistan. A large church stands nearby in the 'park of culture and rest', its unfinished octagonal tower topped by sheets of corrugated iron. It was used as a sports centre in Soviet times, and has not yet been converted back to a religious building. The adjacent new town is focused on the long main street, Niyazov Kochesi, on which most of the main administrative buildings are located. President Niyazov surveys his street from a large billboard at its southern end.

A rusty pontoon bridge provides a crossing of the Amu Darya at Atamurat, linking the town with the settlement of Kerkichi on the river's east bank, from where a road leads to the Kugitang Nature Reserve.

KUGITANG NATURE RESERVE

Straddling the Uzbek border in the far southeast of Turkmenistan, the Kugitang ridge of the Pamir-Alai mountain range presents one of the most attractive natural environments in the country. The limestone range is cut by steep-sided canyons (Kugitang means, roughly, 'Difficult-to-Cross Mountains'), and contains the highest peak in Turkmenistan, at 3,137m. This summit was known as Ayrybaba until September 2004, when the Turkmen parliament adopted a resolution renaming it 'Turkmenbashy the Great Peak'. Several rare species are found here, including the spiral-horned markhor goat, and the Bukhara urial, a mountain sheep. Kugitang was established as a nature reserve in 1986.

Practicalities

The termination of scheduled flights in 2004 to the airports of both Atamurat and Magdanly, the two main towns in the region, has made Kugitang a substantially more difficult place to reach of late. The drive from Turkmenabat, through Atamurat, should take around six hours.

Accommodation options are limited. There are a few chalets, managed by the geological survey, in an attractive setting on the banks of a lake outside the village of Koyten. The nature reserve (☎ 440 31251) has more basic accommodation next to the reserve's central office, close to the hamlet of Hojakarawul, further south. Camping is also an option. The main Turkmen travel companies are experienced in putting together short breaks to Kugitang: given that a visit to the area requires both the appropriate restricted zone permit and the approval of the Ministry of Nature Protection, this is not a straightforward destination to visit independently.

Hojapil

Some of the most interesting places to visit lie in the Hojapil *zakaznik*, in the northern part of the range. To reach this spot, take the road through Koyten, which then runs in an easterly direction towards the Uzbek border. Ammonites found in the rocks here were once believed by local people to be the impressions left by a stamp used by the Emir of Bukhara to mark his territory. Near the lower end of the village of Hojapil, a path up the hillside to the south takes you after a stiff but not difficult 20-minute climb to the **dinosaur plateau**, one of Turkmenistan's more unusual sights. The inclined plateau, some 500m long and 200m wide, was found by scientists in the early 1980s to contain more than 400 footprints of dinosaurs. The three-toed prints make clearly visible depressions in the surface of the limestone. The largest footprints reach diameters of up to 80cm, with the dinosaur step length reaching around 1.5m. Smaller dinosaurs wandered across the plateau too, their tracks the size of a human shoe.

Dinosaur footprints have been discovered at other locations in the Kugitang Mountains too, more than 2,500 in total, dating from the Jurassic period. Turkmen scientists argue that the footprint evidence is suggestive of at least three hitherto unknown dinosaur species, and have suggested the names Gissarosaurus, Hojapilosaurus and Turkmenosaurus. Local villagers believed that the tracks at Hojapil were created either by the elephants of Alexander the Great's army or elephants brought back from India by a local holy man returning from a religious pilgrimage (the name 'Hojapil' derives from the latter legend).

Another worthwhile attraction lies nearby, just outside the village of Hojapil on the road back towards Koyten. This is the canyon and cave of **Kyrk Gyz** ('40 Girls'). The canyon, entered through an incongruously sited wooden gate, is itself impressive: steep-sided and imposing. The path along its floor leads to a cave, surrounded by little pyramidal piles of stones, constructed by visitors to what is considered a sacred place. There is a tomb in the floor of the cave, and a hearth with a couple of upturned cooking pots in the corner, for those wishing to cook a sacrificial meal at this place of pilgrimage. But the most remarkable feature of the cave is the ceiling, from which thousands of strips of material hang, held in place by pats of dried mud. These derive from the principal means of making a wish here: a piece of cloth is attached to some wet mud, which is then flung up against the roof of the cave. If the mud sticks, the wish will be granted.

There are many local legends about the place. In some stories, the 40 girls were warlike Amazons, defeating those who tried to take their land. In others, the girls have a less military role. Facing capture by bandits, the innocent girls prayed for salvation. Protection was granted by the mountain itself, into which the girls found they could miraculously walk. And to this day in the rocks on the floor of the cave can be discerned items such as crumpled piles of clothes, the possessions of those 40 girls.

The Hojapil *zakaznik* also offers fine hiking opportunities, and many places of natural beauty. One site on the itineraries of most tour packages to Kugitang is the steep-sided **Umbardepe Canyon**, containing a waterfall with a drop of 27m.

Hojakarawul and the Karlyuk Caves

The headquarters of the Kugitang Nature Reserve lie south of Hojapil. Follow the road along the Kugitang River valley, through the village of Koyten and the old lead-mining settlement of Svintsovy Rudnik to the hamlet of Hojakarawul. There is a small and eminently missable **museum** here, which features a stuffed markhor, a gypsum model of a dinosaur footprint, glass cases offering displays of minerals and fossils and a mock-up of a cave, replete with stalactites and stalagmites. The latter exhibit reflects one of the other great attractions of

Kugitang; beneath the limestone hills lie one of the most extensive networks of caves in Central Asia. There are references in ancient Greek texts to caves in these mountains, but the complex was not properly explored until the second half of the 20th century. Given the name **Karlyuk**, after the closest settlement, an underground network of some 50km of caves has been mapped. Among the more unusual treasures of this subterranean world is the presence in underground lakes of a rare species of sightless fish, the blind cave loach, which is the only fish endemic to Turkmenistan.

The considerable potential of this area for speleological tourism has not yet properly been tapped, but it is possible for the non-specialist visitor to see something of the Karlyuk Caves in the company of experienced guides from the nature reserve. The entrance to the **Kapkytan Cave**, in the hills to the northeast of Karlyuk, is sealed by a large metal door. This opens to a horizontal shaft, 300m long, cut in Soviet times for the commercial extraction of onyx. At the end of the shaft, the cave network proper: a series of passages, huge galleries and cosier caves. There are stalactites and stalagmites, forming sculptures which, in the universal tradition of cave tourism, are given names reflecting their supposed resemblance to characters of mythology, legend and the animal kingdom. Guides will point out Medusa, with her flowing hair, a chamber containing Father Christmas and the Snow Maiden and, with a snigger, various formations suggesting a passing resemblance to human reproductive organs. The Gulshirin Cave, a few kilometres to the north of here, is another to which local guides will sometimes take visitors.

East of Karlyuk, on the southern edge of the Kugitang range, a hydrogen-sulphide-rich spring known as **Kainar Baba** is a popular local bathing place.

Lebap Region carpet gul

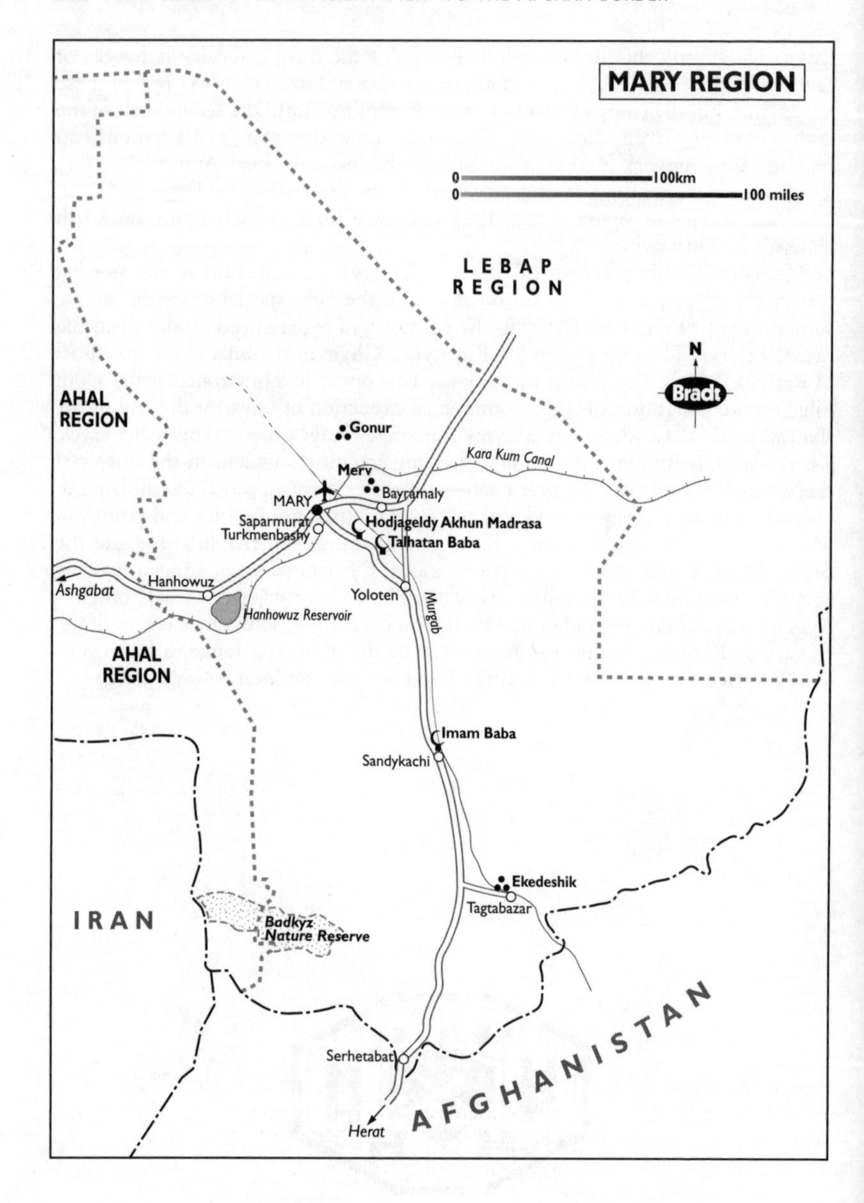
MARY REGION
0 100km
0 100 miles
LEBAP REGION
N
Bradt
AHAL REGION
Gonur
Kara Kum Canal
Merv
Bayramaly
MARY
Saparmurat Turkmenbashy
Hodjageldy Akhun Madrasa
Talhatan Baba
Ashgabat
Hanhowuz
Yoloten
Murgab
Hanhowuz Reservoir
AHAL REGION
Imam Baba
Sandykachi
Ekedeshik
Tagtabazar
IRAN
Badkyz Nature Reserve
Serhetabat
Herat
AFGHANISTAN

8 Mary Region: from Ancient Merv to the Afghan Border

The Murgab River flows northwards into Turkmenistan from the mountains of Afghanistan, its waters fanning out into a great alluvial delta some 300km east of Ashgabat before expiring into the unforgiving sands of the Kara Kum Desert. This delta, the Merv Oasis, has been a centre of human settlement since Bronze Age times, and for 2,500 years was dominated by the city of Merv, which was to become one of the most important cities of the Islamic world, and the eastern capital of the Seljuk Empire.

Given the low annual rainfall of the region, the exploitation of the alluvial soils of the oasis has been a story about irrigation. Dams have been used to harness the waters of the Murgab since the Iron Age. The control of these dams became important military objectives for those seeking to secure the oasis. In 1785, the destruction of the main dam by the forces of the Emir of Bukhara, in their attempt to wrest Merv from Persian control, provoked the economic decline of the area. In 1890, Colonel Sir Colin Scott-Moncrieff of the Royal Engineers, who had spent his career working on irrigation systems in India and Egypt, was asked to advise the Russian government on the irrigation of the newly annexed region of Merv. The Russians were evidently pleased with his work, for Tsar Alexander III presented Sir Colin with a magnificent silver punch bowl, which is now the most valuable item in the Royal Engineers' Mess at Chatham. The construction of the Kara Kum Canal across the region in the late 1950s brought the waters of the Amu Darya to the soils of the Merv Oasis. Coupled with irrigation waters derived from the Murgab, these have made Mary Region an important centre for cotton and wheat production in Turkmenistan.

The archaeological park of Ancient Merv is the single major attraction of Mary Region, and arguably of Turkmenistan as a whole, but there is much else to see here, including the remarkable Bronze Age settlement of Gonur, on the northern edge of the oasis, and the cave settlement of Ekedeshik, close to the Afghan border. The modern regional capital, Mary, serves as the obvious base from which to visit these sites, as well as possessing a worthwhile museum of its own.

MARY

The regional capital, and third largest city of Turkmenistan (telephone code 522), Mary is heir to the city of Ancient Merv, 30km to the east, as the administrative capital of the oasis. Its origins date to the 1820s, when Turkmens built a fortress here, alongside the new banks of the Murgab, in preference to the old city site. This new city of Merv was taken without a fight in 1884 by a Russian lieutenant named Alikhanov, who persuaded the local Tekke Turkmen leaders to accept tsarist authority rather than lose their city and probably their lives. The seizure of Merv by the tsarist forces induced an outbreak of what was described in British newspapers as 'Mervousness', as London fretted about possible Russian designs on British India.

The Russians set about building a new administrative centre here, but Lord Curzon, visiting in 1888, found the place a 'rickety town', and mocked the fancies of 'the brand-new Merv ... that it had inherited some aroma of the ancient renown'. Some would argue that Curzon's words still hold good. The city was renamed Mary in the 1930s. With a population of around 100,000, it is a pleasant enough if unexciting place, offering walks along the Murgab River, a good regional museum, accommodation options to suit most pockets, and plenty of mostly uninspiring places to eat.

Getting there and away

There are two **flights** daily from Ashgabat, by Boeing 717. The flight time is 40 minutes, and tickets cost around 30,000 manat. Since one flight makes the round trip in the early morning, the second in the early evening, it is possible to visit Mary as a day trip from Ashgabat. Local travel companies can organise one-day packages, usually combining a quick tour of Ancient Merv with a visit to Mary Regional Museum. The airport (information office ☎ 522 32472) lies 8km east of the centre of town, off the road to Bayramaly. Taxis await the incoming flights. You should not have to pay more than 20,000 manat. The Turkmenistan Airlines booking office (☎ 522 32777) is in town, on Magtymguly Kochesi. It is open daily, 09.00–20.00, with a lunch-break 14.00–15.00.

The **railway** station is a low-slung white-tiled building in the centre of town, whose function is advertised by a poster depicting a golden statue of President Niyazov, arms outstretched, apparently parting two speeding trains. Three trains daily head west to Ashgabat (7 hours). Two head east, via Turkmenabat (one to Atamurat, the other to Dashoguz), and one south, to Serhetabat on the Afghan border. There is a further train to Turkmenabat, on Tuesdays only.

The **bus** terminal is nearby, a deserted-looking building from which the public buses depart. There are three a day to Ashgabat (21,000 manat), two to Serhetabat and two to Tejen, and a much more frequent service to Bayramaly (32 buses daily, with the first departing at 06.30, the last at 18.10). There is more activity in the open area immediately to the west of the bus terminal. The numerous private vehicles depart from here. There are frequent departures of both minibuses and taxis for Ashgabat, Turkmenabat and Tejen, and options for most towns in the region.

Travel agency

Marysyyahat 58 Mollanepes Shayoly; ☎ 522 39230; **f** 522 37630; **e** marysyyahat@yandex.ru. Based at the Hotel Sanjar, this state travel company can organise letters of invitation as well as tours across Mary Region.

Where to stay

Hotel Margush (28 rooms) Gowshuthan Kochesi; ☎ 522 32328, 34965 or 34832; **f** 522 31213. Opened in 2004, this marble-tiled hotel on the banks of the Murgab River is the only accommodation option at the top end of the range. The rooms run off 2 balconies overlooking a glass-vaulted central lobby. All rooms have central air conditioning, en-suite facilities and satellite TV. Singles cost US$50 a night, doubles US$70, and suites US$150. Breakfast is not included: an unexciting 'standard breakfast' of sausage, cheese and a boiled egg is a pricey 90,000 manat.

Hotel Sanjar 58 Mollanepes Shayoly; ☎ 522 57644. This 8-storey balconied building on Mary's main street has a perfect, central location close to the railway station, and is a textbook example of a run-down former Soviet provincial hotel. It has scuffed wooden flooring, decrepit bathrooms and Soviet-era notices barking out extensive lists of rules in Russian. On the plus side, rooms are air conditioned, there are lifts, and some modernised suites are promised. Singles cost around US$25, doubles US$30, and suites US$50.

Hotel Yrsgal (10 rooms) Ata Kopek Mergena Kochesi; ☎ 522 53976. A 2-storey building a block away from the Sanjar, behind the Altyn Asyr Kafé. Singles cost US$12, doubles from US$20, not all of the air conditioners work and the bathrooms are fairly grim.

Motel Rahat (11 rooms); ☎ 522 34970. Some 5km south of the town centre, on the Serhetabat road, this place is really only a sensible option for those with their own

THE IRISH KHAN OF MERV

One of the more curious episodes of the Great Game played out in Central Asia between Britain and Russia concerned an Irishman named Edmund O'Donovan. With a colourful background including involvement in underground Irish revolutionary movements and a spell in the French Foreign Legion, O'Donovan found himself in the region as a special correspondent of the *London Daily News*. Arriving at Geok Depe in 1881, he found the place in the throes of Russian attack. Determined not to be tardy for battle again, he set out for Merv, reasoning that this was likely to be the Russians' next major target.

When O'Donovan eventually reached Merv, he found not the mythical city of shining domes, but 'some wretched hovels'. He was led to a tent, which immediately became packed out with curious Turkmens, many of whom seemed to have made up their mind that the stranger was a Russian spy. He was held under 'tent arrest' until a letter was eventually received from the British consular agent in Mashhad, confirming his identity. Thereafter, his position gradually improved. The Turkmen leaders evidently felt that, with O'Donovan around, they might be able to secure military support from the British against the advancing Russians. They thus determined both to keep him in Merv, and to accord him progressively greater status. This process culminated in the two local hereditary leaders installing him as the Supreme Ruler of Merv. The people, he was told, had accepted British rule, and looked to him for guidance.

O'Donovan found, however, that life as Supreme Ruler was anything but comfortable. His tent filled at mealtimes with hungry visitors. He acquired a reputation as a physician, and attempted to rid himself of the milling crowds of patients by prescribing everyone dandelion juice. New-born babies were brought to him, their parents having accorded him the honour of naming their child O'Donovan Beg. He was never given any peace. And his position was fraught with potential dangers. The arrival of bundles of newspapers, sent to him from Tehran, caused some difficulties, as the people of Merv assumed they were currency notes of great value. They were only persuaded otherwise by witnessing what O'Donovan did with the newspapers after reading them.

O'Donovan only managed to escape from his 'subjects' by engineering a letter from the British Minister in Tehran, requesting that he be sent to Persia immediately to make a full report. The people of Merv believed that he would return to them, bringing British support against the Russians. But he was never to do so. His travels next took him to the Sudan, where he lost his life accompanying the expedition against the Mahdi.

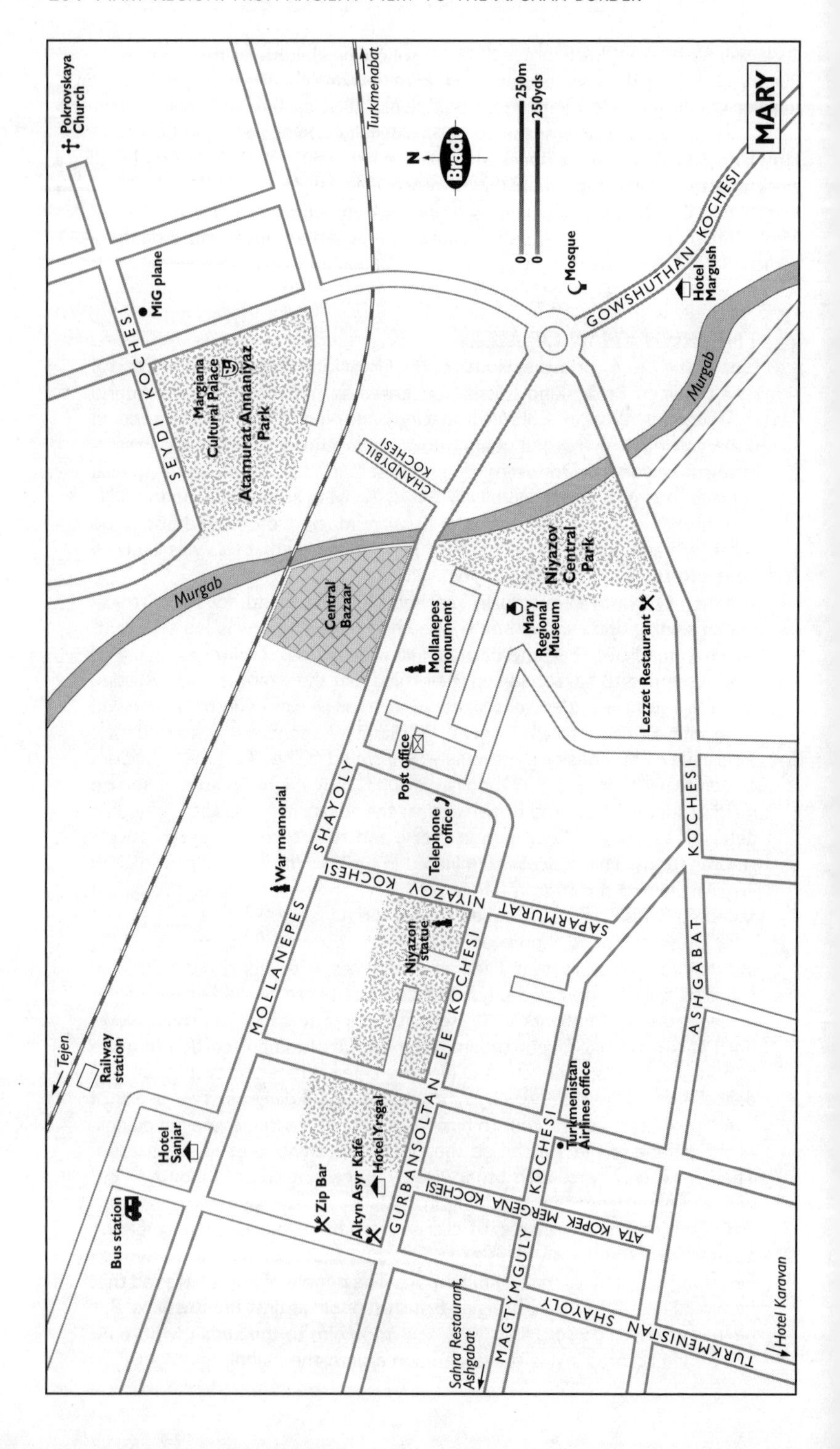
MARY
Bradt
N
0 250m
0 250yds
Turkmenabat
Pokrovskaya Church
MiG plane
SEYDI KOCHESI
Margiana Cultural Palace
Atamurat Annaniyaz Park
Mosque
GOWSHUTHAN KOCHESI
Hotel Margush
Murgab
Murgab
CHANDYBIL KOCHESI
Central Bazaar
Niyazov Central Park
Mary Regional Museum
Mollanepes monument
Lezzet Restaurant
Post office
Telephone office
War memorial
MOLLANEPES SHAYOLY
SAPARMURAT NIYAZOV KOCHESI
Niyazov statue
GURBANSOLTAN EJE KOCHESI
ASHGABAT KOCHESI
Tejen
Railway station
Turkmenistan Airlines office
Hotel Sanjar
Hotel Yrsgal
Altyn Asyr Kafé
Zip Bar
Bus station
ATA KOPEK MERGENA KOCHESI
MAGTYMGULY KOCHESI
TURKMENISTAN SHAYOLY
Hotel Karavan
Sahra Restaurant, Ashgabat

transport. The motel stands next to a lorry park, a couple of hundred metres to the south of a roundabout decorated by a monument resembling an upright Toblerone with 3 circles cut into it. The motel has a central courtyard planted with lemon trees beneath a glass roof. The rooms are air conditioned, have en-suite facilities and are spacious, though rather drab. They are altogether more wholesome than those at the Sanjar. Basic rooms cost 400,000 manat; suites cost 500,000. A 50,000 manat booking fee is also levied. The place has a bar and simple restaurant.

Hotel Karavan (9 rooms) 25 Nesimi Kochesi; ☎ 522 39350, 33464. A private hotel, run by an enterprising family with various local business interests, this is a relaxing place to stay, in a residential area a few blocks south of the town centre. The rooms are clean, though furnished with an alarming number of soft toys, and give out onto a green central courtyard. None of the rooms has its own washing facilities: there are a total of 3 shower-rooms and 1 bathroom, each with a toilet, to serve the place. Single rooms are US$25, doubles US$40, and triples US$51.

Hotel Karavan 2 (7 rooms) 85 Murgab Shosee; ☎ 522 35983. Run by the same family as the Karavan, this offers a similar deal to its sister hotel, with the same prices, and rooms off a courtyard enlivened with rose bushes. But the location of the Karavan 2, not far from the Rahat in Mary's southern suburbs, and close to a busy road, makes this a significantly less attractive option.

Where to eat

Most dining options in Mary are focused around *shashlik*, and this is not a city of stand-out restaurants, but there are plenty of places to have a reasonable and inexpensive meal. Most places offer outdoor seating at plastic tables on warm summer evenings.

Altyn Asyr Kafé Corner of Turkmenistan Shayoly and Gurbansoltan Eje Kochesi; no phone. This white-tiled café offers *shashlik*, plus a few basic Russian and international dishes. It has Turkmen Zip beer on tap and such enticing bar snacks as dried fish and the salty dried curd balls known as *gurt*. It is run by the owners of the Karavan Hotel. Two doors up along Turkmenbashy Shayoly, the **Zip Bar** offers a similar deal. This part of town is at the heart of Mary's nightlife, such as it gets. The **Asia Disco** sits immediately behind the Zip Bar, and there is another disco in the building adjoining the Hotel Sanjar, half a block to the north.

Sahra Restaurant 40 Magtymguly Kochesi; ☎ 522 56177. Just to the west of the town centre, on the Ashgabat road, this place is a minor notch up from the Altyn Asyr. The menu still majors on *shashlik*, served to an accompaniment of Russian MTV. The paper napkins are folded into elegant fans, though.

Lezzet Restaurant Ashgabat Kochesi; ☎ 522 35767. A Turkish restaurant at the southern edge of the Niyazov Central Park, this place offers a reasonable range of Turkish dishes, including *pide* (a kind of Turkish pizza), various kebabs, and *baklava* to follow, but no alcohol and not much atmosphere.

Shopping

The central bazaar lies at the east end of Mollanepes Shayoly, close to the Murgab River. Its main building is topped with a large blue dome, which makes for an unmistakable urban landmark. The fruit and vegetable market is around the back. The bazaar has the official title of 'Merou Shahou Jahan', or 'Merv, Queen of the World', which seems rather to bear out Curzon's critique. The old Soviet Univermag department store is further west along Mollanepes Shayoly, almost opposite the Sanjar Hotel. Several banks and the post office also lie on or close to this street.

What to see

Mary Regional Museum

The museum (☎ 522 34214, 32722), across Mollanepes Shayoly from the main bazaar, is housed in an attractive building built in 1908, apparently for the Russian owner of the local brick factory. Appropriately enough, it is a brick-built dwelling, of two stories around a south-facing courtyard. This is Turkmenistan's best museum outside Ashgabat, whose ground-floor archaeological displays provide an excellent introduction to both Ancient Merv and the Bronze Age sites of the northern part of the oasis. The ethnographic displays upstairs are interesting too. The museum is open daily, 10.00–17.00, with a lunch-break 13.00–14.00.

The first room on the ground floor features a helpful model of the main buildings at the Merv site, though more than a little geographical licence has been used in including in the corner of the Merv model a Bronze Age fire temple from Margush. A long hall lined with display cases follows. The first half of this focuses on the Bronze Age, with some remarkable exhibits from Professor Viktor Sarianidi's excavations at Gonur and Togolok 21, as well as some items from sites further west, including Altyn Depe and Namazga Depe. The skeleton of a Margush woman believed by museum staff to have been a priestess is a replica: the original skeleton was reburied several years back after a series of illnesses and tragedies befell members of the museum team. Among the items from the Bronze Age sites are fine stamp seals, perfume bottles, terracotta female figurines and jewellery.

The second half of the long hall features items from Ancient Merv, from retorts used for the production of gold to Seljuk bronze-ware. A ceramic cup dated to the 11th or 12th centuries depicts a couple in an unmistakably romantic embrace. Most of the labelling at the museum is in Turkmen. Occasional English texts offer such explanations as: 'Parfia's age had been changed by Sasanid's age'. Which does not perhaps add much to human understanding.

The next room offers a presentation of the origins and flowering of the Turkmen people, derived from President Niyazov's book *Ruhnama*. This is followed by a room devoted to the Mongol predations of 1221. A display of Mongol ceramics serves mainly to demonstrate the cultural impoverishment of this period in comparison with those preceding it. Next comes a room emphasising the diverse origins of the materials found on this part of the Silk Road, from Arabic inscriptions to Chinese ceramics. Also here is a display about Turkmen tribal formation in the 16th and 17th centuries. The last room on the ground floor is devoted to the work of the archaeologists who have unearthed the treasures of Merv. A team from University College London, partners in the International Merv Project, here contributes a display in English entitled 'Plants and People at Ancient Merv', reporting the results of the collection of seeds from late Sasanian (AD400–600) soil. Barley and wheat were the most abundant crops, apparently suggesting a staple diet of bread and gruel. But the Sasanians also enjoyed grape, peach and almond. Abundant cottonseeds suggested that, in the Sasanian period as today, cotton was an important local crop, both for yarn and oil.

Upstairs, the museum offers two worthwhile permanent exhibitions, both burdened with wordy titles. The first, 'Material Culture of the Turkmen People', comprises seven rooms of nicely presented ethnographic materials, though labelling here is in Turkmen and Russian only. There are extensive displays of silver jewellery, hunting equipment, talismans, carpet-making and domestic implements. The fourth room is a *yurt*, whose interior furniture includes a crib. A child's dress displayed here is decorated with snake patterns, as talismans against evil. The last room of this exhibition is dedicated to the Turkmen wedding, featuring ornate and heavy wedding dresses, and a *kejebe*, a structure, placed on a camel, in which the bride is precariously seated. A ring hanging from the ceiling has several scarves attached to it; the basis for a wedding game whose rules can best be summarised as 'jump up and grab one'. A metal bowl displayed here is filled at the wedding with sugared water. Bride and groom both drink from this to ensure that their domestic life starts sweetly.

The second of the permanent exhibitions is 'The Material Culture and Historical Survey of Other People Living on Turkmen Soil', a rare example of a display about non-Turkmen peoples in a museum in Turkmenistan. The first room is focused on Turkmenistan's ethnic Baluchi minority, heavily concentrated in rural areas of Mary Region. Three rooms follow about the arrival of the Russians in the 1880s, and the establishment of the Russian administrative centre here. A symbolic chunk of the Transcaspian Railway is on display, as well as domestic items such as *samovars*, a sewing machine and ancient gramophone. There are many interesting photographs from the tsarist era, including of the newly constructed irrigation works, and of Engineer Andreev who supervised them.

Town centre

On the east side of the museum is the shady **Niyazov Central Park**, whose trees conceal a few surprises. There is a bust here of Major General Yaqub Kulievich Kuliev, who died at Stalingrad. Just beyond this hero of the Great Patriotic War are the dodgems, and thereafter the rest of a run-down amusement park, featuring a ropey-looking big wheel and a riverside pavilion filled with arcade games. A few metres away, near the old October Cinema, stands one of the most evocative Soviet-era monuments still surviving in Turkmenistan. A silver rocket zooms off into space. Around its silver trail stand three golden figures, each gesturing heavenwards: a cosmonaut; a sturdy industrial worker in dungarees; and a girl holding a sheaf of wheat in her left hand, though unable to clutch anything in her right, which has fallen off.

West from here, there are several pieces of statuary of varying quality along Mollanepes Shayoly. Just beyond the regional museum sits a thoughtful statue of **Mollanepes**, a well-known local poet of the 19th century, who was also an accomplished jeweller. An Ahal Tekke horse keeps the poet company. Around the statue are laid out garishly painted panels of exotic scenes: the backdrop to snaps taken by local photographers. Two blocks further east is a golden statue of the young Atamurat Niyazov, President Niyazov's father, dressed in military uniform and standing in front of a concrete Turkmen flag. Just across the road from here is a **war memorial** from an earlier regime: a suitably sombre monument to those who died in World War II, comprising a stylised stone flower, with an eternal flame at its base, in front of which stand male and female figures.

A block to the south, an amazingly large expanse of town centre space has been converted into a rather barren **park**. At the west end of this is a concrete stage. In the centre of the park is a golden mother-and-child monument. The child's face is serious, and offers at least a suggestion of the features of the adult President Niyazov. Over the road, looking towards the monument, is a poster of the president, his right hand across his heart, as if paying his respects to his mother opposite. The poster is flanked by two quotes from the president about the glories of motherhood. At the east end of the park is a golden statue of President Niyazov, seated in a comfy armchair, the head out of all proportion to the body. The backdrop to the statue is a tiled carpet design. In front, a low dome is decorated with a map of Turkmenistan.

It is instructive to walk a couple of hundred metres south from here, along Saparmurat Niyazov Kochesi, to a more modestly proportioned silver-painted bust of President Niyazov, a product of an earlier year in the life of independent Turkmenistan. A comparison between this monument and that to the north demonstrates the degree to which the cult of personality around the president has developed.

Towards the Russian Orthodox Church

A pleasant stroll is to be had by walking eastwards along Mollanepes Shayoly from the Niyazov Central Park, crossing the bridge over the Murgab. Take the first turning to the left, along Chandybil Kochesi, and walk (carefully) across the railway tracks at the end of the road. This brings you to the **Atamurat Annaniyaz Park**, which features another golden statue of President Niyazov's father in military uniform, this time accompanied by two of his sons. The park also possesses a concrete flamingo. On the eastern side of the park, the building which in Soviet times housed the Regional House of Culture, the Philharmonia and the Kemine Theatre is now known as the **Margiana Cultural Palace**. The end wall of this building, facing into the park, is covered by a wonderful, vivid mosaic: a Turkmen girl takes flight amid a rainbow, doves fluttering around her. Inside the building there is another large mosaic, albeit a less colourful one, featuring violinists, actors and other cultural types. In the park nearby a concrete base marks the former site of a large statue of the 19th-century Turkmen poet **Kemine**, a mentor of Mollanepes. The statue, a playful piece portraying the head and arms of the poet, has been moved to a suburban location in the east of the city, where it replaced an equestrian statue of the Soviet hero Poltoratskiy.

Walk half a block to the north from the Margiana Cultural Palace, and turn right along Seydi Kochesi, which once carried the name of the Russian poet Pushkin, but now bears that of a Turkmen one. Outside the fire department offices here is the incongruous sight of a **MiG aircraft**, resting on a concrete stick. At the end of Seydi Kochesi, a couple of blocks further east, is the **Pokrovskaya Church**, a red-brick Russian Orthodox church, founded in 1900. Inside, every spare piece of wall is covered by framed icons and other religious works. The part of town through which you have been walking contains some nice single-storey brick buildings dating from the tsarist era.

If you are looking for a longer walk, pathways have been laid out along the Murgab River as Mary's equivalent of the hilltop Serdar Health Path in Ashgabat. The Mary path reportedly stretches for a total of 28km.

BAYRAMALY

Some 30km east of Mary, on the road to Turkmenabat, the town of Bayramaly (telephone code 564) abuts the southern edge of the site of ancient Merv. The walls of the two youngest cities of the Merv site, the Timurid city of Abdullah Khan Kala and the later Bairam Ali Khan Kala, lie across the road from the town's main bazaar. It is from Bairam Ali Khan Kala that the modern town is named. Bairam Ali Khan was ruler of Merv in the latter part of the 18th century, killed in 1785 by Uzbek forces led by Shah Murad of Bukhara. His demise led to the decline of Merv during the following decades.

Most tourists see Bayramaly only through the windows of their Merv-bound transport, but the town is of interest in its own right. In 1887, some 90,000ha close to the ruins of ancient Merv were designated the Murgab Imperial Estate, and a royal lodge built here. A small town grew up near the new Bayramaly railway station to serve the estate. Bayramaly retains the best-preserved tsarist-era centre of any town in Turkmenistan. In the Soviet period, the former royal lodge served as the core of a sanatorium, based around the reported qualities of the

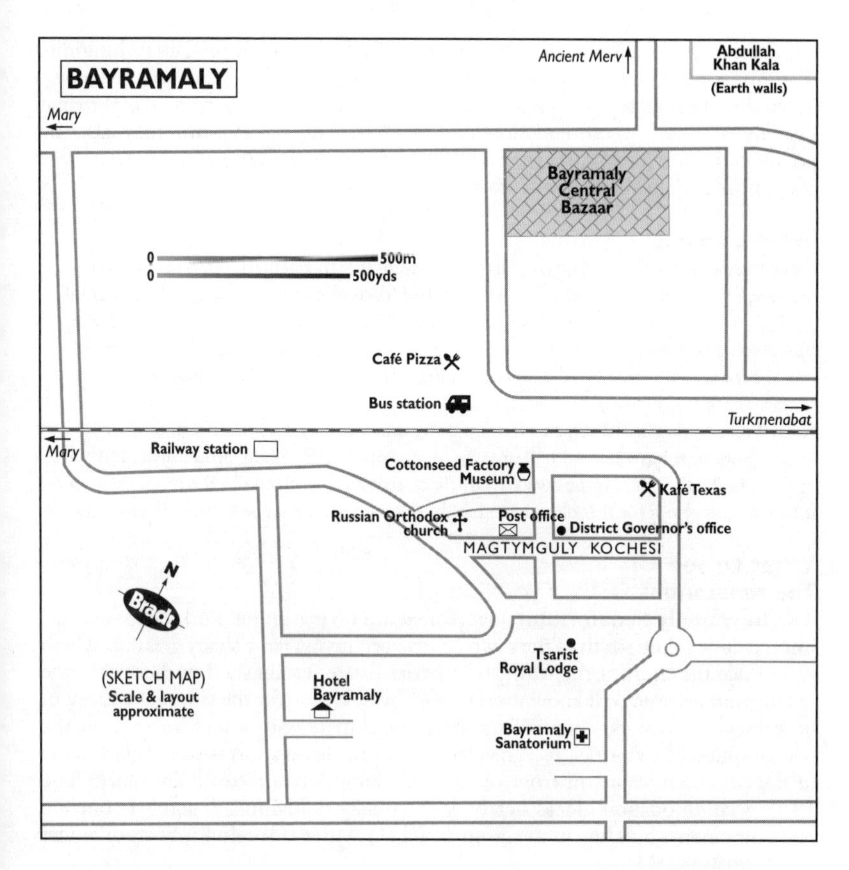

particularly dry and sunny climate here, within dry and sunny Turkmenistan, for the treatment of kidney problems. The roadside monument welcoming visitors to the town features a sun design, in tribute to the source of the town's 20th-century fame.

Getting there and away

The public bus station (☎ 564 26492) lies on the north side of the railway tracks which bisect the town, not far from the main bazaar. There are buses to Mary every 20 minutes or so during the day (1,500 manat), and similarly frequent buses to Yoloten (1,900 manat). Taxis depart from just outside the bus station, though private buses seem to leave from the bazaar, a couple of hundred metres to the north. Together they serve most destinations within Mary Region, as well as a few beyond it, though not to any timetable.

The town's sleepy railway station (☎ 564 22400) looks out southwards from the railway tracks, at the eastern edge of the old town centre. Two trains daily head westwards to Ashgabat. Two head east to Turkmenabat; one going on to Dashoguz, the other to Atamurat.

Where to stay

There is a hotel of sorts here, the **Hotel Bayramaly** (7 habitable rooms); ☎ 564 22795. Close to the Turkmenbashy Bank, off the road heading due south from the railway station, the hotel sits in a partly derelict three-storey building. The air conditioners don't work, the bathrooms are dire, and with Mary so accessible there is really no reason to stay here. The hotel charges 70,000 manat per night. Basic accommodation at the Bayramaly Sanatorium may also be possible, though the place is geared up more to patients undergoing full treatment programmes than short-stay visitors.

Where to eat

Café Pizza ☎ 564 51311. Opposite the bus station, this inexpensive place has a gloomy interior, enlivened by a wooden bar whose inlaid logo offers a witty take on the dollar bill: 'Café Pizza: In God We Trust'. It serves mostly standard Russian-oriented fare, including the ravioli-like *pelmeni* and stuffed cabbage-leaves (*golubtsy*). It does indeed serve pizza, the options for which were described by my waitress thus: 'with meat, without meat, with sausage, with mushrooms'.

Kafé Texas ☎ 564 26363. Open evenings only, this town centre place is a potentially livelier option. It has a billiard hall upstairs, disco ball on the ceiling, loud music, and stays open until 02.00. There must be a Bayramaly craftsman specialising in the production of inlaid wooden bars, for this place has a bar decorated with the logo: 'Camel: Real Leather'.

What to see

The sanatorium

The **Bayramaly Sanatorium**, now named after Saparmurat Turkmenbashy, sits immediately to the south of the town centre, occupying large shady grounds which were once the heart of the Murgab Imperial Estate. Established in the 1930s, the sanatorium became well known across the Soviet Union for the summer treatment of kidney complaints, coupling the hot, dry climate with a diet focused on the consumption of watermelons. The place has a run-down air. A besuited gold statue of the president stands in front of the forbidding-looking treatment block. The 1970s accommodation blocks nearby look equally uninviting. A derelict concrete open-air cinema building in the grounds echoes with the laughing ghosts of Soviet holidaymakers.

The real treasure of the sanatorium lies in the northern part of the complex. The **tsarist royal lodge**, now used as part of the sanatorium administration, is a graceful single-storey brick building. The arched main entrance on the east side of the building is flanked by two small octagonal towers, like mock minarets. An arched portico runs along the exterior of the building, the bases of the arches extending outwards as gentle buttresses. Decorated brickwork running along the tops of the walls is augmented by ornamental crenellations. Altogether a pleasing building, which, however, never accommodated a tsar.

Immediately to the north of the lodge, the original grandeur of the Murgab Imperial Estate is suggested by the conifer-fringed driveway running from the (usually locked) northern entrance of the sanatorium complex. This is an elegant former entrance, which now terminates in a large placard to President Niyazov's book *Ruhnama*. There is a nearby symbol from the intervening age too: a Soviet-era silver-painted statue of a healthy mother and beaming daughter.

Town centre

The tsarist-era single-storey buildings of the quiet, tree-lined centre of town fill the streets to the north. Several of the buildings echo the design of the royal lodge with their pavilion forms, geometrical brick-patterned friezes, crenellations and gentle buttresses. One building, almost opposite the north gate of the sanatorium, suggests a mosque with domed roof and brick minaret. It now houses the local tax office. A block to the northwest, the town's **Russian Orthodox Church** is square in layout and bulky in form. There are two main entrances, on the north and west walls, with arched wooden doors protected beneath porticoes held up by squat columns resembling halved barrels. Inside, the walls are supported by interlocking arches, decorated with medallions of saints and abstract floral designs. The floor, tiled with star motifs is, like the rest of the building, elegant, if battered. The round tower at the centre of the building is now topped with corrugated iron, rather than the original dome. Locals will tell you that an underground passage was built between the royal lodge and the church, to enable the tsar to attend services without having to come into contact with his subjects.

The mildly unpleasant smell which hangs in the air above Bayramaly is a product of the cottonseed oil factory, which sits right in the centre of town. The **Cottonseed Factory Museum**, next to the main gate of the factory, a block east of the church, is well worth a look, as a rare survival in Turkmenistan of a basically Soviet-era museum extolling the achievements of the town's main industrial enterprise. The cotton factory dates from 1903, though became specialised in the production of cottonseed oil from 1936. The museum dates from 1931. It has one large room devoted to the history of the factory. The walls of this room are covered with evocative paintings on white cotton cloth, the work of one Yuri Artamonov. They depict scenes connected with the life of the factory, mostly drawn from photographs: the factory's fire brigade in the 1930s, whose brass bell is also exhibited; a parade led by the local football team, *Pishevik* ('Food Industry Worker'), featuring red flags, banners, and a little barrage balloon marked 'USSR'.

The exhibits are simultaneously mundane and fascinating. There is the shirt of a man named Kulkov, who apparently laid the first brick of the new factory. A wage list from 1903, recording that the highest salary paid was 15 roubles a month. The desk used by an early factory director. A trophy cabinet, commemorating the factory's sporting achievements. The imagery of the banners and shields displayed here is heavy with cotton, grapes, carpet designs, hammers and sickles, wheat, Lenin's head, the sun, the world. There are also photographs of unsmiling children at the kindergarten and a yellowing press article about factory worker Ovezgul Berdieva, elected to the Supreme Soviet of Turkmenistan in 1961. In the centre of the room, the cottonseed oil-making equipment is exhibited. Its role seems essentially to be to heat and squeeze the seeds until the oil is released.

The last items displayed in the main room are the products of the factory: glass bottles of oil, and ugly, brick-like bars of soap. Two small rooms to the side attempt to bring the museum into the independence period; the first an uneventful display of Turkmen ethnographic items, the second a room devoted to President Niyazov and *Ruhnama*.

A candidate for the title of most cloying statue on the planet is to be found nearby, in front of the wedding hall on the central Magtymguly Kochesi. Two intertwined gold rings rest on a bed of red roses. A dove perches on each ring. The two Soviet statues in front of the sports hall next door are little better: well-scrubbed youths playing tennis and football.

The **central bazaar**, on the north side of town towards ancient Merv, is well-stocked. Food and drink are set out on long brick benches beneath roofs of corrugated asbestos. Around these, other stalls are set up under low canopies of billowing cotton supported on poles, giving the place a mystical air and dappled appearance beneath the Bayramaly sun. Carpets and handicraft items are sold from the northeast corner of the bazaar, close to a row of caged ducks and poultry. So a carpet-buying experience in Bayramaly is likely to be accompanied by quacking.

ANCIENT MERV

A significant capital for 2,500 years, Merv was one of the most important oasis cities of the Silk Road, and is among the major archaeological sites of Central Asia. It was declared a World Heritage Site in 1999. Merv first became a significant centre under the Achaemenian Empire, and across the millennia which followed was a regional capital for a succession of controlling dynasties. It was from Merv in the 8th century that Abu Muslim proclaimed the start of the Abbasid revolution. At the height of its importance as the eastern capital of the Seljuk Empire in the 11th and 12th centuries, it was a vital centre of learning. Here Omar Khayyam worked on his celebrated astronomical tables. Merv was sacked by the Mongols in 1221 in devastating fashion, and although archaeologists now question earlier figures of a million or more people massacred in this single event, it was undoubtedly one of great brutality. But the city of Merv was to rise again, albeit never reaching its earlier prominence. It remained in occupation during the Mongol period and later, under the 15th-century Timurid leader Shah Rukh, a new city was established here.

One of the most unusual features of Merv, and one of the reasons for its particular attraction for archaeologists, is its character as what British scholar Georgina Herrmann describes as a 'wandering city'. It is made up of five separate but near adjacent cities. In the geographically unconstrained flat plain of the oasis, and a historical context of continually shifting water-courses, new cities tended to be built alongside rather than on top of the old. The result is a series of easily discernible cities representing different historical periods, scattered across the arid plains to the north of Bayramaly.

Practicalities

The present site's status as the outcome of Merv's 'wanderings' means that it covers a large area. Ignoring the various outlying monuments and the Timurid city of Abdullah Khan Kala, the three oldest city sites alone spread across well over 1,000ha. Merv is not therefore a site which can be comfortably managed on foot, especially in summer. Travel agencies in Turkmenistan are experienced in putting together guided visits to the site. You could also arrange a local guide in Mary. Yevgenia Golubeva, an English-speaking guide who used to be Deputy Director of the Mary Regional Museum, and who has worked with the archaeologists of the International Merv Project, comes highly recommended by visitors (☎ 522 31485). The cheapest option would be simply to hire a taxi in Bayramaly to ferry you between the main monuments.

To get to the site, from the northern side of Bayramaly's central bazaar take the northbound road, away from the town. A concrete monument to 'Gadymy Merw' marks the road, which runs along the western walls of Abdullah Khan Kala. After 4km you will reach another concrete signpost, to the 'State Historical and Cultural Park Ancient Merv'. Turn right here, passing between a curious pair of kinked concrete obelisks, whose design supposedly suggests a Seljuk lamp.

Behind these obelisks are two pillbox-type buildings, which accommodate the small **Margush Archaeological Museum**. The building on the south side of the road is mostly devoted to the Bronze Age sites of the northern part of the oasis. You may also be able to buy a copy of the excellent guidebook to Ancient Merv produced by the International Merv Project. Its partner building over the road concentrates on the Merv site itself, including coverage of the work being done by the International Merv Project to combat the considerable threats to the site. A particular problem has been the rise in the water table which followed the construction of the Kara Kum Canal in the late 1950s. This 'rising damp' is

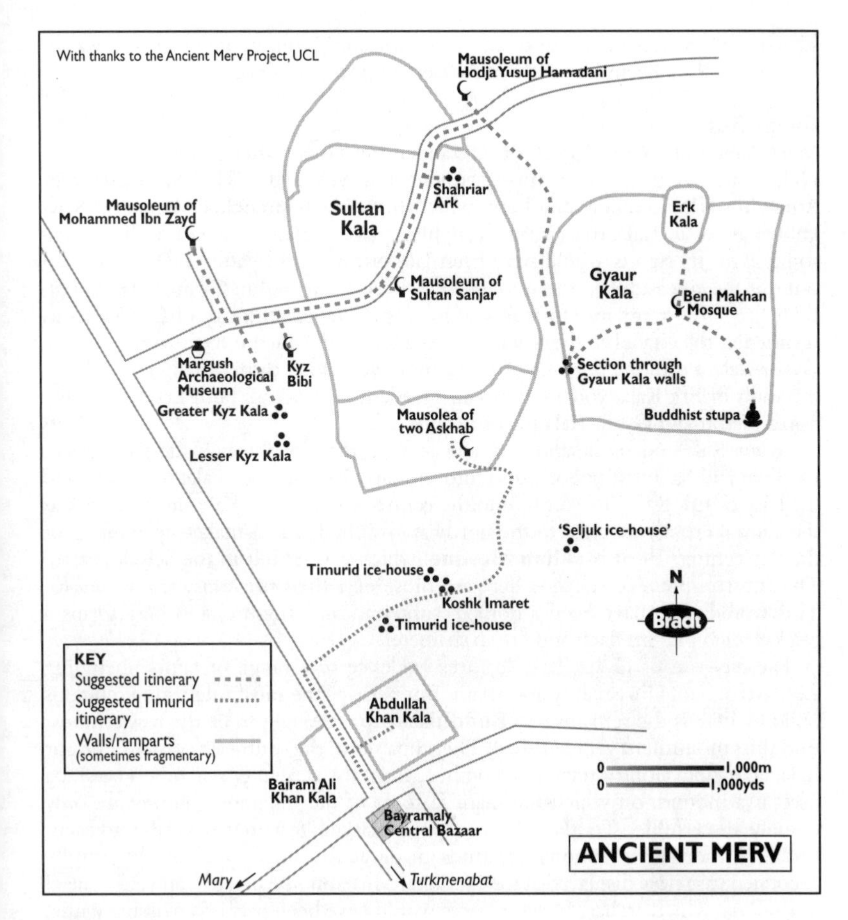

undermining many of the fragile mud-brick walls, at a rate all too clear from a comparison of present-day structures with photographs taken earlier this century. The small museum provides a worthwhile site orientation for visitors who have not seen the much more comprehensive coverage in the Mary Regional Museum.

Suggested itinerary

The following itinerary will take perhaps half a day, driving between each of the sites listed. A full day at Merv could be spent profitably by coupling more in-depth stops at the main sites with coverage of the Timurid monuments set out in the next section. (Bring a picnic and plenty of water, as there is nowhere to buy food or drink on site.) The proposed route starts at one of the furthest points from the main entrance, both to take advantage of the vantage point over the whole site offered by the first suggested port of call, and to structure the visit roughly as a historical chronology.

Erk Kala

Take the road running through the Merv site, past the Sultan Sanjar Mausoleum, the walls of Sultan Kala and Gyaur Kala, all of which you will see on the way back, to arrive at the base of the citadel of Erk Kala. With walls some 25m in height, the structure resembles the crater of an extinct volcano, 500m in diameter. Erk Kala is believed to have been the centre of Achaemenid rule over the oasis.

Gyaur Kala

Merv later fell to the forces of Alexander the Great, after whose early death Hellenistic control was retained, under the Seleucids. The Seleucid ruler Antiochus I built a new city here, which he termed Antiochia Margiana. Now known as Gyaur Kala, this city was roughly square in plan, with each wall running some 2km. Its streets would have been laid out in a grid pattern. The imposing walls of the city aside, no monuments remain standing within Gyaur Kala, though there are some remnant structures of interest. The existing city of Erk Kala was retained as the citadel of the Seleucid city, and is embedded into the north wall of Gyaur Kala. From the remains of a lookout tower which form the highest point of the walls of Erk Kala, you are given an excellent view across both Erk Kala to the north of you and Gyaur Kala to your south.

Gyaur Kala and its northern citadel formed the city through the subsequent Parthian and Sasanian periods, and into the early Islamic one. Take the road from the base of Erk Kala due south, into the centre of the Gyaur Kala site, and park at the central crossroads. Just to the northeast are the hard-to-make-out remains of the 7th-century **Beni Makhan Mosque**, which was rebuilt in the Seljuk period. The most impressive remains here are those of a fired-brick cistern, or *sardoba*. This would once have been a domed, subterranean structure, and now forms a brick-walled pit, 8m deep and 6m in diameter.

The city site of Gyaur Kala features evidence of a range of faiths, including Zoroastrianism, Christianity and Islam. But perhaps the most interesting religious building here is the remains of a **Buddhist stupa**, thought to be the westernmost Buddhist monument yet identified. The stupa sits in the southeast corner of Gyaur Kala, accessible along a track running here from the central crossroads. The stupa itself is a mound, on which the main features of the religious building are only vaguely discernible. To the south, a pock-marked terrain marks the adjacent Buddhist monastery. Among the finds made at the stupa were the beautifully decorated vase now displayed at the National Museum in Ashgabat, and a clay head of Buddha, which archaeologists believe would have been part of a massive statue, more than 3m high.

The archaeologists of the International Merv Project have excavated a cross-section through the southwestern walls of Gyaur Kala. This beautifully demonstrates how the city walls were built up through the centuries: relatively modest and narrow Seleucid walls, of around 280BC, form a core around which extensions were built upwards and outwards, reflecting the more sophisticated threats posed by advances in artillery. Several distinct further phases of wall construction can be identified, including the addition of bastions in the 4th century, which would have provided platforms for defensive artillery pieces, as well as strengthening the walls.

Mausoleum of Hodja Yusup Hamadani

Leaving Gyaur Kala by the central gate in the western wall, take the road to the north, running along the Razik Canal between the walls of Gyaur Kala and Sultan Kala. You will then reach a group of mostly new brick buildings, with a large car park in front. This is the mosque and mausoleum complex of Hodja Yusup Hamadani, one of the most important places of shrine pilgrimage in Turkmenistan. Hodja Yusup was a Sufi scholar of the 12th century, whose teachings formed an important element in the development of Sufism in Central

Asia. He studied theology in Baghdad, and later settled in Merv, where he enjoyed the patronage of Sultan Sanjar. He was buried in the city on his death in 1140.

The mosque here was one of the very few in Turkmenistan allowed to operate, albeit under tight control, during the Soviet period. The open-sided square mausoleum, towards the rear of the complex, is a modern reconstruction. A group of buildings along the west side of this, around a central *iwan*, were probably originally built in the Timurid period.

Sultan Kala

The road heads westwards, entering the third and most extensive of the walled cities of Merv, Sultan Kala. The Abbasid commander Abu Muslim promoted urban development around the Majan Canal, a kilometre to the west of the walls of Gyaur Kala, possibly because of growing difficulties over access to water in the existing city, as the ground level rose with each new phase of building. The old city of Gyaur Kala gradually declined in importance, and the archaeological evidence suggests that it became an industrial suburb of Sultan Kala. The new city reached its peak under the Seljuks. It was walled in the 11th century under Malik Shah. During the reign of Sultan Sanjar, when Merv was one of the most important cities of the world, further northern and southern suburbs were walled, giving the city a total area of some 600ha.

The city had declined by the time of the arrival of a large Mongol force in 1221, but its walls still posed a formidable obstacle for the invaders. The Mongols did not, however, need to attempt to breach them: the defenders of the city negotiated a surrender under which they would be spared, and opened the gates to the Mongol army. The latter promptly forgot about its deal, and massacred everyone. Not much is yet known about the nature of occupation of Merv in the Mongol period, though there is evidence that the city remained in use and even minted its own coins.

To the east side of the road, after passing into Sultan Kala, is a walled citadel known as the **Shahriar Ark**, built in the 12th century to enclose a palace and administrative complex, and the residences of the urban elite. The ruins of the palace are close to the centre of this site: the building was based around a central courtyard, surrounded on each side by *iwans*. The best preserved building in the Shahriar Ark, however, stands to the northeast of the palace. It is a rectangular building some 20m long, and surviving to around 8m in height. Its external walls have a distinctive design of vertical corrugations. The interior is distinctive too, with many square niches. The building is known as a **kepter khana**, or 'pigeon house', based on one theory as to the use to which the niches were put, but there is no academic consensus as to the purpose of this unusual building.

Mausoleum of Sultan Sanjar

The road continues southwestwards to the centre of the Sultan Kala site, where stands the single most impressive building at Merv, the Mausoleum of Sultan Sanjar. Recently restored with finance from the Turkish government, the mausoleum has a square base, with walls 27m in length, and is topped with a double dome, rising to a height of 36m. The original covering of turquoise tiles, visible to the Silk Road traveller when still a day's caravan ride from the city, is, alas, no more. Around the exterior, the base of the dome is surrounded by attractive vaulted arcades. These present five arches along each side of the building, containing latticed balconies with designs based around eight-pointed stars.

The interior of the building is decorated with white stucco, across which red and blue geometrical designs run along the borders of the walls. Most of this is

THE WINDOW IN THE DOME

If you stand inside the Mausoleum of Sultan Sanjar, and look up at the dome, you will see a small, square aperture on its south side. There is a local legend about the origins of this little window.

Sultan Sanjar, they say, fell in love with a beautiful woman. She agreed to be his, but on three conditions. He should never look at her feet, never gaze at her while she was combing her hair, and never embrace her. Of course, Sultan Sanjar's love for this lady caused him to fail to observe any of these. He looked at her feet, to find that they did not actually touch the ground when she walked. He spied on her while she combed her hair, discovering that to do so she removed her head, and combed it while it stood on her dressing table. And he tried to give her a hug, only to find that she consisted entirely of air. She was, in short, a fairy.

Her conditions broken, she turned herself into a beautiful bird, and perched on Sanjar's shoulder. After much pleading, she agreed not to abandon him altogether: she would return from time to time, but only if he constructed a beautiful building, with a little square hole in the dome through which she could fly in and out. Sultan Sanjar agreed, and the mausoleum was duly built. She visited him here from time to time. On his deathbed, Sultan Sanjar asked for her to visit one final time. She did so, this time carrying in her beak the box of treasures he had given to her as a gift when she had been human in form. The fairy bird dropped the box, which became lodged in the dome, where they say it rests still. One tale runs that Russians arriving here at the end of the 19th century heard this tale and took it rather too literally, damaging part of the dome in their search for the treasure.

Locals tell that, on Friday evenings, the fairy bird can still be seen flying around the mausoleum, just beneath the dome.

newly reconstructed: the designs are extrapolations from small fragments of original stucco. There are tall niches in the centre of each wall. The transition between the square plan of the mausoleum and the domed roof is achieved by four large squinches, supporting the roof, between which sit niches. Each of these contain small latticed windows. The name of the architect, Mohammed Ibn Aziz of Serakhs, is found high up on the east wall of the mausoleum. One local legend runs that the man was killed by Sultan Sanjar, to prevent him from designing another building to rival the beauty of this one. The cenotaph on the floor of the mausoleum was a 19th-century addition, and is not the tomb of Sultan Sanjar.

The construction of the mausoleum pre-dated Sultan Sanjar's death in 1157. The building would have originally stood, not in its current isolation, but as part of a complex of religious buildings, including the city's main mosque. The reconstructed bases of the walls of some of these structures surround the mausoleum.

Kyz Bibi

From the Sultan Sanjar Mausoleum, drive due west, leaving Sultan Kala through the western Firuz Gate. South of the road, the small reconstructed square mausoleum, open on all sides, is known as Kyz Bibi. Some scholars have suggested that this may be the burial place of Sultan Sanjar's wife, Turkan-khatun. Who was not a fairy bird, then.

The Kyz Kalas

The next turning to the south takes you to two fascinating monuments. The Greater and Lesser Kyz Kalas are two isolated buildings known as *koshks*, which have distinctive corrugated exterior walls. The Greater Kyz Kala is rectangular in plan, with a length of 45m and width of 38m. Its corrugations are well preserved on the eastern and southern sides of the building, protected against the prevailing wind. The interior of the building preserves squinches and traces of different kinds of vaulting. The Lesser Kyz Kala stands a couple of hundred metres due south: it is roughly square in plan, with sides 20m long, and is more poorly preserved than its neighbour, though does retain the remnants of a stairway in its southeast corner.

'Kyz Kala' means 'Girls' Castle': one story runs that forty girls hid in the Greater Kyz Kala at the time of the Mongol invasion. When they saw what the Mongols had done to the inhabitants of the city of Merv they committed suicide by jumping from the roof. Another local tale identifies the Greater Kyz Kala as the castle for the girls; its smaller neighbour as the boys' castle. It is said that young men wishing to marry the girl of their dreams should fire a projectile from the southern castle, to land in the northern one. Given the distance between the two, there are presumably many local bachelors.

The buildings were elite rural residences, and probably date from the 8th or 9th centuries. There remains much debate about the purpose of their distinctive corrugations: theories include helping to keep the interiors cool, ensuring the rapid run-off of potentially destructive rainwater, and simple decoration.

Mausoleum of Mohammed Ibn Zayd

Retrace your route as far as the road heading westwards from the Firuz Gate. Turn left onto it to reach again the main entrance to the Merv site. But before you leave Merv, turn right in front of the concrete obelisks. You will pass on your right the administrative buildings of the Merv Archaeological Park, before reaching, at the end of this side road, the Mausoleum of Mohammed Ibn Zayd. This is one of the most atmospheric shrine complexes in Turkmenistan. Ibn Zayd was a Shia leader, killed in 740 while leading an uprising against the Umayyads in the city of Kufa in present-day Iraq. The mausoleum at Merv is probably simply a symbolic construction, built by his followers.

The mausoleum at the core of the complex dates from the Seljuk period. It has a square, domed chamber, the dome supported by four squinches, separated by niches. An inscription running around the top of the walls records the date of construction of the mausoleum as 1112. The cenotaph in the centre of the chamber is carved with inscriptions. Unusually, the chamber contains a *mihrab*, a niche in the west wall with a scalloped design. Around the Seljuk mausoleum, two more recent rooms have been added. To the east of the mausoleum, and providing access to it, is a square-domed anteroom. Access to this in turn is through a mosque, which runs along the whole north side of the complex. One of the walls of the mosque comprises what was originally the external north wall of the mausoleum, revealing fine decorated Seljuk brickwork. The complex was much restored in the early part of the 20th century.

Around the mausoleum are several large saxaul trees, considered sacred, from which hang hundreds of strips of material, representing prayers.

The Timurid Monuments

Abdullah Khan Kala

In the southern part of the Merv site, a group of monuments linked to the Timurid rule in the 15th century make for an interesting supplementary itinerary for visitors with the time available for a more in-depth programme. Begin at the city site of Abdullah Khan Kala, immediately across the road from the central market of Bayramaly. This is roughly square in plan, its city walls of crumbling mud brick the most prominent surviving feature. The moat surrounding the walled city can also still be easily discerned. Abdullah Khan Kala, which lies some 3km to the south of Sultan Kala, was built in 1409 by Shah Rukh, who had taken control of the empire of his late father Timur, known as Tamerlane in the West. Covering 46ha, Abdullah Khan Kala was by many standards a sizeable town, but not by those of the great cities which preceded it at Merv. Bar a few short stretches of wall, little remains of **Bairam Ali Khan Kala**, the 18th-century western extension to the Timurid city.

The ice-houses and Koshk Imaret

Take the road north from Bayramaly, as if heading to the Merv Archaeological Park, but turn off it along a rough road to the east, beyond the walls of Abdullah Khan Kala. You will come to a building believed to be a Timurid ice-house, in waste-ground some 500m to the north of Abdullah Khan Kala. Around 13m in diameter, this is a now roofless building of rounded conical form, its interior walls pierced with many beam-slots. Continuing eastwards, you will reach, north of the track, a better preserved ice-house of similar diameter, its form recalling an overturned bowl. The interior of this structure is enlivened with bands of diagonally set bricks. Most archaeologists believe that the buildings were indeed used for the storage of ice, though some sources argue that they may have been water cisterns.

Some 100m to the southeast of this second ice-house is a building known as the Koshk Imaret. This is a Timurid pavilion, which would once have lain in the heart of gardens. It is rectangular in plan, with its main, arched, entrance on the west side of the building, flanked by arched niches. Traces of plaster found on the inside of the building preserve the pink colour in which the pavilion was originally decked out. Nice.

The road continues eastwards, past a brick factory and a Christian cemetery. Another ice-house comes into sight, due south of Gyaur Kala. This is rather different in form to the others, with a taller, steeper design. Fragments of wooden beams survive in many of the slots around the internal walls. Some researchers believe that the building may date from the Seljuk rather than the Timurid period. The presence in this structure of ventilation shafts have led some to question whether it is an ice-house at all.

Mausolea of two Askhab

The most impressive of the Timurid monuments are part of an important place of religious pilgrimage at the southern edge of Sultan Kala. To get here, take the northward-bound road to the west of the final ice-house, turn left before you reach the line of city walls, and follow the road through a large area of cemetery. You can also reach this place by a track running from close by the Greater Kyz Kala. You are making for a reconstructed complex centred around the mausolea of two *Askhab*, or companions of the Prophet. The two black marble cenotaphs mark the tombs of Al Hakim Ibn Amr Al Jafari and Buraida Ibn Al Huseib Al Islami. They lie in modern brick-built mausolea, with low domes. Behind the two mausolea are a pair of heavily reconstructed Timurid *iwans*, built to honour the tombs of the *Askhab*. The mausolea are beautifully framed by the arched *iwans* behind them. The internal walls of the latter are pleasantly decorated with blue and turquoise tiles, in geometric designs.

In front of the *Askhab* complex is a water cistern, probably built at around the same time as the *iwans*, but still in use. Above ground, only a shallow dome and a large arched doorway on the western side are visible. Uneven stone steps lead down to the water. The doorway, decorated with floral-patterned stucco, dates from the 19th century.

THE BRONZE AGE SITES IN THE NORTH OF THE OASIS

The Merv Oasis was an important centre for human settlement long before Achaemenian times. A remarkable Bronze Age civilisation existed here, known variously as Margush, meaning 'lowland', or by the Greek name of Margiana. It has been gradually uncovered since the early 1970s by Professor Viktor Sarianidi, who heads the Margiana Archaeological Expedition. The Bronze Age sites are to be found at or beyond the northern edge of the present-day oasis, in land which is now desert. Climatic change and progressive desertification caused the abandonment of the area, with the result that the ruins of the Bronze Age settlements are well preserved beneath the desert soils. The Margiana sites seem to have had close ties with those at Bactria, in present-day northern Afghanistan. Sarianidi argues that the Bactria-Margiana complex was a major centre of ancient civilisation, and has speculated that Margiana may even have been a birthplace of Zoroastrianism.

Gonur

Practicalities

The Bronze Age Margiana sites are all remote, and you will need a guide to get you here. Yevgenia Golubeva in Mary, or one of the main travel agencies in Ashgabat, can organise a trip to the most worthwhile site for tourist visits, Gonur, which Sarianidi believes to have been the principal settlement. To get here, you need to make for a peasants' association named Turkmenistan, which lies on the northern edge of the oasis, about 50km from Merv. On reaching the village, turn onto a rough track to your right, and then sharp left, so that you skirt around the eastern side of the village. Gonur is some 30km from here, by a track which quickly turns to sand. A 4x4 vehicle is required. The trip from Mary or Bayramaly will take around two hours, each way.

What to see

The Gonur site is fascinating. The single largest excavation is of what Sarianidi describes as a **palace complex**, covering some 10ha and built at the end of the 3rd millennium BC. A vast network of walls have been excavated, like an earthen maze. Sarianidi believes that the palace itself was at the centre of the site, surrounded by administrative buildings, and accessed by a deliberately narrow entrance only 80cm wide. The largest hall in the palace complex, whose mud walls have been recently reconstructed as part of a conservation effort, is known as the throne hall. A stone sceptre was found in one of the two niches here.

Around the palace have been identified a number of structures of apparently Zoroastrian religious use. Thus on the east side of the complex Sarianidi has identified a fire temple; on the west side a 'temple of sacrifice'. South of the complex, a basin some 100m long and 70m wide is suggested as a possible temple of water. Close to this, excavations in 2004 revealed a room roughly 10m square, containing such treasures as a bronze chariot, which Sarianidi thinks might have been a royal tomb. On the north side of the palace complex, a large open area near which a number of ovens have been excavated is described as the square of communal eating. During the later period of occupation of the site, there seems to have been a growing impoverishment faced by the occupants of Gonur. Areas at the heart of the complex were given over to industrial use, including a large double kiln. Green clay has fossilised onto the stone here like globs of glue.

To the southwest of the palace complex, on slightly higher ground, lies the site of what is described as a **temple complex**. Evidence such as the round corner towers suggests that this complex is of a later date than the palace site. Seeds embedded in the plaster covering numerous vessels found here included those of hemp, poppy and ephedra, and appear to have been used in the production of a narcotic drink known as *haoma*, used by the priests. This site was excavated earlier than the palace complex, and is not now as impressive.

A third excavated part of the Gonur site is a large **necropolis**, to the west of the palace site around the present-day irrigation canal. It seems to have been in use from the end of the 3rd millennium to the middle of the 2nd millennium BC. Almost 3,000 burials have been excavated here. Several different types of tombs were identified, from simple pit tombs for the poorest citizens to more elaborate burials for the rich, in which the body was placed in one chamber, the possessions of the deceased next door. Most disquieting were a number of burial pits with round chambers and burnt walls, like ovens. Some of the bones in these showed evidence of diseases, such as osteoporosis. In one of these pits the female occupant was buried upside down.

WEST OF MARY

Hanhowuz

There is one worthwhile stop on the main road west from Mary, towards Tejen. Hanhowuz is the site of one of the main reservoirs of the Kara Kum Canal system, located at the eastern edge of the Tejen Oasis. The reservoir's function is in part to compensate for the erratic flows of the Tejen River, which feeds the oasis from the south. The reservoir itself lies to the south of the road, beyond the village of Hanhowuz; an attractive and expansive circular lake, to which access is, however, restricted.

The presence of the reservoir has helped to foster a thriving small-scale local

THE SONS OF OGUZ HAN

The agricultural district in the west of Mary Region in which the Hanhowuz Reservoir lies takes its post-independence name from Oguz Han, the legendary founder of the Turkmen people. Oguz Han is a major figure in the nation-building texts of President Niyazov, who links Oguz Han with the first Golden Age of the Turkmen. In his book *Ruhnama*, Niyazov identifies six sons of Oguz Han, each of whom had four sons of his own, thus establishing 24 Oguz clans from which he claims that the Turkmen tribes originate.

Niyazov offers a parable. Oguz Han took an arrow from one of his sons, and broke it easily. He took two arrows, and broke them together. Then three. He then took an arrow from each of his six sons, placed them together, and tried to break them. He failed. He then took an arrow from each grandson, and tied the 24 arrows together, to demonstrate what a strong object was created. This demonstrated the importance of unity among the Turkmens.

The peasants' associations of Oguz Han District take their names from the sons of the founder of the Turkmen people. The signs along the main road pointing towards each of these peasants' associations are bows and arrows, each bow drawing not one arrow, but seven.

fishing industry. Along the side of the main road, boys make expansive gestures with their arms to indicate the size of their fish. A 15kg catfish is a typical offering. Stop your car here, and they will pull out the fish from the small canal running along the road. A long line of roadside cafés has sprung up, mostly specialising in fried fish, served with a bowl of spicy tomato sauce, bread and salad. A typical example is the **Café Seljuk**, a two-storey brick building whose name, to judge from the signs adorning the front, should actually be either Café Nescafé or Café TIR-Parking. The promised TIR parking is a flat expanse of ground around the back. This and several of the other cafés offer a few rooms of basic accommodation, mainly targeted at long-distance lorry drivers, but there is little reason to stop overnight here, so close to the wider range of accommodation available in Mary. As a lunch stop this place is, however, recommended.

THE ROAD SOUTH TO AFGHANISTAN

The southern oasis

Heading southeast from Mary on the Serhetabat road, you pass after 9km an elaborate Soviet-era concrete road-sign, featuring a lightning bolt and what appears to be a large conch shell. This marks the road, off to the right, to the Mary power station, the largest in Turkmenistan. The small township built to serve the power station and adjacent factories was named Energetik in Soviet times; it now carries the name **Saparmurat Turkmenbashy**.

Around Taze Durmush

Keeping on the main road south, you will see after a further 30km a turning to the east, marked with a sign to a peasants' association named Taze Durmush ('New Life'). On the northern side of this junction stands, quietly rotting, an interesting example of 19th-century Turkmen architecture. This is the **Hodjageldy Akhun Madrasa**, also known as Kyrk Gummez ('40 Domes') since each of the mud-brick student cells around the central courtyard is topped with a dome. Just to the north are the crumbling remains of a mosque and minaret. An elderly couple still occupies a small part of the *madrasa*. The man, Abdy Halim, told me that he was the grandson of the founder of the place, and took me to see Hodjageldy Akhun's grave.

The village of Taze Durmush, 8km from the main road, is itself worth a visit as one of the centres of Turkmenistan's Baluchi minority. Turkmenistan's Baluchis, most of whom migrated here from countries further south in the early part of the 20th century, number perhaps 30,000 or so, heavily concentrated in agricultural settlements in this part of Mary Region. Their dress is distinctive, especially that of Baluchi women, who wear long red or white headscarves which trail down almost to the ground.

Mosque of Talhatan Baba

Back on the main road, 9km south of the turning to Taze Durmush, you will pass a couple of small signs along the roadside pointing out the graveyard of Talhatan Baba. Take the next, unmarked, turning to the left beyond these, crossing the railway line. The Mosque of Talhatan Baba soon comes into sight on the left side of the road, reachable via the next left turn. Built in 1095, the mosque features some attractive Seljuk decorated brickwork. Approximately 18m long and 12m wide, the mosque has a single brick dome, and opens on its eastern side. Its large central arched entrance and two lateral arches accommodate wooden panelling around doors and windows. Twin tombs, covered by white tiles, lie in the courtyard in front of the main entrance. The brickwork decorating the four blind niches on the western exterior wall of the building is particularly fine. Talhatan Baba was one of the few places of pilgrimage in Turkmenistan which was tolerated during Soviet times. The site has expanded since independence: a new guesthouse, decorated with photographs of the Turkmen president, was opened on Niyazov's birthday in 2004.

Another 13km to the southeast, the main road bypasses the agricultural town of **Yoloten**, known for its now rather forlorn cotton research centre. South of here the flat, fertile land of the Merv Oasis gradually gives way to more undulating, less productive terrain.

Mausoleum of Imam Baba

The long drive south is punctuated by a few sights of passing interest, such as the Mausoleum of Imam Baba, 78km south of Yoloten. Marked by a bright green dome, easily visible from the road, the mausoleum, rebuilt in 1990, contains two graves. The caretaker admitted to me that he knew nothing about their occupants. He produced five pages of carefully handwritten script, recording everything that had been found out about the history of the place during the discussions on its rebuilding. This did not amount to much, though the Russian orientalist Zhukovsky, who carried out a survey of Merv in 1890, reportedly mentioned the site. The caretaker keeps 700 plates in a padlocked lean-to, ready for the large groups of pilgrims who occasionally descend on the place to hold sacrificial meals. Four kilometres further south, the village of **Sandykachi** is known for its winery: bottles of the remarkably sweet product are available from shops here.

Tagtabazar

Some 214km to the south of Mary a border post signals the restricted zone: you cannot travel beyond here without a permit covering Tagtabazar or Serhetabat districts, as required. A road to the east, immediately south of here, heads to the district capital of Tagtabazar, 28km away. Tagtabazar (telephone code 340) is the principal settlement of a small oasis of the Murgab River, close to the Afghan border.

Known in the 19th century as Panjdeh, or Pendi, this sleepy oasis was the unlikely setting for a conflict in 1885 that appeared at one stage to be pitching Britain and Russia towards war. The British government was highly nervous of Russian designs on India, following the Russian capture of Merv the previous year. Russia claimed that Panjdeh was now part of their territory, by virtue of their conquest of Merv. Afghanistan, supported by the British, insisted that it was theirs, and set about strengthening its defences. The issue was settled by the advance of Russian troops under General Komarov, who took Panjdeh on 31 March 1885, leaving more than 800 Afghans dead. This action provoked a period of high tension, with much talk of war, but the extent of Russia's frontiers was eventually settled by the work of the Joint Afghan Boundary Commission. Under the agreed settlement, Russia kept Panjdeh.

The administrative heart of the present-day town is a large roundabout, within which sits a war memorial, shaded by evergreen trees. The district mayor's office and police station abut each other on one side of the roundabout. Behind the latter, on Begnazarova Kochesi, is the **Hotel Pendi** (12 rooms); ☎ 340 21424. It is very basic, has shared facilities, and charges foreigners US$5 a night.

Ekedeshik

The main reason to visit Tagtabazar is the Ekedeshik cave settlement in the sandstone hills north of the town. Head west through town along Magtymguly Kochesi. At the western edge of town, head north towards the line of the hills. Two kilometres on, take the track to the right. The track snakes up the hill for another

1.5km to the entrance to the cave settlement. 'Ekedeshik' means 'single entrance', and the ingress in question is sealed with a metal door. It is open daily from 09.00–17.00. Admission costs US$2, though there are further charges of US$1 for a guide, US$3 for taking photographs, and US$5 for using a video camera.

The place is fascinating, with more than 40 visitable rooms, on two levels. Close to the entrance, the custodian will lift a metal plate from the floor to reveal a steep staircase descending to further, lower, levels, which are in too unsafe a state to be visited. From the entrance, a central barrel-vaulted passage, sloping gently upwards, heads into the hill for some 37m. Off this lead entrances to small rooms on either side. Many of these have circular 'wells' in little adjoining chambers. Cuttings in the walls would have once accommodated candles. One room off the main corridor seems to have had a particularly distinguished occupant or prestigious role, for its entrance is topped by a carved lintel, and its vaulted ceiling bears rectangular carved panels. Reeds have thoughtfully been laid along the floor of the central corridor, to keep down the dust. And the whole place smells of wee.

Among the first people to map the caves was one Captain F de Laessoe, who included a sketch in an article carried in the *Proceedings of the Royal Geographical Society* for 1885. De Laessoe's investigations into the caves and ruins at Panjdeh were, however, brought to an early and sudden end by the Russian advance. There is an ongoing debate about the identity of the builders of the caves. Some scholars believe that they were constructed by early Christian communities. Others suggest that the complex might have been a Buddhist monastery. And of course there are many local legends about the place, including rumours of a subterranean passageway heading into Afghanistan.

There are several smaller cave complexes nearby, including one known as Bashdeshik ('Five Entrances'), but these places, many of which have not been systematically explored, are of more specialist interest.

Serhetabat

Known in Soviet times as Kushka, this town on the Afghan border had the distinction of being the southernmost settlement of the Soviet Union. It sits 90km south of the Tagtabazar turning, a linear settlement of mostly Soviet apartment blocks. The origins of the place as a tsarist garrison town explain the small Orthodox church and the handful of pre-Soviet buildings. Two interesting monuments stand on military property in the hills to the east of the town, overlooking it. A large white-painted cross, with a black border, was erected in tsarist times to mark the southernmost point of the Russian Empire. Similar crosses were placed at the points furthest north, south and west. There is a Soviet monument nearby, to the idealised young war hero Alyosha, which has been given a half-hearted Turkmenising makeover. The Russian inscription has been painted over, with a Turkmen commentary added about the importance of tribal unity.

The Afghan border lies some 5km south of town. The customs post on the Turkmen side is open roughly from 08.00 to dusk. Although the tsarist-era railway does cross a couple of kilometres into Afghan territory, cross-border rail traffic is freight only, and rail passengers can go no further south than Serhetabat.

Badkyz Nature Reserve

Covering almost 90,000ha of remote terrain to the northwest of Serhetabat, at the eastern edge of the Kopet Dag Mountains, Badkyz is one of the most attractive natural environments in Turkmenistan. Most of the reserve comprises an undulating plateau, covered in its western part with the largest area of pistachio trees in Central Asia. The pistachios have short trunks, from which a crown of branches radiate out. Some of the pistachios in the reserve are 700 years old, but there are recently planted groves too, easily distinguished by the regular lines of trees. In spring, the abundance of flowers, including poppies and red and yellow tulips, makes this upland a beautiful sight.

At the southern edge of this plateau, a great sandstone escarpment looks out across the saline depression of **Eroulanduz**. The name means 'The Land Eaten by Salt'. It is a rift valley some 25km long and around 10km wide. Its flat floor is occupied by a series of salt flats, which turn to saline lakes in winter. These are abutted by scattered small cone-shaped hills, the remnants of ancient volcanoes. The salt lakes provide a temporary home for such species as pelicans and cranes. From the top of the escarpment, the valley floor of Eroulanduz makes a stunning view. At the eastern end of Eroulanduz, a V-shaped gorge topped with sheer cliffs runs for 18km into the upland. Up to 400m in height, and not more than a kilometre across, this pink-walled canyon, known as **Gyzyljar**, offers another dramatic panorama. The entrances to ancient cave settlements can be identified high up in the sheer walls of the canyon. One small two-roomed cave is more accessible and, with a guide, can be clambered down to carefully without specialist equipment.

The nature reserve was established here in 1941, primarily to provide a protected area for the local herds of the Central Asian wild ass, or *kulan*. This has proved broadly successful, and a large increase in the population of *kulan* here has allowed the use of Badkyz stocks to populate other reserves across Turkmenistan. The reserve also hosts large populations of goitred gazelle (*jieran*) and of the Transcaspian urial, a curly-horned wild sheep.

Admission to Badkyz requires special permits both as a frontier zone and a nature reserve. A US$15 fee is charged for entry to the reserve. Various other fees may also be levied, including a potentially swingeing photography charge of US$2 per shot. The reserve has three very basic guesthouses, at the ranger posts of Agarcheshme, Pynhancheshme and Gyzyljar, for which the overnight accommodation charge is around US$5. The main routes into the reserve are either south from Serakhs, or west, from the main road running between Mary and Serhetabat. The post of Agarcheshme sits amid pistachio groves, around 90km south of Serakhs. The road is tarmac for the first 40km, but a track thereafter. Gyzyljar, closer to the eastern side of the reserve, is reached by turning westwards onto a track off the Serhetabat road, 50km south of the turning to Tagtabazar. Gyzyljar is 78km from this turning. The headquarters of the nature reserve (☎ 561 21224) lie well outside its boundaries, in Serhetabat.

Mary Region carpet gul

Appendix 1

LANGUAGE

The good news is that the Turkmen language does not require you to memorise genders for every noun, and nor are there any irregular verbs. The bad news includes a complex system of suffixes, and a word order which can be confusing for native English speakers, with the verb coming at the end. But then a language in which the word *beter* means 'worse' is never likely to be straightforward.

A word on script. This appendix uses the characters of the new Turkmen alphabet. Elsewhere in the guide, Turkmen and Russian words are rendered by their approximate Roman alphabet equivalents. The latter has been done more with the aim of readability than through any kind of scientific rigour, and there are many ongoing debates among Turkmen academics. For example, I once witnessed a heated discussion among Turkmen government advisers as to whether *Türkmenbaşy* was properly written in English as *Turkmenbashy* or *Turkmenbashi*. I have plumped for the former, but more out of the need to make a choice than any reasoned argument.

Alphabet

The new alphabet (*täze elipbiý*) now in use in Turkmenistan (see page 17) has nine vowels and 21 consonants. Most of the letters look and sound broadly like their English equivalents. The main exceptions are:

Ç	pronounced 'ch'
Ä	pronounced like the 'a' in 'apple'
Ž	pronounced 'zh'
Ň	pronounced like the 'ng' in 'talking'
Ö	pronounced like the 'ea' in 'early'
Ş	pronounced 'sh'
Ü	pronounced like a rather strained 'u'
W	pronounced 'w' in respect of native Turkmen words, but 'v' in Russian imports
Y	pronounced like the 'i' in 'pit'
Ý	pronounced like the 'y' in 'you'

The Cyrillic script formerly in use in Turkmenistan includes an additional five letters, which are rendered by combinations of two letters in the new script.

Grammar

One of the important features of the Turkmen language is the division of the vowels into two groups. The front vowels, ä, e, i, ö and ü, are more nasal in character; the back vowels, a, y, o and u, are more guttural. Turkmen words, except in the case of loan words of Russian origin, never mix front and back vowels. This 'vowel harmony' is carried through to any suffixes added to the words. Thus, to create a plural, '-ler' is added to a front-vowel word; '-lar' is added to a back-vowel one.

Vowels may also be pronounced in either a short or long form. This can change the meaning. Thus, for example, '*at*' with the 'a' pronounced short means 'horse'; pronounced long and the meaning changes to 'name' or 'title'.

The Turkmen language uses a system of grammatical cases, indicated by suffixes, rather than the extensive usage of prepositions such as 'from', 'with' and 'in', as in English. The basic case endings for nouns are as follows:

Case	***Endings***
Nominative (subject of the phrase)	–
Accusative (direct object)	-y, -i, -ny, -ni
Possessive (possessive relationship)	-yň, -iň, -nyň, -niň
Dative (directed action)	-a, -e, ä, -na, -ne
Time/Place (locality)	-da, -de, -nda, -nde
Instrumental	-dan, -den, -ndan, -nden

Among the many other suffixes used in Turkmen, questions may be formed by adding -my/-mi. The suffix -lik/-lyk/-luk/-lük is used to create abstract nouns. Thus *dost* means 'friend'; *dostluk* is 'friendship'. Verbs end with the infinitive -mak or -mek.

Personal pronouns in the nominative and possessive cases take the following forms:

Nominative		***Possessive***	
Men	I	*Meniň*	my
Sen	you (sing)	*Seniň*	your
Ol	he, she, it	*Onuň*	his, her, its
Biz	we	*Biziň*	our
Siz	you (pl)	*Siziň*	your
Olar	they	*Olaryň*	their

Useful words and phrases

hello	*salam*	tomorrow; morning	*ertir*
thank you; goodbye	*sag bol*	hotel	*myhmanhana*
very many thanks	*köp-köp sag boluň*	cafeteria	*naharhana*
alright; OK	*bolýar*	restaurant	*restoran*
yes	*hawa*	toilet	*hajathana*
no	*ýok*	hospital	*keselhana*
this; that	*bu; şu*	shop	*dukan*
how much?	*näçe?*	bank	*bank*
how much does it cost?	*näçe durýar?*	open	*açyk*
		closed	*ýapyk*
yesterday	*düýn*	carpet	*haly*
today	*bu gün*	welcome!	*hoş geldiňiz!*

And if you need a Turkmen-language toast:

to world peace! *bütin dünýäde parahatçylyk üçin!*

Food and drink

bread	*çörek*	wine	*çakyr*
milk	*süýt*	butter	*ýag*
meat	*et*	cheese	*peýnir*
fish	*balyk*		

Numbers

one	*bir*	four	*dört*
two	*iki*	five	*bäş*
three	*üç*		

Slogans

Among the Turkmen words you will see most frequently are those forming the regime slogans decorating billboards, shopfronts and even hillsides across Turkmenistan. A few words recur frequently in these slogans; with the list below you should be able to understand the gist of most of them.

altyn	gold	*halk*	people; nation; the people
asyr	century; era; age		
baky	eternal; permanent	*mukaddes*	sacred; holy
		şamçyrag	lamp
beýik	great	*serdar*	leader
bitarap	neutral	*şöhrat*	glory
bitaraplyk	neutrality	*watan*	homeland; fatherland
garaşsyz	independent		
garaşsyzlyk	independence	*ýyl*	year

Thus:

Halk Watan Beýik Türkmenbaşy!
Beýik Saparmyrat Türkmenbaşa Şöhrat!
Baky Bitarap Türkmenistan
Ruhnama Şamçyrag
XXI Asyr Türkmen Halkynyň Altyn Asyry!

Appendix 2

GLOSSARY

Turkmen, Russian language and technical terms used in the text

Aksakal	Turkmen elder. Literally 'white beard'.
Alabai	A Central Asian sheepdog.
Bagshy	A folk singer.
Balsam	A herbal liqueur.
Basmachi	Local Central Asian resistance against Soviet power, active in the early years of the Soviet Union.
Caravansaray	A fortified building providing accommodation for travellers.
Chorba	A soup, usually featuring mutton and potato.
Chuwal	A carpet bag, traditionally used to store clothes.
Dacha	Cottage used as weekend or holiday accommodation.
Dayhan birleshik	A peasants' association, successor to the Soviet-era collective farm.
Depe	A small, isolated hill, often marking the site of an ancient settlement.
Destan	An epic sung poem.
Desterkhan	A low table, around which diners squat or lounge.
Dilli-tuyduk	A short reed flute.
Dograma	A heavy soup of torn bread, onions and roasted meat.
Dutar	A two-stringed guitar with a rounded body.
Fitchi	A circular meat and onion pastry.
Gargy-tuyduk	A long reed flute.
Golubtsy	Meat-filled cabbage parcels.
Gopuz	A small metal instrument, placed in the mouth and strummed.
Gul	Repeated motif adorning a Turkmen carpet. Literally 'flower'.
Gupba	Item of female headgear, traditionally made of jewelled silver.
Gurt	Salty balls of dried curd, eaten as a savoury snack.
Gush depdi	A traditional dance from Balkan Region.
Gyjak	A stringed instrument, played with a bow.
Halk Maslahaty	People's Council; in theory the supreme legislative body of Turkmenistan.
Horjun	A carpetwork saddle-bag.
Hudaiyoly	A sacrificial meal.
Hyakim	District or regional governor.
Hyakimlik	Office of the district or regional governor.
Ishlekli	A large round savoury pie.
Iwan	A tall, arched, vaulted area, usually opening onto a courtyard.
Jieran	The goitred gazelle.
Kak	Dried melon. Eaten as a sweet snack.
Kazan	A heavy round cooking pot.
Keche	A felt rug. *Koshma* in Russian.

Kejebe	Elaborate saddle structure, placed on a camel, in which a Turkmen bride traditionally travelled to her wedding.
Koshk	An isolated mud-brick building, often featuring 'corrugated' external walls.
Kulan	The Central Asian wild ass.
Kurban Bayram	The Islamic festival of Eid ul-Adha, marking the willingness of Ibrahim to obey the word of Allah by agreeing to sacrifice his son.
Lyulya	A kebab made with minced lamb.
Mangal	Stand used for cooking *shashlik.*
Manty	Large ravioli, usually filled with minced meat and onion.
Marshrutka	A minivan.
Mejlis	Turkmenistan's parliament.
Nabat	A yellow crystallised sugar.
Namazlyk	A prayer rug, often white in colour.
Nardi	A board game, similar to backgammon.
Novruz Bayram	The spring holiday.
Oraza Bayram	The Islamic festival of Eid ul-Fitr, marking the end of the month of *Ramadan*.
Pelmeni	Small ravioli, often eaten in a broth.
Piyalushka	A small bowl used for drinking tea.
Plov	A rice dish, usually made with meat, onion, garlic and carrot.
Rhyton	Beautifully decorated ivory drinking horn.
Sadaka	A commemorative meal.
Sardoba	A cistern.
Semeni	A caramel-coloured paste made from sprouted wheat and flour.
Shashlik	Skewered kebab.
Somsa	A triangular pastry, usually filled with meat and onion.
Squinch	An arch, lying diagonally across the corner of a room, at the point of transition between the square walls of the room and the round drum carrying the dome above. A common architectural feature of Seljuk-period mausolea, employed to support the weight of the dome.
Suslik	A ground squirrel.
Takhya	An embroidered skull-cap.
Takyr	A hard, flat expanse in the desert, often the remnant of a lake.
Tamdyr	Conical clay oven used for baking bread.
Tapchan	A raised platform, often found in the courtyard of Turkmen houses, on which families dine, rest and sometimes sleep in warm weather.
Tazy	A hunting dog of the borzoi family.
Telpek	A shaggy sheepskin hat.
Torba	A carpet bag, traditionally used to store utensils.
Tugay	Dense forest found along the banks of the Amu Darya.
Yarma	A savoury porridge, containing meat.
Yurt	A circular, wooden-framed, felt-covered dwelling.
Yuzaerlik	A shrub, widely employed as a talisman to ward off the evil eye.
Zapovednik	A nature reserve
Ziarat	Shrine pilgrimage
Ziggurat	A form of temple, built as a pyramid of tiers of decreasing size, with a shrine at the top.

Appendix

FURTHER INFORMATION

Further reading

There are few books in English specifically about Turkmenistan, and most of what is worth reading is difficult to get hold of.

History and archaeology

Herrmann, Georgina *The Ancient Cities of Merv, Turkmenistan: A Visitor's Guide*, International Merv Project, 1996. An excellent short guide written by the former British Director of the International Merv Project, which should be available from the Mary Regional Museum, or the small museum at the entrance to the ancient Merv site.

Herrmann, Georgina *Monuments of Merv: Traditional Buildings of the Karakum*, Society of Antiquaries of London, 1999. A more detailed glossy publication, focusing on the standing monuments of the Merv Oasis.

Knobloch, Edgar *Monuments of Central Asia: A Guide to the Archaeology, Art and Architecture of Turkestan*, I B Tauris, 2001. A scholarly but readable account, revising and much expanding the author's 1972 work, *Beyond the Oxus*.

Masson, V M and Sarianidi, V I *Central Asia: Turkmenia Before the Achaemenids*, Thames and Hudson, 1972. A scholarly guide, by two leading archaeologists, covering the origins of urban settlement in the region. Out of print.

Niyazov, Saparmurat *Ruhnama*, Turkmen State Publishing Service, 2001. Available in an array of languages from Ashgabat bookshops. Turkmenistan's history as viewed by its president.

Sarianidi, Viktor *Margush*, Turkmendowlethabarlary, 2002. Available from bookshops in Turkmenistan. Written in English, Turkmen and the original Russian, this is a well illustrated though confusingly translated account of Sarianidi's excavations at the Bronze Age sites of the Merv Oasis.

The Great Game period and 19th-century travellers' accounts

Hopkirk, Peter *The Great Game: On Secret Service in High Asia*, John Murray, 1990. Classic, highly readable account of the rivalry between Britain and Russia in Central Asia. Includes coverage of the siege of Geok Depe.

Hopkirk, Peter *On Secret Service East of Constantinople*, John Murray, 1994. Hopkirk's account of a later 'Great Game', covering the period around World War I. Includes an account of the background to the murder of the 26 Baku Commissars.

Maclean, Fitzroy *A Person from England and Other Travellers*, Jonathan Cape, 1959. Beautifully written account of some of the leading actors of the Great Game period, including Vambery, Skobelev and O'Donovan. Out of print.

Teague-Jones, Reginald *The Spy Who Disappeared*, Gollancz, 1990. An account by the man who was forced to spend much of his life as Ronald Sinclair, after being accused by the Soviet authorities of complicity in the murder of the 26 Baku Commissars. With an introduction by Peter Hopkirk.

Vambery, Arminius *Travels in Central Asia*, John Murray, 1864. Classic account by an intrepid Hungarian traveller, available in several reprints.

Recent travellers' accounts

A spate of accounts of travels around Central Asia appeared during and immediately following the period of the break-up of the Soviet Union. The following are the most readable.

Akchurin, Marat *Red Odyssey: A Journey Through the Soviet Republics*, HarperCollins, 1992
Thubron, Colin *The Lost Heart of Asia*, Heinemann, 1994
Whittell, Giles *Extreme Continental: Blowing Hot and Cold Through Central Asia*, Gollancz, 1995
Maslow, Jonathan *Sacred Horses: the Memoirs of a Turkmen Cowboy*, Random House, 1994. The author attempts to ride Ahal Tekke horses, but mostly ends up running foul of the local KGB. This Turkmenistan-specific tale is out of print, but well worth hunting out.

Ethnography and culture

Blackwell, Carole *Tradition and Society in Turkmenistan: Gender, Oral Culture and Song*, Curzon, 2001. Looks at the folksongs of Turkmen women.
Kalter, Johannes *The Arts and Crafts of Turkestan*, Thames and Hudson, 1984. Strong on costume and jewellery. Out of print.
Magtymguly Fyragy *Songs from the Steppes of Central Asia*, Society of Friends of Makhtumkuli, 1995. The works of Turkmenistan's most famous poet, translated into English by Youssef Azemoun, and versified by science-fiction writer Brian Aldiss. Copies are occasionally to be found in the souvenir shops of the major Ashgabat hotels.

Natural history

Khramov, Victor (ed) *Nature of Turkmenistan*, Turkmendowlethabarlary, 2002. Ignore the mangled English-language texts in this coffee-table book edited by President Niyazov's private secretary, and enjoy the beautiful photographs of Turkmenistan's wild places. Available at bookshops in Turkmenistan.
Sparks, John *Realms of the Russian Bear*, BBC Books, 1992. Features good coverage of the wildlife of Badkyz and Repetek.

Language

The lack of a good dictionary between English and Turkmen is sorely felt.

Berliner, Juleah and Dietrich, Kyle *Turkmen Language Learning Guide*, Ashgabat, 2004. A compact guide to Turkmen grammar, produced by two Peace Corps volunteers. May be obtainable in Ashgabat.
Frank, Allen and Touch-Werner, Jeren (eds) *Turkmen-English Dictionary*, Dunwoody Press, 1999. A good product, but it covers the Turkmen to English direction only, and uses the old Cyrillic script. May be available in Ashgabat bookshops.

Maps

A dedicated map of Turkmenistan is published by the Russian cartographers Roskartografia. The most up-to-date version was printed in 2001. It is a 1:1,500,000 scale map, which includes a street plan of central Ashgabat and a Russian-language geographical overview of the country. All names on the map are, however, in Cyrillic. The map is available outside Turkmenistan through specialist stores such as Stanfords (12–14 Long Acre, London WC2E 9LP; ☎ 020 7836 1321; **f** 020 7632 8928; **e** sales@stanfords.co.uk). It is also intermittently available in Ashgabat bookshops.

Turkmenistan is also featured on several maps of the wider Central Asian region. The *Central Asia* map published by Nelles (2003) is at a scale of 1:1,750,000, and includes a small street plan of central Ashgabat. A rather eccentric selection of places of tourist interest is marked. The Hungarian company Gizi produces two maps of *Central Asia* (1999), focusing on the road network and physical features respectively, but identical in scale and coverage beyond the difference in emphasis. These are also at 1:1,750,000, but do not cover the whole of Turkmenistan, missing off Balkan Region and the southern part of Mary Region. A larger scale (1:3,000,000) Gizi map, *Silk Road Countries*, does cover the whole of Turkmenistan, along with much of the ground between Syria and China. Useful if you are planning a wider Silk Road trip, though the odd little camel caravans peppering the map are distracting. Another option is the 1:2,000,000 scale *Central Asia* map published by Reise Know-How Verlag, which covers the main physical features, road network and places of interest. These general Central Asia maps are not usually available within Turkmenistan, and should be purchased before you travel.

Decent maps are hard to come by within Turkmenistan itself. Most bookshops in Ashgabat, as well as the gift shops in the major hotels, sell a couple of maps produced by the State Committee for Tourism and Sport for around 35,000–40,000 manat. There is a basic tourist map, which is largely useless for the purpose of navigating around the country, and a rather more helpful street plan of Ashgabat. Make sure you pick up the recently revised version of the latter, which includes the new four digit numbered street names, rather than the out-of-date edition still on sale in many places.

Websites

www.britishembassy.gov.uk/turkmenistan British Embassy in Ashgabat.

www.chaihana.com Peace Corps volunteers who served in Turkmenistan.

www.eurasianet.org/resource/turkmenistan/index.shtml News items about Turkmenistan.

www.eurasianet.org/turkmenistan.project Weekly news brief on Turkmenistan prepared by the Open Society Institute.

www.fco.gov.uk/travel Foreign and Commonwealth Office travel advice.

www.rukhnama.com The book.

www.travel.state.gov US State Department travel advice.

www.turkmen.co.uk Turkmenistan cultural directory, researched by British artist Bridget Tempest. Good coverage of Turkmen painting.

www.turkmenistanembassy.org Turkmen Embassy in Washington.

www.turkmenistan.gov.tm Turkmen Government.

www.turkmens.com A collection of websites, with strong coverage of Turkmen culture.

www.usemb-ashgabat.usia.co.at US Embassy in Ashgabat.

Bradt Travel Guides

Africa Overland	£15.99
Albania	£13.95
Amazon	£14.95
Antarctica: A Guide to the Wildlife	£14.95
The Arctic: A Guide to Coastal Wildlife	£14.95
Armenia with Nagorno Karabagh	£13.95
Azores	£12.95
Baghdad City Guide	£9.95
Baltic Capitals: Tallinn, Riga, Vilnius, Kaliningrad	£11.95
Bosnia & Herzegovina	£13.95
Botswana: Okavango Delta, Chobe, Northern Kalahari	£14.95
British Isles: Wildlife of Coastal Waters	£14.95
Budapest City Guide	£7.95
Cambodia	£11.95
Cameroon	£13.95
Canada: North – Yukon, Northwest Territories	£13.95
Canary Islands	£13.95
Cape Verde Islands	£12.95
Cayman Islands	£12.95
Chile	£16.95
Chile & Argentina: Trekking Guide	£12.95
China: Yunnan Province	£13.95
Cork City Guide	£6.95
Costa Rica	£13.99
Croatia	£12.95
Dubrovnik City Guide	£6.95
East & Southern Africa: Backpacker's Manual	£14.95
Eccentric America	£13.95
Eccentric Britain	£13.99
Eccentric California	£13.99
Eccentric Edinburgh	£5.95
Eccentric France	£12.95
Eccentric London	£12.95
Eccentric Oxford	£5.95
Ecuador, Peru & Bolivia: Backpacker's Manual	£13.95
Ecuador: Climbing & Hiking	£13.95
Eritrea	£12.95
Estonia	£12.95
Ethiopia	£13.95
Falkland Islands	£13.95
Faroe Islands	£13.95
Gabon, São Tomé & Príncipe	£13.95
Galápagos Wildlife	£15.99
Gambia, The	£12.95
Georgia with Armenia	£13.95
Ghana	£13.95
Hungary	£14.99
Iran	£14.99
Iraq	£14.95
Kabul Mini Guide	£9.95
Kenya	£14.95
Kiev City Guide	£7.95
Latvia	£13.99
Lille City Guide	£6.99
Lithuania	£13.99
Ljubljana City Guide	£6.99
London: In the Footsteps of the Famous	£10.95
Macedonia	£13.95
Madagascar	£14.95
Madagascar Wildlife	£14.95
Malawi	£12.95
Maldives	£13.99
Mali	£13.95
Mauritius	£12.95
Mongolia	£14.95
Montenegro	£13.99
Mozambique	£12.95
Namibia	£14.95
Nigeria	£15.99
North Cyprus	£12.95
North Korea	£13.95
Palestine with Jerusalem	£12.95
Panama	£13.95
Paris, Lille & Brussels: Eurostar Cities	£11.95
Peru & Bolivia: Backpacking & Trekking	£12.95
Riga City Guide	£6.95
River Thames: In the Footsteps of the Famous	£10.95
Rwanda	£13.95
St Helena, Ascension, Tristan da Cunha	£14.95
Serbia	£13.99
Seychelles	£13.99
Singapore	£11.95
Slovenia	£12.99
South Africa: Budget Travel Guide	£11.95
Southern African Wildlife	£18.95
Spitsbergen	£14.99
Sri Lanka	£12.95
Sudan	£13.95
Switzerland: Rail, Road, Lake	£12.99
Tallinn City Guide	£6.95
Tanzania	£14.95
Tasmania	£12.95
Turkmenistan	£14.99
Tibet	£12.95
Uganda	£13.95
Ukraine	£14.95
USA by Rail	£13.99
Venezuela	£14.95
Vilnius City Guide	£6.99
Your Child Abroad: A Travel Health Guide	£9.95
Zambia	£15.95
Zanzibar	£12.95

WIN £100 CASH!

READER QUESTIONNAIRE

Send in your completed questionnaire for the chance to win £100 cash in our regular draw

All respondents may order a Bradt guide at half the UK retail price – please complete the order form overleaf.

(Entries may be posted or faxed to us, or scanned and emailed.)

We are interested in getting feedback from our readers to help us plan future Bradt guides. Please complete this quick questionnaire and return it to us to enter into our draw.

Have you used any other Bradt guides? If so, which titles? ....

....

What other publishers' travel guides do you use regularly? ....

....

Where did you buy this guidebook? ....

What was the main purpose of your trip to Turkmenistan (or for what other reason did you read our guide)? eg: holiday/business/charity etc. ....

....

What other destinations would you like to see covered by a Bradt guide?

....

Would you like to receive our catalogue/newsletters?

YES / NO (If yes, please complete details on reverse)

If yes – by post or email? ....

Age (circle relevant category) 16–25 26–45 46–60 60+

Male/Female (delete as appropriate)

Home country ....

Please send us any comments about our guide to Turkmenistan or other Bradt Travel Guides. ....

....

....

....

Bradt Travel Guides

23 High Street, Chalfont St Peter, Bucks SL9 9QE, UK

t +44 (0)1753 893444 f +44 (0)1753 892333

e info@bradtguides.com

www.bradtguides.com

CLAIM YOUR HALF-PRICE BRADT GUIDE!

Order Form

To order your half-price copy of a Bradt guide, and to enter our prize draw to win £100 (see overleaf), please fill in the order form below, complete the questionnaire overleaf, and send it to Bradt Travel Guides by post, fax or email.

Please send me one copy of the following guide at half the UK retail price

Title	*Retail price*	*Half price*
... .	....	....

Please send the following additional guides at full UK retail price

No	*Title*	*Retail price*	*Total*
...	....	....	....
...	....	....	....
...	....	....	....

Sub total ....
Post & packing ....
(£1 per book UK; £2 per book Europe; £3 per book rest of world)
Total ....

Name ....

Address..

Tel .... Email ....

☐ I enclose a cheque for £ .... made payable to Bradt Travel Guides Ltd

☐ I would like to pay by credit card. Number: ....

Expiry date: .../... 3-digit security code (on reverse of card) .....

☐ Please add my name to your catalogue mailing list.

☐ I would be happy for you to use my name and comments in Bradt marketing material.

Send your order on this form, with the completed questionnaire, to:

Bradt Travel Guides/TUR
23 High Street, Chalfont St Peter, Bucks SL9 9QE
t +44 (0)1753 893444 f +44 (0)1753 892333
e info@bradtguides.com www.bradtguides.com

Index

Page numbers in bold indicate major entries; those in italics indicate maps.